Betty Crocker's
MICROWAVE
COOKBOOK

Betty Crocker's

MICROWAVE COOKBOOK

Prentice Hall

New York • London • Toronto • Sydney • Tokyo • Singapore

This special edition celebrates
forty years of Betty Crocker excellence.

PRENTICE HALL GENERAL REFERENCE
15 Columbus Circle
New York, NY 10023

Published simultaneously in Canada by Prentice Hall Canada Inc.

PRENTICE HALL and colophon are registered trademarks of Simon & Schuster, Inc.

BETTY CROCKER is a registered trademark of General Mills, Inc.

Library of Congress Cataloging-in-Publication Data

Crocker, Betty.
    [Microwave cookbook]
    Betty Crocker's microwave cookbook.
        p.   cm.
    ISBN 0-13-073859-X
    1. Microwave cookery. I. Title. II. Title: Microwave cookbook.
TX832.C75 1990
641.5′882—dc20   89-23140
                                                                      CIP

Manufactured in the United States of America
10 9 8 7 6 5 4 3 2 1

GENERAL MILLS, INC.

Editor: Jean E. Kozar
Associate Food Editor: Julie H. Turnbull
Test Kitchen Home Economists: Mary Jane Freidhoff,
Mary Hallin Johnson
Recipe Copy Editors: Lauren Long, Anne Oslund
Nurtrition Department Consultant: Nancy Holmes, R.D.
Administrative Assistant: Phyllis Weinbender
Food Stylists: Cindy Lund, Mary Sethre
Photographer: Nanci E. Doonan
Photography Assistant: Valerie J. Bourassa
Director, Betty Crocker Food and Publications Center:
Marcia Copeland
Assistant Manager, Publications: Lois Tlusty

CONTENTS

. . . .

CONTENTS

INTRODUCTION

· · · · · · · · · · · ·

Did you know that your microwave can . . .

- Poach fish to perfection?
- Make muffins in minutes?
- Precook foods for superfast grilling?
- Give you vegetables with more of their vitamins, color and crunch intact?
- Turn a can of soup into a culinary treasure?
- Let you cook with less added fat?

With your microwave oven, a handful of microwavable utensils and a few simple microwave basics from Betty Crocker, you are on your way to enjoying some of the most delicious, quick and easy dishes you've ever tasted. Memorable meals, crisp salads, delectable desserts, super snacks and treats for nearly instant gratification . . . all with too-good-to-be-true time-saving benefits.

This collection of more than 450 recipes emphasizes the foods the microwave cooks superbly, and makes the best use of the most important innovation in twentieth-century cooking—the microwave! Working with up-to-the-minute technology, we have revised and expanded our repertoire of wonderful microwave recipes, while evaluating the levels of fat, cholesterol and sodium in each and every one. In fact, you will find an extensive nutritional analysis of every recipe at each chapter's end.

The chapter on vegetables provides essential microwave directions for perfect cooking, then goes on to include many additional serving ideas. You can turn to Microwaving Menu Ideas for help in planning meals, even parties. Tips on everything from softening and melting butter to opening oysters to defrosting poultry, special adjustments for high-altitude microwaving, even advice on teaching children to use the microwave . . . it's all here.

As a special convenience, every main-dish recipe taking fewer than thirty minutes to prepare and cook has been identified with this symbol: 🕐

Whether you are a beginner or a seasoned cook, you will find recipes here for every occasion, to satisfy every wish. With this book in hand, you will be able to get the most from your microwave, certainly the "wave of the future."

THE BETTY CROCKER EDITORS

....

MICROWAVING WITH CONFIDENCE

HOW THE MICROWAVE WORKS

There's nothing mysterious about microwaves, even though they can't be seen. They are simply a form of radiant energy, much like radio and television waves. Microwaves are emitted by all objects, from plants to humans to the kitchen sink.

Microwaves for cooking are produced by a magnetron tube that converts household electricity into microwaves. Energy, in the form of a microwave stream, enters the oven cavity through an opening in the metal case, usually at the top. Because microwave energy often is not distributed perfectly evenly throughout the oven cavity, hot spots can lead to unevenly cooked food.

Microwave manufacturers use various methods to distribute microwaves evenly within the oven cavity. Many ovens have a rotating stirrer, similar to a fan blade, to deflect microwaves to different parts of the cavity so all of the microwaves don't follow the same path. Other ovens make use of different solutions, among them a revolving turntable that keeps food moving through the microwave energy field.

Microwaves can't penetrate metal. They are deflected off the metal oven walls at right angles. They adapt well to cooking, however, because of their attraction to moisture.

Consequently, any substance in the oven containing moisture will absorb microwave energy. Microwaves pass through glass, plastic and paper, which is why these materials work so well as containers and packages for microwaving foods.

The microwaves agitate moisture molecules in foods, causing them to vibrate at a speed of about 2½ billion times per second. This agitation produces heat within the food itself, and this heat cooks the food without ever heating the oven interior. When the set time has elasped or the microwave door is opened, the magnetron turns off; the microwaves are no longer produced.

Microwaves penetrate only about one inch into the surface of foods. This means conduction of heat through the food cooks the center (just as in conventional cooking, but much more rapidly). For large, dense or very moist foods, cooking of the center is best accomplished by microwaving at lower power levels and/or by letting food stand after cooking, in order for heat to cook the center before the outside overcooks.

The microwave is one of the safest appliances in the home. The federal government requires that each oven meet strict emission

Fruit Tortillas (page 298), Brandied Butterscotch Fondue (page 31), Rhubarb Crunch (page 288)

1

standards to assure safety of microwave cooking. Like other cooking appliances, the microwave must be operated properly in order to provide safe usage. Be sure to follow the use and care manual for operation and cleaning.

All microwave ovens are not the same. Cooking times vary due to different wattages (the total power of the oven), power setting descriptions and cooking patterns. You may need to adjust recipes and cookware sizes to the workings of your own microwave. Check for doneness at minimum cooking time, and add more cooking time only if necessary. You will need to give more or less attention (stirring, rotating, elevating) to foods while they cook depending on how evenly your microwave cooks.

MICROWAVE COOKING PRINCIPLES

Microwaving involves many of the same principles that conventional cooking does, but because the cooking time is accelerated, these principles are even more important.

Composition of Food. Foods high in moisture, fat and sugar attract microwave energy and will cook faster than other foods. Foods high in natural moisture microwave best with minimal or no added water.

Density. Porous foods such as breads and cakes absorb microwaves quickly and therefore cook quickly, while dense foods such as potatoes, casseroles and meats absorb microwaves less quickly, requiring longer cooking.

Quantity. There are always the same number of microwaves present. If only one potato is being cooked, all the microwaves are concentrated on that one item. If four potatoes are being cooked, the same number of microwaves must be shared by the four potatoes. Consequently, a larger quantity of food needs longer to cook. This means that for large quantities of some foods, microwaving may not be as efficient as conventional cooking.

Shape. Evenly shaped foods or foods placed in evenly shaped dishes—round or ring shaped—microwave best. Unevenly shaped foods require more attention (rearranging or turning) during cooking to cook evenly. Foods microwaved in square or rectangular dishes (cakes, for example) tend to overcook at the corners.

Size. Small pieces of foods cook more rapidly than large pieces. It is important that cut-up or shaped foods such as vegetables and meatballs be uniform in size for even cooking.

Temperature of Food Before Microwaving. Microwave timing is affected by the temperature of the food before cooking. The colder the food, the longer it will take to heat or cook. Testing for this book was done with foods taken directly from their normal storage areas, whether the refrigerator (milk, meats, eggs, poultry, fish), freezer (frozen vegetables, etc.) or cupboard shelf (flour, canned goods).

Stand Time. Standing or "carry-over cooking" is important in microwaving. Foods continue to cook after removal from the microwave. Note the doneness test specified in each recipe and check the food for doneness at the minimum cooking time. The amount of stand time is indicated in each recipe where it is important.

MICROWAVE TECHNIQUES

Foods can cook unevenly in the microwave. Edges cook faster than the center, small pieces faster than large pieces, high-fat, high-sugar foods faster than others. Try some of the easy microwave techniques below to help you cook foods more evenly.

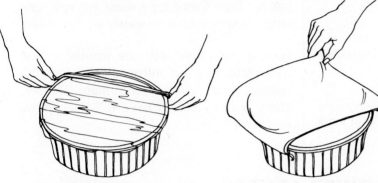

Cover tightly to speed heating. Use lid or plastic wrap with one corner or edge turned back to prevent splitting.

Cover loosely to prevent spattering and/or hold in heat. Use waxed paper, paper towel or napkin, or lid slightly ajar.

Stir to help food cook more quickly. Stir from outside to center to distribute heat; food heats faster on outside.

Rotate to even cooking for foods that cannot be stirred, such as cakes. Rotate ¼ or ½ turn, as directed in recipes.

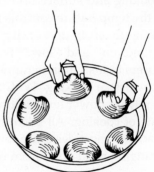

Arrange to take advantage of microwave patterns. Arrange cupcakes, muffins, potatoes or other small foods in circle.

Elevate to assure doneness on the bottom. Place food on inverted dish so bottom center can absorb microwaves.

Rearrange to cook more evenly those foods that can't be sitrred. Reposition food in the dish, moving it from the outside to the inside.

HOW RECIPES WERE TESTED

The recipes for this book were tested in 500-, 600- and 700-watt appliances. There are three different ways wattage is addressed within the recipes:

1. If there is no statement at the end of a recipe, the microwave times given work for all three wattages.

2. If the recipe says "500-watt Microwave: Not recommended," the recipe does not work properly in a 500-watt microwave.

3. If the recipe says "500-watt Microwave: You may need to increase microwave times," the recipe will work in a 500-watt oven but has not been tested for a more accurate time range; you will have to watch for doneness.

Look at your use and care manual or the nameplate on your microwave to find the wattage. Or, contact the manufacturer. Many manufacturers have toll-free phone numbers.

POWER LEVELS

In conventional cooking, we regulate the rate of oven cooking and surface unit cooking by adjusting the temperature controls in degrees or according to such descriptive terms as "high," "medium" and "low." Some range manufacturers tout an infinite number of heat settings for surface cooking. With the microwave, we rely on power level settings to control the rate of cooking. All microwaves offer high power, and most designate lower power settings, ranging most often from two to ten.

Power settings used in this book include

high (100%)
medium-high (70%)
medium (50%)
medium-low (30%)
low (10%) and
defrost

(The percentage is not indicated for high since high is 100%.) To defrost, use the specific setting indicated "defrost" by the manufacturer, since they have determined through testing which setting is best to defrost foods in their appliances.

Percentage of power refers not to the quantity of microwaves the magnetron is producing but to the amount of time it produces them. The higher the percentage of power, the faster food cooks. At high, the magnetron generates power 100% of the time; at medium (50%), it generates microwaves 50% of the time. Microwave manufacturers may have slightly different names for their settings, so consult your use and care manual for more information if necessary.

The appropriate power settings are always stated in each of our recipes. The power levels we use most often are high, medium (50%) and defrost. High is used for such foods as vegetables, sauces, fish, poultry and fruits. Medium (50%) is used for more delicate foods like eggs, cheeses and baked goods to allow heat to penetrate foods more slowly and evenly. Lower power levels are used for defrosting foods. We do not repeat power level settings in recipes, unless a different dish is used. If power levels are to be changed in the course of a recipe, it is always noted.

BASIC MICROWAVE TIPS

The following microwave tips are handy. We refer to many of these tips in the recipes.

Boiling Water. Microwave 1 cup hot water on high 2 to 3 minutes until boiling.

Cooking Bacon. Microwave on rack in dish or paper towel–lined plate. Or, for bacon that tastes conventionally fried, place bacon in baking dish, not on rack or paper towel. Cover with paper towels and microwave on high.

1 to 2 slices	45 seconds to 2 minutes
4 slices	3 to 4 minutes
6 slices	4 to 6 minutes
8 slices	6 to 8 minutes

Melting Margarine or Butter. Microwave uncovered on high in measuring cup, custard cup or casserole. Cover or lower the power if spattering occurs.

1 to 2 tablespoons	15 to 30 seconds
3 to 4 tablespoons	30 to 45 seconds
⅓ to ½ cup	45 to 60 seconds
⅔ to 1 cup	60 to 90 seconds

Softening Margarine or Butter. For easy spreading or mixing, microwave margarine uncovered on medium-low (30%) until softened.

1 to 3 tablespoons	15 to 30 seconds
¼ to 1 cup	30 to 45 seconds

Heating Syrup. Microwave uncovered on high.

½ cup	45 to 60 seconds
1 cup	2 to 2 minutes 30 seconds

Softening Brown Sugar. Cover tightly; microwave on high, checking every 30 seconds.

Toasting Coconut. Microwave uncovered on high, stirring every 30 seconds.

¼ to ⅓ cup	1 minute
½ cup	1 minute 30 seconds
1 cup	2 minutes 30 seconds

Toasting Nuts: pecans, walnuts, hazelnuts, almonds and macadamia nuts. Combine 1 teaspoon margarine and nuts in pie plate and microwave on high, stirring every 30 seconds, until light brown.

2 tablespoons	45 seconds to 1 minute
¼ cup	1 minute 30 seconds to 2 minutes
½ cup	2 minutes 30 seconds to 3 minutes
1 to 1½ cups	3 to 4 minutes

Melting Chocolate Squares. Microwave 1 to 2 squares uncovered on medium (50%) 3 to 4 minutes, stirring after 2 minutes.

Melting Chocolate Chips. Microwave ½ to 1 cup chips on medium (50%) 3 to 4 minutes; stir until smooth.

Toasting Soft Bread Crumbs. Microwave uncovered on high, stirring every 30 seconds. Toss 1 cup crumbs with 1 teaspoon melted margarine, 2 cups crumbs with 1 tablespoon melted margarine.

1 cup	2 to 2 minutes 30 seconds
2 cups	3 to 4 minutes

Melting Caramels. Microwave caramels and water uncovered on high, stirring every 30 to 45 seconds. Mix 1 package (14 ounces) with 2 tablespoons water; mix ½ package (7 ounces) with 1 tablespoon water.

1 package (14 ounces)	3 to 4 minutes
½ package (7 ounces)	1 minute 30 seconds to 2 minutes 30 seconds

Softening Cream Cheese. Remove foil wrapper and microwave uncovered on medium (50%) until softened.

1 package (3 ounces)	30 to 45 seconds
1 package (8 ounces)	60 to 90 seconds

Softening Dried Fruit. For 1 cup raisins, combine 1 teaspoon water and raisins in 2-cup measure. Cover tightly and microwave on high for 1 minute. For 1 cup dried apricots, arrange so apricots are not touching on microwavable plate. Sprinkle with 1 teaspoon water. Cover tightly and microwave on high 45 to 60 seconds.

Melting Crystallized Honey. For an 8-ounce jar, remove lid. Microwave on high 30 seconds to 2 minutes 30 seconds or until honey is fluid and no crystals remain. Cool.

Softening Ice Cream. For ½ gallon, microwave on low (10%) 1 minute 30 seconds to 2 minutes, rotating ½ turn after 1 minute, until slightly soft.

Warming Citrus Fruits. Before squeezing lemons, limes or oranges, microwave on high 20 to 30 seconds or until slightly warm. This will increase the amount of juice that can be squeezed from the fruit.

Crisping Snacks. Microwave popcorn, pretzels, corn chips or potato chips uncovered on high in napkin-lined basket; stir.

2 cups	30 to 60 seconds
4 cups	1 to 2 minutes

Thawing Frozen Vegetables. (10- to 12-ounce packages). Remove outer wrapper from package. Pierce package with fork several times. Place on paper towel and microwave on defrost or medium-low (30%) for the same amount of time recommended on the package for cooking, turning the package over after half the time has elapsed. Microwave until outside edges are thawed and a few ice crystals remain in the center. Break block apart and drain.

Softening Tortillas. Place tortillas between paper towels; microwave uncovered on high until soft.

Four 6-inch tortillas	45 to 60 seconds

BEYOND BASIC TIPS

Opening Clams or Oysters. Soak and scrub oysters or clams in their shells. Arrange six at a time in a circle with hinges toward outside of paper towel–lined plate. Cover tightly and microwave on high.

6 oysters or clams	1 minute to 1 minute 30 seconds

Remove as shells open. Open by holding oyster or clam with hinge toward you; insert knife between shells near hinge; open.

Warming Liquor for Flaming. Microwave liquor in 1-cup measure uncovered on high.

¼ cup	15 seconds
½ cup	30 seconds

Fill metal ladle or serving spoon with liquor; pour remaining liquor over food. Ignite liquor in ladle and pour over food.

Proofing White Yeast Bread Dough. Rising time can be significantly cut with help from the microwave. Place dough (for 2 loaves) in greased bowl and cover with waxed paper. Microwave on low (10%) 10 minutes, rotating bowl ½ turn after 5 minutes. Let stand 10 minutes. Test for rising; press fingertips ½ inch into dough. An indentation should remain. Use the low microwave setting to avoid the possibility of the dough starting to cook or forming a crust before it has a chance to rise. (Timings will vary slightly with different doughs.)

Heating Dampened Finger Towels. Microwave uncovered on high.

2 to 6 towels	1 to 2 minutes

REHEATING FOODS IN THE MICROWAVE

Reheating foods to their ideal serving temperature is a snap in the microwave. A serving temperature of 140°F is recommended. The food is usually hot enough when the center of the bottom of the dish is warm. A temperature probe or microwave thermometer is helpful to determine whether the food is hot enough at its center. If using a conventional thermometer, use it only after microwaving.

Moist foods reheat best. Covering foods speeds and evens heating. Crisp or crunchy foods (pizza, for example) reheat best when a browning dish or a microwave rack is used, so the bottom doesn't get soggy.

- **Reheating a plate of leftovers** is one of the most common microwave uses. For even heating, spread out food with any food that might need more cooking toward the outside of the plate. Leave the center of the plate open, or place any porous foods like breads or food needing a minimum of heating in the center. Cover loosely and microwave on high.

  It takes about three minutes to heat an average plate of food taken straight from the refrigerator. Depending on the portions and the temperature of the food, reheating times will vary.

- **Casseroles and vegetables** should be covered tightly for fastest heating. Stir or rotate once or twice during reheating. Casseroles that can't be stirred benefit from a standing period. Individual servings heat more quickly than full recipes; thus, a portion of lasagne would be ready to serve before an entire pan would.

  Small portions allow microwaves to penetrate more deeply, heating the center more

quickly. A casserole containing eggs, cheese or large chunks of meat should be heated at a lower power setting to avoid overcooking.

- **Meat and poultry** should be thinly sliced or cut into pieces of uniform size, then moistened with broth, meat juices or a sauce and covered loosely. Reheat crisp foods like fried chicken uncovered. The high setting is recommended for small amounts (1 or 2 servings), but a lower setting, medium-high (70%) or medium (50%), is preferred for larger amounts to avoid overcooking, or for meats that are rare or medium doneness.

  Avoid reheating large chunks of meat; for larger amounts, thinly slice and overlap in the dish. Reheat single serving portions on microwavable dishes. Arrange several dishes in a circle in the microwave.

- **Pasta, rice and cereals** should be reheated, tightly covered, on high.

- **Reheating breads, biscuits, muffins and coffee cakes** brings back fresh-baked flavor. To reheat, place the amount needed on a paper towel or napkin or in a napkin-lined basket (do not cover) and follow the directions below. Medium (50%) power is recommended to avoid overheating. Always check at the minimum reheating time because breads are porous and heat quickly.

- **Excessive heating** toughens breads and causes fillings, frostings and fruits in breads to overheat, since the denser, sweet fillings heat more quickly than the surrounding bread. Breads should be warm, not steaming. Increase or decrease microwave times according to the quantity of bread.

Microwave Reheat Directions
for Breads
Medium (50%) Power

Rolls, muffins and biscuits 2 to 3 inches in diameter, coffee cake pieces about 2½ inches square and 2-inch wedges from bundt or ring shapes.

SERVINGS	ROOM TEMPERATURE	FROZEN
1	15 to 30 seconds	45 seconds to 1 minutes 15 seconds
2	25 to 40 seconds	60 seconds to 1 minute 30 seconds
3	35 to 60 seconds	1 minute 15 seconds to 1 minute 30 seconds
4	45 seconds to 1 minute 15 seconds	1 minute 30 seconds to 3 minutes

Pancakes can be refrigerated or frozen for a quick microwave breakfast another time.

Spread the pancakes with a thin layer of margarine or butter to help them heat evenly. Wrap in packets of two or four. Label and freeze no longer than 3 months or refrigerate no longer than 48 hours. Unwrap pancakes and place stack on plate. Cover loosely to microwave.

PANCAKES	ROOM TEMPERATURE	FROZEN
2	1 to 1½ minutes	2 to 3 minutes
4	2 to 3 minutes	3 to 4 minutes

Popovers need conventional dry heat to puff up, hold their shape and bake to crusty brown perfection. You can bake them ahead of time, then wrap, label and freeze no longer than 2 months. The reheated popovers will hold their shape well, become tender, warm and only slightly less crusty than when freshly baked. To microwave fewer than 6, decrease the reheating time. Do not overheat, as popovers can become tough.

POPOVERS	ROOM TEMPERATURE	FROZEN
6	1 to 2 minutes	3 to 4 minutes

MICROWAVE UTENSILS

Use nonmetal utensils: glassware, paper, plasticware, dishwasher-safe plastic containers, ceramic plates and casseroles containing no metals and china without metal decoration.

Look for microwave- and dishwasher-safe utensils that are lightweight, with handles that can be gripped with potholders. If utensils are resistant to conventional heat, they can be used for complementary cooking (they'll move from stove top or oven to the microwave and back).

Avoid metal utensils: They are not suitable for microwaving because arcing (an electric flash, as in welding) can occur. Some manufacturers feel that it is safe to use small pieces of aluminum foil to shield areas of foods that might otherwise cook too quickly. It is common, for example, for the wing tips of a chicken to start to cook while defrosting, or for the corners of bar cookies to overcook. Follow your microwave use and care manual when it comes to using aluminum foil or foil-lined containers.

To test utensils for microwave use, place the utensil in question in the microwave beside 1 cup cool water in a glass measure. Microwave uncovered on high 1 minute. If the water is warm and the utensil remains cool, it can safely be used for microwaving; if the utensil feels warm, it should not be used for microwaving.

Utensil Test

- **Ceramic, stoneware and pottery** are safe for microwaving if there are no traces of metal in the claylike composition or in the glazes. If you are in doubt, test the utensils as described on page 9.

- **China** can be used for microwaving if recommended by the manufacturer. Often this information appears in the label or accompanying leaflet or on the dishes themselves.

- **Glassware** is well suited to microwave cooking and heating. Use oven-tempered glass, because when cooked food becomes hot, that heat is transferred to the glass.

- **Paper** is adequate for reheating if the microwaving time is brief. Microwavable paper towels (designed for direct food contact) are excellent for reheating rolls or muffins, or for absorbing grease during cooking. For cooking, durable microwavable paper containers are available in many shapes and sizes. Avoid color-printed paper towels (color may run) or recycled paper products (they may contain, although rarely, metal fragments).

- **Plastic microwave cookware** is available in many microwave-compatible shapes and sizes. These plastics vary in quality, design, durability and price. When buying plastic cookware, read the package information that advises which foods can be cooked in that utensil. Some plastics can't withstand the temperatures reached in the cooking of high fat– and high sugar–content foods. The manufacturer's recommendation as to where the cookware should be placed in a dishwasher is also a clue; placement on lower racks suggests greater durability.

  Reusable, dishwasher-safe plastic containers can be used for quick reheating, but not for heating or cooking foods with a high fat content such as chili or spaghetti sauce. Very hot food can stain, distort and even melt the plastic.

Plastic cooking pouches of frozen vegetables and entrées can withstand high temperatures and be used in your microwave. Be sure to make a small slit in the pouch to allow steam to escape.

For use in complementary cooking (microwave and conventional), check the plastic manufacturer's directions. Caution: Plastic cookware should never be used for stovetop cooking, broiling or with a browning unit.

- **Wicker baskets, wooden spoons and bread boards** without metal parts can be placed in the microwave for short periods of time.

BASIC MICROWAVE COOKWARE

These pieces of cookware have versatile uses in both everyday and special microwave cooking. Keep the size of your microwave in mind when purchasing cookware. You may need to use alternative sized dishes to some used in our recipes if you own a smaller microwave or have a turntable.

Utensil	Size	Use (Measuring, Mixing or Cooking)
Baking dishes	13 × 9 × 2, 12 × 7½ × 2, 11 × 7 × 1½, 8 × 8 × 2 or 8 × 1½ inch round	Chicken, fish, lasagne, vegetables, cookies, cakes, desserts
Casseroles	1 to 3 quarts	Main dishes, vegetables, fruits
Colander	Size varies	Microwaving and draining ground meats, steaming vegetables
Custard cups	6, 10 ounces	Custards, leftovers, casseroles, eggs
Liquid measures	1, 2, 4, 8 cups	Sauces, puddings, beverages
Microwave or bacon rack	Size varies	Hamburgers, meats, appetizers, sandwiches
Muffin ring	6 cup	Muffins, cupcakes, eggs
Pie plates	9- or 10-inch	Main dishes, pies, appetizers
Ring or bundt dishes	6 to 12 cups	Cakes, coffee cakes, breads

1

APPETIZERS, SNACKS AND BEVERAGES

What we often want in the ideal appetizer, in addition, of course, to marvelous flavor, is quick satisfaction. The microwave not only brings out intense flavors in many foods, it does so rapidly. The microwave can be your best friend when it comes to the things you want without delay: appetizers, snacks and good hot drinks.

- The recipes that follow are well suited to microwaving. Foods that are moist and have color are ideal; those that need to be browned or crisp should be prepared conventionally. Most of them can be prepared and served in the same dishes, and many can be made at leisure and served piping hot at a moment's notice.

- This chapter is a good place for a beginning cook to start. The techniques are so simple that even a child can make a scrumptious cup of hot chocolate or spiced orange cider in the microwave.

Taco Salad Dip (page 15), Cranberry Orange Punch (page 34), Spicy Cheese Dip (page 15), Stacked Quesadillas (page 24)

SPICY CHEESE DIP

MICROWAVE TIME: 3 to 4 minutes

8 ounces process cheese spread loaf with
    jalapeño peppers, cut into cubes
½ teaspoon chili powder
1 small tomato, chopped

1.   Mix all ingredients in 1-quart casserole.
Cover tightly and microwave on high 3 to 4
minutes, stirring after 2 minutes, until cheese
is melted and mixture is hot.

2.   Serve warm with tortilla chips and assorted raw vegetables if desired.   **About 1½
cups dip;** 30 calories per tablespoon.

• • • • • • • • • • •

HOT ARTICHOKE DIP

MICROWAVE TIME: 4 to 5 minutes

½ cup mayonnaise or salad dressing
½ cup grated Parmesan cheese
2 teaspoons lemon juice
1 can (14 ounces) artichoke hearts,
    drained and cut into fourths

1.   Mix all ingredients in 1-quart casserole.
Cover tightly and microwave on medium-
high (70%) 4 to 5 minutes, stirring after 2
minutes, until hot.

2.   Serve warm with thin slices French bread
or rye crakers if desired.   **About 1½ cups dip;**
45 calories per tablespoon.

TACO SALAD DIP

MICROWAVE TIME: 9 to 11 minutes

½ pound ground beef
1 can (16 ounces) refried beans
1 can (8 ounces) tomato sauce
1 package (1¼ ounces) taco seasoning
    mix (dry)
1 small onion, finely chopped (about
    ¼ cup)
¼ cup finely chopped green bell pepper
2 or 3 drops red pepper sauce
1 small clove garlic, finely chopped
Sour Cream Topping (below)
Finely shredded lettuce
Shredded Cheddar cheese

1.   Crumble ground beef into 1½-quart casserole. Cover loosely and microwave on high
2 minutes 30 seconds to 3 minutes 30 seconds or until very little pink remains; break
up beef and drain.

2.   Stir in beans, tomato sauce, seasoning
mix, onion, bell pepper, pepper sauce and
garlic. Cover tightly and microwave 3 minutes; stir. Spread in pie plate, 9 × 1¼ inches.
Cover tightly and microwave on high 3 to 4
minutes or until hot and bubbly.

3.   Prepare Sour Cream Topping. Mound
Sour Cream Topping in center of beef mixture. Sprinkle with lettuce and cheese. Serve
with tortilla chips if desired.   **About 3½ cups
dip;** 25 calories per tablespoon.

Sour Cream Topping

½ cup sour cream
1 tablespoon grated process American
    cheese loaf
½ teaspoon chili powder

Mix all ingredients in small bowl.

SPINACH DIP

This is one of our most popular dips for entertaining. It makes a good, large quantity. Try serving it in a hollowed round loaf of rye or sourdough bread.

MICROWAVE TIME: 9 to 12 minutes

1 package (10 ounces) frozen chopped spinach, thawed and well drained
1 package (8 ounces) cream cheese, softened
2 cups shredded Cheddar cheese (8 ounces)
4 green onions (with tops), sliced
2 medium tomatoes, chopped (about 1½ cups)

1. Mix all ingredients in medium bowl. Cover tightly and microwave on medium (50%) 9 to 12 minutes, stirring every 3 minutes, until Cheddar cheese is melted and mixture is warm.

2. Serve warm with bagel chips or crackers if desired. **About 4 cups dip;** 30 calories per tablespoon.

•••••••••••

HOT HORSERADISH DIP

MICROWAVE TIME: 1 to 2 minutes

1 package (8 ounces) cream cheese, softened
1 tablespoon prepared horseradish
8 drops red pepper sauce
Dash of salt
Chopped fresh chives

1. Mix cream cheese, horseradish, pepper sauce and salt in small bowl.

2. Microwave uncovered on high 1 to 2 minutes, stirring after 30 seconds, until hot. Sprinkle with chives. Serve with assorted raw vegetables if desired. **About 1 cup dip;** 50 calories per tablespoon.

Spinach Dip

Cheddar-Apple Spread

ORANGE DIP WITH FRESH FRUIT

Mix up this sweet dip ahead of time and serve it when the fruit is freshly cut into pieces. A light rub with lemon juice will keep cut fruit from discoloring.

MICROWAVE TIME:	6 to 9 minutes
REFRIGERATION TIME:	2 hours

2 eggs
¼ cup sugar
½ cup orange juice
1 tablespoon grated orange peel
2 cups miniature marshmallows
1 pound grapes
2 pears, cut into wedges
2 kiwifruit, pared and sliced

1. Beat eggs in 4-cup measure with fork; stir in sugar and orange juice. Microwave uncovered on medium (50%) 4 to 7 minutes, stirring every minute, until thickened.

2. Stir in orange peel and marshmallows. Microwave uncovered 2 minutes; stir until marshmallows are melted. Cover and refrigerate at least 2 hours until chilled. Stir before serving. Serve with fruit. Cover and refrigerate any remaining dip. **About 1 cup dip;** 45 calories per tablespoon.

•••••••••••

CHEDDAR-APPLE SPREAD

MICROWAVE TIME:	1 minute

½ cup finely chopped unpared tart apple
¼ cup shredded Cheddar cheese
   (1 ounce)
1 tablespoon mayonnaise or salad
   dressing
1 tablespoon honey

Mix all ingredients in small bowl. Microwave uncovered on medium (50%) about 1 minute or until cheese is softened. Spread on sliced French bread, bagel chips or crackers if desired. **About ¾ cup spread;** 25 calories per tablespoon.

PARTY CHEESE LOG

Try rolling this classic American hors d'oeuvre in pecans, almonds, walnuts . . . anything goes!

MICROWAVE TIME: 1 minute
REFRIGERATION TIME: 3 hours

1 package (8 ounces) cream cheese, softened
¼ cup crumbled blue cheese (2 ounces)
1 cup shredded sharp Cheddar cheese (4 ounces)
1 small onion, finely chopped (about ¼ cup)
2 to 3 tablespoons Worcestershire sauce
⅓ cup finely chopped fresh parsley or chopped nuts

1. Mix all ingredients except parsley in medium bowl. Microwave uncovered on medium (50%) about 1 minute or until cheeses are softened.

2. Beat on low speed until blended. Beat on medium speed about 1 minute, scraping bowl constantly, until fluffy. Cover and refrigerate 1 hour.

3. Shape cheese mixture into 6-inch log, using waxed paper; roll in parsley. Cover and refrigerate about 2 hours or until firm. Serve with crackers if desired. **6 servings; 255 calories per serving.**

BRIE WHEEL

A 14-ounce wheel is sometimes labeled "party brie." Garnished dramatically, this warm cheese is delicious with nuts and dried fruits.

MICROWAVE TIME: 2 to 4 minutes

1 round Brie cheese (14 ounces)
4 teaspoons golden raisins
4 teaspoons finely chopped walnuts
4 teaspoons currants

1. Place cheese on 8-inch plate. Cut rind from top of cheese carefully; score top of cheese into 6 wedges. Press 2 teaspoons each of the raisins, walnuts and currants onto alternate wedges; repeat with remaining wedges.

2. Cover with waxed paper and microwave on medium (50%) 2 to 4 minutes or just until cheese is soft and warm. Serve with crackers and fruit slices if desired. **About 24 servings;** 50 calories per serving.

• • • • • • • • • •

BRIE WITH ALMONDS

MICROWAVE TIME: 1 to 3 minutes

1 small round Brie cheese (about 4½ ounces)
2 tablespoons margarine or butter
¼ cup sliced almonds, toasted
1 tablespoon brandy, if desired

1. Place cheese on 7-inch plate. Microwave uncovered on medium (50%) 1 to 2 minutes or just until soft and warm.

2. Place margarine in 1-cup measure. Microwave uncovered on high 30 to 60 seconds or until melted. Stir in almonds and brandy; pour over cheese. Garnish with chopped fresh parsley and serve with crackers if desired. **About 10 servings;** 85 calories per serving.

Brie Wheel

COCKTAIL WIENER KABOBS

MICROWAVE TIME: 3 to 4 minutes

24 cocktail wieners
1 small zucchini, cut into 12 slices
12 small mushrooms
12 small cherry tomatoes
12 large pimiento-stuffed olives
½ medium green bell pepper, cut into
    1-inch squares

1. Alternate 2 wieners and 4 vegetables on each of twelve 8-inch wooden skewers.

2. Place 6 kabobs on 10-inch plate. Cover with waxed paper and microwave on high 2 minutes 30 seconds to 3 minutes 30 seconds or until hot. Repeat with remaining kabobs. **12 kabobs;** 70 calories per kabob.

• • • • • • • • • • •

GLAZED PORK TENDERLOIN APPETIZERS

MICROWAVE TIME: 12 to 14 minutes

1 pork tenderloin (10 to 12 ounces)
¼ cup tomato preserves or orange
    marmalade
⅛ teaspoon salt
2 drops liquid smoke, if desired
16 slices party rye bread (about 2 inches
    in diameter)

1. Place pork tenderloin on rack in dish. Cover tightly and microwave on medium (50%) 12 to 14 minutes, turning tenderloin over after 6 minutes, until done (160° on meat thermometer).

2. Mix preserves, salt and liquid smoke. Cut pork diagonally into thin slices. Spoon preserves mixture over pork. Place 2 slices pork between 2 slices rye bread. Serve with additional tomato preserves if desired. **8 appetizers;** 175 calories per appetizer.

• • • • • • • • • • •

TROPICAL RUMAKI

Classic rumaki wraps chicken livers into a crunchy-crisp package with water chestnut and bacon. Here, pineapple, papaya and curry give these appetizers an unusual South Seas twist.

MICROWAVE TIME: 12 to 19 minutes

10 slices bacon, cut in half
¼ pineapple, pared and cut into
    1-inch pieces
1 papaya, pared, seeded and cut into
    1-inch pieces
¼ cup packed brown sugar
1 teaspoon curry powder

1. Arrange half of the bacon pieces on rack in dish. Cover with paper towel; arrange remaining bacon pieces on top. Cover with paper towel and microwave on high 8 to 12 minutes or until bacon is almost crisp. Remove bacon from rack; drain on paper towel. Drain fat from dish.

2. Wrap bacon piece around each piece fruit; secure with wooden pick. Mix brown sugar and curry powder. Roll wrapped fruit in sugar mixture; place on rack in dish.

3. Cover with paper towel and microwave on high 4 to 7 minutes or until bacon is crisp. **20 appetizers;** 35 calories per appetizer.

SWEET-AND-SOUR MEATBALLS

MICROWAVE TIME: 16 to 22 minutes
STAND TIME: 3 minutes

1 pound ground beef
½ cup dry bread crumbs
¼ cup milk
1 small onion, finely chopped
    (about ¼ cup)
1 egg
1 teaspoon Worcestershire sauce
½ teaspoon salt
⅛ teaspoon pepper
Sweet-and-Sour Sauce (below)

1. Mix all ingredients except Sweet-and-Sour Sauce. Shape mixture by tablespoonfuls into 1¼-inch balls. (For ease in shaping meatballs, wet hands occasionally with cold water.) Arrange meatballs in rectangular dish, 11 × 7 × 1½ inches.

2. Cover loosely and microwave on high 8 to 10 minutes, rearranging meatballs after 5 minutes, until no longer pink inside. Let stand covered 3 minutes; drain.

3. Prepare Sweet-and-Sour Sauce. Stir meatballs gently into sauce until coated. Cover tightly and microwave 4 to 6 minutes or until hot.   **8 servings (about 3 meatballs each)**; 265 calories per serving.

Sweet-and-Sour Sauce

1 cup chili sauce
½ cup currant jelly
1 teaspoon dry mustard

Mix all ingredients in 2-quart casserole. Cover tightly and microwave on high 4 to 6 minutes or until jelly is almost melted.

GOLDEN MUSHROOMS

MICROWAVE TIME: 8 to 11 minutes

1 pound medium mushrooms (about
    1½ inches in diameter)
1 small onion, chopped (about ¼ cup)
1 small stalk celery, chopped (about
    ¼ cup)
3 tablespoons margarine or butter
1½ cups soft bread crumbs (about 3 slices
    bread)
¼ teaspoon salt
1 teaspoon chopped fresh or ¼ teaspoon
    dried marjoram
¼ teaspoon pepper
⅛ to ¼ teaspoon ground turmeric

1. Cut stems from mushrooms; finely chop enough stems to measure ⅓ cup. Reserve mushroom caps. Mix chopped stems, onion, celery and margarine in 1-quart casserole. Microwave uncovered on high 2 to 3 minutes or until onion is soft. Stir in remaining ingredients except mushroom caps.

2. Fill mushroom caps with onion mixture. Arrange mushrooms, filled sides up and smallest in center, on each of two 10-inch plates. Microwave one plate at a time uncovered on high 3 to 4 minutes, rotating plate ½ turn after 2 minutes, until hot.   **About 30 appetizers**; 20 calories per appetizer.

FILLED NEW POTATOES

MICROWAVE TIME: 12 to 18 minutes
STAND TIME: 10 minutes

12 small new potatoes (about 1½ pounds)
¼ cup plain yogurt
⅛ teaspoon pepper
Toppings (below)

1.   Prepare and microwave pierced potatoes as directed (page 208). Remove potatoes from casserole; let stand about 10 minutes or until cool enough to handle.

2.   Cut thin slice from each potato; scoop out about 1 tablespoon potato from each. Mash scooped-out potato with fork; stir in yogurt and pepper. Fill each potato shell with about 1 tablespoon mashed potato mixture. Place filled potatoes on 10-inch plate.

3.   Microwave uncovered on high 2 to 3 minutes or until hot. Sprinkle each with Toppings.   **12 appetizers;** 50 calories per appetizer.

Toppings: Finely chopped walnuts, finely chopped fully cooked smoked ham, chopped fresh or dried dill weed, cracked black pepper.

• • • • • • • • • • •

APPETIZER BURRITOS

For a Southwest buffet, serve these with the Stacked Quesadillas and Chorizo-stuffed Breads, together with little dishes of salsa, guacamole and chopped fresh cilantro.

MICROWAVE TIME: 4 to 6 minutes

1 can (15 ounces) refried beans
10 flour tortillas (6 inches in diameter)
1½ cups shredded Monterey Jack cheese
    (6 ounces)
3 tablespoons chopped fresh cilantro

1.   Spread about 3 tablespoons beans over each tortilla to within ½ inch of edge; sprin-

Filled New Potatoes

kle each with about 2 tablespoons cheese and 1 teaspoon cilantro. Fold one edge of tortilla up about 1 inch over mixture; fold right and left sides over folded end. Fold remaining end up. Place seam sides down on each of two 10-inch plates.

2.   Cover each plate tightly. Microwave one plate at a time on high 2 to 3 minutes or until hot. Cut each burrito into 3 pieces with sharp knife. Serve with sour cream and guacamole if desired.   **30 appetizers;** 60 calories per appetizer.

Fold one edge of tortilla about 1 inch up over filling.

Fold two opposite sides over folded edge.

Fold remaining open end over to make a roll.

CHORIZO-FILLED BREADS

MICROWAVE TIME: 6 to 8 minutes

¼ pound bulk chorizo or pork sausage
½ teaspoon chili powder
3 green onions (with tops), sliced
6 eggs, beaten
3 pita breads (4 inches in diameter), cut
  in half

1.   Crumble sausage into 1-quart casserole. Cover tightly and microwave on high 2 to 3 minutes, stirring every minute, until done; drain. Stir in chili powder, onions and eggs.

2.   Cover tightly and microwave 3 to 4 minutes, stirring every minute, until set.

3.   Fill each bread half with 2 tablespoons egg mixture. Arrange on each of two 10-inch plates. Cover each plate with paper towel and microwave on high 20 to 30 seconds or until warm. Serve with cilantro and salsa if desired.   **12 appetizers;** 105 calories per appetizer.

STACKED QUESADILLAS

MICROWAVE TIME: 2 to 3 minutes

1 can (4 ounces) chopped green chilies
1 package (3 ounces) cream cheese,
  softened
4 flour tortillas (8 inches in diameter)
½ cup shredded Colby–Monterey Jack
  cheese (2 ounces)

1.   Stir green chilies into cream cheese. Stack tortillas on 10-inch plate, spreading each with about ⅓ cup cream cheese mixture. Sprinkle shredded cheese over top of tortilla.

2.   Microwave uncovered on high 2 to 3 minutes or until shredded cheese is melted. Cut into 12 wedges with sharp knife. Serve with salsa if desired.   **12 appetizers;** 75 calories per appetizer.

Chorizo-filled Breads

Chili-Shrimp with Bacon

CHILI-SHRIMP WITH BACON

REFRIGERATION TIME: 1 hour
MICROWAVE TIME: 10 to 14 minutes

½ cup chili sauce
½ clove garlic, finely chopped
20 peeled and deveined cooked medium
    shrimp
10 slices bacon, cut in half

1. Mix chili sauce and garlic; pour over shrimp in glass bowl. Cover and refrigerate 1 hour.

2. Arrange ⅓ of the bacon pieces in single layer on paper towel–lined 10-inch plate; top with paper towel and another ⅓ of the bacon. Top with paper towel. Arrange remaining bacon on top; cover with paper towel. Microwave on high 4 to 6 minutes or until partially cooked.

3. Wrap bacon piece around each shrimp; secure with wooden pick. Arrange 10 shrimp in circle on paper towel–lined plate. Cover with paper towel. Microwave one plate at a time on high 3 to 4 minutes or until bacon is crisp. Serve with Guacamole (page 90) if desired.   **20 appetizers;** 25 calories per appetizer.

SPICY SHRIMP APPETIZER

This is an easy last-minute appetizer for drop-in guests.

MICROWAVE TIME: 6 minutes

1 jar (8 ounces) Mexican-style process
   cheese spread
½ cup sour cream
2 cans (4¼ ounces each) tiny shrimp,
   rinsed and drained
1 loaf (about 1 pound) French bread, cut
   into ½-inch slices
¼ cup chopped fresh parsley

1.   Place cheese in large bowl. Microwave uncovered on high 30 to 60 seconds or until softened. Stir in sour cream and shrimp.

2.   Spread about 1 tablespoon cheese mixture on each slice bread. Place 8 slices on microwave rack or 10-inch plate. Microwave uncovered on high 1 minute or until cheese mixture is hot. Sprinkle with parsley. Repeat with remaining slices.   **40 slices;** 60 calories per slice.

• • • • • • • • • • •

WINE-MARINATED SHRIMP

MICROWAVE TIME: 6 to 11 minutes
REFRIGERATION TIME: 3 hours

1 cup dry white wine
¼ cup lemon juice
¼ teaspoon salt
¼ teaspoon ground ginger
1 clove garlic, crushed
1 pound fresh or frozen raw medium
   shrimp (15 to 20 in shells), peeled
   and deveined

1.   Mix all ingredients except shrimp in 2-quart casserole. Cover tightly and micro-wave on high 3 to 6 minutes or until boiling. Stir in shrimp.

2.   Cover tightly and microwave 3 to 5 minutes, stirring after 2 minutes, until shrimp are pink and firm. Cover and refrigerate in marinade at least 3 hours until chilled. Drain; serve shrimp with cocktail sauce if desired. **15 to 20 appetizers;** 10 calories per appetizer.

• • • • • • • • • • •

OYSTERS PARMESAN

The microwave makes this turn-of-the-century classic into an everyday treat. Rock salt anchors the shells and keeps them from spilling.

MICROWAVE TIME: 7 to 10 minutes

Rock salt*
12 medium oysters in shells, microwaved
   to open (page 7)
¼ cup sour cream
¼ cup cracker crumbs
2 tablespoons grated Parmesan cheese
1 tablespoon margarine or butter, melted
¼ teaspoon dry mustard

1.   Fill 2 pie plates, 9 × 1¼ inches, ½ inch deep with rock salt (about 2 cups each plate). Place oyster on deep half of shell (drain liquor); discard other half.

2.   Spoon 1 teaspoon sour cream onto oyster in each shell. Mix remaining ingredients. Spoon about 2 teaspoons mixture onto each oyster.

3.   Arrange 6 filled shells in circle on rock salt in each plate. Microwave one plate at a time uncovered on high 2 minutes 30 seconds to 3 minutes 30 seconds, rotating pie plate ½ turn after 1 minute, until oysters are hot and bubbly.   **12 appetizers;** 35 calories per appetizer.

*If desired, omit rock salt; decrease microwave time to 1 minute 30 seconds to 2 minutes 30 seconds.

GINGERED NUTS

MICROWAVE TIME: 2 to 4 minutes

1 cup pecan or walnut halves
¾ teaspoon ground ginger
¼ teaspoon salt
1 tablespoon margarine or butter

1. Place pecans in 1-quart casserole or bowl. Sprinkle with ginger and salt; dot with margarine.

2. Microwave uncovered on high 2 to 4 minutes, stirring after 1 minute, until toasted. Drain on paper towels. Serve warm.   **4 servings (¼ cup each);** 225 calories per serving.

•••••••••••

PRETZEL-CEREAL SNACK

MICROWAVE TIME: 7 to 10 minutes
STAND TIME: 30 minutes

½ cup margarine or butter
1 teaspoon Worcestershire sauce
½ teaspoon garlic powder
½ teaspoon celery salt
4 cups crispy corn puff cereal
2 cups pretzel sticks
2 cups mixed salted nuts

1. Place margarine, Worcestershire sauce, garlic powder and celery salt in 3-quart casserole or bowl. Microwave uncovered on high 45 seconds to 2 minutes or until margarine is melted.

2. Stir in cereal, pretzels and nuts; toss until well coated. Microwave uncovered on high 6 to 8 minutes, stirring every 2 minutes, until toasted. Let stand about 30 minutes or until cool. Store in tightly covered container up to 1 week.   **About 8 cups snack;** 400 calories per cup.

CINNAMON S'MORES SQUARES

MICROWAVE TIME: 2 to 3 minutes
STAND TIME: 1 hour

1 cup milk chocolate chips
⅓ cup light corn syrup
1 tablespoon margarine or butter
½ teaspoon vanilla
¼ teaspoon ground cinnamon
4 cups honey graham cereal
1½ cups miniature marshmallows

1. Grease square pan, 9 × 9 × 2 inches. Mix chocolate chips, corn syrup, margarine, vanilla and cinnamon in 3-quart casserole. Cover tightly and microwave on high 2 to 3 minutes or until boiling; stir.

2. Fold in cereal until completely coated with chocolate; fold in marshmallows. Press evenly in pan, using buttered back of spoon. Let stand about 1 hour or until cool. Cut into about 2-inch squares.   **18 squares;** 110 calories per square.

Hot Orange Cider (page 34), Peanut-Popcorn Balls (page 29), Gingered Nuts (page 27), Fruit-Nut Nibbles

FRUIT-NUT NIBBLES

MICROWAVE TIME: 3 to 4 minutes
STAND TIME: 1 hour

3 cups honey graham cereal
1⅓ cups salted peanuts
1 cup banana chips
2 tablespoons margarine or butter, melted
2 tablespoons honey
½ teaspoon ground cinnamon
¼ teaspoon salt
4 cups popped popcorn (about ¼ cup unpopped)
1 cup flaked coconut
1 cup raisins

1. Mix cereal, peanuts and banana chips in 3-quart casserole or bowl. Mix margarine, honey, cinnamon and salt; pour over cereal mixture, tossing until evenly coated. Microwave uncovered on high 3 to 4 minutes, stirring after 2 minutes, until toasted. Watch carefully so mixture does not burn.

2. Stir in popcorn, coconut and raisins. Sprinkle with additional salt if desired. Let stand about 1 hour or until cool. Store in tightly covered container up to 1 week. **About 12 cups snack;** 130 calories per ½ cup.

PEANUT-POPCORN BALLS

MICROWAVE TIME: 1 to 2 minutes
STAND TIME: 35 minutes

¼ cup packed brown sugar
¼ cup corn syrup
2 tablespoons creamy peanut butter
Dash of salt
4 cups popped popcorn (about ¼ cup unpopped)
½ cup salted peanuts

1. Mix brown sugar, corn syrup, peanut butter and salt in large bowl. Microwave uncovered on high 1 minute to 1 minute 30 seconds or until mixture begins to bubble; stir. Stir in popcorn and peanuts until well coated. Let stand 5 minutes.

2. Shape mixture firmly into four 3-inch balls with hands dipped in cold water. Place on waxed paper; let stand about 30 minutes or until completely cool. Wrap in plastic wrap. **4 popcorn balls;** 310 calories per popcorn ball.

• • • • • • • • • •

CARAMEL-GRANOLA CANDIES

MICROWAVE TIME: 4 to 5 minutes
REFRIGERATION TIME: 45 minutes

12 vanilla caramels
1½ teaspoons water
1 cup granola
¼ cup semisweet chocolate chips
1 tablespoon finely chopped pecans

1. Place caramels and water in 2-cup measure. Microwave uncovered on high 1 to 2 minutes, stirring after 30 seconds, until caramels are melted. Stir until smooth; stir in granola. Drop by teaspoonfuls onto waxed

paper–lined cookie sheet. Refrigerate about 30 minutes or until firm.

2. Place chocolate chips in 1-cup measure. Microwave uncovered on medium (50%) 2 to 3 minutes or until chips are melted; stir until smooth. Spread about ½ teaspoon chocolate over each candy; sprinkle with pecans. Refrigerate about 15 minutes or until chocolate is firm. **About 1½ dozen candies;** 50 calories per candy.

• • • • • • • • • •

ORANGE-DATE BALLS

MICROWAVE TIME: 7 to 8 minutes
STAND TIME: 10 minutes

1 package (16 ounces) chopped dates
½ cup margarine or butter
⅓ cup sugar
1 egg, well beaten
¼ teaspoon salt
2 teaspoons grated orange peel
2 tablespoons orange juice
1 teaspoon vanilla
½ cup chopped nuts
½ cup graham cracker crumbs
4 cups toasted whole wheat flake cereal
1¼ cups finely chopped nuts

1. Mix dates, margarine and sugar in 3-quart casserole. Cover tightly and microwave on high 4 minutes.

2. Stir in egg and salt. Cover tightly and microwave on medium-high (70%) 3 to 4 minutes or until slightly thickened.

3. Stir in orange peel, orange juice, vanilla, ½ cup nuts and the cracker crumbs. Let stand uncovered 10 minutes or until cool.

4. Stir in cereal. Shape into 1-inch balls, using buttered hands. Roll balls in finely chopped nuts. **About 5 dozen balls;** 75 calories per candy.

COCONUT-MOCHA DROPS

MICROWAVE TIME:	About 2 minutes
STAND TIME:	15 minutes

1 tablespoon freeze-dried instant
   coffee (dry)
¼ cup margarine or butter
¼ cup milk
3 cups powdered sugar
2 cups flaked coconut, toasted

1. Mix coffee, margarine and milk in large bowl. Cover loosely and microwave on high 1 minute 30 seconds to 2 minutes or until margarine is almost melted and mixture is hot. Stir until coffee is dissolved.

2. Stir in powdered sugar until smooth. Stir in coconut. Drop by scant teaspoonfuls onto waxed paper. Let stand 15 minutes or until firm. **About 4 dozen candies;** 55 calories per candy.

• • • • • • • • • •

CHOCOLATE-BOURBON BALLS

As good as they are freshly made, the flavor of these bourbon-kissed candies mellows and improves with age.

MICROWAVE TIME:	1 to 2 minutes

½ cup semisweet chocolate chips
2 tablespoons honey
1¼ cups finely crushed vanilla wafers
1 cup ground walnuts
1 tablespoon bourbon whiskey
Sugar

1. Mix chocolate chips and honey in 1½-quart casserole or bowl. Microwave uncovered on high 1 to 2 minutes or until chips are melted; stir.

2. Stir in vanilla wafers, walnuts and whiskey. Shape into 1-inch balls. Roll balls in sugar. Store in tightly covered container up to 10 days. (Flavor will continue to develop as they stand.) **About 1½ dozen candies;** 100 calories per candy.

• • • • • • • • • •

TWO-TONE RUM FUDGE

MICROWAVE TIME:	1 to 2 minutes
REFRIGERATION TIME:	1 hour

3 cups powdered sugar
¼ cup margarine or butter
2 tablespoons milk
¾ teaspoon rum flavoring
½ cup golden raisins
½ cup semisweet chocolate chips, melted

1. Line bottom and sides of loaf pan, 9 × 5 × 3 inches, with waxed paper, leaving 1 inch of waxed paper over sides of pan. Mix powdered sugar, margarine and milk in medium bowl. Microwave uncovered on high 1 to 2 minutes or until margarine is melted and mixture can be stirred smooth.

2. Stir in rum flavoring and raisins. Spread evenly in pan. Drizzle with melted chocolate; spread carefully to edges of pan. Refrigerate about 1 hour or until chocolate is firm. Lift out candy and cut into 1-inch squares. **About 3½ dozen candies;** 60 calories per candy.

Note: Paper bonbon cups, available at specialty shops and some supermarkets, can be used to make about 2½ dozen candies. Spoon into cups.

Double Chocolate Fudge (page 32), Orange-Date Balls (page 29), Chocolate-Bourbon Balls, Peanut Clusters (page 32), Coconut-Mocha Drops

CHOCOLATE-PECAN CLUSTERS

MICROWAVE TIME: 1 to 2 minutes
REFRIGERATION TIME: 30 minutes

1 cup miniature marshmallows
½ cup semisweet chocolate chips
2 tablespoons margarine or butter
1 cup pecan halves
¼ teaspoon vanilla

1. Place marshmallows, chocolate chips and margarine in small bowl. Cover with waxed paper and microwave on high 1 to 2 minutes, stirring every minute, until marshmallows are melted and mixture is smooth.

2. Stir in pecans and vanilla. Drop mixture, with 3 pecan halves per cluster, onto waxed paper–lined cookie sheet. Refrigerate uncovered about 30 minutes or until firm.   **About 20 candies;** 80 calories per candy.

•••••••••••

DOUBLE CHOCOLATE FUDGE

MICROWAVE TIME: 1 to 3 minutes
REFRIGERATION TIME: 2 hours

1 can (14 ounces) sweetened condensed milk
1 package (12 ounces) semisweet chocolate chips (2 cups)
1 ounce unsweetened chocolate
1 teaspoon vanilla
1½ cups chopped nuts

1. Line bottom and sides of square pan, 8 × 8 × 2 inches, with waxed paper, leaving 1 inch of waxed paper over sides of pan. Place milk, chocolate chips and chocolate in medium bowl. Microwave uncovered on high 1 to 3 minutes, stirring after 1 minute, until chocolate is melted and mixture can be stirred smooth.

2. Stir in vanilla and nuts. Spread evenly in pan. Refrigerate about 2 hours or until firm. Lift out candy and cut into 1-inch squares. **About 5½ dozen candies;** 70 calories per candy.

•••••••••••

PEANUT CLUSTERS

MICROWAVE TIME: 2 to 3 minutes
REFRIGERATION TIME: 30 minutes

1 cup sugar
⅓ cup evaporated milk
¼ cup margarine or butter
¼ cup crunchy peanut butter
½ teaspoon vanilla
2 cups quick-cooking or regular oats
½ cup Spanish peanuts
½ cup semisweet chocolate chips

1. Mix sugar, milk and margarine in 2-quart casserole. Microwave uncovered on high 2 to 3 minutes or until boiling.

2. Stir in peanut butter and vanilla until blended. Stir in oats, peanuts and chocolate chips. Drop by tablespoonfuls onto waxed paper–lined cookie sheet. (If mixture becomes too stiff, stir in 1 or 2 drops milk.) Refrigerate about 30 minutes or until firm.   **About 2 dozen candies;** 110 calories per candy.

HOT CHOCOLATE

MICROWAVE TIME: 4 to 6 minutes

3 tablespoons sugar
3 tablespoons cocoa
⅛ teaspoon salt
¾ cup hot water
2¼ cups milk

1.   Mix sugar, cocoa and salt in 4-cup measure. Stir in water. Microwave uncovered on high 1 to 2 minutes or until boiling.

2.   Stir in milk. Microwave uncovered 3 to 4 minutes or until hot (do not boil). Stir in ¼ teaspoon vanilla, if desired.   **5 servings (about ⅔ cup each);** 95 calories per serving.

SPICED TEA MIX

MICROWAVE TIME: 1 to 2 minutes

½ cup orange-flavored instant breakfast drink (dry)
½ cup instant tea (dry)
¼ cup sugar
¼ cup lemonade-flavored drink mix (dry)
¼ teaspoon ground cinnamon
⅛ teaspoon ground cloves

1.   Mix all ingredients; store in tightly covered container at room temperature.

2.   For each serving, stir 4 level teaspoons mixture into ¾ cup water in cup or mug. Microwave uncovered on high 1 to 2 minutes or until hot; stir.   **16 servings (about ¾ cup each);** 30 calories per serving.

Hot Chocolate, Spiced Tea Mix

HOT ORANGE CIDER

MICROWAVE TIME: 6 to 9 minutes

4 cups apple cider
2 tablespoons grenadine syrup
1¼ teaspoons grated orange peel

1. Mix all ingredients in 8-cup measure or 2-quart casserole.

2. Cover tightly and microwave on high 6 to 9 minutes or until hot; stir. Stir in 2 tablespoons brandy if desired.   **4 servings (about 1 cup each);** 130 calories per serving.

• • • • • • • • • •

WASSAIL

MICROWAVE TIME: 11 to 12 minutes

1 bottle (750 ml) dry red wine (about 3 cups)
2 cups apple juice
¼ to ⅓ cup packed brown sugar
1 teaspoon ground cinnamon
½ teaspoon ground nutmeg
½ teaspoon ground ginger
10 whole cloves
10 apple wedges

1. Mix all ingredients except apple wedges in 8-cup measure or 2-quart casserole.

2. Cover tightly and microwave on high 11 to 12 minutes, stirring after 5 minutes, until boiling. Stir in apple wedges. **10 servings (about ½ cup each);** 100 calories per serving.

CRANBERRY ORANGE PUNCH

MICROWAVE TIME: 8 to 12 minutes

1 bottle (32 ounces) cranberry juice cocktail
1 cup dry white wine or orange juice
½ teaspoon grated orange peel
1 cup orange juice
6 cinnamon sticks

1. Mix all ingredients except cinnamon sticks in 8-cup measure or 2-quart casserole.

2. Cover tightly and microwave on high 8 to 12 minutes or until hot. Garnish each serving with cinnamon stick. **6 servings (about 1 cup each);** 200 calories per serving.

• • • • • • • • • •

MULLED TOMATO JUICE

MICROWAVE TIME: 4 to 8 minutes

3 cups tomato juice
1 teaspoon Worcestershire sauce
1 teaspoon chopped fresh or ⅛ teaspoon dried oregano
4 to 6 drops red pepper sauce

1. Mix all ingredients in 4-cup measure.

2. Microwave uncovered on high 4 to 8 minutes or until hot. Serve in small cups or mugs. Garnish each serving with celery stick or green onion if desired. **6 servings (about ½ cup each);** 25 calories per serving.

SPICED MOCHA DRINK

MICROWAVE TIME: 6 to 8 minutes

¾ cup hot water
¼ cup sugar
1 tablespoon plus 2 teaspoons freeze-dried instant coffee (dry)
½ teaspoon ground cinnamon
¼ teaspoon ground nutmeg
Dash of salt
1½ ounces unsweetened chocolate, chopped
2 cups milk

1. Stir water, sugar, coffee, cinnamon, nutmeg and salt in 4-cup measure. Add chocolate. Microwave uncovered on high 3 to 4 minutes, stirring after 2 minutes, until chocolate is melted and can be stirred smooth.

2. Stir in milk. Microwave uncovered 3 to 4 minutes or until hot. Beat with hand beater until foamy. Top each serving with whipped cream if desired. **4 servings (about ⅔ cup each);** 120 calories per serving.

CHOCOLATE CAPPUCCINO

MICROWAVE TIME: 4 to 6 minutes

1 cup hot espresso or double-strength coffee
¼ cup sugar
Dash of salt
1 ounce unsweetened chocolate, chopped
1 cup milk
Whipped cream
Grated orange peel

1. Stir espresso, sugar and salt in 4-cup measure; add chocolate. Microwave uncovered on high 2 to 3 minutes or until chocolate is melted and can be stirred smooth.

2. Stir in milk. Microwave uncovered 2 to 3 minutes or until hot. Beat with hand beater until foamy. Top each serving with whipped cream; sprinkle with orange peel. **4 servings (about ½ cup each);** 140 calories per serving.

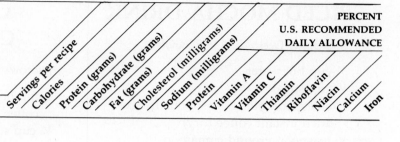

RECIPE, PAGE	Servings per recipe	Calories	Protein (grams)	Carbohydrate (grams)	Fat (grams)	Cholesterol (milligrams)	Sodium (milligrams)	Protein	Vitamin A	Vitamin C	Thiamin	Riboflavin	Niacin	Calcium	Iron
APPETIZERS															
Appetizer Burritos, 23	30	60	2	6	3	0	50	2	0	0	0	0	0	4	0
Brie with Almonds, 18	10	85	3	1	8	15	105	4	2	0	0	4	0	2	0
Brie Wheel, 18	28	50	4	1	4	15	90	4	0	0	0	4	2	2	2
Cheddar-Apple Spread, 17	12	25	0	2	2	2	20	0	0	0	0	0	0	0	0
Chili-Shrimp with Bacon, 25	20	25	1	2	1	10	110	0	0	0	0	0	0	0	0
Chorizo-filled Breads, 24	12	105	6	11	4	135	150	8	6	0	2	4	0	0	2
Cocktail Wiener Kabobs, 20	12	70	3	2	6	10	280	4	6	10	2	4	4	0	2
Filled New Potatoes, 23	12	50	1	12	0	0	5	0	0	2	2	0	2	0	0
Glazed Pork Tenderloin Appetizers, 20	8	175	8	21	7	25	135	12	0	0	14	6	8	0	2
Golden Mushrooms, 21	30	20	0	2	1	0	45	0	0	0	0	4	2	0	0
Hot Artichoke Dip, 15	24	45	1	1	4	0	60	0	0	0	0	0	0	2	0
Hot Horseradish Dip, 16	16	50	1	0	5	15	55	0	4	0	0	0	0	0	0
Orange Dip with Fresh Fruit, 17	16	45	1	9	1	35	100	0	0	2	0	0	0	0	0
Oysters Parmesan, 26	12	35	1	2	3	5	50	0	2	0	0	0	0	2	2
Party Cheese Log, 18	6	255	10	3	22	70	390	14	18	6	0	10	0	22	4
Spicy Cheese Dip, 15	24	30	2	1	2	5	115	2	2	0	0	2	0	4	0
Spicy Shrimp Appetizer, 26	40	60	2	7	2	10	140	4	0	0	2	2	0	4	2
Spinach Dip, 16	64	30	1	0	2	8	35	0	6	0	0	0	0	2	0
Stacked Quesadillas, 24	12	75	2	6	5	10	50	2	4	4	0	2	0	4	0
Sweet-and-Sour Meatballs, 21	8	265	14	27	11	75	635	20	8	6	6	10	14	2	12
Taco Salad Dip, 15	56	25	1	1	2	5	45	2	5	0	2	0	0	0	0
Tropical Rumaki, 20	20	35	1	5	1	25	2	0	6	8	0	0	0	0	0
Wine-marinated Shrimp, 26	20	10	1	0	0	8	10	0	0	0	0	0	0	0	0
SNACKS															
Caramel-Granola Candies, 29	18	50	1	7	2	0	15	0	0	0	0	0	0	0	0
Chocolate-Bourbon Balls, 30	18	100	1	11	6	0	15	2	0	0	0	0	0	0	2
Chocolate-Pecan Clusters, 32	20	80	1	6	6	0	15	0	0	0	2	0	0	0	0
Cinnamon S'mores Squares, 27	18	110	1	19	4	0	75	0	6	2	6	6	4	0	8
Coconut-Mocha Drops, 30	48	55	0	9	2	0	15	0	0	0	0	0	0	0	0

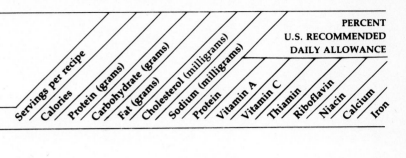

RECIPE, PAGE	Servings per recipe	Calories	Protein (grams)	Carbohydrate (grams)	Fat (grams)	Cholesterol (milligrams)	Sodium (milligrams)	Protein	Vitamin A	Vitamin C	Thiamin	Riboflavin	Niacin	Calcium	Iron
SNACKS, *continued*															
Double Chocolate Fudge, 32	64	70	1	7	4	2	10	2	0	0	0	2	0	2	0
Fruit-Nut Nibbles, 28	½ cup	130	3	18	6	0	130	4	4	2	4	4	8	0	4
Gingered Nuts, 27	14	225	2	6	23	0	45	2	2	0	16	2	0	0	2
Orange-Date Balls, 29	60	75	1	10	4	5	55	0	2	0	2	2	2	0	2
Peanut Clusters, 32	24	110	2	12	6	0	50	2	0	0	0	0	4	0	0
Peanut-Popcorn Balls, 29	4	310	8	43	13	0	110	12	0	0	4	2	22	2	10
Pretzel-Cereal Snack, 27	1 cup	400	7	23	33	0	720	10	22	6	24	18	22	4	12
Two-Tone Rum Fudge, 30	45	60	0	11	2	0	15	0	0	0	0	0	0	0	0
BEVERAGES															
Chocolate Cappuccino, 35	4	140	3	17	8	15	90	4	4	0	0	6	0	8	4
Cranberry Orange Punch, 34	6	200	0	27	0	0	10	0	0	60	2	0	0	2	2
Hot Chocolate, 33	5	95	4	14	3	10	110	6	4	0	2	10	0	12	2
Hot Orange Cider, 34	4	130	0	29	0	0	10	0	0	4	2	2	0	0	4
Mulled Tomato Juice, 34	6	25	1	5	0	0	445	0	12	18	4	2	4	0	4
Spiced Mocha Drink, 35	4	120	5	10	8	10	115	8	4	0	2	12	2	16	4
Spiced Tea Mix, 33	16	30	0	7	0	0	5	0	0	0	0	0	0	0	0
Wassail, 34	10	100	0	13	0	0	5	0	0	0	0	0	0	0	4

2

POULTRY AND
SEAFOOD

Because microwaves do their work in a small, enclosed space, the food cooks not only by microwave energy but by steaming as well. This is good news for poultry and seafood of all kinds. Steaming is one of the kindest ways to cook these foods, resulting in moist perfection.

- To check whether poultry is thoroughly cooked, look to see whether the juices run clear. Cook all white meat *only* until meat thermometer registers 165°. All other poultry should be cooked to an internal temperature of 180°. If juices are still pink, the meat needs a few minutes longer; increase the cooking time by 1-minute intervals until juices run clear. Arrange serving pieces of poultry with the thickest, meatiest pieces toward the outside of the dish, overlapping as little as possible. Poultry is microwaved covered, assuring more even cooking and thorough doneness. The skin will not brown or crisp as it does when cooked conventionally, so you will find many delicious glazes, sauces and even toasted nut coatings in the poultry recipes that follow. Microwaving makes the most of skinned poultry, and removing the skin lowers the calorie count, too.

- Fish is properly cooked when it easily flakes with a fork and meat thermometer registers 160°. Fish fillets are not uniformly thick; usually they are thinner at the tapered (tail) end. Fold the thin end under so that, doubled, it is about as thick as the thickest part. Shrimp turns pink when microwave-cooked, as it does when cooked conventionally. Scallops are done when they turn white or opaque and become firm, and clam and oyster shells open—as if by magic—without the application of a shucking knife.

Lemon Seafood with Pasta (page 100), Chicken with Bell Peppers (page 41)

CHICKEN WITH BELL PEPPERS

This chicken "simmers" in a luscious Italian sauce, savory with sausage and herbs. To reduce the amount of fat, skin the chicken before cooking.

◐ MICROWAVE TIME: 27 to 30 minutes

3- to 3½-pound broiler-fryer chicken, cut up
½ pound Italian sausage links, cut into 1-inch pieces
2 teaspoons chopped fresh or ½ teaspoon dried basil
1 teaspoon chopped fresh or ¼ teaspoon dried thyme
½ teaspoon salt
1 medium onion, chopped (about ½ cup)
1 large red bell pepper, cut into ½-inch strips
1 large green bell pepper, cut into ½-inch strips
1 clove garlic, finely chopped
1 can (15 ounces) tomato sauce with tomato bits

1. Arrange chicken, skin sides up and thickest parts to outside edges, in rectangular dish, 13 × 9 × 2 inches. Add sausage. Cover with waxed paper and microwave on high 15 minutes; drain.

2. Sprinkle with basil, thyme, salt and onion. Arrange bell peppers on top; sprinkle with garlic. Pour tomato sauce over top. Cover with waxed paper and microwave 12 to 15 minutes, rotating dish ½ turn every 5 minutes, until thickest pieces of chicken are done. **6 servings;** 290 calories per serving.

A 500-watt microwave is not recommended.

ITALIAN CHICKEN

◐ MICROWAVE TIME: 26 to 30 minutes

3- to 3½-pound broiler-fryer chicken, cut up
1 can (16 ounces) whole tomatoes, undrained
1 can (8 ounces) tomato sauce
4 ounces fresh mushrooms, sliced (about 1 cup)
1 medium onion, chopped (about ½ cup)
2 cloves garlic, finely chopped
1 bay leaf
¼ cup sliced ripe olives
1 tablespoon chopped fresh or 1 teaspoon dried oregano
1 teaspoon salt
¼ teaspoon pepper
¼ cup chopped fresh parsley
4 cups hot cooked spaghetti

1. Arrange chicken, skin sides up and thickest parts to outside edge, in 3-quart casserole. Cover tightly and microwave on high 12 minutes; drain.

2. Mix remaining ingredients except parsley and spaghetti; break up tomatoes. Stir mixture into chicken. Cover tightly and microwave 14 to 18 minutes or until juices of chicken run clear. Remove bay leaf. Sprinkle with parsley. Serve over spaghetti. **6 servings;** 330 calories per serving.

500-watt microwave: You may need to increase microwave times.

CHICKEN WITH ARTICHOKE HEARTS

MICROWAVE TIME: 27 to 35 minutes

6 slices bacon, cut into ½-inch pieces
3- to 3½-pound broiler-fryer chicken, cut up and skinned
2 teaspoons chopped fresh or ½ teaspoon dried tarragon
½ teaspoon salt
½ teaspoon paprika
4 ounces fresh mushrooms, sliced (about 1½ cups)
½ cup dry white wine or apple juice
1 tablespoon cornstarch
2 tablespoons cold water
1 can (14 ounces) artichoke hearts, drained and cut into halves

1.   Place bacon in rectangular dish, 11 × 7 × 1½ inches. Cover with paper towel and microwave on high 6 to 9 minutes or until crisp. Remove bacon with slotted spoon; drain and reserve. Drain fat from dish.

2.   Arrange chicken, skin sides up and thickest parts to outside edges, in same dish. Mix tarragon, salt and paprika; sprinkle over chicken. Arrange mushrooms on chicken. Pour wine over top. Cover tightly and microwave on high 16 to 20 minutes, rotating dish ½ turn after 10 minutes, until juices run clear. Remove chicken to platter, with slotted spoon; keep warm.

3.   Mix cornstarch and cold water; stir into liquid in dish. Microwave uncovered 3 to 4 minutes, stirring every minute, until slightly thickened. Stir in artichoke hearts. Microwave uncovered 2 minutes. Pour over chicken; sprinkle with bacon.   **6 servings;** 300 calories per serving.

A 500-watt microwave is not recommended.

ORANGE-GLAZED CHICKEN

MICROWAVE TIME: 30 to 35 minutes

3- to 3½-pound broiler-fryer chicken, cut up
½ orange
½ cup orange marmalade
¼ cup orange juice
2 tablespoons cornstarch
2 tablespoons packed brown sugar
2 tablespoons lemon juice
½ teaspoon salt

1.   Arrange chicken, skin sides up and thickest parts to outside edges, in rectangular dish, 11 × 7 × 1½ inches. Cover with waxed paper and microwave on high 15 minutes; drain, reserving juices.

2.   Pare orange; cut into ¼-inch slices. Cut each slice into fourths.

3.   Mix remaining ingredients in 4-cup measure until well blended. Stir in juices from chicken. Microwave uncovered on high 4 minutes 30 seconds to 5 minutes, stirring every minute, until mixture thickens and boils. Stir in orange.

4.   Spoon orange mixture over chicken in dish. Cover with waxed paper and microwave on high 10 to 15 minutes or until juices run clear. Garnish with parsley if desired.
6 servings; 275 calories per serving.

A 500-watt microwave is not recommended.

CHICKEN WITH SUMMER SQUASH

The chicken and the vegetables finish cooking together, then are dressed with a subtle lime and dill sauce and can be served right from the cooking dish.

MICROWAVE TIME: 11 to 14 minutes

4 skinless boneless chicken breast
  halves (about 1½ pounds)
¼ cup margarine or butter
1 tablespoon lime juice
1 tablespoon chopped fresh or 1 teaspoon
  dried dill weed
¼ teaspoon salt
4 small pattypan squash, cut into ¼-inch
  slices
1 small zucchini, cut into thin strips
1 small yellow squash, cut into thin strips
1 small yellow or green bell pepper, cut
  into rings

1. Arrange chicken breast halves with thickest parts to outside edge on 12-inch plate. Cover with waxed paper and microwave on high 8 to 10 minutes, rearranging chicken with uncooked parts to outside edge of plate after 4 minutes, until juices run clear; drain.

2. Place margarine, lime juice, dill weed and salt in 1-cup measure. Microwave uncovered on high about 45 seconds or until margarine is melted; stir.

3. Arrange chicken in center of plate. Arrange vegetables around chicken. Drizzle chicken and vegetables with margarine mixture. Cover with waxed paper and microwave 3 to 4 minutes or until vegetables are crisp-tender. **4 servings;** 325 calories per serving.

A 500-watt microwave is not recommended.

SHERRIED CHICKEN

MICROWAVE TIME: 24 to 32 minutes
STAND TIME: 5 minutes

6 small chicken breast halves (about
  2 pounds)
2 tablespoons margarine or butter, melted
Paprika
½ cup half-and-half
⅓ cup dry sherry or dry white wine
1 can (10¾ ounces) condensed cream of
  chicken soup
1 can (8 ounces) sliced water chestnuts,
  drained
1 can (4 ounces) mushroom stems and
  pieces, drained
1 cup seedless grapes

1. Arrange chicken breast halves, skin sides up and thickest parts to outside edges, in rectangular dish, 12 × 7½ × 2 inches. Pour margarine over chicken; sprinkle generously with paprika. Cover with waxed paper and microwave on high 16 to 20 minutes, rotating dish ½ turn after 10 minutes, until juices run clear; drain.

2. Mix remaining ingredients except grapes; spoon over chicken. Cover tightly and microwave 8 to 12 minutes, rotating dish ½ turn after 5 minutes, until sauce is hot. Sprinkle with grapes. Let stand covered 5 minutes. Garnish with parsley if desired. **6 servings;** 255 calories per serving.

A 500-watt microwave is not recommended.

LEMON-HERB GRILLED CHICKEN

REFRIGERATION TIME: 3 hours
MICROWAVE TIME: 8 to 10 minutes
GRILL TIME: 20 to 25 minutes

3- to 3½-pound broiler-fryer chicken,
  cut up
⅓ cup olive or vegetable oil
¼ cup lemon juice
1 tablespoon chopped fresh or 1 teaspoon
  dried basil
2 teaspoons chopped fresh or ½ teaspoon
  dried thyme
¼ teaspoon salt
¼ teaspoon freshly ground pepper
2 cloves garlic, crushed

1. Arrange chicken, skin sides up and thickest parts to outside edges, in rectangular dish, 11 × 7 × 1½ inches. Shake remaining ingredients in tightly covered container; pour over chicken. Turn chicken to coat well. Cover and refrigerate at least 3 hours.

2. Prepare charcoal fire for grilling. Microwave chicken and marinade tightly covered on high 8 to 10 minutes or until outside edges of chicken begin to cook.

3. Place chicken, skin sides down, 5 to 6 inches from medium coals, on grill; reserve marinade. Cover and grill chicken 10 minutes; turn. Cover and grill 10 to 15 minutes longer, brushing occasionally with marinade, until juices run clear. **6 servings;** 280 calories per serving.

A 500-watt microwave is not recommended.

Microwave-only Directions: Remove skin from chicken. Arrange chicken, thickest parts to outside edges, in rectangular dish, 11 × 7 × 1½ inches. Shake remaining ingredients in tightly covered container; pour over chicken. Turn chicken to coat well. Cover and refrigerate at least 3 hours.

Lemon-Herb Grilled Chicken, Corn (page 198)

Microwave chicken and marinade tightly covered on high 15 to 20 minutes, rotating dish ½ turn after 10 minutes, until juices run clear.

• • • • • • • • • •

LEMON-DILL CHICKEN

MICROWAVE TIME: 9 to 11 minutes
STAND TIME: 5 minutes

2 tablespoons margarine or butter
6 small skinless boneless chicken breast
  halves (about 1½ pounds)
¼ cup dry white wine or water
1 tablespoon lemon juice
1 teaspoon chopped fresh or ⅛ teaspoon
  dried dill weed
¼ teaspoon salt
½ lemon, thinly sliced
2 green onions (with tops), sliced

1. Place margarine in rectangular dish, 11 × 7 × 1½ inches. Microwave uncovered on high 20 to 30 seconds or until melted.

2. Arrange chicken breast halves, thickest parts to outside edges, in margarine. Cover tightly and microwave 4 minutes.

3. Mix wine, lemon juice, dill weed and salt; pour over chicken. Place lemon on chicken. Cover tightly and microwave 4 to 6 minutes or until juices run clear. Let stand covered 5 minutes; sprinkle with onions. **6 servings;** 190 calories per serving.

A 500-watt microwave is not recommended.

RASPBERRY CHICKEN BREASTS

MICROWAVE TIME: 9 to 11 minutes

4 skinless boneless chicken breast
   halves (about 1½ pounds)
2 teaspoons finely chopped gingerroot
⅓ cup raspberry preserves
2 teaspoons raspberry-flavored vinegar

1. Arrange chicken breast halves with thickest parts to outside edge in square dish, 8 × 8 × 2 inches. Sprinkle with gingeroot.

Cover tightly and microwave on high 8 to 10 minutes, rotating dish ½ turn after 4 minutes, until juices run clear.

2. Mix preserves and vinegar in 1-cup measure. Microwave uncovered on high 30 to 60 seconds or until warm. Serve over chicken. Serve with hot cooked rice and garnish with fresh raspberries if desired. **4 servings;** 200 calories per serving.

Raspberry Chicken Breasts

CHICKEN KIEV

🕐 FREEZE TIME: 20 minutes
MICROWAVE TIME: 6 to 8 minutes

¼ cup margarine or butter, softened
2 teaspoons chopped fresh chives
¼ teaspoon garlic powder
¼ teaspoon white pepper
4 skinless boneless chicken breast halves
   (about 1½ pounds)
½ cup cornflake crumbs
1 tablespoon chopped fresh or 1 teaspoon
   dried tarragon
½ teaspoon paprika
¼ cup buttermilk or milk

1. Mix margarine, chives, garlic powder and white pepper. Drop by tablespoonfuls into 4 mounds on waxed paper. Freeze about 20 minutes or until firm.

2. Flatten each chicken breast half to ¼-inch thickness between plastic wrap or waxed paper. Place 1 mound of margarine mixture on center of each chicken breast half. Fold long sides over mound; fold ends up. Secure with wooden picks.

3. Mix cornflake crumbs, tarragon and paprika. Dip chicken into buttermilk; coat evenly with crumb mixture. Arrange chicken, seam sides up, on rack in dish. Cover with waxed paper and microwave on high 6 to 8 minutes or until juices run clear. Remove wooden picks. **4 servings;** 285 calories per serving.

Fold long sides of chicken over margarine.

Fold open ends up and secure with wooden picks.

CHICKEN NUGGETS

These bite-size pieces of chicken are perfect for a party or for an anytime appetizer.

MICROWAVE TIME: 9 to 10 minutes

2 small whole skinless boneless chicken
    breasts (about 1 pound), cut into 1-inch
    pieces
1 tablespoon vegetable oil
½ cup variety baking mix
½ cup cornflake crumbs
¾ teaspoon paprika
¼ teaspoon salt
¼ teaspoon pepper
Apricot-Honey Sauce (page 324)

1. Toss chicken and oil. Mix remaining ingredients except Apricot-Honey Sauce in plastic bag. Shake about 6 pieces chicken at a time in bag until coated. Shake off excess crumbs.

2. Arrange chicken pieces in single layer in pie plate, 10 × 1½ inches. Cover with waxed paper and microwave on high 7 to 8 minutes, rotating pie plate ½ turn after 3 minutes, or until juices run clear. Serve with Apricot-Honey Sauce.   **6 servings;** 180 calories per serving.

CHINESE CHICKEN AND CASHEWS

Plum sauce adds authentic flavor in this easy stir-fry, crunchy with bok choy and nuts.

MICROWAVE TIME: 10 to 12 minutes
REFRIGERATION TIME: 30 minutes

4 skinless boneless chicken breast halves
    (about 1½ pounds), cut into ¾-inch
    pieces
1 tablespoon soy sauce
1 tablespoon dry white wine
2 large stalks bok choy (with leaves),
    chopped (about 2 cups)
3 tablespoons plum sauce
2 green onions (with tops), sliced
    diagonally
1 tablespoon cornstarch
2 tablespoons dry white wine
½ cup dry roasted cashews
2 cups hot cooked rice

1. Mix chicken, soy sauce and 1 tablespoon wine in 2-quart casserole. Cover and refrigerate 30 minutes.

2. Cover chicken tightly and microwave on high 4 minutes, stirring after 2 minutes. Stir in bok choy, plum sauce and onions. Cover tightly and microwave 2 to 3 minutes or until bok choy is crisp-tender.

3. Mix cornstarch and 2 tablespoons wine; stir into chicken mixture. Microwave uncovered 4 to 5 minutes, stirring every minute, until sauce is slightly thickened. Stir in cashews. Serve over rice.   **4 servings;** 370 calories per serving.

500-watt microwave: You may need to increase microwave times.

Curried Chicken Breasts

CURRIED CHICKEN BREASTS

 MICROWAVE TIME: 15 to 17 minutes

6 small skinless boneless chicken breast
  halves (about 1½ pounds)
1 large onion, chopped (about 1 cup)
1 teaspoon chicken bouillon granules
1 cup sour cream
2 teaspoons curry powder
¼ teaspoon salt
⅛ teaspoon ground ginger
⅛ teaspoon ground cumin
Chopped fresh parsley
3 cups hot cooked rice
Condiments (right)

1. Arrange chicken breast halves, thickest
parts to outside edges, in rectangular dish,
11 × 7 × 1½ inches. Sprinkle with onion and
bouillon granules. Cover with waxed paper
and microwave on high 10 to 12 minutes,
rotating dish ½ turn after 5 minutes, until
juices run clear.

2. Remove chicken and onions to serving
dish, using slotted spoon; keep warm. Drain
juices reserving ¼ cup in dish; stir in sour
cream, curry powder, salt, ginger and cumin.
Microwave uncovered on medium (50%)
about 5 minutes, stirring every minute, until
hot. Spoon over chicken. Top with parsley.
Serve with rice and Condiments.   **6 servings;**
350 calories per serving.

A 500-watt microwave is not recommended.

Condiments: Peach Chutney (page 333),
chopped peanuts, toasted coconut, chopped
hard-cooked egg; chopped green onion.

CHICKEN-PINEAPPLE KABOBS

REFRIGERATION TIME: 10 minutes
MICROWAVE TIME: 9 to 12 minutes

2 small whole skinless boneless chicken
    breasts (about 1 pound), cut into
    1-inch pieces
2 tablespoons teriyaki sauce
½ teaspoon sugar
1½ teaspoons vegetable oil
¼ teaspoon ground ginger
1 small clove garlic, finely chopped
1 can (8 ounces) pineapple chunks,
    drained
1 medium green bell pepper, cut into
    1½-inch pieces
2 small onions, cut into fourths

1. Mix chicken, teriyaki sauce, sugar, oil,
ginger and garlic in glass or plastic bowl.
Cover and refrigerate 10 minutes.

2. Remove chicken from marinade. Thread
4 or 5 chicken pieces alternately with pineapple, bell pepper and onion on each of eight
8-inch wooden skewers.

3. Arrange skewers on 12-inch plate. Cover
with waxed paper and microwave on high 9
to 12 minutes or until juices run clear. Serve
with additional teriyaki sauce if desired.
4 servings; 210 calories per serving.

A 500-watt microwave is not recommended.

PAPRIKA CHICKEN

*This Hungarian-inspired recipe takes full ad-
vantage of the rich flavor of dark-meat chicken.
Skinless boneless chicken thighs are available
prepackaged at many grocery stores or from
your butcher.*

MICROWAVE TIME: 13 to 17 minutes

6 skinless boneless chicken thighs
    (about 1 pound), cut in half
1 medium onion, finely chopped (about
    ½ cup)
1 clove garlic, finely chopped
1 tablespoon paprika
1 tablespoon chopped fresh or 1 teaspoon
    dried basil
½ teaspoon salt
⅛ teaspoon ground red pepper (cayenne)
1 can (8 ounces) tomato sauce
1 tablespoon cornstarch
2 tablespoons cold water
¼ cup sour cream
3 cups hot cooked noodles

1. Mix chicken, onion, garlic, paprika, basil,
salt and red pepper in 2-quart casserole. Cover
tightly and microwave on high 8 to 10 minutes, stirring after 4 minutes, until juices run
clear.

2. Stir in tomato sauce. Mix cornstarch and
cold water; stir gradually into tomato mixture. Cover tightly and microwave 5 to 7
minutes, stirring every 2 minutes, until mixture is slightly thickened and hot. Stir in
sour cream. Serve with noodles. **4 servings;**
355 calories per serving.

*500-watt microwave: You may need to in-
crease microwave times.*

GINGERED CHICKEN

◑ MICROWAVE TIME: 19 to 24 minutes

3 pounds chicken drumsticks and
  thighs
⅓ cup honey
⅓ cup chili sauce
⅓ cup soy sauce
1 teaspoon ground ginger
½ teaspoon salt
¼ teaspoon pepper
1 tablespoon cornstarch
2 tablespoons cold water

1. Arrange chicken, thickest parts to outside edges, in rectangular dish, 11 × 7 × 1½
inches. Mix remaining ingredients except
cornstarch and cold water; pour over chicken.
Cover with waxed paper and microwave on
high 17 to 21 minutes, rotating dish ½ turn
and spooning sauce over chicken after 10
minutes, until juices run clear.

2. Remove chicken to platter, with slotted
spoon; keep warm. Skim fat from sauce. Mix
cornstarch and cold water; stir into sauce.
Microwave covered on high 2 to 3 minutes,
stirring every minute, until thickened. Pour
over chicken. **6 servings;** 310 calories per serving.

A 500-watt microwave is not recommended.

EASY MEXICAN CHICKEN

◑ MICROWAVE TIME: 16 to 19 minutes

½ cup variety baking mix
2 tablespoons yellow cornmeal
2 teaspoons chili powder
1 teaspoon paprika
½ teaspoon salt
⅛ teaspoon pepper
8 chicken drumsticks, thighs or wings
  (about 2 pounds)

1. Mix all ingredients except chicken in plastic bag. Shake 2 pieces chicken at a time in
bag until coated.

2. Arrange chicken, thickest parts to outside edges, in square dish, 8 × 8 × 2 inches.
Cover with waxed paper and microwave on
high 16 to 19 minutes, rotating dish ½ turn after
10 minutes, until juices run clear. **4 servings;**
290 calories per serving.

BARBECUED CHICKEN WINGS

🕐 MICROWAVE TIME: 17 to 21 minutes

16 chicken wings (about 3½ pounds)
1 large lemon, cut into 14 thin slices
Zesty Barbecue Sauce (page 324)

1. Cut off and discard chicken wing tips. Arrange chicken and lemon alternately in rectangular dish, 12 × 7½ × 2 inches. Cover tightly and microwave on high 12 to 15 minutes, rotating dish ½ turn after 6 minutes, until juices run clear; drain. Keep warm.

2. Prepare Zesty Barbecue Sauce; pour evenly over chicken. Microwave uncovered 3 to 4 minutes or until sauce is hot.   **4 servings**; 335 calories per serving.

A 500-watt microwave is not recommended.

Cut off and discard chicken wing tip.

Barbecued Chicken Wings

CHICKEN ENCHILADAS

MICROWAVE TIME: 10 to 13 minutes
REFRIGERATION TIME: 1 hour

2 cups cut-up cooked chicken or turkey
1 can (4 ounces) chopped green chilies,
    drained
1 medium tomato, chopped (about
    ¾ cup)
1 medium onion, chopped (about ½ cup)
1 clove garlic, finely chopped
8 six-inch flour tortillas
Guacamole (page 90) or 1 container
    (6 ounces) frozen avocado dip, thawed
1 cup shredded Cheddar cheese
    (4 ounces)

1. Mix chicken, chilies, tomato, onion and garlic in 1½-quart casserole. Cover tightly and microwave on high 5 to 6 minutes, stirring after 2 minutes, until hot.

2. Stack 4 of the tortillas on 10-inch plate. Cover tightly and microwave on high 20 to 30 seconds or until hot. Place about ⅓ cup chicken mixture down center of each tortilla; top each with about 1 tablespoon of the Guacamole. Roll tortillas around filling. Arrange enchiladas, seam sides down, on plate. Sprinkle with ½ cup of the cheese.

3. Microwave uncovered on high 2 to 3 minutes or until enchiladas are hot and cheese is melted. Repeat with remaining tortillas. Serve with taco sauce if desired. **8 enchiladas;** 230 calories per enchilada.

CREOLE CHICKEN CASSEROLE

The satisfying Louisiana flavor of a Creole hot pot, in 21 minutes or less. Look for a smoked ham with pronounced flavor.

MICROWAVE TIME: 17 to 21 minutes

2 cups uncooked instant rice
2 cups chicken broth
½ to ¾ teaspoon red pepper sauce
1 medium onion, chopped (about ½ cup)
1 clove garlic, crushed
2 cups cut-up cooked chicken or turkey
1 cup finely chopped fully cooked
    smoked ham
¼ cup tomato paste
1 small green bell pepper, chopped
    (about ½ cup)
1 can (16 ounces) whole tomatoes,
    undrained
1 can (6½ ounces) shrimp, rinsed and
    drained

1. Mix rice, broth, pepper sauce, onion and garlic in 3-quart casserole. Cover tightly and microwave on high 9 to 11 minutes or until rice is tender and liquid is absorbed.

2. Stir in remaining ingredients; break up tomatoes. Cover tightly and microwave 8 to 10 minutes, stirring after 5 minutes, until hot. **6 servings (about 1⅓ cups each);** 295 calories per serving.

500-watt microwave: You may need to increase microwave times.

Creole Chicken Casserole

CHICKEN CARBONARA

This dish has all the flavors of a classic pasta carbonara, but it features a delightful addition: moist pieces of chicken.

MICROWAVE TIME: 13 to 20 minutes

8 slices bacon, cut into ½-inch pieces
1 medium onion, chopped (about ½ cup)
1 clove garlic, finely chopped
2 cups cut-up cooked chicken or turkey
½ cup grated Parmesan cheese
½ cup whipping (heavy) cream
1 package (7 ounces) spaghetti, cooked and drained

1. Place bacon in 3-quart casserole. Cover with paper towel and microwave on high 8 to 12 minutes, stirring after 5 minutes, until crisp. Remove bacon with slotted spoon; drain and reserve. Drain fat, reserving 1 tablespoon in casserole.

2. Stir onion and garlic into fat in casserole. Cover tightly and microwave 1 to 3 minutes or until onion is tender.

3. Stir in remaining ingredients. Cover tightly and microwave 4 to 5 minutes or until heated through. Toss with bacon. **4 servings (about 1¼ cups each);** 535 calories per serving.

• • • • • • • • • •

CHICKEN NACHOS

MICROWAVE TIME: 8 to 10 minutes

2 cups shredded cooked chicken or turkey
1½ cups shredded Monterey Jack cheese (6 ounces)
½ cup sour cream
1 can (4 ounces) chopped green chilies, drained
½ package (16-ounce size) tortilla chips
1 medium tomato, chopped
1 medium avocado, peeled and sliced

1. Mix chicken, cheese, sour cream and chilies in 2-quart casserole. Cover tightly and microwave on medium (50%) 8 to 10 minutes, stirring every 3 minutes, until cheese is melted and mixture is hot.

2. Place about 2 cups of the tortilla chips on each of 4 serving plates; spoon chicken mixture over chips. Top with tomatoes and avocado. Serve with salsa if desired. **4 servings;** 740 calories per serving.

• • • • • • • • • •

CHICKEN AND SPINACH NOODLE CASSEROLE

MICROWAVE TIME: 8 to 10 minutes

3 cups hot cooked spinach noodles
2 cups cut-up cooked chicken or turkey
½ cup grated Romano cheese
¼ cup margarine or butter, softened
¼ cup milk
1 tablespoon chopped fresh or 1 teaspoon dried basil
¼ teaspoon salt
¼ teaspoon pepper
1 small onion, finely chopped (about ¼ cup)
1 can (4 ounces) mushroom stems and pieces, drained

Mix all ingredients in 2-quart casserole. Cover tightly and microwave on high 8 to 10 minutes, stirring after 4 minutes, until chicken is hot. Serve with additional grated Romano cheese, and garnish with chopped fresh basil if desired. **6 servings (about 1 cup each);** 235 calories per serving.

Chicken and Tortilla Soup

CHICKEN AND TORTILLA SOUP

This uncommon soup can be prepared in advance and served on a moment's notice. It is immensely popular with children of all ages.

◑ MICROWAVE TIME: 12 to 16 minutes

1 small onion, finely chopped (about ¼ cup)
1 clove garlic, finely chopped
2 cups chicken broth
¾ to 1 teaspoon chili powder
1 can (15 ounces) tomato sauce
2 cups cut-up cooked chicken or turkey
2 cups tortilla chips
1 cup shredded Monterey Jack cheese (4 ounces)
1 small avocado, peeled and sliced

1. Place onion and garlic in 2-quart casserole. Cover tightly and microwave on high 3 to 4 minutes or until onion is tender. Stir in broth, chili powder and tomato sauce. Cover tightly and microwave 8 to 10 minutes, stirring after 4 minutes, until boiling.

2. Divide chicken and tortilla chips among 4 soup bowls. Pour soup over chips; sprinkle with cheese. Microwave uncovered on high 1 to 2 minutes or until cheese begins to melt. Top with avocado. **4 servings (about 2 cups each);** 440 calories per serving.

500-watt microwave: You may need to increase cooking times.

CHICKEN SOUP WITH ALMONDS

🕐 MICROWAVE TIME: 12 to 15 minutes

1 tablespoon margarine or butter
1 tablespoon all-purpose flour
¼ teaspoon salt
1 cup chicken broth
2 cups cut-up cooked chicken or turkey
½ cup sliced almonds, toasted
2 cups half-and-half
1 tablespoon chopped fresh cilantro

1. Place margarine in 2-quart casserole. Microwave uncovered on high 20 to 30 seconds or until melted. Stir in flour and salt. Gradually stir in broth. Cover tightly and microwave 2 to 3 minutes, stirring every minute, until mixture thickens and boils.

2. Stir in remaining ingredients. Cover tightly and microwave on medium-high (70%) 10 to 12 minutes, stirring every 4 minutes, until hot. Garnish with additional cilantro if desired. **4 servings (about 1 cup each);** 430 calories per serving.

500-watt microwave: You may need to increase microwave times.

CHICKEN TACO POCKETS

🕐 MICROWAVE TIME: 4 to 5 minutes

1 small avocado, peeled and thinly sliced
1½ teaspoons lemon juice
¼ teaspoon salt
8 pita breads (about 3½-inch diameter)
2 cups chopped cooked chicken or turkey
1 can (4 ounces) chopped green chilies, drained
1 small onion, sliced and separated into rings
1 tablespoon vegetable oil
½ teaspoon salt
2 cups shredded Monterey Jack cheese (8 ounces)
1 cup shredded lettuce
½ cup sour cream
½ cup taco sauce

1. Sprinkle avocado with lemon juice and ¼ teaspoon salt. Split each pita bread halfway around edge with knife; separate to form pocket.

2. Mix chicken, chilies, onion, oil and ½ teaspoon salt in 1½-quart casserole. Cover and microwave on high 4 to 5 minutes, stirring after 2 minutes, until chicken is hot.

3. Spoon about ¼ cup of the chicken mixture into each pita bread. Top with cheese, lettuce and avocado. Serve with sour cream and taco sauce. **8 sandwiches;** 440 calories per sandwich.

CHICKEN CROISSANTS

⏱ MICROWAVE TIME: 2 to 3 minutes

1 cup cut-up cooked chicken or turkey
2 medium stalks celery, chopped (about
   1 cup)
¼ cup mayonnaise or salad dressing
1 tablespoon finely chopped onion
¼ teaspoon salt
⅛ teaspoon pepper
Dash of ground sage
6 croissants or bagels, split
6 slices Cheddar or Monterey Jack cheese

1.   Mix all ingredients except croissants and cheese. Fill croissants with chicken mixture; top with cheese. Arrange croissants in circle on 12-inch plate lined with paper towel.

2.   Microwave uncovered on high 2 to 3 minutes, rotating plate ½ turn after 1 minute, until cheese begins to melt and filling is warm.   **6 sandwiches;** 405 calories per sandwich.

A 500-watt microwave is not recommended.

• • • • • • • • • • •

BARBECUED CHICKEN ON KAISER ROLLS

⏱ MICROWAVE TIME: 6 to 8 minutes

3 cups cut-up cooked chicken or turkey
¾ cup chili sauce
2 tablespoons honey
1 tablespoon soy sauce
¼ teaspoon red pepper sauce
6 kaiser rolls, split

1.   Mix all ingredients except rolls in 2-quart casserole. Cover tightly and microwave on high 6 to 8 minutes, stirring after 3 minutes, until hot.

2.   Fill each roll with about ½ cup chicken mixture.   **6 sandwiches;** 345 calories per sandwich.

FRENCH POTATO SALAD WITH CHICKEN

MICROWAVE TIME: 27 to 33 minutes
REFRIGERATION TIME: 10 minutes

2 chicken breast halves (about
   1¼ pounds)
6 slices bacon, cut into ½-inch pieces
6 green onions (with tops), sliced
1½ pounds small unpared new potatoes
   (about 12), cut into fourths
¼ cup water
¼ cup cider vinegar
½ teaspoon salt
¼ teaspoon pepper

1.   Microwave chicken breast halves as directed (page 73). Refrigerate chicken about 10 minutes or until cool enough to handle. Remove skin and bones. Cut chicken into 2 × ½ × ½-inch strips.

2.   Place bacon in 2-quart casserole. Cover with paper towel and microwave on high 6 to 7 minutes, stirring after 3 minutes, until crisp. Remove bacon with slotted spoon; drain and reserve. Drain fat from casserole, reserving 1 tablespoon.

3.   Place onions, potatoes and water in same casserole. Cover tightly and microwave on high 12 to 14 minutes, stirring every 4 minutes, until potatoes are tender; drain.

4.   Stir chicken, bacon, reserved bacon fat and remaining ingredients into potatoes. Cover tightly and microwave 1 to 2 minutes or until warm. Serve warm.   **4 servings (about 1¼ cups each);** 330 calories per serving.

500-watt microwave: You may need to increase microwave times.

COBB SALAD

MICROWAVE TIME: 14 to 18 minutes
REFRIGERATION TIME: 2 hours 10 minutes

2 chicken breast halves (about
    1¼ pounds)
6 cups finely shredded lettuce
¼ cup crumbled blue cheese (1 ounce)
8 slices bacon, crisply cooked and
    crumbled
4 green onions (with tops), sliced
3 hard-cooked eggs, chopped
2 medium tomatoes, chopped (about
    1½ cups)
1 avocado, peeled and sliced
Lemon Vinaigrette (below)

1. Microwave chicken breast halves as directed (page 73). Refrigerate chicken about 10 minutes or until cool enough to handle. Remove skin and bones. Cut up chicken; cover and refrigerate about 2 hours or until chilled.

2. Divide lettuce among 4 plates. Arrange chicken and remaining ingredients except Lemon Vinaigrette in rows over lettuce. Serve with Lemon Vinaigrette. **4 servings;** 635 calories per serving.

Lemon Vinaigrette

½ cup vegetable oil
¼ cup lemon juice
1 teaspoon sugar
½ teaspoon salt
¼ teaspoon pepper

Shake all ingredients in tightly covered container.

HOT CHICKEN SALAD

MICROWAVE TIME: 8 to 10 minutes

2 cups cut-up cooked chicken or turkey
1 cup thinly sliced celery
2 tablespoons lemon juice
1 tablespoon finely chopped onion
¼ teaspoon salt
¼ teaspoon pepper
½ cup mayonnaise or salad dressing
1 cup seedless grape halves
½ cup slivered almonds, toasted

1. Toss chicken, celery, lemon juice, onion, salt and pepper in large bowl. Stir in mayonnaise. Carefully fold in grapes and ¼ cup of the almonds.

2. Cover loosely and microwave on medium (50%) 8 to 10 minutes, stirring after 4 minutes, until hot. Sprinkle with remaining almonds. **4 servings (about ¾ cup each);** 460 calories per serving.

Cobb Salad

APRICOT-GLAZED GRILLED TURKEY

The microwave provides a wonderful shortcut to traditional grilling techniques, making quick work at the grillside with the same mouth-watering barbecue flavor.

MICROWAVE TIME:	19 to 21 minutes
GRILL TIME:	1 hour to 1 hour 15 minutes
STAND TIME:	10 minutes

1 jar (10 ounces) apricot preserves
2 tablespoons dry white wine
3- to 4-pound fresh or frozen (thawed) boneless turkey breast

1. Prepare charcoal fire for grilling, arranging coals around edge of firebox. Place foil drip pan under grilling area. Mix preserves and wine in 2-cup measure; reserve.

2. Place turkey breast, skin side up, in rectangular dish, 11 × 7 × 1½ inches. Cover tightly and microwave on high 8 minutes. Rotate dish ½ turn.

3. Microwave on medium (50%) 10 to 12 minutes or until outside edges begin to cook.

4. Insert barbecue meat thermometer in center of turkey. Place turkey, skin side up, 5 to 6 inches from medium coals, on grill over drip pan. Cover and grill 1 hour to 1 hour 15 minutes, spooning preserves mixture over turkey 2 or 3 times during last 10 minutes of grilling, until thermometer registers 170°. Remove turkey from grill. Cover with aluminum foil and let stand 10 minutes before slicing.

5. Microwave any remaining preserves mixture uncovered on high 30 to 60 seconds or until boiling; serve with turkey. **12 servings;** 265 calories per serving.

Apricot-glazed Grilled Turkey

A 500-watt microwave is not recommended.

Microwave-only Directions: Mix preserves and wine in 2-cup measure; reserve. Insert microwave meat thermometer in center of turkey breast. Place turkey, skin side down, in rectangular dish, 11 × 7 × 1½ inches. Cover tightly and microwave on high 10 minutes. Rotate dish ½ turn. Microwave on medium (50%) 35 to 40 minutes, turning turkey over after 25 minutes, until thermometer registers 160°.

Spoon about ¼ cup of the preserves mixture over turkey. Cover tightly and microwave on medium (50%) 5 to 10 minutes or until thermometer registers 170°. Let stand covered 10 minutes before slicing. Microwave remaining preserves mixture uncovered on high 30 to 60 seconds or until boiling; serve with turkey.

ALMOND TURKEY CUTLETS

This is almost decadent: moist white meat coated with crunchy almonds and sauced with warm sour cream. Serve this with generous helpings of crisp-tender vegetables.

MICROWAVE TIME: 10 to 13 minutes

1 tablespoon margarine or butter
2 egg whites
½ cup ground toasted almonds
½ cup dry bread crumbs
2 tablespoons chopped fresh parsley
½ teaspoon salt
6 slices cooked turkey breast, each ¼ inch thick (about ¾ pound)
⅓ cup sour cream
¼ cup sliced almonds, toasted

1.   Place margarine on 12-inch plate. Microwave uncovered on high 20 to 30 seconds or until margarine is melted; spread evenly over plate. Beat egg whites until foamy. Mix ground almonds, bread crumbs, parsley and salt. Dip turkey into egg whites; coat evenly with crumb mixture.

2.   Arrange turkey in single layer on plate. Cover with waxed paper and microwave on high 7 to 9 minutes, turning turkey over and rearranging with uncooked parts to outside edge of plate after 4 minutes, until juices run clear.

3.   Microwave sour cream in 1-cup measure uncovered on medium (50%) 2 to 3 minutes, stirring every minute, just until warm. Spoon over turkey; sprinkle with sliced almonds.
4 servings; 370 calories per serving.

A 500-watt microwave is not recommended.

TURKEY SCALLOPINI

Here is an economical take on the elegant favorite with veal, authentic from the crisp crumb coating to the Parmesan cheese and fresh basil. Presliced, uncooked turkey breast makes this faster to prepare.

MICROWAVE TIME: 9 to 11 minutes

2 tablespoons margarine or butter, melted
1 tablespoon lemon juice
1 egg
½ cup Italian-style dry bread crumbs
¼ cup grated Parmesan cheese
1 tablespoon chopped fresh or 1 teaspoon dried basil
¼ teaspoon salt
⅛ teaspoon pepper
8 slices turkey breast, each ¼ inch thick (about 1 pound)
Lemon wedges

1.   Place margarine in medium bowl. Microwave uncovered on high 20 to 30 seconds or just until melted. Beat in lemon juice and egg with fork. Mix bread crumbs, cheese, basil, salt and pepper. Dip turkey slices into egg mixture; coat evenly with crumb mixture.

2.   Arrange turkey in rectangular dish, 13 × 9 × 2 inches. Microwave uncovered on high 8 to 10 minutes, turning turkey over and rearranging with uncooked parts to outside edges of dish after 4 minutes, until juices run clear. Serve with lemon wedges and Garlic Tomato Sauce (page 321) if desired. **4 servings;** 295 calories per serving.

A 500-watt microwave is not recommended.

TURKEY DIVAN

MICROWAVE TIME: 6 to 10 minutes

2 tablespoons margarine or butter
2 tablespoons all-purpose flour
Dash of ground nutmeg
½ cup chicken broth
¼ cup grated Parmesan cheese
1 tablespoon dry white wine or chicken broth
¼ cup whipping (heavy) cream
1 package (10 ounces) frozen broccoli spears, thawed and well drained
3 large slices cooked turkey breast (about ½ pound)
2 tablespoons grated Parmesan cheese

1.   Place margarine in 1-quart casserole. Microwave uncovered on high 20 to 30 seconds or until melted. Stir in flour, nutmeg and broth. Microwave uncovered 1 to 2 minutes, stirring every 30 seconds with wire whisk, until thickened. Stir in ¼ cup cheese and the wine. Beat whipping cream in chilled bowl until stiff. Fold cheese mixture into whipped cream.

2.   Arrange broccoli with stems to outside edge in pie plate, 9 × 1¼ inches; top with turkey. Pour cheese mixture over turkey; sprinkle with 2 tablespoons cheese. Cover tightly and microwave on high 4 to 7 minutes or until hot.   **3 servings;** 345 calories per serving.

Turkey Scallopini, Artichokes (page 181)

MEXICAN TURKEY

◐ MICROWAVE TIME: 5 to 8 minutes

> 1 teaspoon vegetable oil
> 8 slices turkey breast, each ¼ inch thick (about 1 pound)
> ¼ teaspoon chili powder
> ½ cup salsa
> 1 small red bell pepper, cut into 8 rings
> ½ cup shredded Monterey Jack cheese (2 ounces)

1. Brush 12-inch plate with oil. Arrange turkey breast slices around edge of plate; sprinkle with chili powder

2. Cover with waxed paper and microwave on high 3 to 5 minutes, rotating plate ½ turn after 2 minutes, until juices run clear; drain.

3. Top each turkey slice with 1 tablespoon salsa and bell pepper ring. Microwave uncovered 1 to 2 minutes or until salsa is hot. Sprinkle with cheese. Microwave uncovered 30 seconds or until cheese begins to melt. Serve with sour cream if desired.   **4 servings;** 230 calories per serving.

A 500-watt microwave is not recommended.

DEVILED TURKEY PATTIES

◐ MICROWAVE TIME: 7 to 11 minutes
STAND TIME: 2 minutes

> 1 pound ground turkey
> ¼ cup dry bread crumbs
> 1 teaspoon chopped fresh or ¼ teaspoon dried thyme
> ½ teaspoon garlic powder
> ¼ teaspoon salt
> ¼ teaspoon pepper
> 3 tablespoons sour cream
> 1 tablespoon Dijon mustard
> 1 tablespoon chopped fresh parsley

1. Mix all ingredients except sour cream, mustard and parsley. Shape into 4 patties, each about ¾ inch thick. Arrange patties on rack in dish. Cover with waxed paper and microwave on high 6 to 9 minutes, rotating dish ½ turn every 3 minutes, until patties are no longer pink in center. Let stand covered 2 minutes.

2. Mix remaining ingredients in 1-cup measure. Microwave uncovered on medium (50%) 1 to 2 minutes or until hot. Spoon over patties.   **4 servings;** 150 calories per serving.

TURKEY CASSEROLE

MICROWAVE TIME: 16 to 24 minutes

2 turkey tenderloins (about 1½ pounds),
  cut into 1-inch pieces
6 green onions (with tops), sliced
1 cup sour cream
¼ cup dry sherry or chicken broth
1 teaspoon chopped fresh or ½ teaspoon
  dried rosemary, crushed
2 cups cooked rice
8 ounces fresh mushrooms, sliced (about
  3 cups)
1 can (14 ounces) artichoke hearts,
  drained and cut into fourths
¼ cup grated Parmesan cheese

1.   Mix turkey and onions in 3-quart casserole. Cover and microwave on high 8 to 10 minutes, stirring after 4 minutes, until turkey is done; drain.

2.   Stir in sour cream, sherry and rosemary. Stir in rice, mushrooms and artichoke hearts carefully. Cover tightly and microwave 8 to 14 minutes, stirring every 4 minutes, until hot. Sprinkle with cheese.   **6 servings (about 1⅓ cups each);** 380 calories per serving.

500-watt microwave: You may need to increase microwave times.

TURKEY-STUFFING CASSEROLE

MICROWAVE TIME: 23 to 29 minutes

Cranberry Relish (page 329)
⅓ cup margarine or butter
3 cups herb-seasoned stuffing mix (dry)
¼ cup water
1 can (10¾ ounces) condensed cream of
  mushroom soup
1 package (10 ounces) frozen green peas
⅓ cup milk
3 tablespoons finely chopped onion or
  2 teaspoons instant minced onion
2 cups coarsely chopped cooked turkey
  or chicken
2 tablespoons chopped pimiento

1.   Prepare Cranberry Relish. Place margarine in round dish, 8 × 1½ inches. Cover loosely and microwave on high 45 to 60 seconds or until melted. Add stuffing and water; toss to coat. Reserve 1 cup stuffing. Spread remaining stuffing evenly in dish.

2.   Mix soup, peas, milk and onion in 1½-quart casserole. Cover tightly and microwave on high 6 to 7 minutes, stirring after 3 minutes, until hot and bubbly.

3.   Stir in turkey and pimiento. Spread over stuffing. Sprinkle with reserved stuffing. Microwave uncovered on high 7 to 9 minutes or until hot and bubbly. Serve with Cranberry Relish.   **6 servings (about 1½ cups each);** 380 calories per serving.

500-watt microwave: You may need to increase microwave times.

TURKEY-SAUSAGE CASEROLE

MICROWAVE TIME: 14 to 18 minutes

½ pound pork sausage links, cut into
  1-inch pieces
2 medium stalks celery, thinly sliced
  (about 1 cup)
1 medium onion, chopped (about ½ cup)
¾ cup sour cream
2 cups cut-up cooked turkey or chicken
2 cups hot cooked noodles
1 medium unpared red all-purpose apple, chopped
2 tablespoons sliced almonds

1.   Place sausage, celery and onion in 3-quart
casserole. Cover tightly and microwave on
high 6 to 8 minutes or until sausage is no
longer pink; drain.

2.   Stir in sour cream. Add remaining ingredients except almonds; toss. Cover tightly
and microwave 8 to 10 minutes, stirring after
5 minutes, until hot. Sprinkle with almonds.
6 servings (about 1⅓ cups each); 330 calories per
serving.

*500-watt microwave: You may need to in-
crease microwave times.*

ORIENTAL TURKEY AND VEGETABLES

MICROWAVE TIME: 22 to 31 minutes

1 package (16 ounces) frozen Oriental-
  style vegetables
2 cups cut-up cooked turkey or chicken
1 teaspoon finely chopped gingerroot or
  1 teaspoon ground ginger
1 can (10¾ ounces) condensed chicken
  broth
3 tablespoons cornstarch
½ cup cold water
2 cups chow mein noodles

1.   Place frozen vegetables in 3-quart casserole. Cover tightly and microwave as directed
on package until crisp-tender. Stir in turkey,
gingerroot and broth.

2.   Mix cornstarch and cold water; stir into
turkey mixture. Cover tightly and microwave
on high 3 minutes; stir. Cover tightly and
microwave 5 to 6 minutes, stirring every minute, until mixture thickens and boils. Serve
over chow mein noodles.   **4 servings;** 320 calories per serving.

*500-watt microwave: You may need to in-
crease microwave times.*

Turkey Chowder with Vegetables

TURKEY CHOWDER WITH VEGETABLES

MICROWAVE TIME: 29 to 34 minutes

2 tablespoons margarine or butter
3 medium carrots, thinly sliced
1 medium potato, cut into ½-inch pieces
1 small onion, finely chopped (about
  ¼ cup)
1 package (10 ounces) frozen whole
  kernel corn
2 tablespoons all-purpose flour
1 can (14½ ounces) chicken broth
2 cups cut-up cooked turkey or chicken
2 cups milk
¼ teaspoon salt
⅛ teaspoon pepper

1. Place margarine, carrots, potato and onion in 3-quart casserole. Cover tightly and microwave on high 8 to 10 minutes, stirring after 5 minutes, until vegetables are crisp-tender.

2. Stir in frozen corn. Cover tightly and microwave 7 to 8 minutes or until corn is hot. Shake flour and ½ cup of the broth in tightly covered container. Stir flour mixture, remaining broth and remaining ingredients into vegetables.

3. Cover tightly and microwave 14 to 16 minutes, stirring every 4 minutes, until hot and slightly thickened. Garnish with snipped fresh parsley if desired.   **6 servings (about 1⅓ cups each);** 260 calories per serving.

500-watt microwave: You may need to increase microwave times.

Wild Rice and Turkey Salad

WILD RICE AND TURKEY SALAD

Make this colorful, tarragon-scented salad ahead for guests.

MICROWAVE TIME: 7 to 10 minutes
REFRIGERATION TIME: 3 hours

1 pound turkey breast tenderloin, cut
    into 1½ × ½ × ½-inch strips
1 medium red bell pepper, chopped
1 medium yellow bell pepper, chopped
1 medium onion, chopped (about ½ cup)
3 cups cooked wild rice
½ cup slivered almonds, toasted
Tarragon Dressing (right)

1. Place turkey in 2-quart casserole. Cover tightly and microwave on high 6 to 8 minutes, stirring after 3 minutes, until done; drain. Stir in bell peppers and onion. Cover tightly and microwave 1 to 2 minutes or until vegetables are crisp-tender.

2. Stir in wild rice and almonds. Prepare Tarragon Dressing; toss with turkey mixture. Cover and refrigerate at least 3 hours until chilled. **6 servings (about 1⅓ cups each);** 540 calories per serving.

500-watt microwave: You may need to increase microwave times.

Tarragon Dressing

1 cup mayonnaise or salad dressing
½ cup tarragon vinegar
2 tablespoons chopped fresh or 2 teaspoons dried tarragon
½ teaspoon salt
¼ teaspoon pepper

Mix all ingredients.

EASY SLOPPY JOES

This delicious, lower-fat version of an American classic is easy for kids to prepare themselves.

MICROWAVE TIME: 10 to 14 minutes

1 pound ground turkey
1 medium onion, chopped (about ½ cup)
2 teaspoons Worcestershire sauce
3 drops red pepper sauce
1 can (10¾ ounces) condensed tomato
    soup
6 hamburger buns, split

1.   Crumble turkey into 2-quart casserole; add onion. Cover with waxed paper and microwave on high 6 to 8 minutes, stirring after 4 minutes, until turkey is no longer pink; drain. Break up turkey.

2.   Stir in remaining ingredients except buns. Cover tightly and microwave 4 to 6 minutes, stirring after 3 minutes, until hot. Fill buns with turkey mixture.   **6 sandwiches;** 275 calories per sandwich.

DUCKLING WITH TANGY SAUCE

MICROWAVE TIME: 38 to 45 minutes
STAND TIME: 10 minutes

4- to 5-pound duckling
2 tablespoons orange juice
½ teaspoon browning sauce
½ cup orange juice
¼ cup orange marmalade
1 tablespoon lemon juice
⅛ teaspoon ground ginger
⅛ teaspoon salt
2 teaspoons cornstarch
1 tablespoon cold water
1 orange, pared and sectioned

1.   Fasten neck skin of duckling to back with wooden skewers. Lift wing tips up and over back for natural brace. Pierce skin with fork. Mix 2 tablespoons orange juice and the browning sauce; brush half of mixture over duckling. Place duckling, breast side down, on rack in dish. Cover with waxed paper and microwave on medium-high (70%) 18 minutes; drain.

2.   Turn duckling breast side up; brush with remaining orange juice mixture. Cover with waxed paper and microwave 18 to 23 minutes or until drumstick meat feels very soft when pressed between fingers. Cover with aluminum foil; let stand 10 minutes.

3.   Mix ½ cup orange juice, the marmalade, lemon juice, ginger and salt in 2-cup measure. Microwave uncovered on high 1 to 2 minutes or until boiling.

4.   Mix cornstarch and cold water; stir into orange juice mixture. Microwave uncovered on medium-high (70%) 1 to 2 minutes, stirring every minute, until mixture thickens and boils. Stir in orange. Brush duckling with orange sauce; serve with remaining sauce. **4 servings;** 560 calories per serving.

A 500-watt mirowave is not recommended.

PLUM-GLAZED CORNISH HENS

MICROWAVE TIME: 17 to 21 minutes
STAND TIME: 5 minutes

2 Rock Cornish hens (about 1½ pounds
   each)
½ cup plum preserves
2 tablespoons chili sauce
1 tablespoon lemon juice
1 teaspoon Dijon mustard
Paprika

1. Cut each hen lengthwise in half; place meaty sides down in rectangular dish, 11 × 7 × 1½. Mix remaining ingredients except paprika; brush mixture lightly over hens. Cover with waxed paper and microwave on high 8 minutes.

2. Turn hens meaty sides up; rearrange. Brush lightly with preserves mixture; sprinkle with paprika. Cover with waxed paper and microwave 8 to 12 minutes longer or until juices run clear. Let stand covered 5 minutes.

3. Microwave remaining preserves mixture uncovered on high 30 to 60 seconds or until boiling. Serve with hens.   **4 servings;** 275 calories per serving.

MICROWAVING POULTRY

Arrange poultry pieces skin side up with thickest parts to outside edge in a dish large enough to hold pieces in single layer. Cover tightly and microwave as directed below until juices run clear. Cook all white meat *only* until meat thermometer registers 165°. All other poultry should be cooked to an internal temperature of 180°. Let stand about 5 minutes after cooking.

TYPE	AMOUNT	POWER LEVEL	TIME
Chicken			
Broiler-fryer chicken, cut up	3 to 3½ pounds	High	15 to 20 minutes, rotating dish ½ turn after 10 minutes
Chicken breast halves, with skin and bones	About 1¼ pounds (two)	High	8 to 10 minutes, rotating dish ½ turn after 4 minutes
Chicken breast halves, skinless boneless	About 1½ pounds (four)	High	8 to 10 minutes, rotating dish ½ turn after 4 minutes
Chicken drumsticks, thighs	2 pounds	High	16 to 19 minutes, rotating dish ½ turn after 10 minutes
Chicken wings	3 to 3½ pounds	High	12 to 15 minutes, rotating dish ½ turn after 6 minutes

Turkey

For whole boneless turkey breast place skin side down. Cover and begin microwaving on high; continue on medium (50%), turning over after half the time. Microwave until meat thermometer registers 170°. Let stand covered 10 minutes before slicing.

TYPE	AMOUNT	POWER LEVEL	TIME
Boneless whole turkey breast	4 to 5 pounds	High Medium (50%)	10 minutes, rotating dish ½ turn 40 to 50 minutes, turning over after 25 minutes
Turkey tenderloins	About 1½ pounds (two)	High	8 to 10 minutes, rotating dish ½ turn after 4 minutes
Turkey breast slices	1 pound	High	3 to 5 minutes, rotating dish ½ turn after 2 minutes
Ground turkey	1 pound	High	6 to 8 minutes, stirring after 4 minutes

Rock Cornish Hens

TYPE	AMOUNT	POWER LEVEL	TIME
Rock Cornish hens, whole	1 to 1½ pounds (one)	High	10 to 13 minutes, turning over after 5 minutes
	2 to 3 pounds (two)	High	15 to 20 minutes, turning over after 10 minutes

DEFROSTING POULTRY

Place unwrapped poultry in shallow dish. Microwave uncovered on defrost setting as directed below until pieces can be separated; move the pieces most frozen to outside edge of dish. Microwave until few ice crystals remain in center. Edges should not begin to cook. Let stand 10 to 15 minutes.

TYPE	AMOUNT	TIME
Chicken		
Broiler-fryer, cut up	3 to 3½ pounds	20 to 25 minutes, turning over or separating every 10 minutes
Breast halves, with skin and bones	About 1¼ pounds (two)	12 to 15 minutes, turning over and separating after 8 minutes
Breast halves, skinless boneless	About 1½ pounds (four)	15 to 20 minutes, turning over and separating after 10 minutes
Drumsticks, thighs	2 pounds	12 to 15 minutes, separating after 8 minutes
Wings	1½ pounds	10 to 12 minutes, separating after 6 minutes
Turkey		
Tenderloins	About 1½ pounds (two)	10 to 12 minutes, separating after 5 minutes
Breast slices	1 pound	8 to 10 minutes, turning over after 4 minutes
Ground	1 pound	10 to 12 minutes, turning over or separating every 4 minutes
Rock Cornish Hens		
Whole	About 1½ pounds (one)	10 to 12 minutes, turning over after 5 minutes (let stand 30 minutes in cold water)
	About 3 pounds (two)	15 to 18 minutes, turning over after 8 minutes (let stand 30 minutes in cold water)

FLOUNDER WITH CREAMY HERB STUFFING

MICROWAVE TIME: 6 to 8 minutes
STAND TIME: 3 minutes

1 pound flounder or sole fillets
½ cup ricotta cheese
2 tablespoons chopped fresh parsley
1 tablespoon chopped fresh or 1 teaspoon dried tarragon
¼ teaspoon salt
⅛ teaspoon pepper
½ medium lemon
Paprika

1. If fish fillets are large, cut into 4 serving pieces; pat dry. Mix cheese, parsley, tarragon, salt and pepper.

2. Place about 2 tablespoons cheese mixture on center of each piece fish. Roll up; place seam sides down in square dish, 8 × 8 × 2 inches. Squeeze lemon over fish; sprinkle with paprika.

3. Cover with waxed paper and microwave on high 6 to 8 minutes or until fish flakes easily with fork. Let stand covered 3 minutes. Serve with melted margarine or butter if desired. **4 servings;** 240 calories per serving.

500-watt microwave: You may need to increase microwave time.

SOLE WITH RED GRAPES

MICROWAVE TIME: 10 to 12 minutes

1½ pounds sole fillets
1 tablespoon lemon juice
½ teaspoon salt
¼ teaspoon pepper
3 green onions (with tops), sliced
¾ cup water
¼ cup dry white wine
½ cup whipping (heavy) cream
2 tablespoons all-purpose flour
1 cup seedless red or green grapes

1. If fish fillets are large, cut into 6 serving pieces; pat dry. Arrange fish, thickest parts to outside edges, in rectangular dish. 11 × 7 × 1½ inches. Sprinkle with lemon juice, salt, pepper and onions.

2. Cover tightly and microwave on high 7 to 8 minutes, rotating dish ½ turn after 4 minutes, until fish flakes easily with fork. Let stand covered.

3. Place water and wine in 4-cup measure. Shake whipping cream and flour in tightly covered container; stir gradually into wine mixture. Microwave uncovered on high 3 to 4 minutes, stirring every minute, until boiling. Stir in grapes. Serve sauce over fish.
6 servings; 315 calories per serving.

CRUNCHY PECAN FILLETS

Toast all of the pecans at the same time and set aside ¼ cup before grinding to garnish the fish.

 MICROWAVE TIME: 7 to 9 minutes

1 tablespoon margarine or butter
2 egg whites
¾ cup ground toasted pecans
¼ cup unseasoned dry bread crumbs
1 teaspoon chopped fresh or ¼ teaspoon
   dried rosemary, crushed
½ teaspoon salt
1 pound grouper or sole fillets
¼ cup pecan halves, toasted
6 lemon wedges

1.   Place margarine on 12-inch plate. Microwave uncovered on high 15 to 30 seconds or until melted; spread evenly over plate.

2.   Beat egg whites until foamy. Mix ground pecans, bread crumbs, rosemary and salt. If fish fillets are large, cut into 4 serving pieces; pat dry. Dip fish into egg whites; coat with pecan mixture. Arrange fish, thickest parts to outside edge, in single layer on plate.

3.   Cover with waxed paper and microwave 6 to 8 minutes, turning fish over after 4 minutes, until fish flakes easily with fork. Top with pecan halves; serve with lemon wedges. **4 servings;** 300 calories per serving.

   A 500-watt microwave is not recommended.

SOLE AU GRATIN

MICROWAVE TIME: 10 to 14 minutes
STAND TIME: 3 minutes

2 tablespoons margarine or butter
2 tablespoons all-purpose flour
1 teaspoon chicken bouillon granules
Dash of ground nutmeg
1 cup milk
⅔ cup shredded Cheddar cheese
1 package (10 ounces) frozen chopped
   broccoli, thawed and well drained
1 tablespoon lemon juice
1 pound sole fillets
½ teaspoon salt
2 tablespoons grated Parmesan cheese
Paprika

1.   Place margarine in 4-cup measure. Microwave uncovered on high 20 to 30 seconds or until melted. Stir in flour, bouillon granules and nutmeg; stir in milk. Microwave uncovered 3 to 4 minutes, stirring every minute, until thickened; stir in Cheddar cheese.

2.   Spread broccoli in square dish, 8 × 8 × 2 inches; sprinkle with lemon juice. If fish fillets are large, cut into 4 serving pieces; pat dry. Arrange fish, thickest parts to outside edges, on broccoli; sprinkle with salt. Spread sauce over fish and broccoli.

3.   Cover with waxed paper and microwave on high 7 to 9 minutes, rotating dish ½ turn after 4 minutes, until fish flakes easily with fork. Let stand covered 3 minutes. Sprinkle with Parmesan cheese and paprika.   **4 servings;** 360 calories per serving.

STUFFED PERCH FILLETS

MICROWAVE TIME: 6 to 8 minutes

1 medium onion, chopped (about ½ cup)
2 tablespoons margarine or butter
1 cup soft bread crumbs (about 1½ slices bread)
¼ cup chopped fresh parsley
¾ teaspoon salt
¼ teaspoon ground nutmeg
1 egg, slightly beaten
1 pound perch fillets
1 tablespoon margarine or butter, melted
1½ teaspoons vinegar
Paprika
Chopped fresh parsley

1. Place onion and 2 tablespoons margarine in 1-quart casserole. Microwave uncovered on high about 2 minutes or until crisp-tender. Stir in bread crumbs, ¼ cup parsley, the salt, nutmeg and egg.

2. If fish fillets are large, cut into 4 serving pieces; pat dry. Spread stuffing evenly over fish. Roll up; arrange seam sides down in circle in round dish, 8 × 1½ inches. Mix 1 tablespoon melted margarine and the vinegar; drizzle over fish. Sprinkle with paprika.

3. Cover tightly and microwave on high 4 to 6 minutes, rotating dish ½ turn after 2 minutes, until fish flakes easily with fork. Garnish with parsley. **4 servings;** 325 calories per serving.

SALMON-STUFFED FLOUNDER

This is a pretty dish. A pale pink salmon mixture is rolled up into white flounder paupiettes, *rolls that the French call "corks" because of their shape.*

MICROWAVE TIME: 12 to 15 minutes
STAND TIME: 3 minutes

1 can (6½ ounces) salmon, drained
⅛ teaspoon white pepper
1 egg
1 teaspoon chopped fresh or ½ teaspoon dried dill weed
1½ pounds flounder or sole fillets
3 tablespoons dry white wine or chicken broth
Lemon-Dill Sauce (page 321)

1. Place salmon, white pepper and egg in food processor workbowl fitted with steel blade or in blender container. Cover and process until smooth; stir in dill weed.

2. If fish fillets are large, cut into 6 serving pieces; pat dry. Place about 2 tablespoons salmon mixture on center of each piece fish. Roll up; place seam sides down in square dish, 8 × 8 × 2 inches. Drizzle with wine.

3. Cover tightly and microwave on high 8 to 10 minutes, rotating dish ½ turn after 5 minutes, until fish flakes easily with fork. Let stand covered.

4. Prepare Lemon-Dill Sauce, serve with fish.
6 servings; 315 calories per serving.

500-watt microwave: You may need to increase microwave time.

Salmon-stuffed Flounder, Herbed Carrots and Zucchini (page 196), Savory French Bread (page 252)

WHITEFISH WITH BROCCOLI

◑ MICROWAVE TIME: 11 to 13 minutes

3 cups broccoli flowerets (about
    ½ pound)
¼ cup water
1 egg white
½ cup sour cream
1 tablespoon prepared horseradish
1 pound whitefish or cod fillets
¼ teaspoon salt
⅛ teaspoon pepper

1. Place broccoli and water in 1½-quart casserole. Cover tightly and microwave on high 4 to 5 minutes or until crisp-tender; drain and reserve.

2. Beat egg white until soft peaks form; fold in sour cream and horseradish.

3. If fish fillets are large, cut into 4 serving pieces; pat dry. Arrange fish, thickest parts to outside edges, in rectangular dish, 11 × 7 × 1½ inches. Sprinkle with salt and pepper; top with broccoli. Spoon sour cream mixture evenly over broccoli. Cover with waxed paper and microwave on high 7 to 8 minutes or until fish flakes easily with fork. **4 servings;** 280 calories per serving.

A 500-watt microwave is not recommended.

SOUTHWEST SNAPPER FILLETS

◑ MICROWAVE TIME: 5 to 7 minutes
   STAND TIME: 2 minutes

1 pound skinless red snapper or cod
    fillets
½ medium lime
1 tablespoon chopped fresh cilantro
½ teaspoon chili powder
½ cup salsa

1. If fish fillets are large, cut into 4 serving pieces; pat dry. Arrange fish, thickest parts to outside edges, in square dish, 8 × 8 × 2 inches. Squeeze lime over fish; sprinkle with cilantro and chili powder.

2. Cover tightly and microwave on high 5 to 7 minutes, rotating dish ½ turn after 3 minutes, until fish flakes easily with fork. Let stand covered 2 minutes. Serve with salsa and, if desired, lime wedges. **4 servings;** 205 calories per serving.

SOLE TIMBALES WITH SPINACH

🌙 MICROWAVE TIME: 6 to 8 minutes

1 pound sole fillets
¼ teaspoon salt
¼ teaspoon ground nutmeg
⅛ teaspoon pepper
1 package (10 ounces) frozen chopped
    spinach, thawed and well drained
4 teaspoons margarine or butter
4 lemon wedges

1. Grease four 10-ounce custard cups. If fish fillets are large, cut into 4 pieces; pat dry. Cut each piece lengthwise into halves. Line each custard cup with 2 half-pieces fish, facing darker side of fish into cups.

2. Mix salt, nutmeg, pepper and spinach; divide evenly among cups. Top each with 1 teaspoon margarine.

3. Cover with waxed paper and microwave on high 6 to 8 minutes or until fish flakes easily with fork. Invert each onto plate; remove cup. Serve with lemon wedges and, if desired, Hollandaise Sauce (page 322). **4 servings;** 240 calories per serving.

500-watt microwave: You may need to increase microwave time.

Line each custard cup with 2 half-pieces of fish, placing darker side of fish towards inside cup.

Sole Timbales with Spinach

SOLE IN PARCHMENT

Cooking in parchment is simple but very dramatic. It ensures moist, flavorful fish. To present, simply cut an X into the top of each parchment packet before serving.

MICROWAVE TIME: 7 to 8 minutes
STAND TIME: 3 minutes

1 pound sole or orange roughy fillets
½ teaspoon salt
1 tablespoon lemon juice
1 small yellow or red bell pepper, coarsely chopped
1 medium tomato, seeded and coarsely chopped
1 large clove garlic, crushed
Four 12-inch circles cooking parchment paper

1. Pat fish fillets dry; cut into 1-inch pieces. Mix remaining ingredients. Place one-fourth of the fish on half of each parchment circle. Place one-fourth of the vegetable mixture on fish. Fold other half of circle over fish and vegetables.

2. Beginning at one end, roll edge up tightly 2 or 3 times to seal. Twist each end several times to secure. Arrange packets in circle in microwave.

3. Microwave on high 7 to 8 minutes, rearranging packets after 4 minutes, until fish is done. Let stand 3 minutes.

4. Place each packet on plate. To serve, cut a large X shape on top of each packet; fold back corners. **4 servings;** 210 calories per serving.

500-watt microwave: You may need to increase microwave time.

Beginning at one end, roll edge up tightly 2 or 3 times to seal.

Twist each end several times to secure.

Sole in Lettuce Packets

SOLE IN LETTUCE PACKETS

STAND TIME: 1 to 2 minutes
MICROWAVE TIME: 9 to 10 minutes

6 large lettuce leaves
1 medium carrot, shredded
1 small zucchini, shredded
1½ pounds sole or cod fillets
1 tablespoon chopped fresh or 1 teaspoon dried marjoram
Salt and pepper to taste
Margarine or butter

1. Place a few lettuce leaves at a time in hot water. Let stand until wilted, 1 to 2 minutes; drain.

2. Cut fish fillets into 6 serving pieces; pat dry. Mound a portion of carrot and zucchini near stem end of each lettuce leaf. Place 1 piece fish on vegetables. Sprinkle with marjoram, salt and pepper; dot with margarine. Fold lettuce leaf over fish; place seam sides down in rectangular dish, 11 × 7 × 1½ inches.

3. Cover tightly and microwave on high 9 to 10 minutes, rotating dish ½ turn after 4 minutes, until fish is done. **6 servings;** 240 calories per serving.

Fold one edge of lettuce over fish. Fold the two opposite sides over. Fold over to make into a roll.

RED SNAPPER WITH ZUCCHINI

MICROWAVE TIME: 7 to 9 minutes

1 pound red snapper fillets
½ teaspoon salt
Tomato-Chili Sauce (below)
2 tablespoons grated Parmesan cheese
2 small zucchini (about ½ pound) cut crosswise into ¼-inch slices
¼ teaspoon garlic salt
¼ cup coarsely shredded carrot

1. If fish fillets are large, cut into 4 serving pieces; pat dry. Arrange fish, thickest parts to outside edge, in pie plate, 9 × 1¼ inches; sprinkle with salt. Cover tightly and microwave on high 3 minutes; drain.

2. Prepare Tomato-Chili Sauce. Spread 1 tablespoon of the sauce over each piece fish; sprinkle with 1 tablespoon of the cheese. Arrange zucchini on fish; sprinkle with garlic salt and remaining cheese.

3. Cover tightly and microwave 3 to 4 minutes or until fish flakes easily with fork. Top with carrot, and serve with remaining Tomato-Chili Sauce. **4 servings;** 280 calories per serving.

Tomato-Chili Sauce

1 cup chili sauce
2 teaspoons prepared horseradish
2 teaspoons lemon juice
¼ teaspoon Worcestershire sauce

Mix all ingredients in 2-cup measure. Microwave uncovered on high 1 to 2 minutes or until hot; stir before serving.

GARLIC COD

MICROWAVE TIME: 8 to 11 minutes
STAND TIME: 3 minutes

2 tablespoons margarine or butter, melted
1 tablespoon lemon juice
½ teaspoon onion powder
¼ teaspoon paprika
¼ teaspoon salt
Dash of pepper
1 pound cod fillets
5 large cloves garlic, finely chopped
2 tablespoons margarine or butter
1 tablespoon olive or vegetable oil
5 lemon wedges

1. Mix melted margarine, lemon juice, onion powder, paprika, salt and pepper in square dish, 8 × 8 × 2 inches. If fish fillets are large, cut into 4 serving pieces; pat dry.

2. Place fish in margarine mixture; turn fish over to coat. Arrange fish with thickest parts to outside edges of dish.

3. Cover tightly and microwave on high 4 to 6 minutes, rotating dish ½ turn after 2 minutes, until fish flakes easily with fork. Let stand covered 3 minutes.

4. Place garlic, 2 tablespoons margarine and the oil in 2-cup measure. Cover loosely and microwave on high 4 to 5 minutes or until garlic is brown; pour over fish. Serve with lemon wedges. **4 servings;** 330 calories per serving.

Red Snapper with Zucchini

ORANGE ROUGHY WITH SHRIMP SAUCE

◑ MICROWAVE TIME: 11 to 15 minutes

1 pound orange roughy fillets
1 tablespoon lemon juice
½ teaspoon salt
⅛ teaspoon pepper
Shrimp Sauce (page 324)
2½ to 3 cups hot cooked macaroni shells

1.   If fish fillets are large, cut into 4 serving pieces; pat dry. Arrange fish, thickest parts to outside edges, in rectangular dish, 12 × 7½ × 2 inches. Sprinkle with lemon juice, salt and pepper.

2.   Cover tightly and microwave on high 5 to 7 minutes, rotating dish ½ turn after 3 minutes, until fish flakes easily with fork. Remove fish to platter; keep warm.

3.   Prepare Shrimp Sauce. Spoon macaroni around fish; pour sauce over. Garnish with cucumber slices or parsley sprigs if desired. **4 servings;** 410 calories per serving.

PARMESAN SOLE WITH MUSHROOMS

◑ MICROWAVE TIME: 8 to 10 minutes

4 ounces fresh mushrooms, sliced
1 small onion, chopped (about ¼ cup)
1 tablespoon margarine or butter
1 pound sole fillets
½ teaspoon salt
⅛ teaspoon pepper
½ cup sour cream
3 tablespoons grated Parmesan cheese
2 tablespoons dry bread crumbs
Paprika
Chopped fresh parsley

1.   Place mushrooms, onion and margarine in 1-quart casserole. Cover tightly and microwave on high about 2 minutes or until onion is crisp-tender; stir.

2.   If fish fillets are large, cut into 4 serving pieces, pat dry. Arrange fish, thickest parts to outside edges, in rectangular dish, 11 × 7 × 1½ inches. Spoon mushroom mixture over fish; sprinkle with salt and pepper. Cover with waxed paper and microwave on high 3 minutes.

3.   Mix sour cream and cheese; spread over mushroom mixture. Sprinkle with bread crumbs. Microwave uncovered 3 to 5 minutes or until fish flakes easily with fork. Sprinkle with paprika and parsley.   **4 servings;** 330 calories per serving.

HADDOCK WITH ASPARAGUS

🕐 MICROWAVE TIME: 12 to 13 minutes

1 package (10 ounces) frozen
    asparagus spears
1 pound haddock fillets
Salt and pepper
Paprika
1 tablespoon margarine or butter

1. Place frozen block of asparagus in rectangular dish, 11 × 7 × 1½ inches. Cover tightly and microwave on high 3 minutes; drain. Arrange asparagus spears lengthwise, with tips in center, in center of dish. Cover tightly and microwave 3 minutes longer. Let stand covered.

2. If fish fillets are large, cut into 4 serving pieces; pat dry. Arrange fish, thickest parts to outside edge, in pie plate, 9 × 1¼ inches. Sprinkle with salt, pepper and paprika; dot with margarine. Cover tightly and microwave on high 3 minutes.

3. Arrange fish on both ends of asparagus in dish. Cover tightly and microwave 3 to 4 minutes or until fish flakes easily with fork. Serve with Hollandaise Sauce (page 322), if desired.   **4 servings;** 235 calories per serving.

•••••••••••

BELL PEPPER COD

🕐 MICROWAVE TIME: 8 to 12 minutes
STAND TIME: 3 minutes

1 pound cod fillets
1 tablespoon soy sauce
1 small clove garlic, crushed
Dash of ground ginger
2 medium bell peppers (green, red or
    yellow), cut into 1-inch pieces
8 ounces fresh mushrooms, cut in half

1. If fish fillets are large, cut into 4 serving pieces; pat dry. Arrange fish, thickest parts to outside edges, in square dish, 8 × 8 × 2 inches. Mix soy sauce, garlic and ginger; brush on fish. Top with vegetables.

2. Cover tightly and microwave on high 8 to 12 minutes, rotating dish ½ turn after 4 minutes, until fish flakes easily with fork and vegetables are crisp-tender. Let stand covered 3 minutes.   **4 servings;** 230 calories per serving.

•••••••••••

BREADED LEMON PERCH

🕐 MICROWAVE TIME: 4 to 6 minutes

20 round buttery crackers, crushed
    (½ cup)
¼ teaspoon salt
⅛ teaspoon white pepper
¼ cup margarine or butter, melted
2 tablespoons lemon juice
1 pound perch fillets
Paprika

1. Reserve 2 tablespoons cracker crumbs. Mix remaining cracker crumbs, the salt and white pepper. Mix margarine and lemon juice.

2. If fish fillets are large, cut into 4 serving pieces; pat dry. Dip fish into margarine mixture, then into cracker crumbs. Arrange fish, thickest parts to outside edges, on rack in dish; sprinkle with paprika.

3. Microwave uncovered on high 4 to 6 minutes, rotating dish ½ turn after 2 minutes, until fish flakes easily with fork. Sprinkle with reserved cracker crumbs. Garnish with lemon slices if desired.   **4 servings;** 340 calories per serving.

SAVORY BUTTER-DIPPED SOLE

◑ MICROWAVE TIME: 7 to 9 minutes
STAND TIME: 3 minutes

Flavored butter (below)
1½ pounds sole or flounder fillets, each
    ½ to ¾ inch thick

1. Prepare one of the flavored butters. If fish fillets are large, cut into 6 serving pieces; pat dry. Pour flavored butter into square dish, 8 × 8 × 2 inches. Dip fish in butter; turn fish to coat well. Arrange fish, thickest parts to outside edges, in dish.

2. Cover tightly and microwave on high 7 to 9 minutes, rotating dish ½ turn after 4 minutes, until fish flakes easily with fork. Let stand covered 3 minutes.   **6 servings;** 230 calories per serving.

Garlic Butter

2 tablespoons margarine or butter,
    melted
1 teaspoon chopped fresh or ½ teaspoon
    dried oregano
½ teaspoon paprika
1 clove garlic, crushed
Dash of freshly ground pepper

Mix all ingredients.

Lemon Butter

2 tablespoons margarine or butter,
    melted
½ teaspoon grated lemon peel
1 tablespoon lemon juice
½ teaspoon Worcestershire sauce

Mix all ingredients.

Parmesan Butter

2 tablespoons margarine or butter, melted
2 tablespoons grated Parmesan cheese
1 teaspoon chopped fresh or ½ teaspoon
    dried basil
1 teaspoon chopped fresh parsley

Mix all ingredients.

• • • • • • • • • • •

HALIBUT WITH STEAMED VEGETABLES

◑ MICROWAVE TIME: 12 to 15 minutes

4 small halibut steaks, each about
    1 inch thick (about 1½ pounds)
1 tablespoon chopped fresh or 1 teaspoon
    dried savory
Salt and pepper
4 thin slices lemon
1 tablespoon margarine or butter
1 medium onion, sliced and separated
    into rings
1 small yellow bell pepper, cut into
    ¼-inch slices
1 small red bell pepper, cut into ¼-inch
    slices
½ pound spinach, coarsely chopped
    (about 6 cups)

1. Pat fish steaks dry. Arrange fish, thickest parts to outside edges, in square dish, 8 × 8 × 2 inches. Sprinkle with savory, salt and pepper; place lemon slice on each fish steak.

2. Cover tightly and microwave on high 8 to 9 minutes, rotating dish ½ turn after 5 minutes, until fish flakes easily with fork. Let stand covered.

3. Place margarine, onion and bell peppers in 1½-quart casserole. Cover tightly and microwave on high 3 to 4 minutes or until vegetables are crisp-tender; stir in spinach. Cover tightly and microwave 1 to 2 minutes or just until spinach is hot. Serve fish over vegetables.   **4 servings;** 350 calories per serving.

LEMONY HERB SWORDFISH

MICROWAVE TIME: 9 to 11 minutes
STAND TIME: 3 minutes

4 small swordfish or halibut steaks, each
    about ¾ inch thick (about 1½ pounds)
¼ teaspoon salt
¼ teaspoon pepper
2 tablespoons chopped fresh or
    1 teaspoon dried chervil
1 tablespoon lemon juice
¼ cup magarine or butter

1. Pat fish steaks dry. Arrange fish, thickest
parts to outside edges, in square dish, 8 × 8
× 2 inches. Sprinkle with salt, pepper and
chervil; drizzle with lemon juice.

2. Cover tightly and microwave on high 8
to 10 minutes, rotating dish ½ turn after 4
minutes, until fish flakes easily with fork.
Let stand covered 3 minutes; drain.

3. Place margarine in 1-cup measure. Cover
with paper towel and microwave on medium
(50%) 1 to 2 minutes or until hot and bubbly;
pour over fish. **4 servings;** 395 calories per
serving.

POACHED SALMON SALAD

MICROWAVE TIME: 6 to 8 minutes
STAND TIME: 3 minutes

1 pound salmon steaks, each about
    1 inch thick (about 2 medium)
¼ teaspoon salt
¼ cup dry white wine or chicken broth
4 cups shredded lettuce
½ cup croutons
¼ cup chopped fresh parsley
½ small red onion, sliced and separated
    into rings
Dijon Vinaigrette (below)

1. Pat salmon steaks dry. Arrange fish,
thickest parts to outside edges, in square
dish, 8 × 8 × 2 inches; sprinkle with salt.
Pour wine over fish.

2. Cover tightly and microwave on high 6
to 8 minutes or until fish flakes easily with
fork. Let stand covered 3 minutes; drain.
Remove skin and bones; break salmon into
1-inch pieces.

3. Mix remaining ingredients except Dijon
Vinaigrette in large salad bowl; top with
salmon. Drizzle vinaigrette over salad.
4 servings; 365 calories per serving.

*500-watt microwave: You may need to in-
crease microwave time.*

Dijon Vinaigrette

¼ cup vegetable oil
2 tablespoons lemon juice
2 tablespoons finely chopped green
    onion (with top)
2 teaspoons chopped fresh or ½ teaspoon
    dried tarragon
1 teaspoon Dijon mustard
Dash of freshly ground pepper

Mix all ingredients.

HALIBUT STEAKS WITH GUACAMOLE

REFRIGERATION TIME: 1 hour
MICROWAVE TIME: 8 to 10 minutes
STAND TIME: 3 minutes

6 small halibut steaks, each about ¾ inch
   thick (about 1½ pounds)
1 teaspoon grated lemon peel
¼ cup lemon juice
¼ cup water
3 tablespoons soy sauce
1 teaspoon ground ginger
½ teaspoon garlic powder
Guacamole (below) or 1 package
   (6 ounces) frozen avocado dip, thawed
Lemon wedges

1. Pat fish steaks dry. Place in shallow glass
or plastic dish. Mix lemon peel, lemon juice,
water, soy sauce, ginger and garlic powder;
pour over fish. Cover and refrigerate at
least 1 hour, spooning marinade over fish
occasionally.

2. Drain fish, reserving marinade. Arrange
fish, thickest parts to outside edge, in circle
on 12-inch plate. Cover tightly and microwave on high 8 to 10 minutes, brushing with
marinade and rotating plate ½ turn after 4
minutes, until fish flakes easily with fork.
Let stand covered 3 minutes. Serve with Guacamole and lemon wedges. **6 servings;** 280
calories per serving.

Guacamole

1 ripe avocado, peeled and pit removed
1 clove garlic, finely chopped
¼ cup chopped tomato
1 tablespoon lime juice
⅛ teaspoon salt

Mash avocado until slightly lumpy. Stir in
remaining ingredients. Cover and refrigerate
1 hour.

HALIBUT STEAKS WITH WINE

MICROWAVE TIME: 6 to 8 minutes
STAND TIME: 3 minutes

2 large halibut steaks, each about ¾ inch
   thick (about 1 pound)
2 tablespoons dry white wine
¼ teaspoon salt
1 teaspoon chopped fresh or ¼ teaspoon
   dried oregano
1 tablespoon dry bread crumbs
1 tablespoon grated Parmesan cheese
1 tablespoon margarine or butter, melted
1 green onion (with top), finely chopped

1. Pat halibut steaks dry. Arrange fish,
thickest parts to outside edges, in rectangular dish, 11 × 7 × 1½ inches. Sprinkle with
wine, salt and oregano.

2. Cover tightly and microwave on high 3
minutes; drain. Sprinkle with bread crumbs
and cheese; drizzle with margarine. Rotate
dish ½ turn.

3. Microwave uncovered 3 to 5 minutes or
until small ends of fish flake easily with fork.
Let stand uncovered 3 minutes. Sprinkle with
onion. **4 servings;** 220 calories per serving.

*Poached Salmon Steaks (page 94), Halibut Steaks with
Guacamole*

SWORDFISH STEAKS WITH VEGETABLE JULIENNE

MICROWAVE TIME: 11 to 13 minutes
STAND TIME: 5 minutes

2 medium carrots, coarsely shredded
1 medium leek, cut into thin strips
1 medium zucchini, cut into thin strips
1 medium stalk celery, cut into thin
    strips
4 medium swordfish steak, each about
    1 inch thick (about 2 pounds)
2 tablespoons margarine or butter, melted
1 teaspoon salt
1½ teaspoons chopped fresh or
    ½ teaspoon dried marjoram
1½ teaspoons chopped fresh or
    ½ teaspoon dried rosemary, crushed
4 thin slices lemon

1. Mix vegetables; arrange evenly in rectangular dish, 11 × 7 × 1½ inches. Arrange fish steaks on vegetables with thickest parts to outside edges of casserole. Drizzle with margarine; sprinkle with salt and herbs. Place lemon slice on each piece fish.

2. Cover tightly and microwave on high 11 to 13 minutes, rotating dish ½ turn after 5 minutes, until fish flakes easily with fork. Let stand covered 5 minutes.   **4 servings;** 430 calories per serving.

PEPPER TUNA STEAKS

MICROWAVE TIME: 4 to 5 minutes

4 small tuna or shark steaks, each
    about ¾ inch thick (about 1½ pounds)
2 tablespoons margarine or butter, melted
1 tablespoon chopped fresh or
    ½ teaspoon dried thyme
Freshly ground pepper
Paprika

1. Preheat large microwave browning dish as directed by manufacturer. Pat fish steaks dry; brush both sides with margarine. Sprinkle with thyme, pepper and paprika; press into fish.

2. Place fish on hot browning dish. Microwave uncovered on high 4 to 5 minutes, turning fish over after 2 minutes, until fish flakes easily with fork. Serve with lemon wedges if desired.   **4 servings;** 295 calories per serving.

A 500-watt microwave is not recommended.

Swordfish Steaks with Vegetable Julienne

POACHED SALMON STEAKS

Fish steaks poached by microwaves are invariably moist, if you watch the cooking time with care.

MICROWAVE TIME: 8 to 10 minutes
STAND TIME: 3 minutes
REFRIGERATION TIME: 2 hours, if desired

4 medium salmon steaks, each about 1 inch thick (about 2 pounds)
¼ teaspoon salt
4 sprigs fresh dill weed
4 slices lemon
5 black peppercorns
¼ cup dry white wine or water
Mustard-Dill Sauce (below) or Creamy Cucumber Sauce (right)

1. Pat salmon steaks dry. Arrange fish, thickest parts to outside edges, in rectangular dish, 11 × 7 × 1½ inches; sprinkle with salt. Place dill weed sprig and lemon slice on each. Add peppercorns; pour wine over fish.

2. Cover tightly and microwave on high 8 to 10 minutes, rotating dish ½ turn after 4 minutes, until fish flakes easily with fork. Let stand covered 3 minutes; drain. Serve hot with Mustard-Dill Sauce. Or cover and refrigerate about 2 hours or until chilled. Serve cold with Creamy Cucumber Sauce. **4 servings;** 450 calories per serving.

500-watt microwave: You may need to increase microwave time.

Mustard-Dill Sauce

1 tablespoon sugar
1 tablespoon chopped fresh or ½ teaspoon dried dill weed
2 tablespoons Dijon mustard
2 tablespoons vegetable oil
1 tablespoon vinegar

Mix all ingredients.

Creamy Cucumber Sauce

½ cup plain yogurt
2 tablespoons chopped fresh parsley
1 teaspoon lemon juice
¼ teaspoon salt
Dash of white pepper
1 medium cucumber, pared, seeded and shredded

Mix all ingredients; cover and refrigerate at least 1 hour.

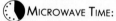

SALMON STEAKS WITH ASPARAGUS AND PEAS

MICROWAVE TIME: 9 to 10 minutes

4 small salmon or halibut steaks, each about 1 inch thick (about 1½ pounds)
½ teaspoon salt
2 teaspoons chopped fresh or ½ teaspoon dried rosemary, crushed
1 tablespoon lemon juice
½ pound asparagus, cut into 2-inch pieces
1 cup fresh or frozen green peas
Lemon wedges

1. Pat fish steaks dry. Arrange fish, thickest parts to outside edges, in square dish, 8 × 8 × 2 inches. Sprinkle with salt, rosemary and lemon juice. Arrange asparagus and peas on fish.

2. Cover tightly and microwave on high 9 to 10 minutes, rotating dish ½ turn after 5 minutes, until fish flakes easily with fork and vegetables are crisp-tender. Serve with lemon wedges. **4 servings;** 305 calories per serving.

Salmon Cakes with Mustard Mayonnaise, Colorful Coleslaw (page 222)

SALMON CAKES WITH MUSTARD MAYONNAISE

MICROWAVE TIME: 7 to 8 minutes
REFRIGERATION TIME: 15 minutes

2 cups soft bread crumbs (about 4 slices bread)
¼ cup chopped fresh parsley
¼ cup mayonnaise or salad dressing
1 tablespoon Dijon mustard
2 green onions (with tops), finely chopped
1 egg
1 can (15½ ounces) salmon, drained and flaked
¼ teaspoon paprika
1 tablespoon margarine or butter
Mustard Mayonnaise (right)

1. Mix 1½ cups of the bread crumbs, the parsley, mayonnaise, mustard, onions, egg and salmon. Cover and refrigerate about 15 minutes or until slightly firm.

2. Mix remaining bread crumbs and the paprika. Shape salmon mixture into 4 patties, each about ¾ inch thick; coat with bread crumb mixture.

3. Place margarine on 10-inch plate. Microwave uncovered on high 20 to 30 seconds or until melted. Spread margarine evenly over plate; arrange patties on top. Cover with waxed paper and microwave 6 to 7 minutes, turning patties over after 4 minutes, until hot. Serve with Mustard Mayonnaise. **4 servings;** 450 calories per serving.

Mustard Mayonnaise

⅓ cup mayonnaise or salad dressing
1 tablespoon Dijon mustard

Mix ingredients.

HOT SEAFOOD SANDWICHES

Sometimes sold as "sea legs" or "surimi," imitation crabmeat is considerably less expensive than the real item.

 MICROWAVE TIME: 3 to 4 minutes

1 cup bite-size pieces cooked crabmeat or lobster (about 4 ounces)
1 cup shredded Swiss cheese (4 ounces)
⅓ cup mayonnaise or salad dressing
1 green onion (with top), thinly sliced
Dash of red pepper sauce
4 slices whole-grain bread, toasted
½ cup alfalfa sprouts

1. Mix all ingredients except toast and sprouts. Arrange sprouts on toast; top with seafood mixture. Arrange on microwave rack or 12-inch plate.

2. Microwave uncovered on high 3 to 4 minutes, rotating rack ½ turn after 2 minutes, until cheese begins to melt and mixture is hot. **4 open-face sandwiches;** 315 calories per sandwich.

• • • • • • • • • •

TUNA CHEDDAR SANDWICHES

MICROWAVE TIME: 3 to 4 minutes

1 can (6½ ounces) tuna, drained
¾ cup chopped cucumber (about ½ medium)
¼ cup mayonaise or salad dressing
2 teaspoons chopped fresh or ½ teaspoon dried dill weed
3 English muffins, split and toasted
6 slices Cheddar or Colby–Monterey Jack cheese (about 4 ounces)

1. Mix all ingredients except muffins and cheese. Spread tuna mixture over cut side of each muffin half. Arrange on microwave rack or 10-inch plate.

2. Microwave uncovered on high 2 to 3 minutes or until mixture is hot. Top with cheese. Microwave uncovered 30 to 60 seconds or until cheese begins to melt. **6 open-face sandwiches;** 265 calories per sandwich.

• • • • • • • • • •

CREAMY SHRIMP SANDWICHES

MICROWAVE TIME: 2 to 3 minutes

1 can (4¼ ounces) shrimp, rinsed and drained
1 package (3 ounces) cream cheese, softened
2 tablespoons mayonnaise or salad dressing
1 tablespoon lemon juice
2 teaspoons chopped fresh or ½ teaspoon dried dill weed
2 bagels, split and toasted
1 small avocado, peeled and sliced

1. Mix all ingredients except bagels and avocado. Top each cut side of bagel with shrimp mixture. Arrange on microwave rack or 10-inch plate.

2. Microwave uncovered on high 2 to 3 minutes or until mixture is hot. Top with avocado slices. **4 open-face sandwiches;** 285 calories per sandwich.

CRAB BISQUE

This soup is rich with pieces of crabmeat and the flavor of sherry. Consider serving it with a grinding of cracked pepper.

◔ MICROWAVE TIME: 17 to 21 minutes

1 tablespoon margarine or butter
2 medium carrots, thinly sliced
   (about 1 cup)
1 small onion, finely chopped
   (about ¼ cup)
8 ounces fresh mushrooms, sliced
1 teaspoon chopped fresh or ¼ teaspoon
   dried thyme
½ teaspoon salt
2 cups half-and-half
2 packages (6 ounces each) frozen
   crabmeat, thawed, drained and
   cartilage removed
2 tablespoons dry sherry or half-and-half
2 tablespoons chopped fresh parsley

1.   Place margarine, carrots, onions and mushrooms in 2-quart casserole. Cover tightly and microwave on high 7 to 9 minutes, stirring after 4 minutes, until carrots are tender; drain.

2.   Stir in remaining ingredients except parsley. Cover tightly and microwave on medium-high (70%) 10 to 12 minutes, stirring after 5 minutes, until hot. Stir in freshly ground pepper if desired. Sprinkle with parsley. **4 servings (about 1 cup each);** 280 calories per serving.

500-watt microwave: You may need to increase microwave times.

CRAB NEWBURG

◔ MICROWAVE TIME: 10 to 12 minutes

¼ cup margarine or butter
¼ cup all-purpose flour
½ teaspoon dry mustard
¼ teaspoon salt
¼ teaspoon pepper
2 cups milk
2 cups cut-up cooked crabmeat or
   imitation crabmeat
2 tablespoons dry white wine, if desired
6 slices bread, toasted

1.   Place margarine in 2-quart casserole. Microwave on high about 45 seconds or until melted. Stir in flour, mustard, salt and pepper until smooth. Stir in milk gradually.

2.   Microwave uncovered on high 7 to 8 minutes, stirring every minute, until mixture thickens and boils. Stir in crabmeat and wine. Cover tightly and microwave on high 2 to 3 minutes or until hot. Serve over toast.   **6 servings;** 220 calories per serving.

500-watt microwave: You may need to increase microwave times.

EASY SHRIMP TORTILLAS

🌙 MICROWAVE TIME: 5 to 7 minutes

  2 cans (4¼ ounces each) shrimp, rinsed
    and drained
  Guacamole (page 90) or 1 container
    (6 ounces) frozen avocado dip, thawed
  ½ teaspoon chili powder
  8 flour tortillas (about 7 inches in diameter)
  1 cup shredded Monterey Jack cheese
    (4 ounces)

1. Mix shrimp, Guacamole and chili powder. Spread about ¼ cup mixture down center of each tortilla. Roll up; place seam sides down in rectangular dish, 11 × 7 × 1½ inches. Cover with damp paper towel and microwave on high 3 to 4 minutes or until hot.

2. Sprinkle with cheese. Microwave uncovered on high 2 to 3 minutes or until cheese is melted. Serve with sour cream and salsa if desired.   **4 servings;** 330 calories per serving.

  A 500-watt microwave is not recommended.

• • • • • • • • • •

LEMON SHRIMP

🌙 MICROWAVE TIME: 12 to 14 minutes
   STAND TIME: 5 minutes

  1½ pounds frozen peeled and deveined
    raw medium shrimp
  ¼ cup soy sauce
  ¼ cup lemon juice
  2 tablespoons sugar
  2 tablespoons dry white wine
  ¼ teaspoon ground ginger
  2 cups hot cooked rice

1. Arrange frozen shrimp in rectangular dish, 11 × 7 × 1½ inches. Mix remaining ingredients except rice; stir into shrimp.

2. Cover tightly and microwave on high 12 to 14 minutes, stirring after 6 minutes, until shrimp are pink and firm. Let stand covered 5 minutes.

3. Remove shrimp with slotted spoon; arrange on serving plate over rice. Garnish with green onion tops if desired.   **4 servings;** 250 calories per serving.

• • • • • • • • • •

SHRIMP IN BEER

Arrange the shrimp with their tails toward the center of the plate, slightly overlapping. Beer adds a surprisingly subtle flavor to the seafood. Serve this casual dish with chewy sourdough bread and mustardy-dressed green salad.

🌙 MICROWAVE TIME: 6 to 8 minutes
   STAND TIME: 3 minutes

  ½ cup room-temperature beer
  ¼ teaspoon salt
  1 large clove garlic, crushed
  1 pound fresh or frozen (thawed) raw
    medium shrimp in shells
  ½ cup margarine or butter

1. Mix beer, salt and garlic in pie plate, 10 × 1½ inches. Arrange shrimp, with tails to center, spoke fashion in pie plate.

2. Cover tightly and microwave on high 5 to 7 minutes or until shrimp are pink and firm. Let stand covered 3 minutes.

3. Place margarine in 2-cup measure. Cover with paper towel and microwave about 1 minute or until melted and hot. Serve shrimp with melted margarine and, if desired, lemon wedges.   **4 servings;** 280 calories per serving.

GINGER SHRIMP WITH RICE

 MICROWAVE TIME: 13 to 17 minutes

1 pound fresh or frozen (thawed) raw
    large shrimp, peeled and deveined
1 package (10 ounces) frozen green peas
1 large onion, sliced
2 medium stalks celery, cut into ¼-inch
    diagonal slices (about 1 cup)
1 can (8 ounces) sliced water chestnuts
2 tablespoons soy sauce
1 tablespoon dry white wine or sherry
1 teaspoon crushed gingerroot or
    ½ teaspoon ground ginger
¼ teaspoon salt
1 tablespoon cornstarch
½ teaspoon chicken bouillon granules
⅓ cup cold water
4 cups hot cooked rice

1. Mix shrimp, frozen peas, onion, celery,
water chestnuts, soy sauce, wine, gingerroot
and salt in 2-quart casserole. Cover tightly
and microwave on high 9 to 11 minutes,
stirring every 3 minutes, until shrimp are
pink and firm and vegetables are crisp-tender.

2. Mix cornstarch, bouillon granules and water; stir into shrimp mixture. Cover tightly
and microwave 4 to 6 minutes, stirring after
2 minutes, until thickened. Serve over rice.
6 servings; 275 calories per serving.

LEMON SEAFOOD WITH PASTA

*Few dishes are as beautiful as this, with pink
shrimp, pale scallops, bright yellow bell pepper, two kinds of summer squash and snips
of bright dill. In the microwave, the seafood
is perfectly cooked while the vegetables stay
crisp.*

MICROWAVE TIME: 11 to 14 minutes
STAND TIME: 5 minutes

½ pound fresh or frozen (thawed) raw
    medium shrimp, peeled and deveined
½ pound bay scallops
1 medium zucchini, cut into ¼-inch slices
    (about 1½ cups)
1 medium yellow squash, cut into ¼-inch
    slices (about 1½ cups)
1 small yellow or green bell pepper, cut
    into ¼-inch strips
1 cup chicken broth
¼ cup lemon juice
2 tablespoons cornstarch
1 tablespoon chopped fresh or 1 teaspoon
    dried dill weed
¼ teaspoon salt
2 cups hot cooked rotini pasta

1. Mix shrimp, scallops, zucchini, squash
and bell pepper in 3-quart casserole. Cover
tightly and microwave on high 8 to 10 minutes, stirring every 3 minutes, until shrimp
are pink and firm. Drain; let stand covered 5
minutes.

2. Mix broth, lemon juice, cornstarch, dill
weed and salt in 2-cup measure until smooth.
Microwave uncovered on high 3 to 4 minutes, stirring every minute, until mixture
thickens and boils. Stir into seafood mixture;
serve over pasta. Garnish with fresh dill weed
if desired.   **4 servings;** 190 calories per serving.

*500-watt microwave: You may need to in-
crease microwave times.*

Spicy Oysters, Green Beans Vinaigrette (page 184)

SPICY OYSTERS

MICROWAVE TIME: 9 to 11 minutes

1 tablespoon margarine or butter
1½ cups corn bread stuffing (dry)
¼ to ½ teaspoon ground red pepper
   (cayenne)
¼ teaspoon salt
¼ teaspoon garlic powder
1 pint shucked oysters, rinsed and
   drained

1. Place margarine in square dish, 8 × 8 ×
2 inches. Microwave uncovered on high 20
to 30 seconds or until melted; spread evenly
in dish.

2. Mix remaining ingredients except oysters. Coat oysters with stuffing mixture; arrange in single layer in dish. Sprinkle any remaining stuffing mixture evenly over top. Cover with waxed paper and microwave on medium (50%) 8 to 10 minutes, rotating dish ½ turn after 4 minutes, until oysters are hot.   **4 servings;** 295 calories per serving.

500-watt microwave: You may need to increase microwave times.

OYSTERS WITH BUTTERED CRUMBS

MICROWAVE TIME: 7 to 10 minutes

1 pint shucked oysters, rinsed, drained
   and cut into halves
⅓ cup half-and-half
1 cup crushed saltine crackers (about
   20 squares)
¼ teaspoon salt
⅛ teaspoon pepper
Dash of ground nutmeg
⅓ cup margarine or butter, melted

1.   Arrange oysters in round dish, 8 × 1½
inches; pour half-and-half over oysters. Mix
remaining ingredients; sprinkle over top.

2.   Microwave uncovered on high 7 to 10
minutes, rotating dish ½ turn after 4 minutes, until oysters are hot.   **4 servings;** 310
calories per serving.

•••••••••••

PARSLEY SCALLOPS

MICROWAVE TIME: 6 to 9 minutes
REFRIGERATION TIME: 4 hours

1½ pounds sea scallops
⅓ cup oil-and-vinegar dressing
3 tablespoons chopped fresh parsley
1 clove garlic, finely chopped
Paprika

1.   If scallops are large, cut into halves. Place
scallops in 2-quart casserole. Cover tightly
and microwave on high 6 to 9 minutes, stirring after 4 minutes, until scallops turn white;
drain.

2.   Mix dressing, parsley and garlic; pour
over scallops. Refrigerate about 4 hours, stirring occasionally. Sprinkle with paprika.
About 4 servings; 175 calories per serving.

CITRUS SCALLOP SALAD

*The fresh, sprightly flavors of citrus and kiwi-
fruit make for a summery scallop dish.*

MICROWAVE TIME: 6 to 9 minutes
REFRIGERATION TIME: 2 hours

1½ pounds sea scallops
½ teaspoon salt
¼ pound spinach, torn into bite-size
   pieces (about 4 cups)
2 kiwifruit, pared and sliced
2 medium oranges, pared and sliced
Citrus Dressing (below)

1.   If scallops are large, cut into halves. Mix
scallops and salt in 2-quart casserole. Cover
tightly and microwave on high 6 to 9 minutes, stirring after 4 minutes, until scallops
are white in center; drain. Cover and refrigerate at least 2 hours until chilled.

2.   Drain scallops; toss with spinach and fruit.
Drizzle with Citrus Dressing.   **4 servings;** 230
calories per serving.

*500-watt microwave: You may need to in-
crease microwave time.*

Citrus Dressing

1 teaspoon grated orange peel
¼ cup orange juice
2 tablespoons vegetable oil
2 tablespoons lemon juice

Shake all ingredients in tightly covered
container.

Citrus Scallop Salad

Hot and Sour Fish Soup

HOT AND SOUR FISH SOUP

MICROWAVE TIME: 14 to 17 minutes

½ pound cod fillets
2 tablespoons white vinegar
2 teaspoons soy sauce
2 medium carrots, shredded
  (about 1 cup)
2 bottles (8 ounces each) clam juice or
  2 cups fish or chicken broth
1 jar (7 ounces) sliced shiitake mushrooms, undrained
2 tablespoons cornstarch
2 tablespoons water
1 teaspoon red pepper sauce
4 ounces fresh Chinese pea pods or
  1 package (6 ounces) frozen Chinese
  pea pods, thawed

1. Pat fish fillets dry; cut into 1-inch pieces. Mix fish, vinegar, soy sauce, carrots, clam juice and mushrooms in 3-quart casserole. Cover tightly and microwave on high 5 minutes.

2. Mix cornstarch and water; stir into fish mixture. Cover tightly and microwave 8 to 10 minutes, stirring every 2 minutes, until mixture thickens and boils.

3. Stir in red pepper sauce and pea pods. Cover tightly and microwave 1 to 2 minutes or until pea pods are hot. **4 servings (about 1¼ cups each); 85 calories per serving.**

DILLED SALMON CHOWDER

 MICROWAVE TIME: 20 to 23 minutes

2 medium unpared potatoes, cut into
½-inch cubes
2 medium stalks celery, sliced
1 medium carrot, sliced
1 medium onion, chopped (about ½ cup)
1 can (10¾ ounces) condensed chicken
broth
1 broth can water
1 tablespoon chopped fresh or 1 teaspoon
dried dill weed
½ teaspoon salt
¼ teaspoon pepper
2 cups half-and-half
1 can (15½ ounces) salmon, drained and
flaked

1. Mix all ingredients except half-and-half and salmon in 3-quart casserole. Cover tightly and microwave on high 16 to 18 minutes, stirring after 8 minutes, until vegetables are crisp-tender.

2 . Stir in half-and-half and salmon. Cover tightly and microwave 4 to 5 minutes, stirring every 2 minutes, until hot. **6 servings (about 1½ cups each);** 280 calories per serving.

VEGETABLE-CLAM CHOWDER

MICROWAVE TIME: 18 to 22 minutes

2 tablespoons margarine or butter
1 package (16 ounces) frozen corn and
broccoli mixture
2 cans (6½ ounces each) minced clams,
drained
3 cups milk
1 teaspoon salt
⅛ teaspoon pepper

1. Place margarine and frozen vegetables in 3-quart casserole. Cover tightly and microwave on high 8 to 10 minutes or until hot.

2. Stir in remaining ingredients. Cover tightly and microwave on medium-high (70%) 10 to 12 minutes, stirring after 5 minutes, until hot. **4 servings (about 1¼ cups each);** 230 calories per serving.

500-watt microwave: You may need to increase microwave time.

MANHATTAN CLAM CHOWDER

MICROWAVE TIME: 22 to 25 minutes

4 slices bacon, cut into ½-inch pieces
2 medium unpared potatoes, cut into
    ½-inch cubes
1 small onion, finely chopped (about
    ¼ cup)
1 stalk celery, finely chopped (about
    ½ cup)
1 small green bell pepper, finely chopped
2 cans (6½ ounces each) minced clams,
    undrained
1 teaspoon chopped fresh or ¼ teaspoon
    dried thyme
¼ teaspoon salt
¼ teaspoon pepper
1 can (28 ounces) whole tomatoes,
    undrained
¼ cup chopped fresh parsley

1.   Place bacon in 3-quart casserole. Cover with paper towel and microwave on high 5 to 6 minutes or until crisp. Drain, reserving 1 tablespoon fat and the bacon in casserole.

2.   Stir potatoes, onion, celery and bell pepper into bacon in casserole. Cover tightly and microwave 7 minutes.

3.   Stir in remaining ingredients except parsley; break up tomatoes. Cover tightly and microwave 10 to 12 minutes, stirring after 5 minutes, until potatoes are tender and mixture is hot. Sprinkle with parsley.   **6 servings (about 1¼ cups each);** 155 calories per serving.

500-watt microwave: You may need to increase microwave times.

CREAMY TUNA CASSEROLE

MICROWAVE TIME: 14 to 17 minutes

4 to 5 cups hot cooked noodles
2 cans (6½ ounces each) tuna, drained
1 can (4 ounces) mushroom stems and
    pieces, drained
1 can (2 ounces) sliced pimientos, drained
1½ cups sour cream
⅔ cup milk
½ teaspoon salt
¼ teaspoon pepper
¼ cup dry bread crumbs
¼ cup grated Parmesan cheese
2 tablespoons margarine or butter, melted
Chopped fresh parsley

1.   Mix noodles, tuna, mushrooms, pimientos, sour cream, milk, salt and pepper in 2-quart casserole. Cover tightly and microwave on medium (50%) 10 minutes; stir.

2.   Mix bread crumbs, cheese and margarine; sprinkle evenly over tuna mixture. Microwave uncovered until hot and bubbly, 4 to 7 minutes longer. Sprinkle with parsley. **6 servings;** 370 calories per serving.

MICROWAVING SEAFOOD

TYPE	AMOUNT	TIME

Fish

Arrange fish with thickest parts to outside edge in a dish large enough to hold pieces in single layer. Fold thin fillet ends under to prevent overcooking. Cover tightly and microwave on high as directed below or until fish flakes easily with fork and meat thermometer registers 160°. Let stand about 3 minutes after cooking.

TYPE	AMOUNT	TIME
Fillets, ½ to ¾ inch thick	1 pound	5 to 7 minutes, rotating dish ½ turn after 3 minutes
	1½ pounds	7 to 9 minutes, rotating dish ½ turn after 4 minutes
Steaks, 1 inch thick	1 pound (about 2)	5 to 7 minutes, rotating dish ½ turn after 3 minutes
	2 pounds (about 4)	8 to 10 minutes, rotating dish ½ turn after 4 minutes

Shellfish

Cut large scallops into halves. Place shellfish in dish. Cover tightly and microwave on high as directed below or until scallops are white or opaque or shrimp are pink and firm.

TYPE	AMOUNT	TIME
Scallops	1½ pounds	6 to 9 minutes, stirring after 4 minutes
Shrimp in shells	1 pound	5 to 7 minutes, stirring after 3 minutes
Shrimp, peeled and deveined	1 pound	6 to 8 minutes, stirring after 3 minutes

DEFROSTING SEAFOOD

Type	Amount	Time

Fish

Place unwrapped fish in shallow dish. Cover tightly and microwave on defrost setting as directed below until pieces can be separated. Microwave until few ice crystals remain in center. Edges should not begin to cook.

Type	Amount	Time
Fillets, ½ to ¾ inch thick	1 pound	6 to 8 minutes, rearranging after 3 minutes
	1½ pounds	8 to 10 minutes, rearranging after 4 minutes
Steaks, 1 inch thick	1 pound (about 2)	6 to 8 minutes, rearranging after 3 minutes
	2 pounds (about 4)	14 to 16 minutes, rearranging after 7 minutes

Shellfish

Place unwrapped shellfish in shallow dish. Cover tightly and microwave on defrost setting as directed below until pieces can be separated. Microwave until few ice crystals remain in center. Let stand 5 to 10 minutes.

Type	Amount	Time
Crabmeat	6 ounces	5 to 7 minutes, breaking up after 3 minutes
Imitation crabmeat	8 ounces	4 to 6 minutes, breaking up after 2 minutes
Lobster tails	2 pounds (about 4)	8 to 10 minutes, rotating dish ½ turn after 5 minutes
Scallops	1 pound	8 to 10 minutes, stirring after 4 minutes
Shrimp in shells or peeled and deveined	1 pound	6 to 8 minutes, stirring after 3 minutes

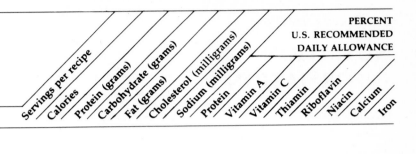

RECIPE, PAGE	Servings per recipe	Calories	Protein (grams)	Carbohydrate (grams)	Fat (grams)	Cholesterol (milligrams)	Sodium (milligrams)	Protein	Vitamin A	Vitamin C	Thiamin	Riboflavin	Niacin	Calcium	Iron
POULTRY															
Almond Turkey Cutlets, 63	4	370	32	1	21	75	480	70	6	0	6	22	36	10	14
Apricot-glazed Grilled Turkey, 62	12	265	43	20	1	120	80	96	0	0	4	10	52	2	12
Barbecued Chicken on Kaiser Rolls, 59	6	345	26	42	8	65	905	56	8	4	18	18	44	8	14
Barbecued Chicken Wings, 53	4	335	43	16	11	120	455	94	10	8	6	12	52	2	12
Chicken with Artichoke Hearts, 42	6	300	29	15	10	85	335	64	4	6	10	20	48	2	12
Chicken with Bell Peppers, 41	6	290	32	10	13	100	490	70	42	80	20	18	50	2	14
Chicken Carbonara, 56	4	535	33	36	28	125	360	72	10	2	20	20	42	18	14
Chicken Croissants, 59	6	405	18	19	29	90	600	38	14	0	20	14	16	22	8
Chicken Enchiladas, 54	8	230	16	16	12	50	260	34	10	10	6	8	18	16	8
Chicken Kiev, 47	4	285	28	9	15	75	300	62	14	0	6	8	62	4	6
Chicken Nachos, 56	4	740	37	46	47	75	675	82	30	20	14	28	42	42	16
Chicken Nuggets, 49	6	180	19	12	6	50	325	28	4	0	8	6	42	2	6
Chicken-Pineapple Kabobs, 51	4	210	25	12	7	65	350	56	4	50	8	6	44	2	8
Chicken Soup with Almonds, 58	4	430	28	10	31	110	650	60	14	0	8	24	36	18	8
Chicken and Spinach Noodle Casserole, 56	6	235	17	10	14	80	395	36	14	0	4	8	24	4	6
Chicken with Summer Squash, 43	4	325	39	6	16	105	365	60	18	40	10	10	86	4	12
Chicken Taco Pockets, 58	8	440	27	44	19	40	735	58	10	12	2	12	18	22	4
Chicken and Tortilla Soup, 57	4	440	32	25	24	65	1670	70	38	46	10	20	42	28	20
Chinese Chicken and Cashews, 49	4	370	31	36	11	70	825	68	28	12	14	14	62	6	18
Cobb Salad, 61	4	635	37	11	50	290	605	80	40	40	18	22	66	10	18
Creole Chicken Casserole, 54	6	295	27	32	6	80	1105	58	10	30	26	12	38	6	16
Curried Chicken Breasts, 50	6	350	31	30	11	95	750	68	6	4	12	14	64	6	12
Deviled Turkey Patties, 66	4	150	19	6	5	60	300	42	2	0	4	10	20	2	8
Duckling with Tangy Sauce, 71	4	560	27	23	40	120	165	60	8	30	20	24	34	4	22

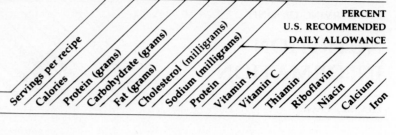

Per Serving or Unit **NUTRITION INFORMATION** RECIPE, PAGE	Servings per recipe	Calories	Protein (grams)	Carbohydrate (grams)	Fat (grams)	Cholesterol (milligrams)	Sodium (milligrams)	Protein	Vitamin A	Vitamin C	Thiamin	Riboflavin	Niacin	Calcium	Iron
POULTRY, *continued*															
Easy Mexican Chicken, 52	4	290	30	11	14	95	565	64	16	0	10	18	34	4	12
Easy Sloppy Joes, 71	6	275	16	32	9	36	600	36	8	8	14	14	22	8	14
French Potato Salad with Chicken, 59	4	330	28	32	10	70	425	62	18	12	8	10	58	10	64
Gingered Chicken, 52	6	310	30	21	12	95	1360	64	4	2	6	14	34	2	10
Hot Chicken Salad, 61	4	460	24	12	36	65	360	52	2	6	8	16	34	6	18
Italian Chicken, 41	6	330	31	33	9	80	885	68	20	26	18	22	54	6	20
Lemon-Dill Chicken, 45	6	190	25	2	7	70	200	56	6	8	4	6	54	2	6
Lemon-Herb Grilled Chicken, 45	6	280	26	1	19	80	170	56	0	2	4	8	40	2	6
Mexican Turkey, 66	4	230	33	4	9	90	290	72	28	34	4	12	34	12	10
Orange-glazed Chicken, 42	6	275	26	28	7	80	265	56	0	10	4	10	40	2	6
Oriental Turkey and Vegetables, 68	4	320	29	26	12	65	780	64	36	34	6	14	44	6	10
Paprika Chicken, 51	4	355	27	35	12	85	660	58	38	24	16	20	6	6	20
Plum-glazed Cornish Hens, 72	4	275	28	30	5	70	200	42	4	2	4	14	52	2	12
Raspberry Chicken Breasts, 46	4	200	24	19	3	68	60	60	52	0	2	2	4	52	04
Sherried Chicken, 43	5	255	20	16	11	60	500	42	10	2	4	8	40	4	6
Turkey Casserole, 67	6	380	34	25	15	90	425	74	18	10	14	30	40	12	18
Turkey Chowder with Vegetables, 69	6	260	20	25	9	50	660	42	100	2	8	16	28	12	16
Turkey Divan, 65	3	345	31	10	19	100	470	48	48	30	6	14	34	20	10
Turkey-Sausage Casserole, 68	6	330	21	20	18	90	320	46	6	2	18	14	28	6	10
Turkey Scallopini, 65	4	295	34	10	12	162	460	74	6	0	4	12	36	0	12
Turkey-Stuffing Casserole, 67	6	380	21	33	18	45	1220	46	16	6	22	16	34	6	16
Wild Rice and Turkey Salad, 70	6	540	28	21	39	55	445	60	32	70	12	20	30	6	18

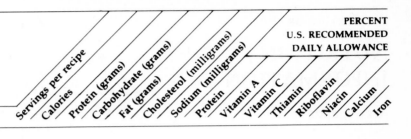

PER SERVING OR UNIT ## NUTRITION INFORMATION RECIPE, PAGE	Servings per recipe	Calories	Protein (grams)	Carbohydrate (grams)	Fat (grams)	Cholesterol (milligrams)	Sodium (milligrams)	PERCENT U.S. RECOMMENDED DAILY ALLOWANCE							
								Protein	Vitamin A	Vitamin C	Thiamin	Riboflavin	Niacin	Calcium	Iron
FISH															
Bell Pepper Cod, 87	4	230	31	7	9	55	415	46	22	80	12	22	60	2	14
Breaded Lemon Perch, 87	4	340	29	6	22	55	495	44	24	0	6	6	48	2	6
Creamy Tuna Casserole, 106	6	370	15	32	20	45	745	22	16	6	12	14	20	16	10
Crunchy Pecan Fillets, 77	4	300	31	5	16	55	535	48	16	0	8	8	48	2	6
Dilled Salmon Chowder, 104	6	280	21	18	14	30	835	32	78	6	6	18	38	26	26
Flounder with Creamy Herb Stuffing, 75	4	240	32	2	10	65	330	48	18	0	4	8	46	19	6
Garlic Cod, 85	4	330	29	2	23	55	425	44	24	0	4	4	46	2	4
Haddock with Asparagus, 87	4	235	30	2	11	55	735	46	28	14	8	8	50	2	6
Halibut Steaks with Guacamole, 90	6	280	30	5	15	60	870	46	18	4	6	6	50	2	8
Halibut Steaks with Wine, 90	4	220	29	2	11	60	360	65	20	0	4	6	45	4	6
Halibut with Steamed Vegetables, 88	4	350	45	7	15	85	850	68	100	68	12	14	74	8	18
Hot and Sour Fish Soup, 105	4	185	18	17	5	30	720	28	100	4	6	12	38	4	6
Lemony Herb Swordfish, 89	4	395	43	0	23	85	500	66	32	0	4	6	70	2	6
Orange Roughy with Shrimp Sauce, 86	4	410	38	24	17	145	550	58	24	2	14	16	52	12	14
Parmesan Sole with Mushrooms, 86	4	330	32	8	18	75	570	50	28	2	6	16	54	10	8
Pepper Tuna Steaks, 93	4	295	47	0	10	56	230	72	68	0	4	4	92	4	12
Poached Salmon Salad, 89	4	365	28	7	21	45	345	42	12	6	12	4	48	14	10
Poached Salmon Steaks with Creamy Cucumber Sauce, 94	4	450	56	4	15	95	530	86	8	6	22	12	98	32	16
Poached Salmon Steaks with Mustard-Dill Sauce, 94	4	450	55	4	22	95	470	84	6	0	20	6	98	26	14
Red Snapper with Zucchini, 85	4	280	32	18	9	60	1285	48	76	10	8	8	52	6	8
Salmon Cakes with Mustard Mayonnaise, 95	4	450	23	9	36	70	755	34	18	4	8	16	36	26	12

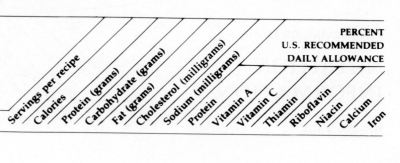

	PER SERVING OR UNIT NUTRITION INFORMATION RECIPE, PAGE	Servings per recipe	Calories	Protein (grams)	Carbohydrate (grams)	Fat (grams)	Cholesterol (milligrams)	Sodium (milligrams)	PERCENT U.S. RECOMMENDED DAILY ALLOWANCE							
									Protein	Vitamin A	Vitamin C	Thiamin	Riboflavin	Niacin	Calcium	Iron
FISH, continued																
Salmon Steaks with Asparagus and Peas, 94		4	305	45	3	12	85	505	68	32	16	10	10	74	4	10
Salmon-stuffed Flounder, 78		6	315	36	3	15	105	415	54	18	2	4	10	58	10	8
Savory Butter-dipped Sole, 88		6	230	28	0	12	55	200	44	18	0	2	4	46	2	4
Sole au Gratin, 77		4	360	36	10	19	75	770	56	54	34	8	18	50	22	8
Sole in Lettuce Packets, 83		6	240	29	2	12	55	565	44	90	2	4	4	48	2	6
Sole in Parchment, 82		4	210	29	4	8	55	430	44	26	36	6	6	48	2	8
Sole with Red Grapes, 75		6	315	29	8	15	85	345	44	26	2	6	6	48	4	6
Sole Timbales with Spinach, 81		4	240	30	2	12	55	365	46	88	8	6	8	48	6	10
Southwest Snapper Fillets, 80		4	205	29	2	8	55	295	44	16	2	2	4	48	0	6
Stuffed Perch Fillets, 78		4	325	32	7	18	125	740	48	34	6	8	10	48	4	10
Swordfish Steaks with Vegetable Julienne, 93		4	430	65	8	14	75	875	98	100	6	10	8	100	8	20
Tuna Cheddar Sandwiches, 97		6	265	15	15	16	35	570	22	4	0	6	8	18	18	6
Whitefish with Broccoli, 80		4	280	32	5	14	70	330	48	34	28	6	14	48	12	8
SHELLFISH																
Citrus Scallop Salad, 102		4	230	22	21	8	45	525	32	44	84	6	6	8	16	20
Crab Bisque, 98		4	280	14	15	18	90	480	20	100	8	12	28	18	20	8
Crab Newburg, 98		6	220	13	15	11	50	790	20	18	0	10	14	8	14	6
Creamy Shrimp Sandwiches, 97		4	285	8	16	22	50	460	12	12	4	8	8	10	4	8
Easy Shrimp Tortillas, 99		4	330	17	27	18	45	475	26	12	2	6	10	8	34	16
Ginger Shrimp with Rice, 100		6	275	13	49	2	110	1120	20	6	10	22	14	16	12	16
Hot Seafood Sandwiches, 97		4	315	16	12	23	55	345	24	20	2	6	8	6	32	4
Lemon Seafood with Pasta, 100		4	190	17	25	3	120	460	26	12	38	12	10	16	14	16

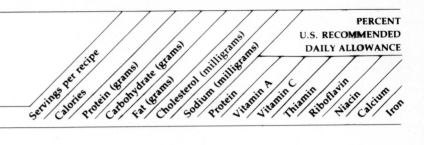

PER SERVING OR UNIT NUTRITION INFORMATION RECIPE, PAGE	Servings per recipe	Calories	Protein (grams)	Carbohydrate (grams)	Fat (grams)	Cholesterol (milligrams)	Sodium (milligrams)	Protein	Vitamin A	Vitamin C	Thiamin	Riboflavin	Niacin	Calcium	Iron
SHELLFISH, *continued*															
Lemon Shrimp, 99	4	250	21	30	4	310	1050	32	2	0	10	12	16	30	16
Manhattan Clam Chowder, 106	6	155	8	22	5	5	565	12	20	50	8	6	12	8	34
Oysters with Buttered Crumbs, 102	4	310	12	17	22	65	540	18	20	28	14	16	18	16	38
Parsley Scallops, 102	4	175	13	3	13	30	405	20	4	2	0	0	2	6	10
Shrimp in Beer, 99	4	280	10	2	25	170	490	16	18	0	2	4	6	16	4
Spicy Oysters, 101	4	295	14	23	15	75	930	20	10	26	8	20	10	6	38
Vegetable-Clam Chowder, 104	4	230	15	24	10	15	1010	22	44	32	8	24	10	26	12

3

MEATS, EGGS AND CHEESE

There are two keys to successful meat cookery in the microwave. First, select good quality cuts. Chops, most steaks, tenderloin, ground meat, ham, sausages and bacon are the best choices for microwave cooking. Large cuts, like roasts, are better cooked conventionally. Such cuts as steaks can be successfully microwaved with the help of browning dishes, and microwaving meats first can cut cooking time on a grill dramatically, with delicious results.

Second, choose pieces of meat (or trim them yourself) of approximately the same size, similar in shape and thickness. This way, they are more likely to be done at the same time. Trim off visible fat, too; this will not only cut calories, it will keep those portions of meat near the fat from overcooking, since fat attracts microwave energy.

- Always arrange pieces of meat with thickest parts toward the outside of the dish for even cooking. Because meats don't brown as they do with conventional cooking, many recipes include sauces and glazes. The microwave provides extraordinary grilling shortcuts. You can microwave meats until nearly done, then transfer them to a charcoal grill for delicious outdoor-cooked results in record time.

- Cook beef steaks and tenderloin to desired doneness: 140° for rare, 160° for medium and 170° for well done. Ground meats and sausages should be cooked until no longer pink, and 160°. Cook all pork until the meat thermometer registers 170°. Cover tightly and rearrange, stir or turn during cooking to be sure it is fully and evenly cooked.

- Most egg and cheese recipes make use of medium microwave power. This prevents eggs from becoming rubbery and cheese from getting tough or stringy. Remember to pierce egg yolks before poaching to prevent eggs from exploding. Notice that cheese is often added to a dish after it has been cooked; the heat of the food melts the cheese gently.

Barbecued Meatloaf (page 130), Eggs with Tomatoes and Bell Peppers (page 163)

GOURMET GRILLED STEAK

REFRIGERATION TIME: 1 hour
MICROWAVE TIME: 8 to 10 minutes
GRILL TIME: 7 to 8 minutes

2-pound beef boneless top round steak, about 1¼ inches thick
½ cup dry red wine or beef broth
2 tablespoons vegetable oil
1 tablespoon Worcestershire sauce
2 cloves garlic, crushed
8 ounces fresh mushrooms, sliced
4 green onions (with tops), diagonally sliced
1 can (2¼ ounces) sliced ripe olives, drained

1. Trim fat from beef steak. Pierce beef several times on both sides with fork. Place beef in rectangular dish, 11 × 7 × 1½ inches. Mix wine, oil, Worcestershire sauce and garlic; pour over beef. Cover and refrigerate at least 1 hour, turning beef over occasionally.

2. Prepare charcoal fire for grilling. Just before grilling, cover beef and marinade tightly and microwave on high 4 minutes.

3. Place beef, 5 to 6 inches from medium coals, on grill; reserve marinade. Cover and grill beef 7 to 8 minutes, turning beef over after 4 minutes, until desired doneness.

4. Place ¼ cup of the reserved marinade, the mushrooms, onions and olives in 4-cup measure. Cover tightly and microwave on high 4 to 6 minutes, stirring after 3 minutes, until boiling. Serve with beef. **8 servings;** 255 calories per serving.

A 500-watt microwave is not recommended.

Microwave-only Directions: Prepare and refrigerate beef steak as directed in step 1 (above). Cover tightly and microwave beef and marinade on high 9 to 10 minutes, turning beef over after 5 minutes, until desired doneness.

Remove beef to warm platter; cover and keep warm. Drain marinade, reserving ¼ cup in dish; stir in mushrooms, onions and olives. Cover tightly and microwave on high 4 to 5 minutes, stirring after 3 minutes, until mushrooms are hot.

•••••••••••

BRANDY BEEF STEAKS

Browning dishes make it possible to quickly sear foods in the microwave, sealing in juices and giving a nice, browned appearance. Always follow the manufacturer's instructions in using these dishes.

◑ MICROWAVE TIME: 6 to 9 minutes

4 beef tenderloin steaks (about 4 ounces each), about 1 inch thick
2 large cloves garlic, crushed
Freshly ground pepper
1 teaspoon vegetable oil
¼ cup beef broth
2 tablespoons brandy or beef broth
2 tablespoons chopped fresh parsley

1. Preheat large microwave browning dish as directed by manufacturer for steak. Coat both sides beef steaks with garlic; sprinkle with pepper. Brush browning dish with oil. Place beef in hot browning dish, pressing beef against dish with spatula.

2. Microwave uncovered on high 4 to 6 minutes, turning beef over after 2 minutes, until beef is brown and medium doneness. Remove beef; keep warm.

3. Pour broth and brandy onto browning dish. Microwave uncovered 2 to 3 minutes or until hot; stir in parsley. Pour sauce over beef. Sprinkle with salt if desired. **4 servings;** 215 calories per serving.

A 500-watt microwave is not recommended.

Mushroom Steaks, Noodles Romanoff (page 265)

MUSHROOM STEAKS

MICROWAVE TIME: 9 to 10 minutes
STAND TIME: 5 minutes

4 beef cubed steaks (about 1 pound)
¼ teaspoon salt
¼ teaspoon lemon pepper
1 can (4 ounces) sliced mushrooms,
  drained
¼ cup chopped green bell pepper
1 small onion, chopped (about ¼ cup)
2 tablespoons dry white or red wine

1. Arrange beef steaks in square dish, 8 × 8 × 2 inches. Sprinkle with salt and lemon pepper. Top with mushrooms, bell pepper and onion; drizzle with wine.

2. Cover with waxed paper and microwave on high 9 to 10 minutes, rotating dish ½ turn after 5 minutes, until beef is tender and no longer pink. Let stand covered 5 minutes. Serve with hot cooked rice, noodles or potatoes if desired. **4 servings;** 200 calories per serving.

BEEF BURGUNDY

This version of a French classic has the rich flavor of the conventionally cooked original, but it is ready to enjoy in half the time.

MICROWAVE TIME: 29 to 38 minutes

1½ pounds beef boneless sirloin steak, about ¾ inch thick
2 tablespoons margarine or butter
1 medium onion, finely chopped (about ½ cup)
⅓ cup all-purpose flour
2 teaspoons chopped fresh or ½ teaspoon dried thyme
½ cup dry red wine or water
½ teaspoon salt
1 can (10½ ounces) condensed beef broth
½ package (16-ounce size) frozen small whole onions
1 pound mushrooms, cut in half

1.   Trim fat from beef steak. Cut beef into ¾-inch pieces.

2.   Place margarine and chopped onion in 3-quart casserole. Cover tightly and microwave on high 3 to 4 minutes or until onion is soft. Stir in flour and beef. Cover and microwave 6 to 8 minutes, stirring after 4 minutes, until outside of beef is no longer pink.

3.   Stir in remaining ingredients except mushrooms. Cover tightly and microwave 12 to 16 minutes, stirring every 5 minutes, until slightly thickened and boiling. Stir in mushrooms.

4.   Cover tightly and microwave on medium (50%) 8 to 10 minutes, stirring after 4 minutes, until beef is tender. Serve with hot cooked noodles, rice or French bread if desired. **4 servings (about 1½ cups each);** 645 calories per serving.

500-watt microwave: You may need to increase microwave times.

SPICY BEEF

MICROWAVE TIME: 10 to 15 minutes

1 pound beef boneless sirloin steak, about 1 inch thick
1 package (9 ounces) frozen cut green beans
½ teaspoon crushed red pepper
2 cloves garlic, crushed
1 can (8 ounces) sliced water chestnuts, drained
1 teaspoon cornstarch
1 tablespoon red wine vinegar
2 teaspoons soy sauce
2 cups hot cooked rice

1.   Trim fat from beef steak. Cut beef across grain into 2 × ⅛-inch slices.

2.   Place green beans in square dish, 8 × 8 × 2 inches. Cover with waxed paper and microwave on high 4 to 5 minutes or until hot. Stir in beef, red pepper, garlic and water chestnuts. Mix cornstarch, vinegar and soy sauce; stir into beef and vegetable mixture.

3.   Cover with waxed paper and microwave 6 to 10 minutes, stirring every 3 minutes, until beef is no longer pink. Serve with rice. **4 servings (about 1¼ cups each);** 475 calories per serving.

BEEF TERIYAKI WITH BROCCOLI

Partially freeze the beef round steak so that it is easier to slice thinly. After as few as 6 minutes cooking time, the beef is tender and thoroughly cooked, while the vegetables are crisp.

REFRIGERATION TIME: 20 minutes
MICROWAVE TIME: 8 to 11 minutes

1 pound beef boneless round steak, about ¾ inch thick
3 tablespoons teriyaki sauce
1 tablespoon lemon juice
2 teaspoons cornstarch
1 teaspoon finely chopped fresh gingerroot
1½ cups chopped fresh broccoli
1 small onion, finely chopped (about ¼ cup)
1 clove garlic, crushed
1 small red or green bell pepper, cut into thin strips

1.   Trim fat from beef steak. Cut beef across grain into 2 × ⅛-inch slices. Mix teriyaki sauce, lemon juice, cornstarch and gingerroot in square dish, 8 × 8 × 2 inches. Stir in beef; cover and refrigerate at least 20 minutes.

2.   Drain beef, reserving marinade. Stir broccoli, onion and garlic into beef in square dish. Cover tightly and microwave on high 6 to 8 minutes, stirring after 4 minutes, until beef is no longer pink.

3.   Stir in bell pepper and marinade. Cover tightly and microwave 2 to 3 minutes or until sauce is slightly thickened and boils. Serve with hot cooked rice if desired.   **4 servings (about 1 cup each);** 265 calories per serving.

500-watt microwave: You may need to increase microwave times.

Beef Teriyaki with Broccoli, Marmalade Pears (page 241)

BEEF KABOBS

MICROWAVE TIME: 15 to 21 minutes

1½ pounds beef boneless top loin or sirloin steak
¼ cup soy sauce
1 small fresh pineapple, cut into ½-inch pieces*
36 fresh mushroom caps
1 large green bell pepper, cut into 1-inch pieces
1 cup honey
2 teaspoons dry mustard
1 teaspoon ground cloves

1.   Trim fat from beef steak. Cut beef into 1-inch cubes. Toss beef cubes and soy sauce. Alternate beef cubes, pineapple and vegetables on each of eighteen 8-inch wooden skewers.

2.   Mix honey, mustard and cloves in 2-cup measure. Microwave uncovered on medium-high (70%) about 1 minute or until warm.

3.   Brush kabobs with honey mixture. Place 9 of the kabobs on 10-inch plate. Microwave uncovered on medium-high (70%) 7 to 10 minutes, turning kabobs over, rearranging and brushing with honey mixture after 4 minutes, until beef is almost done; keep warm. Repeat with remaining kabobs. Garnish each kabob with cherry tomato if desired.   **6 servings;** 465 calories per serving.

One can (20 ounces) pineapple chunks, drained, can be substituted for the fresh pineapple.

BEEF ROLLS

MICROWAVE TIME: 28 to 34 minutes
STAND TIME: 5 minutes

½ pound bulk pork sausage
1 cup soft bread crumbs (about 1½ slices
   bread)
¼ cup chopped celery
2 tablespoons finely chopped onion
1 teaspoon chopped fresh or ¼ teaspoon
   ground sage
1 teaspoon chopped fresh or ¼ teaspoon
   dried basil
4 beef cubed steaks (about 1 pound)
1 can (10¾ ounces) condensed tomato
   soup
2 tablespoons water
1 teaspoon chopped fresh or ¼ teaspoon
   dried basil
About 3 cups hot cooked rice

1.   Crumble sausage into 2-quart casserole.
Cover loosely and microwave on high 3 to 4
minutes, breaking up and stirring after 2 minutes, until no longer pink; drain.

2.   Mix in bread crumbs, celery, onion,
sage and 1 teaspoon basil. Spread about ½
cup mixture over each beef steak. Roll up,
beginning at short side; secure with wooden
picks.

3.   Place beef rolls in 2-quart casserole. Mix
soup, water and 1 teaspoon basil; pour over
beef rolls.

4.   Cover tightly and microwave on medium
(50%) 25 to 30 minutes, rearranging beef rolls
after 15 minutes, until beef is tender. Let
stand covered 5 minutes. Serve beef rolls on
rice; pour sauce over beef rolls.   **4 servings;**
510 calories per serving.

MEXICAN CUBED STEAKS

MICROWAVE TIME: 8 to 11 minutes
STAND TIME: 2 minutes

4 beef cubed steaks (about 1½ pounds)
1 cup salsa
½ cup shredded Monterey Jack cheese
   (2 ounces)
½ medium avocado, peeled and sliced

1.   Place beef steaks in square dish, 8 × 8
× 2 inches. Cover with waxed paper and
microwave on high 6 to 8 minutes, turning
beef over after 3 minutes, until almost done;
drain.

2.   Top each steak with ¼ cup salsa. Cover
with waxed paper and microwave 2 to 3
minutes or until salsa is hot. Sprinkle each
with 2 tablespoons cheese; cover and let stand
about 2 minutes or until cheese is melted.
Top with avocado. Serve with warm flour
tortillas if desired.   **4 servings;** 410 calories per
serving.

SPAGHETTI WITH MEAT SAUCE

MICROWAVE TIME: 15 to 18 minutes

1 pound ground beef
⅓ cup chopped onion
3 tablespoons finely chopped green bell
  pepper
1 large clove garlic, finely chopped
1 can (15 ounces) tomato sauce
1 can (4 ounces) mushroom stems and
  pieces, drained
½ cup dry red wine
¼ teaspoon pepper
2 teaspoons chopped fresh or ¼ teaspoon
  dried basil
3 cups hot cooked spaghetti

1. Crumble ground beef into 2-quart casserole; add onion, bell pepper and garlic. Cover loosely and microwave on high 5 to 6 minutes, breaking up beef and stirring after 3 minutes, until beef is no longer pink; drain.

2. Stir in remaining ingredients except spaghetti. Cover tightly and microwave 10 to 12 minutes, stirring after 6 minutes, until hot and bubbly.

3. Pour sauce over hot spaghetti. Serve with grated Parmesan cheese if desired. **4 servings;** 460 calories per serving.

MEATBALLS IN RED WINE SAUCE

MICROWAVE TIME: 10 to 14 minutes
STAND TIME: 3 minutes

1 pound ground beef
1 can (8 ounces) water chestnuts, chopped
½ cup dry bread crumbs
1 medium onion, chopped (about ¼ cup)
¼ cup water
1 egg
1 small clove garlic, finely chopped
¼ teaspoon Worcestershire sauce
⅛ teaspoon pepper
Red Wine Sauce (page 323)

1. Mix all ingredients except Red Wine Sauce. Shape mixture by teaspoonfuls into 1-inch balls. Arrange, sides not touching, in rectangular dish, 11 × 7 × 1½ inches. Cover loosely and microwave on high 7 to 10 minutes, rearranging meatballs every 3 minutes, until no longer pink inside. Let stand covered 3 minutes. Remove meatballs to serving dish, using slotted spoon; keep warm.

2. Prepare Red Wine Sauce. Pour hot sauce over meatballs; gently stir to coat. Garnish with chopped fresh parsley if desired. **4 servings;** 475 calories per serving.

IMPOSSIBLE LASAGNE PIE

MCROWAVE TIME: 23 to 28 minutes
STAND TIME: 5 minutes

1 pound ground beef
1 cup ricotta cheese
¼ cup grated Parmesan cheese
2 cups shredded mozzarella cheese
   (8 ounces)
1 tablespoon chopped fresh or
   ½ teaspoon dried basil
1 can (6 ounces) tomato paste
1 cup milk
2 eggs
⅔ cup variety baking mix
½ teaspoon salt

1. Crumble ground beef into pie plate, 10 × 1½ inches. Cover loosely and microwave on high 5 to 6 minutes, stirring after 3 minutes, until no longer pink. Remove beef; drain.

2. Layer ricotta and Parmesan cheeses in same pie plate. Mix cooked ground beef, ½ cup of the mozzarella cheese, 2 teaspoons of only the fresh basil and the tomato paste; spoon evenly over cheese in pie plate.

3. Beat milk, eggs, baking mix and salt with hand beater or wire whisk 1 minute or until smooth. Pour evenly over beef mixture; sprinkle with remaining fresh basil or ½ teaspoon dried basil.

4. Elevate pie plate on inverted dinner plate in microwave oven. Microwave uncovered on medium-high (70%) 18 to 22 minutes, rotating pie plate ¼ turn every 6 minutes, until knife inserted in center comes out clean. Sprinkle with remaining mozzarella cheese. Let stand 5 minutes. **6 servings;** 480 calories per serving.

500-watt microwave: You may need to increase microwave times.

Impossible Lasagne Pie

BEEF AND CORN PIE

◐ MICROWAVE TIME: 11 to 17 minutes

¾ pound ground beef
2 tablespoons chopped onion
1 small clove garlic, finely chopped
1 can (8 ounces) whole tomatoes, drained
     and ½ cup liquid reserved
1 cup whole kernel corn
12 pitted ripe olives, sliced
1½ to 2½ teaspoons chili powder
1 egg
½ cup yellow cornmeal
½ cup shredded Cheddar cheese
     (2 ounces)
Paprika

1.   Crumble ground beef into 1½-quart casserole; add onion and garlic. Cover loosely and microwave on high 4 to 5 minutes, breaking up beef and stirring after 2 minutes, until beef is no longer pink; drain.

2.   Stir in tomatoes, corn, olives and chili powder. Cover tightly and microwave 4 to 6 minutes or until hot and bubbly; stir.

3.   Beat egg in small bowl; stir in cornmeal and reserved tomato liquid. Pour over beef mixture; sprinkle with cheese and paprika. Microwave uncovered 3 to 6 minutes or until topping is no longer doughy.   **4 servings;** 355 calories per serving.

STUFFED GREEN PEPPERS

MICROWAVE TIME: 18 to 22 minutes
STAND TIME: 15 minutes

¾ cup hot water
⅓ cup uncooked bulgur
1 small onion, chopped (about ¼ cup)
¼ teaspoon salt
⅛ teaspoon garlic powder
6 medium green bell peppers
1 pound ground beef
1 can (15 ounces) tomato sauce
¾ cup shredded Cheddar cheese
     (3 ounces)

1.   Mix water, bulgur, onion, salt and garlic powder in 2-quart casserole. Cover tightly and microwave on high 6 to 8 minutes or until boiling; stir. Cover and let stand until water is absorbed, about 10 minutes.

2.   Cut thin slice from stem end of each bell pepper. Remove seeds and membranes; rinse. Arrange peppers, cut ends up, in circle in pie plate, 9 × 1¼ or 10 × 1½ inches.

3.   Crumble ground beef into bulgur mixture; stir in 1 cup of the tomato sauce. Fill each pepper with about ½ cup mixture. Pour remaining tomato sauce over peppers. Cover tightly and microwave on high 12 to 14 minutes, rotating pie plate ½ turn after 7 minutes, until beef mixture is done (160° on meat thermometer). Sprinkle peppers with cheese; let stand uncovered 5 minutes.   **6 servings;** 335 calories per serving.

BEEF WITH CRACKED WHEAT

MICROWAVE TIME: 19 to 22 minutes
STAND TIME: 1 minute

1 pound ground beef
1 medium onion, chopped (about ½ cup)
1 small clove garlic, finely chopped
1½ cups beef broth
½ cup uncooked cracked wheat
2 tablespoons chopped fresh parsley
¼ teaspoon salt
1 teaspoon chopped fresh or ¼ teaspoon dried oregano
¼ teaspoon pepper
¼ cup grated Parmesan cheese
1 medium tomato, chopped (about ¾ cup)

1. Crumble ground beef into 1½-quart casserole; add onion and garlic. Cover loosely and microwave on high 5 to 6 minutes, breaking up beef and stirring after 3 minutes, until beef is no longer pink; drain.

2. Stir in remaining ingredients except cheese and tomato. Cover tightly and microwave 14 to 16 minutes or until cracked wheat is tender and liquid is absorbed.

3. Stir in cheese and tomato. Cover and let stand 1 minute. Sprinkle with additional grated Parmesan cheese, and garnish with chopped fresh parsley if desired. **4 servings (about 1 cup each)**; 395 calories per serving.

BEEF STROGANOFF

 MICROWAVE TIME: 11 to 14 minutes

1 pound ground beef
1 medium onion, chopped (about ½ cup)
1 can (10¾ ounces) condensed cream of chicken soup
1 can (4 ounces) mushroom stems and pieces, drained
¼ teaspoon salt
¼ teaspoon pepper
½ cup sour cream or plain yogurt
2 cups hot spinach noodles
1 medium carrot, finely shredded

1. Crumble ground beef into 2-quart casserole; add onion. Cover loosely and microwave on high 5 to 6 minutes, breaking up beef and stirring after 3 minutes, until beef is no longer pink; drain.

2. Stir in soup, mushrooms, salt and pepper. Cover tightly and microwave 5 to 6 minutes, stirring after 3 minutes, until boiling. Stir in sour cream. Cover and microwave 1 to 2 minutes or until hot. Serve over hot noodles; sprinkle with carrot. **4 servings (about 1¼ cups each)**; 380 calories per serving.

Lamb Stroganoff: Substitute 1 pound ground lamb for the ground beef. 435 calories per serving.

Stuffed Acorn Squash

STUFFED ACORN SQUASH

MICROWAVE TIME:	21 to 29 minutes
STAND TIME:	4 minutes

2 small acorn squash (about 1 pound each)
1 pound ground beef
2 cups chopped unpared tart all-purpose apples (about 2 medium)
¼ cup raisins
¼ teaspoon salt
½ teaspoon ground nutmeg
4 teaspoons sugar
2 tablespoons margarine or butter, melted

1. Prepare and microwave squash as directed on page 219.

2. Crumble ground beef into 2-quart casserole. Cover loosely and microwave on high 5 to 6 minutes, breaking up and stirring after 3 minutes, until no longer pink; drain. Stir in apple, raisins, salt and nutmeg.

3. Remove stems and cut thin slice from pointed ends of squash, if necessary, to prevent tipping. Scoop squash from rind, leaving ¼-inch-thick shell. Stir squash into beef mixture; spoon into shells. Sprinkle 1 teaspoon sugar over mixture in each shell; drizzle with margarine.

4. Cover loosely and microwave on high 7 to 9 minutes or until hot. Uncover and let stand 3 minutes. **4 servings;** 475 calories per serving.

BEEF AND NOODLE CASSEROLE

MICROWAVE TIME: 13 to 16 minutes

1 pound ground beef
1 medium onion, chopped (about ½ cup)
1 clove garlic, finely chopped
1 can (10¾ ounces) condensed cream of mushroom soup
2 jars (4½ ounces each) sliced mushrooms, drained and ⅓ cup liquid reserved
2 tablespoons all-purpose flour
1 tablespoon chopped fresh or 1 teaspoon dried dill weed
¼ teaspoon pepper
1 cup sour cream or plain yogurt
2 to 3 cups chow mein noodles
2 tablespoons chopped fresh parsley

1.   Crumble ground beef into 2-quart casserole; add onion and garlic. Cover loosely and microwave on high 5 to 6 minutes, breaking up beef and stirring after 3 minutes, until beef is no longer pink; drain.

2.   Stir in soup, mushrooms, reserved liquid, the flour, dill weed, and pepper. Cover tightly and microwave 8 to 10 minutes, stirring after 5 minutes, until hot and bubbly.

3.   Stir in sour cream; serve over chow mein noodles. Sprinkle with parsley.   **4 servings (about 1⅓ cups each)**; 620 calories per serving.

BEEF GOULASH

MICROWAVE TIME: 28 to 34 minutes

1½ pounds ground beef
1 medium onion, chopped (about ½ cup)
1 medium stalk celery, sliced (about ½ cup)
1 can (16 ounces) stewed tomatoes, undrained
1 package (7 ounces) uncooked elbow macaroni (2 cups)
1 can (6 ounces) tomato paste
1½ cups hot water
1 tablespoon paprika
1 teaspoon Worcestershire sauce
½ teaspoon pepper

1.   Crumble ground beef into 3-quart casserole. Cover with waxed paper and microwave on high 8 to 9 minutes, breaking up and stirring after 4 minutes, until beef is no longer pink; drain.

2.   Stir in remaining ingredients. Cover tightly and microwave about 10 minutes or until bubbly around edge; stir. Cover tightly and microwave 10 to 15 minutes, stirring every 5 minutes, until macaroni is tender and liquid is absorbed.   **6 servings (about 1 cup each)**; 335 calories per serving.

Italian Sausage Goulash: Substitute 1½ pounds bulk Italian sausage for the ground beef. Omit pepper. 390 calories per serving.

Chunky Chili con Carne

CHUNKY CHILI CON CARNE

🕐 MICROWAVE TIME: 18 to 27 minutes

1 pound coarsely ground beef
1 small green bell pepper, chopped
   (about ½ cup)
1 medium onion, chopped (about ½ cup)
2 cloves garlic, finely chopped
1 can (16 ounces) stewed tomatoes,
   undrained
1 can (15½ ounces) kidney beans, drained
1 can (8 ounces) tomato sauce
2 tablespoons all-purpose flour
1 to 2 tablespoons chili powder
¼ teaspoon salt

1. Crumble ground beef into 3-quart casserole. Add bell pepper, onion and garlic. Cover tightly and microwave on high 6 to 9 minutes, breaking up beef and stirring after 4 minutes, until beef is no longer pink.

2. Stir in remaining ingredients. Cover tightly and microwave 12 to 18 minutes, stirring every 6 minutes, until boiling. **4 servings (about 1½ cups each);** 420 calories per serving.

BARBECUED MEAT LOAF

MICROWAVE TIME: 28 to 34 minutes
STAND TIME: 5 minutes

1½ pounds ground beef
1 cup dry bread crumbs
1 cup milk
1 tablespoon Worcestershire sauce
½ teaspoon dry mustard
¼ teaspoon pepper
¼ teaspoon ground sage
1 small onion, chopped (about ¼ cup)
½ small green bell pepper, chopped
   (about ¼ cup)
1 egg
3 tablespoons barbecue sauce

1. Mix all ingredients except barbecue sauce. Spread mixture evenly in loaf dish, 9 × 5 × 3 inches.

2. Cover with waxed paper and microwave on medium-high (70%) 25 to 30 minutes, rotating dish ½ turn every 10 minutes, until center is no longer pink (160° on meat thermometer).

3. Spread barbecue sauce over top of meat loaf. Cover with waxed paper and microwave on high 3 to 4 minutes or until hot. Let stand covered 5 minutes.   **6 servings**; 400 calories per serving.

Mexican Meat Loaf: Substitute 1 to 2 tablespoons chopped green chilies for the bell pepper and 2 tablespoons taco sauce for the barbecue sauce. Arrange 3 slices process American cheese on meat loaf before letting stand 5 minutes. Serve with chopped tomatoes, shredded lettuce and additional taco sauce if desired.   450 calories per serving.

VEGETABLE-BEEF SOUP

MICROWAVE TIME: 23 to 28 minutes

1 pound ground beef
1 medium onion, chopped (about ½ cup)
1 large carrot, chopped (about ⅔ cup)
⅔ cup chopped celery
⅔ cup ½-inch pieces potato
¼ cup water
½ teaspoon salt
¼ teaspoon pepper
1 teaspoon chopped fresh or ⅛ teaspoon
   dried basil
1 bay leaf
1¾ cups hot water
1 can (16 ounces) whole tomatoes,
   undrained

1. Crumble ground beef into 3-quart casserole; add onion. Cover loosely and microwave on high 5 to 6 minutes, breaking up beef and stirring after 2 minutes, until beef is no longer pink; drain.

2. Stir in remaining ingredients except 1¾ cups hot water and the tomatoes. Cover tightly and microwave 9 to 11 minutes, stirring after 5 minutes, until vegetables are tender.

3. Stir in water and tomatoes; break up tomatoes. Cover tightly and microwave 9 to 11 minutes, stirring after 5 minutes, until boiling. Remove bay leaf.   **4 servings (about 1½ cups each)**; 335 calories per serving.

LENTIL SOUP

MICROWAVE TIME: 34 to 41 minutes

1 pound ground beef
1 large carrot, cut into ⅛-inch slices
   (about ¾ cup)
1 medium onion, chopped (about ½ cup)
1 clove garlic, finely chopped
2 cups hot water
1 can (16 ounces) stewed tomatoes,
   undrained
1 can (4 ounces) mushroom stems and
   pieces, undrained
¾ cup uncooked dried lentils
1 medium stalk celery, sliced (about
   ½ cup)
2 tablespoons chopped fresh or
   2 teaspoons dried parsley
½ teaspoon salt
1 teaspoon Worcestershire sauce
¼ teaspoon pepper
1 bay leaf
1 cup hot water

1.   Crumble ground beef into 3-quart casserole; add carrot, onion and garlic. Cover loosely and microwave on high 7 to 8 minutes, breaking up beef and stirring after 4 minutes, until beef is no longer pink; drain.

2.   Stir in remaining ingredients except 1 cup hot water. Cover tightly and microwave 24 to 28 minutes, stirring every 6 minutes, until vegetables are tender.

3.   Stir in 1 cup hot water. Cover tightly and microwave 3 to 5 minutes or until bubbly. Remove bay leaf.   **6 servings (about 1½ cups each);** 300 calories per serving.

PIZZA BURGERS

 MICROWAVE TIME: 11 to 15 minutes

1 can (8 ounces) tomato sauce
1 pound ground beef
½ cup dry bread crumbs
2 teaspoons chopped fresh or ½ teaspoon
   dried oregano
¼ teaspoon salt
1 cup shredded mozzarella cheese
   (4 ounces)
2 English muffins, split into halves and
   toasted

1.   Reserve ¼ cup of the tomato sauce. Mix remaining tomato sauce, the ground beef, bread crumbs, oregano and salt. Shape mixture into 4 patties, each about ¾ inch thick. Pinch edge of each patty to form ¼-inch rim. Arrange in circle on rack in dish.

2.   Cover with waxed paper and microwave on high 5 minutes. Spread reserved tomato sauce over patties; rotate dish ½ turn. Cover and microwave 5 to 8 minutes or until edges are brown and firm and beef is medium doneness (160° on meat thermometer).

3.   Sprinkle cheese over patties. Microwave uncovered 1 minute to 1 minute 30 seconds or until cheese begins to melt. Serve on muffin halves.   **4 open-face sandwiches;** 495 calories per sandwich.

BACON BURGERS

MICROWAVE TIME: 10 to 13 minutes
STAND TIME: 3 minutes

4 slices bacon, cut in half
1 pound ground beef
¼ cup dry bread crumbs
2 tablespoons ketchup
¼ teaspoon salt
1 small onion, finely chopped (about
  ¼ cup)
½ small green bell pepper, finely
  chopped (about ¼ cup)
4 hamburger buns, split and toasted

1. Place bacon on rack in dish. Cover with paper towel and microwave on high 3 to 4 minutes or until almost crisp; drain and reserve. Drain fat from dish.

2. Mix remaining ingredients except hamburger buns. Shape mixture into 4 patties, each about ¾ inch thick. Arrange in circle on rack in dish. Crisscross 2 half-slices bacon on each patty.

3. Cover with paper towel and microwave on high 7 to 9 minutes, rotating dish ½ turn after 3 minutes, until beef is medium doneness (160° on meat thermometer). Let stand covered 3 minutes. Serve in hamburger buns. **4 sandwiches;** 465 calories per sandwich.

PICADILLO TACOS

MICROWAVE TIME: 7 to 9 minutes

1 pound ground beef
1 medium onion, chopped (about ½ cup)
1 clove garlic, finely chopped
¼ cup raisins
½ teaspoon salt
¼ teaspoon ground cinnamon
1 small green bell pepper, chopped
  (about ½ cup)
¼ cup slivered almonds, toasted
¼ cup sliced pimiento-stuffed olives
1 medium tomato, coarsely chopped
  (about ¾ cup)
8 taco shells

1. Crumble ground beef into 2-quart casserole; add onion and garlic. Cover loosely and microwave on high 5 to 6 minutes, breaking up beef and stirring after 3 minutes, until beef is no longer pink; drain.

2. Stir in raisins, salt, cinnamon and bell pepper. Cover tightly and microwave 2 to 3 minutes or until hot.

3. Stir in almonds, olives and tomato. Serve in taco shells. Garnish with sour cream and lime wedges if desired. **4 servings;** 490 calories per serving.

ORIENTAL COLD NOODLES AND BEEF

Linguine is similar to Chinese noodles. Serve this chilled salad, a perfect do-ahead dish, with either steamed Chinese buns or crusty bread.

MICROWAVE TIME: 8 to 10 minutes
REFRIGERATION TIME: 2 hours

½ package (16-ounce size) linguine
1 pound beef boneless sirloin steak, about
   1 inch thick
1 clove garlic, crushed
½ cup sliced green onions (with tops)
2 medium carrots, thinly sliced (about
   1 cup)
4 ounces fresh Chinese pea pods, tips
   and strings removed
8 ounces fresh mushrooms, sliced (about
   2 cups)
Oriental Dressing (right)

1.   Cook linguine as directed on package; drain. Rinse with cold water; drain and reserve.

2.   Trim fat from beef steak. Cut beef across grain into 2 × ⅛-inch slices. Place beef and garlic in 3-quart casserole. Cover tightly and microwave on high 5 to 6 minutes, stirring after 3 minutes, until beef is no longer pink.

3.   Stir in onions, carrots and pea pods. Cover tightly and microwave 2 to 3 minutes or until vegetables are crisp-tender. Stir in mushrooms. Microwave uncovered 1 minute; drain.

4.   Mix linguine and beef mixture. Toss with Oriental Dressing. Refrigerate at least 2 hours until chilled. Toss before serving.   **6 servings (about 1½ cups each);** 420 calories per serving.

500-watt microwave: You may need to increase microwave times.

Oriental Dressing

¼ cup dry sherry
3 tablespoons soy sauce
2 tablespoons sesame oil
2 teaspoons ground gingerroot or
   ½ teaspoon ground ginger
⅛ teaspoon pepper
1 clove garlic, crushed

Shake all ingredients in tightly covered container.

• • • • • • • • • • •

REUBEN SANDWICHES

MICROWAVE TIME: 2 to 3 minutes

⅓ cup mayonnaise or salad dressing
1 tablespoon chili sauce
8 slices rye bread, toasted if desired
4 slices cooked corned beef (about
   1 ounce each)
4 slices Swiss cheese (about 1 ounce each)
1 can (8 ounces) sauerkraut, well drained

1.   Mix mayonnaise and chili sauce; spread over each slice bread. Layer corned beef, cheese and sauerkraut on 4 slices bread; top with remaining slices bread.

2.   Arrange sandwiches in circle on paper towel–lined 12-inch plate. Cover with paper towel and microwave on high 2 to 3 minutes, rotating plate ½ turn after 1 minute, until cheese is melted and filling is hot. **4 sandwiches;** 480 calories per sandwich.

SAVORY TOSTADAS

MICROWAVE TIME: 4 to 6 minutes

2 cups bite-size pieces cooked beef
   (about ¾ pound)
1 teaspoon chili powder
1 teaspoon ground cumin
1 can (8 ounces) tomato sauce
1 clove garlic, finely chopped
4 tostada shells
1 medium zucchini, shredded (about
   1 cup)
1 small onion, finely chopped (about
   ¼ cup)
1 medium tomato, coarsely chopped
   (about ¾ cup)
1 cup shredded Monterey Jack cheese
   (4 ounces)

1. Mix beef, chili powder, cumin, tomato sauce and garlic in 2-quart casserole. Cover tightly and microwave on high 4 to 6 minutes, stirring after 3 minutes, until hot.

2. Spoon about ½ cup beef mixture onto each tostada shell. Top each tostada with remaining ingredients. **4 tostadas;** 415 calories per tostada.

GREEK BEEF SALAD

MICROWAVE TIME: 8 to 10 minutes
REFRIGERATION TIME: 2 hours

1 pound beef flank steak
1 tablespoon chopped fresh or 1 teaspoon
   dried oregano
1 teaspoon vegetable oil
½ teaspoon salt
1 clove garlic, crushed
3 green onions (with tops), sliced
1 small green bell pepper, cut into ½-inch
   strips
3 tablespoons red wine vinegar
1 medium tomato, coarsely chopped
½ medium cucumber, seeded and
   chopped

1. Cut beef across grain into 2 × ⅛-inch slices. Mix beef, oregano, oil, salt and garlic in square dish, 8 × 8 × 2 inches. Cover tightly and microwave on high 6 to 7 minutes, stirring after 3 minutes, until beef is no longer pink.

2. Stir in onions and bell pepper. Cover tightly and microwave 2 to 3 minutes or until bell pepper is crisp-tender; drain.

3. Stir in remaining ingredients. Cover and refrigerate at least 2 hours until chilled. Serve with pita bread and plain yogurt if desired. **4 servings (about 1¼ cups each);** 180 calories per serving.

Greek Beef Salad, German Pork Salad (page 154)

GRILLED PORK TENDERLOINS

MICROWAVE TIME: 5 minutes
GRILL TIME: 25 to 30 minutes

2 pork tenderloins (about ¾ pound each)
1 tablespoon grated orange peel
½ cup orange juice
¼ cup dry white wine
1 tablespoon chopped fresh or 1 teaspoon dried tarragon
1 tablespoon soy sauce

1.   Prepare charcoal fire for grilling. Place pork tenderloins in rectangular dish, 11 × 7 × 1½ inches. Mix remaining ingredients; pour over pork.

2.   Cover tightly and microwave on high 5 minutes.

3.   Insert barbecue meat thermometer in center of one of the pork tenderloins. Place pork, 5 to 6 inches from medium coals, on grill; reserve orange juice mixture. Cover and grill pork 25 to 30 minutes, turning and brushing with orange juice mixture several times, until thermometer registers 170°.   **6 servings;** 320 calories per serving.

A 500-watt microwave is not recommended.

Microwave-only Directions: Prepare pork tenderloins and orange juice mixture as directed in step 1 (above). Cover tightly and microwave on high 8 minutes; turn pork over. Cover tightly and microwave on medium (50%) 8 to 10 minutes, turning pork over after 5 minutes, until pork is done in center (170° on meat thermometer). Slice pork; spoon juices over top.

Grilled Pork Tenderloins, Apple and Wild Rice Dressing (page 256)

SWEET-AND-SOUR PORK TENDERLOIN

REFRIGERATION TIME: 2 hours
MICROWAVE TIME: 13 to 18 minutes

10- to 12-ounce pork tenderloin
1 can (8 ounces) pineapple chunks in juice, drained and 2 tablespoons juice reserved
2 tablespoons dry white wine
1 tablespoon soy sauce
1 tablespoon chili sauce
1 green onion (with top), thinly sliced
1 clove garlic, finely chopped
1 slice gingerroot, crushed
3 tablespoons honey
2 teaspoons cornstarch
1 tablespoon cold water
3 cups hot cooked rice

1.   Place pork tenderloin in rectangular dish, 10 × 6 × 1½ inches. Mix pineapple chunks, reserved juice, the wine, soy sauce, chili sauce, onion, garlic and gingerroot; pour over pork. Cover and refrigerate 2 hours, turning pork over once.

2.   Drain pork, reserving marinade in medium bowl. Place pork on rack in same dish. Brush pork with half of the honey. Cover with waxed paper and microwave on medium (50%) 6 minutes, rotating dish ¼ turn after 3 minutes.

3.   Turn pork over; brush with remaining honey. Cover with waxed paper and microwave 5 to 9 minutes, rotating dish ¼ turn every 3 minutes, until pork is done (170° on meat thermometer). Remove to serving platter; keep warm.

4.   Mix cornstarch and water; stir into marinade. Cover tightly and microwave on high 2 to 3 minutes or until mixture thickens and boils. To serve, cut pork diagonally into ¼-inch slices. Serve pork and pineapple sauce over rice. Garnish with parsley if desired.   **4 servings;** 365 calories per serving.

PORK CHOPS WITH APPLE STUFFING

MICROWAVE TIME: 20 to 23 minutes

4 pork loin chops, each about ½ inch thick
Paprika
2 cups herb stuffing mix (dry)
½ cup apple juice
2 tablespoons margarine or butter, melted
1 medium unpared all-purpose apple, finely chopped

1.   Arrange pork chops, meaty parts to outside edges, in rectangular dish, 11 × 7 × 1½ inches; sprinkle with paprika.

2.   Mix remaining ingredients. Mound in center of dish. Cover tightly and microwave on medium (50%) 20 to 23 minutes, rotating dish ½ turn every 7 minutes, until pork is done (170° on meat thermometer).   **4 servings;** 405 calories per serving.

A 500-watt microwave is not recommended.

ORANGE-SPICED PORK CHOPS

MICROWAVE TIME: 23 to 27 minutes

4 pork loin chops, each about ½ inch thick
1 small onion, thinly sliced
1 tablespoon grated orange peel
⅓ cup orange juice
¼ cup medium red wine
2 tablespoons packed brown sugar
¼ teaspoon ground cloves
1 small clove garlic, finely chopped
1 small orange, thinly sliced
2 teaspoons cornstarch
1 tablespoon cold water

1.   Arrange pork chops, meaty parts to outside edges, in square dish, 8 × 8 × 2 inches. Arrange onion slices on pork.

2.   Mix orange peel, orange juice, wine, brown sugar, cloves and garlic; pour over pork. Cover tightly and microwave on medium (50%) 10 minutes, rotating dish ¼ turn after 5 minutes. Arrange orange slices on pork; rotating dish ½ turn. Cover and microwave 12 to 15 minutes, rotating dish ¼ turn every 5 minutes, until pork is done (170° on meat thermometer).

3.   Remove pork to serving platter; keep warm. Pour 1 cup of liquid from dish into 2-cup measure. Mix cornstarch and water; stir into liquid. Cover loosely and microwave on high 1 to 2 minutes or until mixture thickens and boils. Serve pork with sauce on mixture of white and wild rice if desired. Spoon sauce over pork.   **4 servings;** 325 calories per serving.

Pork Chops with Apple Stuffing, Asparagus with Cheddar Sauce (page 182)

CURRANT-GLAZED GRILLED PORK RIBS

MICROWAVE TIME: 11 to 14 minutes
GRILL TIME: 20 to 25 minutes

3 pounds pork back ribs, cut into
    serving pieces
¼ cup chili sauce
2 tablespoons currant jelly
1 teaspoon soy sauce

1. Prepare charcoal fire for grilling. Arrange pork ribs, meaty sides up, in rectangular dish, 11 × 7 × 1½ inches. Cover tightly and microwave on high 10 to 12 minutes, rearranging pork after 5 minutes, until almost no pink remains.

2. Mix remaining ingredients in 1-cup measure. Cover and microwave on high 1 to 2 minutes or until jelly is melted; stir and reserve.

3. Place pork, bone sides down and 5 to 6 inches from medium coals, on grill. Cover and grill 20 to 25 minutes, brushing with sauce several times during last 10 minutes of grilling, until done (170° on meat thermometer).   **4 servings;** 570 calories per serving.

A 500-watt microwave is not recommended.

Microwave-only Directions: Arrange pork ribs, meaty sides up, in rectangular dish, 11 × 7 × 1½ inches. Cover tightly and microwave on high 10 to 12 minutes, rearranging pork after 5 minutes, until almost no pink remains; drain. Prepare sauce mixture as directed in step 2 (above). Cover pork tightly and microwave on medium (50%) 25 to 30 minutes, rearranging pork after 10 minutes, until done (170° on meat thermometer). Brush pork with sauce. Microwave uncovered on high 4 to 6 minutes or until sauce is set.

Currant-glazed Grilled Pork Ribs

PEPPER PORK WITH NOODLES

MICROWAVE TIME: 36 to 40 minutes
STAND TIME: 5 minutes

1½ pounds pork boneless shoulder
3 medium onions, sliced
½ teaspoon salt
½ teaspoon paprika
¼ teaspoon pepper
⅛ to ¼ teaspoon crushed red pepper
   (cayenne)
¾ teaspoon cornstarch
1 tablespoon cold water
1 medium tomato, chopped (about
   ¾ cup)
1 medium green bell pepper, cut into
   strips
⅓ cup shredded Cheddar cheese
4 cups hot cooked noodles

1. Trim fat from pork shoulder. Cut pork into ½-inch strips. Mix pork and onions in 3-quart casserole. Cover tightly and microwave on medium (50%) 12 to 14 minutes, stirring every 3 minutes, until pork is no longer pink; drain.

2. Stir in salt, paprika, pepper and red pepper. Cover tightly and microwave 12 minutes, stirring every 3 minutes. Mix cornstarch and water; stir into pork. Stir in tomato. Cover and microwave 12 to 14 minutes, stirring every 3 minutes, until pork is tender.

3. Stir in bell pepper. Cover and let stand 5 minutes. Sprinkle with cheese; serve with noodles.   **6 servings;** 365 calories per serving.

GINGER PORK WITH NECTARINES

REFRIGERATION TIME: 20 minutes
MICROWAVE TIME: 13 to 15 minutes

1 pound pork boneless shoulder or loin
2 tablespoons dry white wine
1 teaspoon cornstarch
1 teaspoon sugar
1 teaspoon finely chopped gingerroot or
   1 teaspoon ground ginger
1 green bell pepper, cut into 1-inch pieces
1 can (8 ounces) sliced water chestnuts,
   drained
¾ cup chicken broth
2 tablespoons cornstarch
¼ cup cold water
2 large nectarines, sliced
½ cup salted nuts

1. Trim fat from pork shoulder. Cut pork into ½-inch pieces. Toss pork, wine, 1 teaspoon cornstarch, the sugar and gingerroot in 2-quart casserole. Cover tightly and refrigerate 20 minutes.

2. Microwave tightly covered on high 7 to 8 minutes, stirring after 4 minutes, until no longer pink. Stir in bell pepper, water chestnuts and broth.

3. Mix 2 tablespoons cornstarch and the water; stir into pork mixture. Cover tightly and microwave 2 minutes; stir. Cover and microwave 4 to 5 minutes, stirring every minute, until boiling. Stir in nectarines; sprinkle with nuts. Serve with hot cooked rice if desired. **4 servings;** 525 calories per serving.

PORK AND CARROTS WITH PASTA

MICROWAVE TIME: 38 to 42 minutes

1 pound pork boneless shoulder
3 medium carrots, cut into ¼-inch slices
   (about 1½ cups)
1 medium onion, chopped (about ½ cup)
2 cloves garlic, finely chopped
¾ cup chicken broth
2 teaspoons chopped fresh or ¾ teaspoon
   dried basil
¼ teaspoon salt
¼ teaspoon pepper
1 tablespoon cornstarch
2 tablespoons cold water
3 cups hot cooked spaghetti

1. Trim fat from pork shoulder. Cut pork into ¾-inch pieces. Mix pork, carrots, onion and garlic in 2-quart casserole. Cover tightly and microwave on medium (50%) 9 to 11 minutes, stirring every 3 minutes, until pork is no longer pink and vegetables are crisp-tender.

2. Stir in broth, basil, salt and pepper. Cover tightly and microwave 27 to 29 minutes, stirring every 6 minutes, until pork is tender.

3. Mix cornstarch and water; stir into pork mixture. Cover tightly and microwave on high 1 minute 30 seconds to 2 minutes or until mixture thickens and boils.

4. Serve pork and vegetables over spaghetti. Sprinkle with Parmesan cheese if desired. **4 servings;** 340 calories per serving.

SZECHUAN PORK

REFRIGERATION TIME: 20 minutes
MICROWAVE TIME: 15 to 18 minutes

1 pound pork boneless loin or leg
1 tablespoon soy sauce
1 tablespoon cornstarch
½ teaspoon ground red pepper (cayenne)
1 clove garlic, finely chopped
3 cups broccoli flowerets or 1 package
   (16 ounces) frozen broccoli cuts,
   thawed and drained
2 small onions, cut into eighths
1 can (8 ounces) whole water chestnuts,
   drained
¼ cup chicken broth
½ cup peanuts
2 cups hot cooked rice

1. Trim fat from pork loin. Cut pork across grain into 2 × 1 × ⅛-inch slices. Toss pork, soy sauce, cornstarch, red pepper and garlic in 3-quart casserole. Cover tightly and refrigerate 20 minutes.

2. Microwave tightly covered on high 9 to 10 minutes, stirring after 4 minutes, until pork is no longer pink.

3. Stir in broccoli, onions, water chestnuts and broth. Cover tightly and microwave 6 to 8 minutes, stirring after 3 minutes, until broccoli is crisp-tender. Stir in peanuts. Serve with rice.   **4 servings;** 600 calories per serving.

GREEN CHILI

This recipe has Southwestern roots. Green chili stew is often made with either lamb or pork. For a spicier chili, add chopped jalapeño chilies.

MICROWAVE TIME: 19 to 24 minutes

1 pound pork boneless shoulder
1 small onion, finely chopped (about ¼ cup)
2 cloves garlic, crushed
2 teaspoons chopped fresh or ½ teaspoon dried oregano
½ teaspoon ground cumin
½ teaspoon salt
2 cans (4 ounces each) chopped green chilies, drained
1 can (14½ ounces) whole tomatoes, undrained

1. Trim fat from pork shoulder. Cut pork into ½-inch cubes. Place pork, onion and garlic in 2-quart casserole. Cover tightly and microwave on high 6 to 8 minutes, stirring after 4 minutes, until pork is no longer pink.

2. Stir in remaining ingredients; break up tomatoes. Cover tightly and microwave 5 to 6 minutes or just to boiling; stir.

3. Cover tightly and microwave on medium-high (70%) 8 to 10 minutes or until pork is tender. Serve with sour cream and shredded Cheddar cheese if desired.   **4 servings (about 1 cup each);** 210 calories per serving.

Green Chili

GRILLED PORK AND FRUIT KABOBS

Here is a decidedly different combination of flavors on one skewer. The dried peaches and prunes plump in peach brandy. These rich fruits are delicious with grilled pork.

MICROWAVE TIME:	5 to 7 minutes
REFRIGERATION TIME:	1 hour
GRILL TIME:	10 to 15 minutes

1 jar (12 ounces) peach preserves
⅓ cup peach brandy or peach nectar
1 pound pork boneless loin
1 package (8 ounces) dried peaches
1 package (12 ounces) dried pitted prunes

1. Mix preserves and brandy in 2-cup measure. Microwave uncovered on high 1 to 2 minutes or until hot. Trim fat from pork loin. Cut pork into 1-inch cubes. Mix pork, peaches, prunes and preserves mixture. Cover and refrigerate at least 1 hour.

2. Prepare charcoal fire for grilling. Remove pork from preserves mixture; place pork in 2-quart casserole. Cover tightly and microwave on medium (50%) 4 to 5 minutes, stirring after 2 minutes, until partially cooked.

3. Alternate pork, peaches and prunes on each of twelve 10-inch metal skewers. Reserve preserves mixture.

4. Place kabobs, 5 to 6 inches from medium coals, on grill. Cover and grill 10 to 15 minutes, turning and brushing kabobs 2 or 3 times with preserves mixture, until pork is done (170° on meat thermometer). **6 servings;** 600 calories per serving.

500-watt microwave: You may need to increase microwave times.

Microwave-only Directions: Prepare and refrigerate pork as directed in step 1 (above). Alternate pork, peaches and prunes on each of twelve 10-inch wooden skewers. Reserve preserves mixture. Place 6 of the kabobs on 10-inch plate. Cover with waxed paper and microwave on medium (50%) 10 to 12 minutes, rearranging kabobs and brushing with preserves mixture every 4 minutes, until pork is done (170° on meat thermometer). Repeat with remaining kabobs.

• • • • • • • • • • •

PORK AND PEA PODS

The microwave does not call for added fat in this stir-fry, a bonus in addition to the quick, authentic-tasting results.

MICROWAVE TIME:		15 to 20 minutes

1 pound pork boneless loin
1 tablespoon cornstarch
1 tablespoon soy sauce
2 tablespoons dry sherry or apple juice
8 ounces fresh Chinese pea pods, cut in half
8 ounces fresh bean sprouts

1. Trim fat from pork loin. Cut pork into 2 × ⅛-inch strips. Toss pork, cornstarch and soy sauce in 3-quart casserole. Cover tightly and microwave on medium (50%) 9 to 12 minutes, stirring every 3 minutes, until no longer pink.

2. Stir in sherry, pea pods and bean sprouts. Cover tightly and microwave on high 6 to 8 minutes, stirring after 4 minutes, until pea pods are crisp-tender. Serve with hot cooked rice if desired. **4 servings (about 1¼ cups each);** 360 calories per serving.

PORK PAPRIKA WITH SAUERKRAUT

MICROWAVE TIME: 38 to 42 minutes
STAND TIME: 5 minutes

1 pound pork boneless shoulder, cut into 1-inch pieces
1 medium onion, chopped (about ½ cup)
1 small clove garlic, finely chopped
1 can (16 ounces) sauerkraut, drained
½ cup chicken broth
1 tablespoon all-purpose flour
1 tablespoon paprika
½ teaspoon caraway seed
½ cup sour cream or plain yogurt
Chopped parsley
3 cups hot cooked noodles

1. Mix pork, onion and garlic in 2-quart casserole. Cover tightly and microwave on medium (50%) 11 to 13 minutes, stirring after 6 minutes, until pork is no longer pink and onion is tender.

2. Stir in remaining ingredients except sour cream, parsley and noodles. Cover tightly and microwave 27 to 29 minutes, stirring after 15 minutes, until pork is tender.

3. Stir in sour cream. Cover and let stand 5 minutes. Sprinkle with parsley, and serve over hot noodles.   **4 servings;** 380 calories per serving.

••••••••••

APRICOT PORK PATTIES

MICROWAVE TIME: 7 to 9 minutes

1 pound ground pork
¼ cup dry bread crumbs
¼ teaspoon salt
¼ teaspoon ground cinnamon
¼ teaspoon ground cloves
¼ cup apricot preserves

1. Mix all ingredients except apricot preserves. Shape mixture into 4 patties, each about ¾ inch thick. Arrange in circle on rack in dish.

2. Cover with waxed paper and microwave on high 6 to 8 minutes, turning patties over after 4 minutes, until no longer pink (170° on meat thermometer).

3. Place preserves in 1-cup measure. Microwave uncovered on high 30 to 60 seconds or until hot; spoon over patties.   **4 servings;** 280 calories per serving.

500-watt microwave: You may need to increase microwave times

••••••••••

PORK AND RICE CASSEROLE

MICROWAVE TIME: 12 to 15 minutes
STAND TIME: 5 minutes

2 medium stalks celery, cut into ¼-inch diagonal slices (about 1 cup)
1 medium onion, chopped (about ½ cup)
1 tablespoon margarine or butter
2 cups 1-inch pieces cooked pork
1 cup uncooked instant rice
1 cup hot water
2 tablespoons soy sauce
1 medium green bell pepper, chopped (about 1 cup)

1. Place celery, onion and margarine in 2-quart casserole. Cover tightly and microwave on high 4 to 5 minutes, stirring after 2 minutes, until celery is crisp-tender.

2. Stir in pork, rice, water and soy sauce. Cover tightly and microwave 8 to 10 minutes, stirring after 4 minutes, until water is absorbed. Stir in bell pepper. Cover and let stand 5 minutes.   **4 servings;** 390 calories per serving.

PORK WITH CHINESE VEGETABLES

MICROWAVE TIME: 11 to 13 minutes

1½ cups ¾-inch pieces cooked pork
1½ cups pork or beef gravy
2 medium stalks celery, cut into ¼-inch diagonal slices (about 1 cup)
1 can (16 ounces) Chinese vegetables, rinsed and drained*
1 can (4½ ounces) sliced mushrooms, drained
1 jar (2 ounces) sliced pimientos, drained
2 teaspoons soy sauce

1. Mix all ingredients in 2-quart casserole.

2. Cover tightly and microwave on high 11 to 13 minutes, stirring after 6 minutes, until hot and bubbly. Serve over chow mein noodles if desired.   **4 servings;** 245 calories per serving.

One package (16 ounces) frozen Oriental vegetables, thawed and drained, can be substituted for the canned vegetables.

• • • • • • • • • • •

GRILLED HAM WITH PLUM GLAZE

MICROWAVE TIME: 17 minutes
GRILL TIME: 1 hour to 1 hour 15 minutes

3-pound fully cooked boneless smoked ham
¼ cup water
¼ cup plum jam
1 teaspoon lemon juice
⅛ teaspoon ground ginger

1. Prepare charcoal fire for grilling, arranging coals around edge of firebox. Place foil drip pan under grilling area. Place ham, fat side down, in 3-quart casserole; add water. Cover tightly and microwave on high 5 minutes; turn ham over.

2. Cover tightly and microwave on medium (50%) 12 minutes. Mix remaining ingredients; reserve.

3. Insert barbecue meat thermometer in center of ham. Place ham, fat side up and 5 to 6 inches from medium coals, on grill over drip pan. Cover and grill 1 hour to 1 hour 15 minutes. Score top surface lightly, cutting uniform diamond pattern ¼ inch deep and spoon plum glaze over ham occasionally during last 10 minutes of grilling, until thermometer registers 140°. Serve with any remaining plum glaze.   **12 servings;** 195 calories per serving.

500-watt microwave: You may need to increase microwave times.

Microwave-only Directions: Place ham, fat side down, in 3-quart casserole; add water. Cover tightly and microwave on high 5 minutes; turn ham over. Cover tightly and microwave on medium (50%) 25 to 35 minutes, turning ham over every 12 minutes, until 140° on meat thermometer. Let stand covered 10 minutes. Mix remaining ingredients; reserve. Score fat surface of ham in diamond pattern ¼ inch deep. Spoon about half of the plum glaze over ham. Microwave uncovered 4 to 5 minutes or until glaze is hot. Serve with remaining plum glaze.

CURRIED HAM WITH PEAR CHUTNEY

REFRIGERATION TIME: 2 hours
MICROWAVE TIME: 18 to 22 minutes

Pear Chutney (page 333)
1 fully cooked smoked ham slice, about
    1 inch thick (about 1 pound)
1 tablespoon margarine or butter, melted
1 tablespoon lemon juice
1 teaspoon curry powder
¼ teaspoon dry mustard

1. Prepare Pear Chutney and refrigerate at least 2 hours. Slash outer edge of fat on ham slice diagonally at 1-inch intervals to prevent curling. Place ham in rectangular dish, 11 × 7 × 1½ inches.

2. Mix remaining ingredients. Brush half of the mixture over ham. Cover with waxed paper and microwave on medium-high (70%) 8 to 10 minutes, turning ham over and brushing with remaining margarine mixture after 4 minutes, until hot. Serve with Pear Chutney. **4 servings;** 205 calories per serving.

• • • • • • • • • •

GLAZED HAM

MICROWAVE TIME: 32 to 39 minutes
STAND TIME: 10 minutes

3-pound fully cooked boneless smoked
    ham
⅓ cup orange marmalade
2 tablespoons sweet white wine or
    apple juice
1 teaspoon prepared horseradish
Dash of ground cloves
Corn Relish (page 330), if desired

1. Place ham, fat side down, on rack in dish. Cover tightly and microwave on medium (50%) 17 minutes; turn ham over.

2. Score fat surface of ham lightly, cutting uniform diamond shapes ¼ inch deep. Mix remaining ingredients; spoon over ham. Cover tightly and microwave on medium (50%) 15 to 22 minutes or until meat thermometer registers 135°. Cover with aluminum foil; let stand 10 minutes. (Ham will continue to cook while standing.) Serve with Corn Relish. **10 servings;** 250 calories per serving.

• • • • • • • • • •

HAM WITH MUSTARD FRUITS

MICROWAVE TIME: 18 to 25 minutes

1 fully cooked smoked ham slice, about
    1 inch thick (about 2 pounds)
1 can (30 ounces) apricot halves, drained
1 can (15 ounces) pineapple chunks,
    drained
¼ cup margarine or butter, melted
2 tablespoons prepared mustard
2 tablespoons honey
1 teaspoon prepared horseradish
1 medium clove garlic, crushed

1. Slash outer edge of fat on ham slice diagonally at 1-inch intervals to prevent curling. Place ham in rectangular dish, 11 × 7 × 1½ inches. Cover with waxed paper and microwave on medium-high (70%) 8 minutes. Turn ham over; arrange fruit on ham.

2. Mix remaining ingredients; pour over fruit and ham. Cover with waxed paper and microwave 10 to 17 minutes, rotating dish ½ turn after 5 minutes, until ham is hot. **8 servings;** 335 calories per serving.

LINGUINE WITH HAM

This may be the easiest version of pasta carbonara ever imagined. Grated lemon adds a fresh note, very nice with the smoked ham.

MICROWAVE TIME: 9 to 13 minutes

    1 tablespoon vegetable oil
    2 cloves garlic, crushed
    1 medium onion, chopped (about ½ cup)
    2 cups finely chopped fully cooked
        smoked ham (about ¾ pound)
    ½ package (16-ounce size) linguine,
        cooked and drained
    ½ cup grated Parmesan cheese
    ½ cup half-and-half
    2 to 3 teaspoons grated lemon peel

1. Mix oil, garlic and onion in 3-quart casserole. Cover tightly and microwave on high 4 to 5 minutes or until onion is tender.

2. Stir in remaining ingredients except lemon peel. Cover tightly and microwave 5 to 8 minutes, stirring after 3 minutes, until heated through. Sprinkle with lemon peel; toss. **4 servings (about 1½ cups each);** 320 calories per serving.

Linguine with Ham

Green Pea Soup with Ham

GREEN PEA SOUP WITH HAM

MICROWAVE TIME: 11 to 15 minutes

1 package (16 ounces) frozen green peas
1 cup milk
2 tablespoons margarine or butter
2 tablespoons all-purpose flour
¾ teaspoon salt
⅛ teaspoon pepper
½ cup half-and-half
Ground ginger
2 cups ¼-inch strips fully cooked smoked ham

1. Microwave peas in 1½-quart casserole as directed on package; drain. Place peas and milk in workbowl of food processor fitted with steel blade or in blender container. Cover and process until uniform consistency.

2. Place margarine in 1½-quart casserole. Cover with waxed paper and microwave on high 30 to 60 seconds or until melted. Stir in flour, salt and pepper. Gradually stir in pea mixture.

3. Cover with waxed paper and microwave 5 to 6 minutes, stirring every minute, until boiling. Stir in half-and-half. Cover with waxed paper and microwave 30 to 60 seconds or just until hot (do not boil). Garnish each serving with dash of ginger and ½ cup ham.   **4 servings (about ¾ cup each);** 260 calories per serving.

HAM WITH BEANS AND PINEAPPLE

◖ MICROWAVE TIME: 10 to 12 minutes

1 cup ½-inch pieces fully cooked smoked ham
1 can (15½ ounces) butter beans, drained
1 can (16 ounces) baked beans in molasses sauce
1 can (8½ ounces) lima beans, drained
1 small onion, chopped (about ¼ cup)
1 teaspoon prepared mustard
1 can (8 ounces) pineapple chunks in juice, drained

1. Mix all ingredients except pineapple in 2-quart casserole.

2. Cover tightly and microwave on high 10 to 12 minutes, stirring after 5 minutes, until hot and bubbly. Top with pineapple chunks. **5 servings (1 cup each);** 270 calories per serving.

• • • • • • • • • • •

BRATWURST AND SAUERKRAUT

◖ MICROWAVE TIME: 10 to 12 minutes

1 pound fully cooked bratwurst
2 cans (16 ounces each) sauerkraut, drained
⅓ cup packed brown sugar

1. Arrange bratwurst evenly in square dish, 8 × 8 × 2 inches. Cover with sauerkraut; sprinkle with brown sugar.

2. Cover tightly and microwave on high 10 to 12 minutes, rotating dish ½ turn every 5 minutes, until hot. **6 servings;** 315 calories per serving.

CANADIAN BACON WITH SWEET POTATOES

◖ MICROWAVE TIME: 18 to 27 minutes

1½ pounds sweet potatoes (about 4 medium)*
6 slices fully cooked Canadian-style bacon, each about ½ inch thick (about 1¼ pounds)
1 can (8 ounces) crushed pineapple, drained
2 tablespoons packed brown sugar
¼ teaspoon ground cinnamon

1. Prepare and microwave sweet potatoes as directed (page 210). Pare and cut crosswise into thirds.

2. Arrange Canadian bacon in rectangular dish, 11 × 7 × 1½ inches. Place 2 sweet potato pieces on each slice bacon; top with pineapple. Mix brown sugar and cinnamon; sprinkle over pineapple.

3. Cover tightly and microwave on medium-high (70%) 10 to 12 minutes, rotating dish ½ turn after 5 minutes, until hot. **6 servings;** 240 calories per serving.

A 500-watt microwave is not recommended.

One can (18 ounces) vacuum-packed sweet potatoes can be substituted for the fresh sweet potatoes.

LASAGNE

MICROWAVE TIME: 41 to 50 minutes
STAND TIME: 15 minutes

1 pound bulk Italian sausage
1 jar (32 ounces) spaghetti sauce
1 container (16 ounces) small curd
   creamed cottage cheese
¼ cup grated Parmesan cheese
2 tablespoons chopped fresh parsley
1 tablespoon chopped fresh or 1 teaspoon
   dried basil
1 egg
8 uncooked lasagne noodles
2 cups shredded mozzarella cheese
   (8 ounces)

1. Crumble sausage into 2-quart casserole. Cover with waxed paper and microwave on high 6 to 7 minutes, breaking up and stirring after 4 minutes, until no longer pink; drain.

2. Stir in spaghetti sauce. Cover tightly and microwave 3 to 5 minutes, stirring after 2 minutes, until hot.

3. Mix cottage cheese, Parmesan cheese, parsley, basil and egg.

4. Spread 1⅓ cups of the sauce mixture evenly in rectangular dish, 12 × 7½ × 2 or 13 × 9 × 2 inches. Overlap 4 uncooked lasagne noodles on sauce. Spread 1 cup of the cheese mixture evenly over noodles; sprinkle with 1 cup of the mozzarella cheese. Repeat layers with sauce mixture, noodles and cheese mixture. Top with remaining sauce mixture. Cover tightly and microwave on high 10 minutes; rotate dish ½ turn.

5. Microwave on medium (50%) 22 to 28 minutes or until noodles are tender. Sprinkle with remaining mozzarella cheese. Let stand uncovered 15 minutes. **8 servings;** 370 calories per serving.

A 500-watt microwave is not recommended.

GRILLED ITALIAN SAUSAGE KABOBS

Microwaving the sausage first in the microwave rids it of some of the fat and helps avoid flare-ups on the grill.

MICROWAVE TIME: 4 to 5 minutes
GRILL TIME: 15 to 20 minutes

1½ pounds Italian sausage links, cut
   crosswise into fourths
2 medium zucchini, cut into 1-inch slices
1 large red bell pepper, cut into 1½-inch
   pieces
½ cup spaghetti sauce

1. Prepare charcoal fire for grilling. Place sausage pieces in 2-quart casserole. Cover tightly and microwave on high 4 to 5 minutes, stirring after 2 minutes, until partially cooked.

2. Alternate sausage, zucchini and bell pepper on each of 4 metal skewers, leaving small space between foods.

3. Place kabobs, 5 to 6 inches from medium coals, on grill. Cover and grill 15 to 20 minutes, turning and brushing kabobs 2 or 3 times with spaghetti sauce, until sausage is no longer pink. Serve with corn on the cob if desired. **4 servings;** 210 calories per serving.

A 500-watt microwave is not recommended.

Microwave-only Directions: Prepare and microwave sausage pieces as directed in step 1 (above). Alternate sausage, zucchini and bell pepper on each of eight 10-inch wooden skewers, leaving small space between foods. Place kabobs on 12-inch plate. Spoon half of the spaghetti sauce evenly over kabobs. Cover with waxed paper and microwave on high 8 to 10 minutes, rearranging kabobs and brushing with remaining sauce after 4 minutes, until sausage is no longer pink.

Grilled Italian Sausage Kabobs, Italian Risotto with Peas (page 260)

BURRITOS

MICROWAVE TIME: 20 to 28 minutes

1 pound bulk pork sausage
1 tablespoon chili powder
½ teaspoon salt
½ teaspoon ground cumin
1 medium tomato, coarsely chopped
    (about ¾ cup)
1 clove garlic, crushed
8 flour tortillas (6 inches in diameter)
1 can (16 ounces) refried beans
1 cup shredded Cheddar cheese
    (4 ounces)

1. Crumble pork sausage into 2-quart casserole. Cover with paper towel and microwave on high 7 to 9 minutes, breaking up and stirring after 4 minutes, until no longer pink; drain.

2. Stir in chili powder, salt, cumin, tomato and garlic. Cover tightly and microwave 3 to 5 minutes or until hot.

3. Place 4 of the tortillas between damp paper towels on 10-inch plate. Microwave on high 1 to 2 minutes or until softened and hot (keep tortillas covered while working with filling).

4. Spread about ¼ cup refried beans over each warm tortilla. Spoon about ⅓ cup sausage mixture onto center of each tortilla; sprinkle each with 2 tablespoons cheese. Roll up; arrange seam sides down on 10-inch plate. Cover with paper towel and microwave on high 4 to 5 minutes or until filling is hot. Repeat with remaining tortillas and filling. **8 burritos;** 315 calories per burrito.

GERMAN PORK SALAD

This warm salad brings out the juicy nature of pork tenderloin.

MICROWAVE TIME: 13 to 17 minutes

¾-pound pork tenderloin
4 cups bite-size pieces romaine
4 ounces fresh mushrooms, sliced (about
    1 cup)
2 green onions (with tops), thinly sliced
2 medium tomatoes, cut into wedges
2 teaspoons cornstarch
⅓ cup cold water
3 tablespoons vegetable oil
3 tablespoons white wine vinegar
1 tablespoon Dijon mustard
Freshly ground pepper

1. Place pork tenderloin in rectangular dish, 11 × 7 × 1½ inches. Cover tightly and microwave on medium (50%) 11 to 14 minutes, turning pork over after 6 minutes, until done (170° on meat thermometer).

2. Divide romaine, mushrooms, onions and tomatoes among 4 salad plates. Cut pork into ¼-inch slices; arrange on vegetables.

3. Mix cornstarch and water in 2-cup measure. Stir in oil, vinegar and mustard. Microwave uncovered on high 2 to 3 minutes, stirring every minute, until mixture thickens and boils. Pour over salads; serve immediately. Sprinkle with pepper. **4 servings;** 340 calories per serving.

A 500-watt microwave is not recommended.

OPEN-FACE HAM AND MUSHROOM SANDWICHES

◐ MICROWAVE TIME: 9 to 12 minutes

1 tablespoon margarine or butter
8 ounces fresh mushrooms, sliced (about 2 cups)
1 small onion, thinly sliced and separated into rings
1 clove garlic, crushed
4 thin slices fully cooked smoked ham (about 4 ounces)
4 slices dark rye bread, toasted
8 thin slices tomato
1 cup shredded Cheddar cheese (4 ounces)

1.   Place margarine, mushrooms, onion and garlic in 1-quart casserole. Cover tightly and microwave on high 4 to 6 minutes, stirring after 2 minutes, until onion is crisp-tender.

2.   Place 1 slice ham on each slice toast. Place about ¼ of the mushroom mixture on each slice ham, using slotted spoon.

3.   Arrange 2 sandwiches on paper towel–lined 10-inch plate. Microwave uncovered on high 2 minutes. Top each sandwich with 2 slices tomato; sprinkle each with ¼ cup cheese. Microwave uncovered 30 to 60 seconds or until cheese is melted. Repeat with remaining sandwiches. **4 open-face sandwiches;** 275 calories per sandwich.

VEAL WITH SOUR CREAM

◐ MICROWAVE TIME: 24 to 29 minutes

1 medium onion, chopped (about ½ cup)
1 tablespoon margarine or butter
1 can (4 ounces) mushroom stems and pieces, drained
⅓ cup beef broth
2 teaspoons grated lemon peel
½ teaspoon paprika
1 teaspoon chopped fresh or ¼ teaspoon dried dill weed
⅛ teaspoon pepper
1-pound veal shoulder steak, ½ to ¾ inch thick, cut into 4 serving pieces
1 tablespoon plus 1 teaspoon cornstarch
2 tablespoons cold water
½ cup sour cream or plain yogurt

1.   Place onion and margarine in 4-cup measure. Microwave uncovered on high 2 to 3 minutes or until onion is crisp-tender. Stir in mushrooms, broth, lemon peel, paprika, dill weed and pepper.

2.   Arrange veal in square dish, 8 × 8 × 2 inches. Pour onion mixture over veal. Cover tightly and microwave on medium (50%) 20 to 23 minutes, rotating dish ½ turn after 10 minutes, until veal is medium doneness (160° on meat thermometer).

3.   Remove veal to warm platter; keep warm. Mix cornstarch and water; gradually stir into onion mixture. Stir in sour cream. Microwave uncovered on medium-high (70%) 2 to 3 minutes, stirring every minute, until thickened. Pour over veal. **4 servings;** 300 calories per serving.

VEAL WITH ARTICHOKES

MICROWAVE TIME: 17 to 21 minutes
STAND TIME: 5 minutes

4 veal loin chops, about 1 inch thick
¼ teaspoon salt
⅛ teaspoon pepper
1 can (14 ounces) artichoke hearts, drained and cut into fourths
2 tablespoons lemon juice
1 tablespoon milk
4 ounces Fontina or Swiss cheese, cut into ½-inch pieces

1. Arrange veal chops, thickest parts to outside edges, in rectangular dish, 11 × 7 × 1½ inches. Cover tightly and microwave on medium-high (70%) 8 minutes; turn veal over.

2. Sprinkle veal with salt and pepper. Arrange artichoke hearts on veal; drizzle with lemon juice. Cover tightly and microwave on medium-high (70%) 7 to 10 minutes or until veal is medium doneness (160° on meat thermometer). Let stand covered 5 minutes.

3. Place milk and cheese in 1-cup measure. Cover with waxed paper and microwave on medium (50%) 2 to 3 minutes, stirring every minute, until melted and smooth. Serve over veal. Sprinkle with chopped fresh parsley if desired.   **4 servings;** 305 calories per serving.

A 500-watt microwave is not recommended.

LAMB PATTIES WITH VEGETABLES

MICROWAVE TIME: 11 to 13 minutes

1 pound ground lamb or turkey
½ teaspoon garlic salt
¼ teaspoon pepper
2 small onions, cut into fourths
1 small green bell pepper, cut into 1-inch pieces
1 small summer squash, cut into ½-inch slices
1 tablespoon chopped fresh or 1 teaspoon dried marjoram

1. Mix lamb, garlic salt and pepper. Shape mixture into 4 patties, each about ½ inch thick.

2. Arrange patties in circle on rack in dish. Cover with waxed paper and microwave on high 4 minutes.

3. Arrange vegetables on and around lamb; sprinkle with marjoram. Cover with waxed paper and microwave 7 to 9 minutes, rotating dish ½ turn after 4 minutes, until vegetables are crisp-tender and lamb is medium doneness (170° on meat thermometer).   **4 servings;** 265 calories per serving.

Veal with Artichokes, Curried Rice with Almonds (page 257)

LAMB WITH LEMON SAUCE

 MICROWAVE TIME: 5 to 7 minutes

2 tablespoons margarine or butter
2 tablespoons all-purpose flour
1 tablespoon chopped fresh or 1 teaspoon
   dried dill weed
⅔ cup chicken broth
3 tablespoons lemon juice
2 cups bite-size pieces cooked lamb
Paprika

1. Place margarine in 1½-quart casserole. Microwave uncovered on high 15 to 30 seconds or until melted.

2. Stir in flour, dill weed, broth and lemon juice. Microwave uncovered about 2 minutes, stirring every minute, until thickened.

3. Stir in lamb until coated. Cover tightly and microwave 2 to 4 minutes or until lamb is hot; stir. Sprinkle with paprika. Serve with hot cooked rice or noodles if desired. **2 servings (1 cup each);** 400 calories per serving.

MEATBALLS WITH MINT

Mint is a natural accompaniment to lamb. Even those who are not confirmed fans of lamb will like these juicy meatballs.

MICROWAVE TIME: 8 to 10 minutes

1 pound ground lamb or turkey
¼ cup dry bread crumbs
1 small onion, finely chopped (about
   ¼ cup)
3 tablespoons chopped fresh or
   1 tablespoon dried mint
½ teaspoon lemon pepper
1 egg
Mint Sauce (below)

1. Mix all ingredients except Mint Sauce. Shape mixture by tablespoonfuls into 1½-inch balls. Arrange, sides not touching, in square dish, 8 × 8 × 2 inches.

2. Cover with waxed paper and microwave on high 6 to 8 minutes, rearranging meatballs after 3 minutes, until no longer pink inside; drain. Prepare Mint Sauce; serve with meatballs. **4 servings (about 6 meatballs each);** 395 calories per serving.

Mint Sauce

½ cup mint jelly
1 tablespoon vinegar
1 tablespoon chopped fresh or 1 teaspoon
   dried mint

Mix all ingredients in 1-cup measure. Microwave uncovered on high 30 seconds to 1 minute or until jelly is melted; stir.

MICROWAVING MEATS

Type	Amount	Power Level	Time

Place ground meat in dish, meatballs or patties on rack in dish. Cover loosely and microwave as directed below or until no longer pink. Meat thermometer registers 160° for medium or 170° for well-done beef and pork.

Type	Amount	Power Level	Time
Ground			
crumbled	1 pound	High	5 to 6 minutes, stirring after 3 minutes
meatballs	1 pound (24 balls)	High	6 to 8 minutes, rotating dish after 3 minutes
patties, ¾ inch thick	1 pound (4 patties)	High	6 to 8 minutes, rearranging after 3 minutes

For ribs, place in shallow dish; cover tightly. Microwave as directed below or until meat thermometer registers 170°.

Type	Amount	Power Level	Time
Ribs, back	3 pounds	High	10 minutes, rearranging after 5 minutes; drain
		Medium (50%)	25 to 30 minutes

For bacon slices, place on rack in dish; cover with paper towels. Microwave as directed below or until bacon is crisp.

Type	Amount	Power Level	Time
Bacon	2 slices	High	1 minute 30 seconds to 2 minutes
	4 slices	High	3 to 4 minutes
	6 slices	High	4 to 6 minutes
	8 slices	High	6 to 8 minutes

Place frankfurters or sausages on paper towel–lined plate. Pierce several times with fork. Cover loosely and microwave as directed below or until done (170° on meat thermometer for raw sausages).

Type	Amount	Power Level	Time
Frankfurters (10 per pound)	1	High	30 to 45 seconds
	2	High	1 minute to 1 minute 15 seconds
	4	High	1 minute 15 seconds to 1 minute 30 seconds
Sausages, cooked (bratwurst, Italian—6 per pound)	2	High	1 minute 30 seconds to 2 minutes 30 seconds, rearranging after 1 minute
	4	High	3 to 4 minutes, rearranging after 2 minutes
Sausages, uncooked (bratwurst, Polish—6 per pound)	2	High	2 minutes to 3 minutes 30 seconds, rearranging after 1 minute
	4	High	4 to 5 minutes, rearranging after 3 minutes

DEFROSTING MEATS

Meats may be defrosted in the wrapper. Check after half the time to separate and place in dish. As soon as possible, arrange thickest parts to outside edges. Pierce bacon, frankfurter and sausage package with fork. Microwave on defrost setting as directed below until few ice crystals remain in center. Let stand 5 to 10 minutes to complete defrosting.

TYPE	AMOUNT	TIME
Steak		
½ inch thick	1 pound	7 to 9 minutes, turning over after 4 minutes
1 inch thick	1 pound	8 to 11 minutes, turning over after 4 minutes
Chops, ½ inch thick	1 pound (about 4)	6 to 9 minutes, rearranging after 4 minutes
Ribs, back	1 pound	7 to 9 minutes, rearranging after 4 minutes
Ground	1 pound	8 to 10 minutes, turning over after 4 minutes
meatballs, cooked	1 pound (24 balls)	7 to 9 minutes, separating after 3 minutes
patties, ¾ inch thick	1 pound (4 patties)	8 to 10 minutes, turning over after 4 minutes
Bacon, sliced	1 pound	5 to 6 minutes
Frankfurters	1 pound (about 10)	5 to 7 minutes, turning over after 3 minutes
	½ pound	2 to 4 minutes
Sausages, cooked or uncooked (bratwurst, Italian, Polish)	1 pound (about 6)	6 to 8 minutes, turning over after 3 minutes

GARDEN HARVEST FRITTATA

A frittata is the Italian version of a thick omelet, often filled with vegetables, sometimes with sausage or potatoes. The frittata below boasts of summertime, with zucchini, corn, carrots, red bell pepper and fresh dill.

MICROWAVE TIME: 6 to 11 minutes

1 medium zucchini, thinly sliced (about 2 cups)
2 medium carrots, coarsely shredded (about 1 cup)
¼ cup whole kernel corn
4 eggs, beaten
¼ cup milk
1 tablespoon chopped fresh or 1 teaspoon dried dill weed
⅛ teaspoon salt
⅛ teaspoon pepper
4 red bell pepper rings

1.   Arrange zucchini evenly in ungreased pie plate, 9 × 1¼ inches. Top with carrots and corn. Mix remaining ingredients except bell pepper; pour over vegetables.

2.   Elevate pie plate on inverted dinner plate in microwave. Cover with waxed paper and microwave on high 6 to 11 minutes, rotating pie plate ½ turn after 3 minutes, until eggs are set. Top with bell pepper.   **4 servings;** 130 calories per serving.

Garden Harvest Frittata

WESTERN OMELET

Microwaved omelets do not brown on the bottom but they cook rapidly and are easily folded in half. The use of a round pie plate helps shape a perfect omelet. To cook an un-flavored, basic omelet, refer to Microwaving Eggs (page 167).

 MICROWAVE TIME: 4 to 5 minutes

1 tablespoon margarine or butter
3 eggs, beaten
¼ cup finely chopped fully cooked
   smoked ham
2 tablespoons finely chopped onion
1 tablespoon finely chopped green bell
   pepper
Salt and pepper to taste

1.   Place margarine in pie place, 9 × 1¼ inches. Microwave uncovered on high 20 to 30 seconds or until melted.

2.   Mix eggs, ham, onion and bell pepper; pour into pie plate. Cover with waxed paper and microwave on high 2 minutes 30 seconds to 3 minutes 30 seconds, pushing cooked edge of omelet to center after 1 minute 30 seconds, until center is set but still moist.

3.   Loosen edge of omelet; fold just to center. Slide omelet onto serving plate so folded side rolls over again and edge is on bottom, or fold in half. Sprinkle with salt and pepper.   **1 serving;** 360 calories.

Cheddar Omelet: Just before folding omelet, sprinkle with ¼ cup shredded Cheddar cheese (1 ounce).   460 calories.

Herb Omelet: Just before folding omelet, sprinkle with 1 tablespoon chopped fresh parsley and 1 tablespoon chopped fresh chives.   345 calories.

• • • • • • • • • • •

BACON-CHEDDAR FRITTATA

MICROWAVE TIME: 12 to 14 minutes

6 eggs, beaten
8 slices bacon, crisply cooked and
   crumbled
1 cup shredded Cheddar cheese
   (4 ounces)
¼ cup chopped fresh parsley
¼ teaspoon pepper
2 tablespoons chopped fresh chives

1.   Grease pie plate, 9 × 1¼ inches. Mix all ingredients except chives; pour into pie plate. Elevate pie plate on inverted dinner plate in microwave oven. Microwave uncovered on medium (50%) 12 to 14 minutes, rotating pie plate ¼ turn every 4 minutes, until set.

2.   Sprinkle with chives. Serve with sour cream if desired.   **6 servings;** 205 calories per serving.

500-watt microwave: You may need to increase microwave time.

EGGS WITH TOMATOES AND BELL PEPPERS

◔ MICROWAVE TIME: 14 to 19 minutes

2 medium green bell peppers, sliced
2 small onions, sliced
1 small clove garlic, finely chopped
2 teaspoons chopped fresh or ½ teaspoon dried basil
2 medium tomatoes, cut into wedges
8 eggs
½ cup sour cream
½ teaspoon salt
¼ teaspoon pepper

1.   Mix bell peppers, onions, garlic and basil in 2-quart casserole. Cover tightly and microwave on high 5 to 7 minutes, stirring after 3 minutes, until bell pepper is crisp-tender.

2.   Stir in tomatoes. Cover tightly and microwave 2 to 3 minutes or until tomatoes are hot; drain. Arrange vegetables around edge of platter; cover to keep warm.

3.   Mix remaining ingredients in same casserole. Microwave uncovered on high 7 to 9 minutes, stirring every 2 minutes, until eggs are set. Mound egg mixture in center of vegetables.   **4 servings;** 260 calories per serving.

• • • • • • • • • •

ANYTIME SCRAMBLED EGGS

◔ MICROWAVE TIME: 3 to 4 minutes

4 eggs
¼ cup milk
¼ teaspoon salt
Dash of pepper
¼ cup shredded cheese, crumbled cooked bacon, chopped fresh chives, sliced green onions or chopped canned mushrooms

1.   Beat egg, milk, salt and pepper in 1-quart casserole, using fork. Stir in cheese.

2.   Cover tightly and microwave on high 3 to 4 minutes, stirring every minute, until eggs are puffy and set but still moist. Stir before serving.   **2 servings;** 175 calories per serving.

Note: Recipe can be doubled. Increase microwave time to 6 to 8 minutes, stirring every 2 minutes.

• • • • • • • • • •

FLUFFY EGGS WITH BROCCOLI

◔ MICROWAVE TIME: 15 to 19 minutes

1 package (10 ounces) frozen chopped broccoli
9 eggs
½ cup shredded Cheddar cheese (2 ounces)
2 tablespoons finely chopped onion
2 tablespoons milk
½ teaspoon salt
1 teaspoon chopped fresh or ½ teaspoon dried basil
¼ teaspoon garlic powder
2 tomatoes, sliced

1.   Place frozen broccoli in square dish, 8 × 8 × 2 inches. Cover tightly and microwave on high 6 to 8 minutes, stirring after 4 minutes, until crisp-tender; drain well.

2.   Beat eggs in medium bowl. Stir in cheese, onion, milk, salt, basil and garlic powder. Pour over broccoli. Elevate dish on inverted dinner plate in microwave. Cover loosely and microwave on medium-high (70%) 9 to 11 minutes, pushing cooked edges to center, until center is almost set. Arrange tomato slices on top.   **4 servings;** 275 calories per serving.

MEXICAN EGGS WITH CHILIES

MICROWAVE TIME: 20 to 23 minutes

1 cup shredded Cheddar cheese
    (8 ounces)
1 can (4 ounces) chopped green chilies,
    drained
1 cup shredded Monterey Jack cheese
    (8 ounces)
3 eggs
⅓ cup all-purpose flour
2 cans (5⅓ ounces each) evaporated milk
1 can (8 ounces) tomato sauce

1.   Layer Cheddar cheese, chilies and Monterey Jack cheese in square dish, 8 × 8 × 2 inches.

2.   Beat eggs, flour and milk in 4-cup measure. Microwave uncovered on medium (50%) 4 minutes, stirring with fork every minute, until hot. Quickly and evenly pour egg mixture over cheese.

3.   Elevate dish on inverted dinner plate in microwave. Cover and microwave on medium (50%) 15 to 17 minutes, rotating dish ½ turn every 5 minutes, until center is set.

4.   Pour tomato sauce into small bowl. Microwave uncovered on high 1 to 2 minutes or until hot. Serve with eggs.   **6 servings;** 280 calories per serving.

VEGETABLE–EGG SALAD SANDWICHES

MICROWAVE TIME: 6 to 8 minutes

1 cup broccoli flowerets
¼ cup finely chopped onion (about
    1 small)
3 hard-cooked eggs, chopped
3 tablespoons mayonnaise or salad
    dressing
1 teaspoon prepared mustard
¼ teaspoon salt
4 slices whole wheat bread, toasted
1 medium tomato, sliced
½ cup shredded Monterey Jack cheese
    (2 ounces)

1.   Place broccoli and onion in ungreased pie plate, 9 × 1¼ inches. Cover tightly and microwave on high 3 to 4 minutes or until broccoli is crisp-tender.

2.   Mix eggs, mayonnaise, mustard and salt; spread on toast. Top with tomato, broccoli mixture and cheese. Place on paper towel–lined plate. Microwave uncovered on high 3 to 4 minutes, rotating plate ½ turn after 1 minute 30 seconds, until cheese is melted.
4 open-face sandwiches; 260 calories per sandwich.

Vegetable–Egg Salad Sandwiches

CHEESE AND EGG PIE

MICROWAVE TIME: 8 to 11 minutes

1 cup coarsely crushed cornflakes
2 tablespoons margarine or butter, melted
8 eggs
½ cup milk
1 tablespoon chopped fresh chives
¼ teaspoon seasoned salt
⅛ teaspoon pepper
6 slices bacon, crisply cooked and
    crumbled
3 slices process American cheese, cut
    diagonally in half

1.   Mix cornflakes and margarine; reserve ¼ cup. Spread remaining mixture in pie plate, 9 × 1¼ inches. Beat eggs, milk, chives, seasoned salt and pepper in 1½-quart casserole, using hand beater; stir in bacon.

2.   Cover tightly and microwave on high 6 to 8 minutes, stirring every 2 minutes, until eggs are puffy and set but still moist. Quickly spoon into pie plate. Arrange cheese, overlapping slightly, around edge of pie plate; sprinkle with reserved cornflake mixture. Microwave uncovered on medium (50%) 2 to 3 minutes or until cheese is melted.   **6 servings;** 260 calories per serving.

EGGS FOO YONG CASSEROLE

MICROWAVE TIME: 11 to 14 minutes

Oriental Sauce (below)
1 can (16 ounces) bean sprouts, rinsed
    and drained
1 can (8 ounces) sliced water chestnuts,
    drained
1 small green bell pepper, chopped
    (about ½ cup)
1 small onion, chopped (about ¼ cup)
6 eggs
1 tablespoon chopped pimiento
¼ teaspoon salt

1.   Prepare Oriental Sauce; keep warm.

2.   Mix bean sprouts, water chestnuts, bell pepper and onion in 1½-quart casserole. Cover tightly and microwave on high 5 to 6 minutes, stirring after 3 minutes, until hot; drain.

3.   Beat eggs, pimiento and salt; pour over vegetables. Cover tightly and microwave 3 to 4 minutes, stirring after 2 minutes, until eggs are set but still moist. Spoon sauce over each serving.   **4 servings;** 185 calories per serving.

Oriental Sauce

⅔ cup water
3 tablespoons soy sauce
1 tablespoon cornstarch
1 teaspoon sugar
1 teaspoon vinegar

Mix all ingredients in 2-cup measure. Microwave uncovered on high 3 to 4 minutes, stirring every minute, until mixture boils and thickens.

MICROWAVING EGGS

Type	Amount		Power Level	Time	Stand Time

Poached Eggs

For each egg, microwave 2 tablespoons water in 6-ounce custard cup uncovered on high 30 to 60 seconds or until boiling. Carefully break egg into custard cup. Pierce egg yolk several times with wooden pick. Cover tightly and microwave as directed below until eggs are almost set (eggs will continue to cook while standing).

	1 egg		Medium (50%)	1 minute to 1 minute 30 seconds	1 minute (covered)
	2 eggs		Medium (50%)	1 minute 30 seconds to 2 minutes	1 minute (covered)

Scrambled Eggs

Microwave margarine in 1-quart casserole until melted. Add eggs and milk; beat. Microwave uncovered as directed below, stirring every minute, until eggs are puffy and set but still moist.

	1 serving: 1 teaspoon margarine or butter 2 eggs 2 tablespoons milk or water	High	1 minute 30 seconds to 2 minutes
	2 servings: 1 teaspoon margarine or butter 4 eggs ¼ cup milk or water	High	3 to 4 minutes

Omelets

Microwave margarine in pie plate until melted. Pour beaten eggs into pie plate. Cover with waxed paper and microwave as directed below, pushing cooked edge of omelet to center after 1 minute 30 seconds until eggs are puffy and set but still moist.

	1 serving: 1 tablespoon margarine or butter 3 eggs, beaten	High	2 minutes 30 seconds to 3 minutes 30 seconds

SAUSAGE AND CHEESE STRATA

This recipe is ideal for refrigerating overnight and serving for brunch the following day. Pull it from the microwave, fragrant and steaming, just when you are ready to serve.

MICROWAVE TIME:	23 to 33 minutes
REFRIGERATION TIME:	2 to 24 hours

½ pound bulk pork sausage
3 cups seasoned croutons
1½ cups shredded Gruyère or Swiss cheese (6 ounces)
4 green onions (with tops), sliced
1¼ cups milk
½ teaspoon dry mustard
4 eggs

1. Spread sausage in ungreased pie plate, 9 × 1¼ inches. Cover tightly and microwave on high 3 to 4 minutes or until no longer pink; crumble. Drain sausage; drain fat from pie plate.

2. Arrange half of the croutons in same pie plate. Layer with cheese, sausage, onions and remaining croutons. Beat milk, mustard and eggs; pour evenly over croutons. Cover and refrigerate at least 2 hours but no longer than 24 hours.

3. Elevate pie plate on inverted dinner plate in microwave oven. Microwave uncovered on high 2 to 5 minutes.

4. Microwave uncovered on medium (50%) 18 to 24 minutes, rotating dish ½ turn after 10 minutes, until knife inserted in center comes out clean. **6 servings;** 380 calories per serving.

500-watt microwave: You may need to increase microwave times.

SWISS CHEESE FONDUE

Use only natural, aged Swiss cheese for fondue. It is the only way the fondue will have its authentic, distinctively nutty flavor and the proper consistency.

◔ MICROWAVE TIME: 7 to 12 minutes

2 cups shredded natural Swiss cheese*
   (8 ounces)
2 teaspoons cornstarch
1 tablespoon margarine or butter
1 clove garlic, crushed
¾ cup dry white wine or chicken broth
1 teaspoon Dijon mustard
⅓ loaf (1-pound size) French bread, cut
   into 1-inch cubes

1. Toss cheese and cornstarch; reserve. Mix margarine and garlic in 2-quart casserole. Microwave uncovered on high 1 to 2 minutes or until garlic is soft.

2. Stir in wine. Microwave uncovered 2 to 4 minutes or until boiling.

3. Stir in mustard and cheese mixture. Microwave uncovered on medium (50%) 4 to 6 minutes, stirring after 2 minutes, until cheese is melted and smooth. Pour into earthenware fondue dish; keep warm over low heat. Spear bread cubes with fondue forks; dip and swirl in fondue with stirring motion. **3 servings;** 440 calories per serving.

500-watt microwave: You may need to increase microwave times.

Swiss cheese should be aged at least 6 months.

SPINACH-CHEESE PIE

MICROWAVE TIME:	20 to 22 minutes
STAND TIME:	5 minutes

1½ cups small curd creamed cottage cheese
¼ cup grated Parmesan cheese
¼ cup sliced green onions (with tops)
¼ teaspoon ground nutmeg
1 package (10 ounces) frozen chopped spinach, thawed and well-drained
⅔ cup variety baking mix
½ cup milk
2 eggs
¼ teaspoon salt
½ cup shredded Swiss cheese (2 ounces)
¼ cup chopped red bell pepper

1. Grease pie plate, 10 × 1½ inches. Mix cottage cheese, Parmesan cheese, onions, nutmeg and spinach; spoon into pie plate. Beat baking mix, milk, eggs and salt with hand beater or wire whisk 1 minute or until smooth. Pour evenly over spinach mixture.

2. Elevate pie plate on inverted dinner plate in microwave oven. Microwave uncovered on medium-high (70%) 20 to 22 minutes, rotating pie plate ¼ turn every 6 minutes, until knife inserted in center comes out clean.

3. Sprinkle with Swiss cheese and bell pepper. Cover with waxed paper and let stand 5 minutes. **6 servings;** 210 calories per serving.

A 500-watt microwave is not recommended.

MACARONI PIE WITH GARLIC TOMATO SAUCE

MICROWAVE TIME:	21 to 26 minutes
STAND TIME:	10 minutes

⅓ cup dry bread crumbs
2 tablespoons grated Parmesan cheese
2 tablespoons margarine or butter
1 package (7 ounces) macaroni rings, cooked and drained
1 cup small curd creamed cottage cheese
¾ cup shredded sharp Cheddar cheese (3 ounces)
2 eggs, slightly beaten
⅛ teaspoon pepper
1 cup Garlic Tomato Sauce (page 321)

1. Mix bread crumbs, Parmesan cheese and margarine in 2-cup measure. Microwave uncovered on high 1 to 2 minutes, stirring every 30 seconds, until light brown.

2. Grease pie plate, 9 × 1¼ inches. Mix hot macaroni, cottage cheese, Cheddar cheese, eggs and pepper. Turn into pie plate. Cover with waxed paper and microwave on medium (50%) 8 minutes.

3. Sprinkle with crumb mixture. Microwave uncovered 8 to 10 minutes or until center is almost set. Let stand uncovered 10 minutes. Serve with Garlic Tomato Sauce. **6 servings;** 310 calories per serving.

CHEESE AND TOMATO PIE IN RICE CRUST

MICROWAVE TIME:	17 to 20 minutes
STAND TIME:	10 minutes

2 cups hot cooked rice
1 tablespoon chopped fresh chives
1 egg white
⅓ cup finely chopped onion
1 cup shredded mozzarella or Monterey Jack cheese (4 ounces)
3 eggs plus 1 egg yolk
1 can (13 ounces) evaporated milk
⅛ teaspoon salt
1 teaspoon chopped fresh or ¼ teaspoon dried sage
4 drops red pepper sauce
6 tomato slices
Chopped fresh chives

1. Mix rice, 1 tablespoon chives and egg white with fork. Spread evenly over bottom and halfway up side of pie plate, 10 × 1½ inches (do not leave any holes). Microwave uncovered on high 2 minutes.

2. Sprinkle onion and mozzarella cheese over crust. Beat eggs, milk, salt, sage and pepper sauce in 4-cup measure. Microwave uncovered on medium-high (70%) 4 minutes, stirring every minute, until hot. Pour carefully over cheese in crust.

3. Elevate pie plate on inverted dinner plate in microwave. Cover with waxed paper and microwave on medium-high (70%) 11 to 14 minutes, rotating pie plate ½ turn after 6 minutes, until center is almost set. Top with tomato; sprinkle with chives. Cover with waxed paper and let stand 10 minutes. **6 servings;** 275 calories per serving.

MACARONI AND CHEESE

 MICROWAVE TIME: 19 to 23 minutes

2 cups uncooked macaroni (about 7 ounces)
2 cups hot water
⅓ cup margarine or butter
1 small onion, chopped (about ¼ cup)
¼ teaspoon salt
¼ teaspoon pepper
¼ teaspoon dry mustard
1¼ cups milk
8 ounces process American cheese loaf, cut into cubes
⅓ cup all-purpose flour

1. Mix macaroni, water, margarine, onion, salt, pepper and mustard in 2-quart casserole. Cover tightly and microwave on high 5 minutes; stir.

2. Cover tightly and microwave on medium (50%) 4 to 6 minutes or until boiling.

3. Stir in remaining ingredients. Cover tightly and microwave on high 10 to 12 minutes, stirring every 4 minutes, until mixture is bubbly and macaroni is tender. **4 servings (about 1¼ cups each);** 660 calories per serving.

Macaroni and Cheese with Franks: Stir in 4 frankfurters, cut into 1-inch pieces, with the cheese.   780 calories per serving.

Ricotta Shells

RICOTTA SHELLS

🕐 MICROWAVE TIME: 6 to 7 minutes

1 cup ricotta cheese
½ cup shredded mozzarella cheese
    (2 ounces)
¼ cup grated Parmesan cheese
1 tablespoon chopped fresh parsley
¼ teaspoon pepper
1 egg
12 jumbo pasta shells, cooked and
    drained
1 cup spaghetti sauce

1. Mix all ingredients except pasta shells and spaghetti sauce. Fill each pasta shell with about 2 tablespoons cheese mixture.

2. Arrange stuffed shells in circle around edge of pie plate, 9 × 1¼ inches. Pour spaghetti sauce over shells. Cover tightly and microwave on high 6 to 7 minutes, rotating pie plate ½ turn after 3 minutes, until hot. **4 servings (3 shells each);** 310 calories per serving.

500-watt microwave: You may need to increase microwave time.

RICH CAULIFLOWER SOUP

MICROWAVE TIME: 7 to 9 minutes

1 cup ½-inch cauliflowerets (about ¼ pound)
2 tablespoons margarine or butter
1 cup chicken broth
½ cup half-and-half
⅛ teaspoon salt
Dash of ground nutmeg
Dash of ground allspice
6 ounces process American cheese spread loaf, cut into ½-inch cubes
¼ cup dry white wine
¼ cup finely chopped green bell pepper
Paprika

1. Place cauliflowerets and margarine in 2-quart casserole. Cover tightly and microwave on high 2 minutes or until crisp-tender.

2. Stir in chicken broth, half-and-half, salt, nutmeg, allspice and cheese. Cover tightly and microwave on medium-high (70%) 3 minutes.

3. Stir in wine. Cover tightly and microwave 2 to 4 minutes or until hot. Sprinkle with bell pepper and paprika. **4 servings (about 1 cup each);** 270 calories per serving.

BEER-CHEESE SOUP

Don't let the soup boil after the cheese has been added, or it may separate. This makes for an unusual wintertime lunch, especially fun when garnished with fresh popcorn.

MICROWAVE TIME: 12 to 16 minutes

¼ cup margarine or butter
1 small onion, finely chopped (about ¼ cup)
¼ cup all-purpose flour
1 teaspoon dry mustard
⅛ teaspoon ground red pepper (cayenne)
3 cups milk
½ cup beer
8 ounces sharp process American cheese loaf, shredded

1. Place margarine and onion in 2-quart casserole. Cover tightly and microwave on high 3 to 4 minutes or until onion is tender. Stir in flour, mustard and red pepper. Gradually stir in milk and beer.

2. Microwave uncovered 6 to 8 minutes, stirring after 4 minutes, until boiling. Stir in cheese. Microwave uncovered 3 to 4 minutes or until cheese is melted and mixture is hot. Garnish with shredded carrot or popcorn if desired. **4 servings (1⅓ cups each);** 455 calories per serving.

500-watt microwave: You may need to increase microwave times.

Swiss Cheese–Veggie Sandwiches

SWISS CHEESE–VEGGIE SANDWICHES

MICROWAVE TIME: 3 to 4 minutes

1 cup shredded Swiss cheese (4 ounces)
1 cup shredded zucchini (about 1 small)
   or carrots (about 2 small)
1 small tomato, chopped (about ½ cup)
½ cup thinly sliced small cauliflowerets
2 tablespoons mayonnaise or salad
   dressing
2 teaspoons chopped fresh or ½ teaspoon
   dried dill weed
¼ teaspoon salt
3 English muffins, cut into halves and
   toasted

1. Mix all ingredients except muffin halves; spread evenly over muffin halves. Arrange in circle on rack in dish.

2. Microwave uncovered on high 3 to 4 minutes or until hot and bubbly. **6 open-face sandwiches;** 150 calories per sandwich.

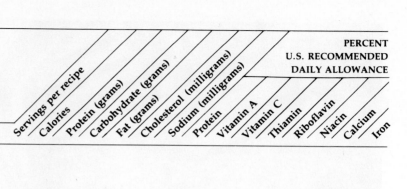

Per Serving or Unit # NUTRITION INFORMATION RECIPE, PAGE	Servings per recipe	Calories	Protein (grams)	Carbohydrate (grams)	Fat (grams)	Cholesterol (milligrams)	Sodium (milligrams)	Protein	Vitamin A	Vitamin C	Thiamin	Riboflavin	Niacin	Calcium	Iron
BEEF															
Bacon Burgers, 132	4	465	29	31	25	85	570	44	4	22	20	20	34	8	24
Barbecued Meat Loaf, 130	6	400	28	19	22	130	725	42	4	10	8	18	26	8	20
Beef Burgundy, 119	4	645	37	27	41	115	985	56	24	10	18	48	56	6	36
Beef and Corn Pie, 125	4	355	24	14	23	145	520	36	22	6	8	14	18	12	18
Beef with Cracked Wheat, 126	4	395	29	22	21	85	580	44	28	22	2	16	28	12	28
Beef Goulash, 128	6	335	33	34	7	110	430	50	22	22	32	26	46	4	32
Beef Kabobs, 121	6	465	20	51	21	70	735	30	2	32	10	18	26	2	20
Beef and Noodle Casserole, 128	4	620	30	29	43	110	930	46	10	4	8	18	28	10	20
Beef Rolls, 122	4	510	25	56	20	55	1430	38	8	34	26	20	34	4	28
Beef Stroganoff, 126	4	380	32	21	18	130	360	50	100	4	10	20	32	8	24
Beef Teriyaki with Broccoli, 121	4	265	24	9	15	70	500	36	18	50	8	18	24	8	20
Brandy Beef Steaks, 117	4	215	25	1	10	75	110	38	2	0	4	10	24	0	16
Chunky Chili con Carne, 129	4	420	30	29	21	80	1115	46	56	60	20	20	34	8	34
Gourmet Grilled Steak, 117	8	255	22	2	16	70	160	34	6	6	6	18	26	2	18
Greek Beef Salad, 133	4	180	24	5	7	70	315	36	18	28	6	12	18	2	20
Impossible Lasagne Pie, 124	6	480	34	19	30	195	895	52	28	10	14	30	22	44	20
Lentil Soup, 131	6	300	24	22	13	55	370	36	64	14	14	12	22	4	28
Meatballs in Red Wine Sauce, 123	4	475	31	33	22	150	1130	46	20	4	12	22	32	4	24
Mexican Cubed Steaks, 122	4	410	37	7	25	110	495	56	14	2	8	22	34	12	24
Mexican Meat Loaf, 130	6	450	31	19	26	145	930	46	6	10	8	22	26	16	20
Mushroom Steaks, 118	4	200	19	3	10	65	320	30	0	10	4	8	18	0	14
Oriental Cold Noodles and Beef, 133	6	420	19	31	23	50	560	28	100	10	20	24	30	2	20
Picadillo Tacos, 132	4	490	28	37	26	80	870	42	8	26	14	16	28	14	28
Pizza Burgers, 131	4	495	34	29	26	100	770	52	18	20	14	20	32	22	28
Reuben Sandwiches, 133	4	480	20	31	31	55	1110	30	6	6	8	12	4	32	16
Savory Tostadas, 134	4	415	31	23	22	70	520	46	32	26	8	18	24	24	24

PER SERVING OR UNIT **NUTRITION INFORMATION** RECIPE, PAGE	Servings per recipe	Calories	Protein (grams)	Carbohydrate (grams)	Fat (grams)	Cholesterol (milligrams)	Sodium (milligrams)	PERCENT U.S. RECOMMENDED DAILY ALLOWANCE Protein	Vitamin A	Vitamin C	Thiamin	Riboflavin	Niacin	Calcium	Iron
BEEF, *continued*															
Spaghetti with Meat Sauce, 123	4	460	29	36	20	80	640	44	26	46	20	18	34	4	34
Spicy Beef, 119	4	475	23	35	27	80	605	34	8	6	12	16	26	4	22
Stuffed Acorn Squash, 127	4	475	26	38	26	80	270	40	100	18	18	14	30	6	22
Stuffed Green Peppers, 125	6	335	22	21	19	70	700	34	36	100	16	16	24	14	30
Vegetable-Beef Soup, 130	4	335	25	14	20	80	670	38	100	18	10	14	28	6	28
PORK															
Apricot Pork Patties, 146	4	280	24	19	11	80	200	36	0	0	36	18	22	2	8
Bratwurst and Sauerkraut, 151	6	315	12	19	22	45	1330	18	2	16	26	8	12	8	18
Burritos, 154	8	315	13	27	18	15	690	20	12	2	8	8	6	12	8
Canadian Bacon with Sweet Potatoes, 151	6	240	21	29	5	40	1445	30	100	42	48	10	30	2	8
Currant-glazed Grilled Pork Ribs, 140	4	570	39	11	40	160	410	60	4	2	36	30	36	6	14
Curried Ham with Pear Chutney, 148	4	205	28	1	9	65	1540	42	2	0	50	16	28	0	6
German Pork Salad, 154	4	340	18	7	27	60	100	26	48	40	40	24	26	2	10
Ginger Pork with Nectarines, 141	4	525	30	39	28	80	615	46	4	42	36	22	42	2	16
Glazed Ham, 148	10	250	34	7	8	75	1810	52	0	0	60	20	34	0	6
Green Chili, 144	4	210	24	8	9	80	520	36	16	32	32	18	26	4	12
Green Pea Soup with Ham, 150	4	260	16	22	12	30	985	24	22	8	34	18	16	12	10
Grilled Ham with Plum Glaze, 147	12	195	28	5	6	65	1505	42	0	0	50	16	28	0	6
Grilled Italian Sausage Kabobs, 152	4	210	10	7	16	35	355	14	12	42	24	8	12	4	8
Grilled Pork and Fruit Kabobs, 145	6	600	17	98	15	55	50	26	38	4	30	22	30	4	22
Grilled Pork Tenderloins, 137	6	320	21	3	22	80	230	32	0	8	42	16	24	0	6
Ham with Beans and Pineapple, 151	5	270	16	48	3	15	600	25	4	10	24	10	18	4	14
Ham with Mustard Fruits, 148	8	335	29	27	12	65	1630	44	22	2	54	18	30	2	8
Italian Sausage Goulash, 128	6	390	14	36	21	30	800	20	22	22	42	18	28	4	18
Lasagne, 152	8	370	21	14	25	70	1230	32	16	0	10	16	8	24	6

PER SERVING OR UNIT **NUTRITION INFORMATION** RECIPE, PAGE	Servings per recipe	Calories	Protein (grams)	Carbohydrate (grams)	Fat (grams)	Cholesterol (milligrams)	Sodium (milligrams)	PERCENT U.S. RECOMMENDED DAILY ALLOWANCE Protein	Vitamin A	Vitamin C	Thiamin	Riboflavin	Niacin	Calcium	Iron

PORK, *continued*

Recipe, page															
Linguine with Ham, 149	4	320	16	37	12	30	465	22	4	4	22	14	12	18	8
Open-face Ham and Mushroom Sandwiches, 155	4	275	18	20	14	45	730	28	14	8	22	28	20	22	10
Orange-spiced Pork Chops, 138	4	325	18	16	20	70	190	26	2	24	44	18	20	2	4
Pepper Pork with Noodles, 141	6	365	29	32	12	120	385	44	12	34	40	22	28	6	18
Pork and Carrots with Pasta, 142	4	340	29	34	9	80	370	42	100	6	42	22	28	4	16
Pork with Chinese Vegetables, 147	4	245	16	13	14	50	700	24	6	12	28	14	20	2	10
Pork Chops with Apple Stuffing, 138	4	405	19	18	28	70	380	28	8	0	44	18	22	2	6
Pork Paprika with Sauerkraut, 146	4	380	29	31	16	90	850	44	26	14	40	24	30	8	24
Pork and Pea Pods, 145	4	360	26	14	22	80	35	40	6	16	58	24	34	2	14
Pork and Rice Casserole, 146	4	390	20	31	20	65	1120	30	6	42	44	20	26	2	12
Sweet-and-Sour Pork Tenderloin, 137	4	365	19	61	3	50	920	28	4	4	46	20	22	2	14
Szechuan Pork, 142	4	600	33	49	31	80	765	50	34	64	64	42	52	16	22

VEAL

Veal with Artichokes, 157	4	305	29	7	18	100	290	44	6	4	6	20	22	28	14
Veal with Sour Cream, 155	4	300	24	7	19	95	235	36	10	2	6	16	26	4	16

LAMB

Lamb with Lemon Sauce, 158	2	400	41	8	22	140	495	62	8	4	16	26	44	2	18
Lamb Patties with Vegetables, 157	4	265	22	6	16	85	325	34	4	36	10	16	24	2	10
Lamb Stroganoff, 126	4	435	25	21	28	130	950	38	100	4	14	20	26	8	12
Meatballs with Mint, 158	4	395	24	34	18	150	125	36	0	0	10	16	24	2	14

EGGS

Anytime Scrambled Eggs, 163	2	175	13	3	12	560	430	28	10	0	6	20	0	8	12
Bacon-Cheddar Frittata, 162	6	205	13	1	15	255	305	28	12	2	4	14	2	16	8

RECIPE, PAGE	Servings per recipe	Calories	Protein (grams)	Carbohydrate (grams)	Fat (grams)	Cholesterol (milligrams)	Sodium (milligrams)	PERCENT U.S. RECOMMENDED DAILY ALLOWANCE Protein	Vitamin A	Vitamin C	Thiamin	Riboflavin	Niacin	Calcium	Iron

PER SERVING OR UNIT

NUTRITION INFORMATION

EGGS, *continued*

RECIPE, PAGE	Servings	Calories	Protein	Carb	Fat	Chol	Sodium	Protein	Vit A	Vit C	Thiamin	Riboflavin	Niacin	Calcium	Iron
Cheddar Omelet, 162	1	460	26	2	38	870	805	38	30	0	8	32	0	28	18
Cheese and Egg Pie, 166	6	260	13	10	18	390	585	28	22	4	22	32	18	12	12
Egg Foo Yong Casserole, 166	4	185	12	15	9	420	1020	28	12	24	6	18	4	6	16
Eggs with Tomatoes and Bell Peppers, 163	4	260	15	11	18	570	570	22	36	80	12	26	2	10	18
Fluffy Eggs with Broccoli, 163	4	275	20	9	18	645	815	44	62	42	12	28	2	22	18
Garden Harvest Frittata, 161	4	130	9	9	7	285	210	18	100	14	8	12	2	10	8
Herb Omelet, 162	1	345	19	2	28	840	630	40	24	0	8	26	0	8	16
Mexican Eggs with Chilies, 164	6	280	17	11	19	175	310	24	14	6	4	22	2	42	6
Vegetable–Egg Salad Sandwiches, 164	4	260	12	16	18	205	470	26	28	20	6	14	4	16	10
Western Omelet, 162	1	360	19	4	29	840	665	28	26	10	10	28	0	8	18

CHEESE

RECIPE, PAGE	Servings	Calories	Protein	Carb	Fat	Chol	Sodium	Protein	Vit A	Vit C	Thiamin	Riboflavin	Niacin	Calcium	Iron
Beer-Cheese Soup, 172	4	455	20	18	33	70	1040	44	30	2	6	30	4	58	2
Cheese and Tomato Pie in Rice Crust, 170	6	275	14	25	14	210	500	20	12	2	10	26	6	28	8
Macaroni and Cheese, 170	4	660	24	61	35	60	1300	52	28	0	24	30	14	46	12
Macaroni and Cheese with Franks, 170	4	380	29	62	46	80	1790	44	28	0	28	34	20	46	16
Macaroni Pie with Garlic Tomato Sauce, 169	6	310	15	33	13	115	520	20	15	20	15	15	8	15	10
Rich Cauliflower Soup, 172	4	270	11	4	23	50	820	24	18	26	2	12	0	30	2
Ricotta Shells, 171	4	310	17	29	14	105	525	36	24	4	10	16	8	32	8
Sausage and Cheese Strata, 168	6	380	21	23	23	235	685	46	12	0	16	20	4	38	6
Spinach-Cheese Pie, 169	6	210	16	14	10	115	620	34	82	12	10	20	4	28	8
Swiss Cheese Fondue, 168	3	440	24	19	25	70	410	52	14	0	4	18	2	74	4
Swiss Cheese–Veggie Sandwiches, 173	6	150	7	10	9	20	270	16	8	8	4	6	2	20	2

VEGETABLES AND SALADS

If you crave perfectly cooked, crisp-tender, intensely colored vegetables, your microwave is your best friend. Not only a time-saver, although it does cook a baked potato in only 4 minutes, the microwave also saves nutrients since little or no water is needed. Because you needn't add butter or oil either, vegetables remain deliciously unfattening, too. Most cooked vegetables are as delicious at room temperature or chilled as they are hot.

Just a few tips to keep in mind for flawless vegetables every time in next-to-no time:

- For whole vegetables like squash and potatoes, simply pierce the skin with a fork or knife to prevent steam buildup from bursting the skin of the vegetable.

- For cut-up vegetables, be sure the pieces are approximately the same size to ensure even cooking.

- When cooking an assortment of vegetables, arrange large or dense vegetables toward the outside of the plate, tender, small pieces in the center, and they'll all be done at the same time. Summer squash, asparagus, bell peppers, mushrooms and other tender vegetables should be placed in the center, with carrots, broccoli, green beans, cabbage and the like toward the outside of the dish.

- Season vegetables after microwaving. Salting them first, without dissolving the salt in water, may leave brown spots. You'll be surprised how little salt they need after microwaving.

- Cooked vegetables are only as good as the raw product, so we've included what to look for in the market as well as how to prepare and serve them.

Colorful Dilled Vegetables (page 194)

ARTICHOKES, GLOBE

4 ARTICHOKES YIELD 4 SERVINGS; 75 CALORIES PER SERVING

When Shopping: Look for plump globes that are heavy in relation to size. Globes should be compact, inner leaves fresh and green with no signs of shriveling.

To Prepare: Remove any discolored leaves and the small leaves at base of artichoke; trim stem even with base of artichoke. Cutting straight across, slice 1 inch off top; discard top. Snip off points of the remaining leaves with scissors. Rinse artichoke under cold water.

To Microwave: Place 1 cup water, 1 teaspoon lemon juice, 1 small clove garlic, cut into fourths, and artichokes in 3-quart casserole. Cover tightly and microwave on high 14 to 20 minutes, rotating casserole ½ turn after 7 minutes, until leaves pull out easily. Remove artichokes carefully (use tongs or two large spoons); place upside down to drain.

To Serve:

- Dip leaves in mayonnaise, lemon butter or Hollandaise Sauce (page 322).
- Drizzle with melted margarine or butter.

• • • • • • • • • •

ARTICHOKES, JERUSALEM

4 ARTICHOKES YIELD 4 SERVINGS; 105 CALORIES PER SERVING.

When Shopping: Look for smooth, firm tubers with the fewest protrusions (knobs). Tubers should be light colored and free of blotches, green-tinged areas and sprouting.

To Prepare: Scrub artichokes; pare thinly. Cut into ¼-inch slices; place in cold water with small amount of lemon juice before cooking to prevent discoloration.

To Microwave: Place artichokes and ¼ cup water in 1½-quart casserole. Cover tightly and microwave on high 6 to 12 minutes, stirring every 5 minutes, until crisp-tender. Let stand covered 5 minutes; drain.

To Serve:

- Mash and mix together with mashed potatoes or turnips.
- Mix hot cooked artichokes with hot cooked green beans, and drizzle with melted butter.
- Use uncooked as garnish for soups.
- Serve uncooked slices cold with dips as a snack.

• • • • • • • • • •

ASPARAGUS

1½ POUNDS YIELD 4 SERVINGS; 45 CALORIES PER SERVING.

When Shopping: Look for smooth, tender, medium-size green spears with closed tips.

To Prepare: Break off tough ends as far down as stalks snap easily. Wash asparagus. Remove scales if sandy or tough. (If necessary, remove sand particles with a vegetable brush.) Leave spears whole or cut into 1-inch pieces.

To Microwave: For spears, arrange asparagus with tips toward center, in square dish, 8 × 8 × 2 inches; add ¼ cup water. Cover tightly and microwave on high 6 to 9 minutes, rotating dish ½ turn after 3 minutes, until crisp-tender. Let stand covered 1 minute; drain.

For pieces, place asparagus in 1½-quart casserole; add ¼ cup water. Cover tightly and microwave on high 6 to 9 minutes, stirring after 3 minutes, until crisp-tender. Let stand covered 1 minute; drain.

To Serve:

- Chopped fresh dill weed, marjoram or savory brings out the springtime flavor of asparagus.
- Hollandaise Sauce (page 322) spooned over asparagus is a special seasonal treat.

ASPARAGUS WITH CHEDDAR SAUCE

MICROWAVE TIME: 12 to 17 minutes
STAND TIME: 5 minutes

Crunchy Herb Topping (below)
1½ pounds asparagus*
Cheddar Cheese Sauce (page 323)

1.   Prepare Crunchy Herb Topping. Prepare and microwave asparagus spears as directed (page 181)—except decrease microwave time to 5 to 8 minutes or until almost tender. Let stand covered 5 minutes.

2.   Prepare Cheddar Cheese Sauce. Drain asparagus; pour cheese sauce over top. Sprinkle with Crunchy Herb Topping.   **6 servings;** 185 calories per serving.

Two packages (10 ounces each) frozen asparagus spears, cooked and drained, can be substituted for the fresh asparagus.

Crunchy Herb Topping

½ cup crushed corn puff cereal
2 tablespoons margarine or butter
1 teaspoon chopped fresh or ¼ teaspoon dried marjoram

1.   Mix all ingredients in small bowl.

2.   Microwave uncovered on high 3 to 4 minutes, stirring every minute, until toasted.

ASPARAGUS WITH ORANGE SAUCE

While you might expect lemon-flavored Hollandaise sauce on your asparagus, the citrusy sweetness of orange scented with nutmeg is a pleasant surprise.

MICROWAVE TIME: 7 to 10 minutes
STAND TIME: 1 minute

1½ pounds asparagus*
3 tablespoons margarine or butter
2 tablespoons orange juice
Dash of ground nutmeg

1.   Prepare and microwave asparagus spears as directed (page 181).

2.   Place margarine, orange juice and nutmeg in 1-cup measure. Cover loosely and microwave on high 45 to 60 seconds or until margarine is melted; stir. Pour over asparagus.   **4 servings;** 105 calories per serving.

Two packages (10 ounces each) frozen asparagus spears, cooked and drained, can be substituted for the fresh asparagus.

ASPARAGUS WITH WATER CHESTNUTS

MICROWAVE TIME:　　9 to 12 minutes

2 pounds asparagus
1 can (8 ounces) sliced water chestnuts, drained
¼ cup margarine or butter
½ teaspoon salt
⅛ teaspoon pepper

1. Prepare asparagus as directed (page 181)—except cut diagonally. Place asparagus and remaining ingredients in 2-quart casserole.

2. Cover tightly and microwave on high 9 to 12 minutes, stirring every 4 minutes, until asparagus is crisp-tender. **6 servings (about ½ cup each);** 120 calories per serving.

Asparagus with Water Chestnuts

BEANS—GREEN, WAX

1 POUND YIELDS 4 SERVINGS; 40 CALORIES PER SERVING.

When Shopping: Look for bright, smooth, crisp pods. Just-picked beans will feel pliable and velvety.

To Prepare: Wash beans; remove ends. Cut crosswise into 1-inch pieces.

To Microwave: Place beans and ½ cup water in 1½-quart casserole. Cover tightly and microwave on high 9 to 14 minutes, stirring every 5 minutes, until tender. Let stand covered 5 minutes; drain.

To Serve:
- Drizzle with a mustard-flavored vinaigrette.
- Toss beans with lemon juice, and top with crumbled cooked bacon.
- Sprinkle with chopped fresh basil, marjoram, savory or thyme.

• • • • • • • • • •

GREEN BEANS WITH ALMONDS

MICROWAVE TIME: 12 to 19 minutes

1 pound green beans*
¼ cup slivered almonds
1 tablespoon margarine or butter
1 teaspoon chopped fresh or ¼ teaspoon dried thyme
¼ teaspoon salt

1. Prepare green beans as directed (above). Place almonds and margarine in 1-quart casserole. Microwave uncovered on high 3 to 5 minutes, stirring every minute, until golden. Remove almonds from casserole.

2. Place green beans and thyme in same casserole. Cover tightly and microwave on high 9 to 14 minutes, stirring after 3 minutes, until beans are tender. Stir in salt and almonds.   **4 servings (about ⅔ cup each);** 95 calories per serving.

*One package (9 ounces) frozen cut green beans can be substituted for the fresh green beans.

• • • • • • • • • •

GREEN BEANS VINAIGRETTE

MICROWAVE TIME: 10 to 14 minutes

¼ cup water
3 cups fresh or frozen cut green beans
1 small onion, sliced and separated into rings
3 tablespoons vegetable oil
1 tablespoon wine vinegar
2 teaspoons chopped fresh or ½ teaspoon dried oregano
1 teaspoon Dijon mustard
½ teaspoon salt
Freshly ground pepper

1. Place water, green beans and onion in 1½-quart casserole. Cover tightly and microwave on high 10 to 14 minutes, stirring every 4 minutes, until beans are tender; drain.

2. Shake remaining ingredients in tightly covered container; toss with beans.   **4 servings (about ⅔ cups each);** 135 calories per serving.

Hot Pepper Limas

HOT PEPPER LIMAS

MICROWAVE TIME: 10 to 14 minutes

2 tablespoons water
¼ teaspoon salt
1 package (10 ounces) frozen baby lima beans
½ cup cut-up process American cheese spread loaf with jalapeño peppers
2 tablespoons milk

1.   Place water, salt and lima beans in 1-quart casserole. Cover tightly and microwave on high 9 to 12 minutes, stirring every 4 minutes, until beans are tender.

2.   Stir in cheese and milk. Cover tightly and microwave 1 to 2 minutes or until cheese is melted; stir.   **4 servings (about ½ cup each);** 165 calories per serving.

DILLED LIMA BEANS WITH WATER CHESTNUTS

MICROWAVE TIME:	8 to 11 minutes
STAND TIME:	5 minutes

3 tablespoons water
2 teaspoons chopped fresh or ½ teaspoon dried dill weed
¼ teaspoon salt
1 package (10 ounce) frozen lima beans
1 can (8 ounces) sliced water chestnuts, drained

1. Place all ingredients in 1-quart casserole.

2. Cover tightly and microwave on high 8 to 11 minutes, stirring after 4 minutes, until lima beans are tender. Let stand covered 5 minutes. **4 servings (about ½ cup each);** 75 calories per serving.

• • • • • • • • • •

BEETS

1¼ POUNDS (ABOUT 5 MEDIUM) YIELD 4 SERVINGS; 65 CALORIES PER SERVING.

When Shopping: Look for firm, round, smooth beets of a deep red color; unwilted tops.

To Prepare: Cut off all but 1 inch of beet tops. Wash beets and leave whole with root ends attached. Pierce each beet with knife.

To Microwave: Place beets and ½ cup water in 1½-quart casserole. Cover tightly and microwave on high 18 to 25 minutes, stirring every 5 minutes, until tender. Let stand covered 5 minutes. Run cold water over beets; slip off skin and remove root ends.

To Serve:
• Slice, dice or cut cooked beets into julienne strips.

• Dot with margarine or butter; sprinkle with salt and pepper.
• Sprinkle with red wine or raspberry vinegar to bring out the sweetness of fresh beets.

• • • • • • • • • •

BEETS WITH GARDEN HERBS

The earthy flavor and vibrant color of fresh beets are enhanced by the addition of spritely green herbs. The microwave makes beets quick to fix and a snap to peel—the skins slip right off after cooking.

MICROWAVE TIME:	24 to 32 minutes
STAND TIME:	5 minutes

1¼ pounds beets (about 5 medium)*
2 tablespoons margarine or butter
1 teaspoon chopped fresh or ¼ teaspoon dried savory
1 teaspoon chopped fresh or ¼ teaspoon dried basil
¼ teaspoon salt

1. Prepare and microwave beets as directed (left); cut into slices.

2. Place beets and remaining ingredients in 1½-quart casserole. Cover tightly and microwave on high 6 to 7 minutes, stirring after 3 minutes, until hot. **4 servings (about ½ cup each);** 100 calories per serving.

One can (16 ounces) sliced beets, drained, can be substituted for the fresh beets.

Beets with Garden Herbs

HARVARD BEETS

MICROWAVE TIME: 22 to 31 minutes
STAND TIME: 5 minutes

1¼ pounds fresh beets (about 5 medium)*
1 tablespoon sugar
1 tablespoon cornstarch
¼ teaspoon salt
Dash of pepper
½ cup water
2 tablespoons vinegar

1. Prepare and microwave beets as directed (page 186).

2. Mix sugar, cornstarch, salt and pepper in 1-quart casserole. Gradually stir in water and vinegar. Microwave uncovered on high 2 to 3 minutes, stirring every minute, until mixture thickens and boils.

3. Stir in beets. Cover tightly and microwave 2 to 3 minutes or until beets are hot.
4 servings (about ½ cup each); 80 calories per serving.

One can (16 ounces) sliced beets, drained and liquid reserved, can be substituted for the fresh beets. Substitute beet liquid for the water.

•••••••••••

BROCCOLI

1½ POUNDS YIELD 4 SERVINGS; 55 CALORIES PER SERVING.

When Shopping: Look for firm, compact dark green clusters. Avoid thick, tough stems.

To Prepare: Trim off large leaves; remove tough ends of lower stems (spears should be about 4 inches long). Wash broccoli. Peel stems if desired. For spears, cut lengthwise into stalks about ½ inch wide. For pieces, cut lengthwise into stalks, then cut crosswise into 1-inch lengths.

To Microwave: For spears, arrange broccoli, flowerets toward center, in square dish, 8 × 8 × 2 inches. Add 1 cup hot water. Cover tightly and microwave on high 9 to 12 minutes, rotating dish ¼ turn every 4 minutes, until almost tender. Let stand covered 5 minutes; drain.

For pieces, place broccoli in 2-quart casserole. Add 1 cup hot water. Cover tightly and microwave on high 9 to 12 minutes, stirring every 4 minutes, until almost tender. Let stand covered 5 minutes; drain.

To Serve:
• Broccoli is wonderful with eggs; use in omelets or quiches.
• Drizzle with Lemon-Dill Sauce (page 321).
• Sprinkle with lemon pepper, ground nutmeg or oregano.

•••••••••••

BROCCOLI WITH CHEESE SAUCE

MICROWAVE TIME: 10 to 14 minutes

1 package (10 ounces) frozen chopped broccoli
½ can (11-ounce size) condensed Cheddar cheese soup (⅔ cup)
½ cup French fried onions

1. Place broccoli in 1-quart casserole. Cover tightly and microwave on high 8 to 11 minutes, stirring after 5 minutes, until tender.

2. Stir in soup. Cover and microwave 2 to 3 minutes or until hot. Sprinkle with onions.
4 servings (about ½ cup each); 85 calories per serving.

BROCCOLI MORNAY

Broccoli and cheese are a classic flavor combination and so traditional Mornay Sauce with its two cheeses is a natural enchancement here. With the microwave, you can make the sauce in three minutes flat.

MICROWAVE TIME: 10 to 13 minutes
STAND TIME: 5 minutes

1½ pounds broccoli
Mornay Sauce (below)

1. Prepare and microwave broccoli spears as directed (page 188). Cover to keep warm.

2. Prepare Mornay Sauce. Serve over broccoli. **6 servings;** 75 calories per serving.

Mornay Sauce

1 tablespoon margarine or butter
1 tablespoon all-purpose flour
⅛ teaspoon salt
Dash of ground nutmeg
¾ cup milk
⅓ cup shredded Swiss cheese
2 tablespoons grated Parmesan cheese

1. Place margarine in 2-cup measure. Microwave uncovered on high 30 to 60 seconds or until melted. Stir in flour, salt and nutmeg until smooth. Gradually stir in milk.

2. Microwave uncovered 2 to 3 minutes, stirring every minute, until mixture thickens and boils. Stir in cheeses until melted.

DILLED BROCCOLI

MICROWAVE TIME: 10 to 13 minutes
STAND TIME: 5 minutes

1½ pounds broccoli
2 tablespoons margarine or butter
2 teaspoons chopped fresh or ½ teaspoon dried dill weed
Dash of salt
Dash of pepper
2 tablespoons half-and-half

1. Prepare and microwave broccoli spears as directed (page 188).

2. Place margarine, dill weed, salt and pepper in 1-cup measure. Microwave uncovered on high about 45 seconds or until bubbly; stir in half-and-half. Pour over broccoli. **4 servings;** 110 calories per serving.

• • • • • • • • • • •

BRUSSELS SPROUTS

1 POUND YIELDS 4 SERVINGS; 55 CALORIES PER SERVING.

When Shopping: Look for unblemished, bright green sprouts; compact heads with tightly wrapped leaves.

To Prepare: Remove any discolored leaves. Cut off stem ends; wash sprouts. Cut larger sprouts in half.

To Microwave: Place Brussels sprouts and ¼ cup water in 1½-quart casserole. Cover tightly and microwave on high 8 to 13 minutes, stirring after 5 minutes, until tender. Let stand covered 5 minutes; drain.

To Serve:
• Sprinkle with garlic salt, caraway seed, cumin, marjoram or savory.
• Toss with toasted hazelnuts.
• Top with crumbled cooked bacon.

LEMONY SPROUTS AND CARROTS

MICROWAVE TIME: 9 to 10 minutes

2 tablespoons water
½ teaspoon salt
2 teaspoons chopped fresh or ½ teaspoon
   dried basil
1 package (8 ounces) frozen Brussels
   sprouts
2 small carrots, cut into ¼-inch slices
2 tablespoons margarine or butter, melted
1 tablespoon lemon juice

1. Place water, salt, basil, Brussels sprouts and carrots in 1-quart casserole. Cover tightly and microwave on high 8 to 9 minutes, stirring after 4 minutes, until vegetables are tender; drain.

2. Place margarine and lemon juice in 1-cup measure. Microwave uncovered on high 30 to 60 seconds or until margarine is melted; drizzle over vegetables. **4 servings (about ½ cup each);** 100 calories per servings.

Chinese Cabbage and Broccoli (page 191), Lemony Sprouts and Carrots, Savory Tomatoes (page 221)

CABBAGE, CHINESE

1 POUND (1 MEDIUM HEAD) YIELDS 4 SERVINGS; 10 CALORIES PER SERVING.

When Shopping: Look for crisp, green heads with no signs of browning. The leaves can be firm or leafy.

To Prepare: Remove root ends. Wash cabbage; shred (about 6 cups shredded).

To Microwave: Place cabbage and ¼ cup water in 2-quart casserole. Cover tightly and microwave on high 4 to 7 minutes, stirring after 2 minutes, until crisp-tender. Let stand covered 1 minute; drain.

To Serve:
• Top with grated Parmesan cheese or buttered bread crumbs.
• Stir-fry uncooked cabbage with broccoli and Chinese pea pods.
• Drizzle with Hoisin sauce.

• • • • • • • • • • •

CHINESE CABBAGE WITH BROCCOLI

MICROWAVE TIME: 11 to 13 minutes

1 pound Chinese cabbage
1 pound broccoli
2 medium onions, sliced
1 can (8 ounces) sliced water chestnuts, drained
2 tablespoons water
1 tablespoon vegetable oil
2 tablespoons soy sauce

1. Prepare Chinese cabbage as directed (above), except slice. Prepare broccoli pieces as directed (page 188), except use only flowerets (about 3 cups).

2. Mix vegetables and remaining ingredients except soy sauce in 3-quart casserole.

3. Cover tightly and microwave on high 11 to 13 minutes, stirring after 5 minutes, until hot; drain. Toss with soy sauce. **8 servings (about ¾ cup each);** 65 calories per serving.

• • • • • • • • • • •

CABBAGE— GREEN, RED

1 POUND (1 SMALL HEAD) YIELDS 4 SERVINGS; 25 CALORIES PER SERVING.

When Shopping: Look for firm heads that are heavy in relation to size. Outer leaves should have good color and be free of blemishes.

To Prepare: Remove outside leaves; wash cabbage. Cut cabbage into 4 wedges and trim core to within ¼ inch of leaves, or shred cabbage and discard core.

To Microwave: For shredded, place shredded cabbage and ¼ cup water in 2-quart casserole. Cover tightly and microwave on high 8 to 10 minutes, stirring after 4 minutes, until crisp-tender. Let stand covered 5 minutes; drain.

For wedges, arrange cabbage with core ends toward outside edges of 2-quart casserole; add ½ cup water. Cover tightly and microwave on high 10 to 14 minutes, rotating casserole ½ turn after 5 minutes, until crisp-tender. Let stand covered 5 minutes; drain.

To Serve:
• Sprinkle with caraway seed, oregano, ground nutmeg or dill weed.
• Top with whipping (heavy) cream or Garlic Tomato Sauce (page 321).

CABBAGE WITH BELL PEPPER AND CHEESE

MICROWAVE TIME: 13 to 19 minutes
STAND TIME: 5 minutes

¾ to 1 pound green cabbage (1 small head)
¼ cup chopped red or green bell pepper
1 small clove garlic, finely chopped
2 tablespoons margarine or butter
1 tablespoon all-purpose flour
¼ teaspoon salt
Dash of pepper
½ cup milk
¼ cup shredded Cheddar cheese (1 ounce)

1. Prepare and microwave cabbage wedges as directed (page 191).

2. Place bell pepper, garlic and margarine in 2-cup measure. Microwave uncovered on high 1 to 2 minutes or until bell pepper is crisp-tender. Stir in flour, salt and pepper thoroughly; gradually stir in milk. Microwave uncovered 2 to 3 minutes, stirring every minute, until mixture boils and thickens.

3. Pour sauce over cabbage; sprinkle with cheese.   **4 servings;** 130 calories per serving.

Cabbage with Bell Pepper and Cheese

SAVORY CABBAGE

Fresh, chopped oregano adds life to an old-fashioned favorite, shredded cabbage tenderized in milk and butter and topped with grated Parmesan. This is comfort food with an update.

MICROWAVE TIME: 8 to 10 minutes

¾ to 1 pound green cabbage (1 small head)
⅓ cup milk
1 tablespoon magarine or butter
1 teaspoon chopped fresh or ¼ teaspoon dried oregano
¼ teaspoon salt
Dash of pepper
Grated Parmesan cheese

1. Prepare and shred cabbage as directed (page 191). Place cabbage and milk in 2-quart casserole. Cover tightly and microwave on high 8 to 10 minutes, stirring after 4 minutes, until crisp-tender.

2. Stir in margarine, oregano, salt and pepper. Serve with cheese. **6 servings (about ½ cup each)**; 40 calories per serving.

• • • • • • • • • •

CELERY

1¼ POUNDS (1 MEDIUM BUNCH) YIELD 4 SERVINGS; 35 CALORIES PER SERVING.

When Shopping: Look for crisp, unblemished stalks; fresh leaves.

To Prepare: Remove leaves and any coarse strings. Trim off root ends; wash celery. Cut stalks into 1-inch pieces (about 4 cups).

To Microwave: Place celery and 2 tablespoons water in 1½-quart casserole. Cover tightly and microwave on high 7 to 11 minutes, stirring after 4 minutes, until tender. Let stand covered 1 minute; drain.

To Serve:
• Sprinkle with grated Parmesan cheese or shredded Cheddar cheese.
• Serve with a vinaigrette or Italian dressing.

• • • • • • • • • •

CARROTS

1 POUND (6 TO 7 MEDIUM) YIELDS 4 SERVINGS; 50 CALORIES PER SERVING.

When Shopping: Look for firm, nicely shaped carrots of good color.

To Prepare: Pare carrots and remove ends. Cut carrots crosswise into ¼-inch slices.

To Microwave: Place carrots and ¼ cup water in 1-quart casserole. Cover tightly and microwave on high 6 to 8 minutes, stirring after 4 minutes, until tender. Let stand covered 1 minute; drain.

To Serve:
• Sprinkle with chopped fresh parsley, mint or chives or chopped green onion.
• Toss with melted margarine or butter and honey. Top with plain yogurt and chopped fresh dill weed.

CARROTS AND CAULIFLOWER

MICROWAVE TIME: 8 to 10 minutes
STAND TIME: 5 minutes

3 medium carrots
1½ cups small cauliflowerets (about
    ½ pound)
2 tablespoons margarine or butter
½ teaspoon salt
⅛ teaspoon ground nutmeg

1. Prepare carrots as directed (page 193).
Place carrots and remaining ingredients in
1-quart casserole.

2. Cover tightly and microwave on high 8
to 10 minutes, stirring after 4 minutes, until
vegetables are crisp-tender. Let stand covered 5 minutes. Sprinkle with chopped fresh
parsley if desired. **4 servings (about ½ cup
each);** 90 calories per serving.

• • • • • • • • • •

DILLED VEGETABLE PLATTER

MICROWAVE TIME: 10 to 16 minutes
STAND TIME: 5 minutes

2 small carrots
1 small yellow squash
1 cup small whole mushrooms (about
    4 ounces)
1 cup small broccoli flowerets
1 cup small cauliflowerets
1 teaspoon chopped fresh or ¼ teaspoon
    dried dill weed
Wine-Cheese Sauce (page 197)

1. Prepare carrots as directed (page 193)—
except cut into ⅛-inch slices. Prepare squash
as directed (page 217)—except cut into ⅛-inch
slices.

2. Mound mushrooms in center of 10-inch
plate. Arrange squash around mushrooms.
Arrange broccoli, cauliflowerets and carrots
around edge of plate. Sprinkle with dill weed.

3. Cover tightly and microwave on high 7
to 11 minutes, rotating plate ½ turn after 3
minutes, until vegetables are crisp-tender.
Let stand covered 5 minutes; keep warm.

4. Prepare Wine-Cheese Sauce; serve with
vegetables.   **4 servings (about 1 cup each);** 160
calories per serving.

• • • • • • • • • •

COLORFUL DILLED VEGETABLES

MICROWAVE TIME: 13 to 15 minutes

5 medium carrots
¼ cup water
½ teaspoon salt
1 small onion, sliced and separated into
    rings
1 teaspoon chopped fresh or ½ teaspoon
    dried dill weed
1 package (10 ounces) frozen green peas
1 medium red or green bell pepper, cut
    into ¼-inch strips

1. Prepare carrots as directed (page 193)—
except cut into ½-inch diagonal slices. Place
water, salt, carrots, onion and dill weed in
2-quart casserole. Cover tightly and microwave on high 6 minutes.

2. Stir in peas and bell pepper. Cover tightly
and microwave 7 to 9 minutes, stirring after
5 minutes, until vegetables are tender; drain.
6 servings (about ⅔ cup each); 70 calories per
serving.

Dilled Vegetable Platter

Herbed Carrots and Zucchini

HERBED CARROTS AND ZUCCHINI

MICROWAVE TIME: 9 to 12 minutes

3 medium carrots
3 small onions, cut into fourths
2 tablespoons water
½ teaspoon salt
1 teaspoon chopped fresh or ¼ teaspoon dried dill weed
½ teaspoon chopped fresh or ⅛ teaspoon dried rosemary, crushed
2 small zucchini (about ½ pound)

1. Prepare carrots as directed (page 193). Place carrots and remaining ingredients except zucchini in 1½-quart casserole. Cover tightly and microwave on high 6 minutes.

2. Prepare zucchini as directed for Summer Squash (page 217)—except cut crosswise in half; cut each half lengthwise into fourths. Stir zucchini into carrots. Cover tightly and microwave 3 to 6 minutes or until vegetables are tender; drain. **6 servings (about ½ cup each);** 35 calories per serving.

CAULIFLOWER

2 POUNDS (1 MEDIUM HEAD) YIELD 4 SERVINGS; 60 CALORIES PER SERVING.

When Shopping: Look for clean, tightly closed flower clusters (the white portion); green outer leaves.

To Prepare: Remove outer leaves and stalk. Cut off any discoloration; wash cauliflower. Leave whole, cutting cone-shaped center from core, or separate into flowerets.

To Microwave: For whole, place cauliflower and ¼ cup water in 2-quart casserole. Cover tightly and microwave on high 12 to 14 minutes, rotating casserole ½ turn after 6 minutes, until tender. Let stand covered 1 minute; drain.

For cauliflowerets, place cauliflowerets and ¼ cup water in 2-quart casserole. Cover tightly and microwave on high 12 to 14 minutes, stirring after 6 minutes, until tender. Let stand covered 1 minute; drain.

To Serve:
- Buttered toasted whole wheat or rye bread crumbs add not only flavor but interesting color contrast.
- Sprinkle with chopped fresh basil, curry powder, celery seed or poppy seed.
- Top with grated Parmesan cheese or Cheddar Cheese Sauce (page 323).

CAULIFLOWER WITH WINE-CHEESE SAUCE

Crisp-tender cauliflower is a sure thing with the microwave. Cook the whole head in as little as 12 minutes. For the most even cooking, remove part of the core with a sharp knife. White wine and cheese create a 4-minute sauce reminiscent of a flavorful fondue.

MICROWAVE TIME:	16 to 19 minutes
STAND TIME:	1 minute

2 pounds cauliflower (1 medium head)
Wine-Cheese Sauce (below)

1. Prepare and microwave whole cauliflower as directed (left). Cover to keep warm.

2. Prepare Wine-Cheese Sauce. Pour over cauliflower. Sprinkle with paprika if desired. **4 servings (about 1 cup each); 155 calories per serving.**

Wine-Cheese Sauce

1 tablespoon margarine or butter
1 tablespoon all-purpose flour
½ teaspoon dry mustard
⅛ teaspoon salt
Dash of pepper
¼ cup half-and-half
¼ cup dry white wine
½ cup shredded sharp process American cheese (2 ounces)

1. Place margarine in 2-cup measure. Microwave uncovered on high 30 to 60 seconds or until melted. Stir in flour, mustard, salt and pepper until smooth. Gradually stir in half-and-half and wine (mixture may appear curdled).

2. Microwave uncovered 2 to 3 minutes, stirring every minute, until mixture thickens and boils. Stir in cheese. Microwave uncovered 30 to 60 seconds or until cheese is melted.

CORN

4 EARS YIELD 4 SERVINGS; 90 CALORIES PER SERVING.

When Shopping: Look for bright green, tight-fitting husks, fresh-looking silk, plump but not too large kernels.

To Prepare: Refrigerate unhusked corn until ready to use. (Corn is best when eaten as soon after picking as possible.) Husk ears and remove silk just before cooking, or microwave in the husk.

To Microwave: For unhusked corn, microwave on a paper towel as directed, without water. For 4 ears, place corn and ¼ cup water in square dish, 8 × 8 × 2 inches. Cover tightly and microwave on high 9 to 14 minutes, rearranging ears after 5 minutes, until tender. Let stand covered 5 minutes.

For 2 ears, place corn and ¼ cup water in square dish, 8 × 8 × 2 inches. Cover tightly and microwave on high 5 to 7 minutes, rearranging ears after 3 minutes, until tender. Let stand covered 5 minutes.

To Serve:
• Remove husks carefully from hot corn.
• Dip ears into herb-flavored melted butter.
• Sprinkle with chili powder, chopped fresh basil or celery seed.
• Cut kernels from cooked corn, and mix with chopped bell pepper or chilies.

•••••••••••

GARLIC CORN WITH CHILIES

MICROWAVE TIME: 7 minutes

1 package (10 ounces) frozen whole kernel corn*
2 tablespoons chopped green chilies
1 tablespoon margarine or butter
1 tablespoon chopped pimiento
1 clove garlic, finely chopped
¼ teaspoon salt
⅛ teaspoon ground red pepper (cayenne)

1. Microwave corn as directed on package—except use 1-quart casserole; drain.

2. Stir in remaining ingredients. Cover tightly and microwave on high about 2 minutes or until hot. **4 servings (about ½ cup each);** 90 calories per serving.

Four ears corn on the cob, microwaved and kernels cut off the cob, can be substituted for the frozen corn.

•••••••••••

GREENS—BEET TOPS, CHICORY, ESCAROLE, MUSTARD GREENS, SPINACH

1 POUND YIELDS 4 SERVINGS; 25 CALORIES PER SERVING.

When Shopping: Look for tender, young, unblemished leaves of bright green color.

To Prepare: Remove root ends and imperfect leaves. Wash several times in water, lifting out of water each time; drain.

To Microwave: Place greens with just the water that clings to the leaves in 3-quart casserole. Cover tightly and microwave on high 8 to 10 minutes, stirring after 5 minutes, until tender. Let stand covered 1 minute; drain.

To Serve:
• Sprinkle with chopped, fresh dill weed, marjoram, mint or rosemary.
• Sprinkle with chopped cooked green onions or shallots.
• Serve with nutmeg-flavored white sauce or horseradish sauce.

SPINACH WITH BACON

MICROWAVE TIME: 12 to 15 minutes

3 slices bacon, cut into 1-inch pieces
1 package (10 ounces) frozen chopped
   spinach
1 small onion, thinly sliced
¼ teaspoon salt
Dash of pepper

1. Place bacon in 1-quart casserole. Cover and microwave on high 4 to 5 minutes or until crisp; drain bacon and reserve. Drain fat from casserole.

2. Place remaining ingredients in same casserole. Cover tightly and microwave on high 8 to 10 minutes, breaking up spinach and stirring after 4 minutes, until spinach is tender; drain. Sprinkle with bacon. **3 servings (about ½ cup each)**; 60 calories per serving.

• • • • • • • • • •

SPINACH AND BROCCOLI

MICROWAVE TIME: 14 to 16 minutes

2 tablespoons water
1 teaspoon salt
1 package (10 ounces) frozen chopped
   spinach
1 package (10 ounces) frozen chopped
   broccoli
1 tablespoon margarine or butter
1 tablespoon lemon juice

1. Place water, salt, spinach and broccoli in 1½-quart casserole. Cover tightly and microwave on high 14 to 16 minutes, breaking up and stirring after 8 minutes, until tender; drain.

2. Stir in margarine and lemon juice. **6 servings (about ½ cup each)**; 40 calories per serving.

ORIENTAL SPINACH

Garlic, ginger and soy sauce add an Oriental air to fresh, green spinach, but it still has under a hundred calories per serving.

MICROWAVE TIME: 10 to 13 minutes

1 pound spinach (about 12 cups)
1 tablespoon vegetable oil
1 teaspoon finely chopped gingerroot
1 small onion, chopped (about ¼ cup)
1 clove garlic, finely chopped
1 cup sliced mushrooms
1 can (8 ounces) sliced water chestnuts,
   drained
1 tablespoon soy sauce
1 teaspoon sugar

1. Prepare spinach as directed for greens (page 198). Mix oil, gingerroot, onion and garlic in 3-quart casserole. Cover tightly and microwave on high 4 to 6 minutes, stirring after 2 minutes, until onion is soft.

2. Stir in spinach and remaining ingredients. Cover tightly and microwave 6 to 7 minutes, stirring after 3 minutes, until spinach is hot and crisp-tender. **4 servings (about ¾ cup each)**; 95 calories per serving.

EGGPLANT

1½ POUNDS (1 MEDIUM) YIELD 4 SERVINGS; 30 CALORIES PER SERVING.

When Shopping: Look for smooth, glossy, taut-skinned eggplant that is free of blemishes or rust spots. Fuzzy green caps and stems should be intact and free of mold.

To Prepare: Just before cooking, wash eggplant and, if desired, pare. Cut into ¼-inch slices or ½-inch cubes.

To Microwave: For slices, overlap eggplant slices in a circle around edge of pie plate, 9 × 1¼ inches; add 2 tablespoons water. Cover tightly and microwave on high 5 to 7 minutes, rotating pie plate ½ turn after 3 minutes, until tender; drain.

For cubes, place eggplant and 2 tablespoons water in 1½-quart casserole. Cover tightly and microwave on high 8 to 10 minutes, stirring every 2 minutes, until tender; drain.

To Serve:
- Sprinkle with grated Parmesan cheese or shredded mozzarella cheese.
- Top with chopped tomato and cooked sliced onion.

•••••••••••

KOHLRABI

1½ POUNDS (6 TO 8 MEDIUM) YIELD 4 SERVINGS; 35 CALORIES PER SERVING.

When Shopping: Look for small or medium-size smooth bulbs with no blemishes. Smaller bulbs have more delicate flavor and texture. Leaves should be fresh and green.

To Prepare: Trim off root ends and vinelike stems. Wash and pare. Cut into ¼-inch slices.

To Microwave: Place kohlrabi and ¼ cup water in 1-quart casserole. Cover tightly and microwave on high 6 to 11 minutes, stirring after 3 minutes, until tender. Let stand covered 1 minute; drain.

To Serve:
- Stir in sour cream.
- Purée with margarine or butter and whipping (heavy) cream.
- Uncooked slices may be served with other vegetables and dips.

•••••••••••

LEEKS

2 POUNDS (6 MEDIUM) YIELD 4 SERVINGS; 140 CALORIES PER SERVING.

When Shopping: Look for white bulbs with pliable, crisp green tops. Bulbs less than 1½ inches in diameter are the most tender.

To Prepare: Remove green tops to within 2 inches of white part (save greens for soup or stew). Peel outside layer of bulbs. Wash leeks several times in cold water; drain. Cut large leeks lengthwise into fourths.

To Microwave: Place leeks and ¼ cup water in square dish, 8 × 8 × 2 inches. Cover tightly and microwave on high 6 to 11 minutes, rotating dish ½ turn after 3 minutes, until tender. Let stand covered 1 minute; drain.

To Serve:
- Top with Garlic Tomato Sauce (page 321), and serve with lemon wedges.
- Use as a garnish for roast beef.

MUSHROOMS

1 POUND YIELDS 4 SERVINGS; 30 CALORIES PER SERVING.

When Shopping: Look for creamy white to light brown caps, closed around the stems; if slightly open, gills should be tan.

To Prepare: Rinse mushrooms and trim off stem ends. Do not peel. Slice parallel to stem if desired.

To Microwave: Place mushrooms (sliced) in 1½-quart casserole. Cover tightly and microwave on high 5 to 6 minutes, stirring after 3 minutes, or until tender. Let stand covered 1 minute; drain.

To Serve:
• Toss with 1 to 2 tablespoons wine or melted butter.
• Sprinkle with fresh herbs or crumbled bacon.
• Top with Mozzarella Sauce (page 323) or spaghetti sauce.

• • • • • • • • • •

GARLIC MUSHROOMS

MICROWAVE TIME: 3 to 4 minutes

2 tablespoons margarine or butter
1½ teaspoons cornstarch
¼ teaspoon salt
8 ounces mushrooms, cut into ¼-inch slices (about 3 cups)
1 small clove garlic, finely chopped
Chopped fresh parsley

1. Place margarine, cornstarch and salt in 1-quart casserole; add mushrooms and garlic.

2. Cover tightly and microwave on high 3 to 4 minutes, stirring after 2 minutes, until hot. Sprinkle with parsley. **4 servings (about ¼ cup each);** 70 calories per serving.

ONIONS, SMALL— WHITE, YELLOW

1½ POUNDS (8 TO 10 SMALL) YIELD 4 SERVINGS; 60 CALORIES PER SERVING.

When Shopping: Look for firm, well-shaped onions with unblemished, papery skins and no sign of sprouting.

To Prepare: Peel onions under running cold water (to prevent eyes from watering).

To Microwave: Place onions and ¼ cup water in 2-quart casserole. Cover tightly and microwave on high 6 to 11 minutes, stirring after 4 minutes, until tender. Let stand covered 1 minute; drain.

To Serve:
• Sprinkle with chopped basil, oregano, thyme, rosemary, cilantro or ground ginger.
• Serve with Mornay Sauce (page 189).

Glazed Onions, Brandy Beef Steaks (page 117)

GLAZED ONIONS

Microwave Time: 9 to 11 minutes

8 small white or yellow onions (about
    1½ pounds)
¼ cup packed brown sugar
⅛ teaspoon ground cloves
1 tablespoons margarine or butter

1. Prepare onions as directed (page 202).
Place onions in 1½-quart casserole. Cover
tightly and microwave on high 8 to 10 minutes, stirring after 4 minutes, until tender.

2. Sprinkle with brown sugar and cloves;
dot with margarine. Cover and microwave
about 1 minute or until brown sugar and
margarine are melted; stir. **4 servings;** 135
calories per serving.

OKRA

1 POUND YIELDS 4 SERVINGS; 45 CALORIES PER SERVING.

When Shopping: Look for tender, plump, unblemished, bright green pods, less than 4 inches long.

To Prepare: Wash okra; remove ends and cut into ½-inch slices.

To Microwave: Place okra and ¼ cup water in 1½-quart casserole. Cover tightly and microwave on high 5 to 9 minutes, stirring after 3 minutes, until tender; drain. Let stand covered 1 minute.

To Serve:
• Add dash of vinegar or lemon juice.
• Mix with stewed tomatoes.
• Use in Southern-style gumbos and stews.

• • • • • • • • • •

OKRA WITH CORN AND TOMATOES

MICROWAVE TIME: 18 to 23 minutes

½ pound okra*
4 slices bacon, cut into ½-inch pieces
1 cup frozen whole kernel corn
½ cup chopped onion
¼ teaspoon salt
¼ teaspoon red pepper sauce
2 medium tomatoes, cut into eighths

1. Prepare okra as directed (above). Place bacon in 2-quart casserole. Cover loosely and microwave on high 4 to 6 minutes or until crisp. Remove bacon with slotted spoon; drain and reserve.

2. Stir okra, corn, onion, salt and pepper sauce into bacon fat in casserole. Cover tightly and microwave on high 12 to 14 minutes, stirring after 5 minutes, until corn is tender.

3. Stir in tomatoes. Cover and microwave 2 to 3 minutes or until hot. Stir in bacon. Sprinkle with freshly cracked pepper if desired. **6 servings (about ⅔ cup each);** 150 calories per serving.

One package (10 ounces) frozen cut okra can be substituted for the fresh okra.

• • • • • • • • • •

PEPPERS, BELL

½ POUND (2 MEDIUM) YIELDS 4 SERVINGS; 25 CALORIES PER SERVING.

When Shopping: Look for well-shaped, shiny, bright-colored peppers (green, red, yellow, purple and orange) with firm sides without wrinkles or soft spots.

To Prepare: Wash bell peppers; remove stems, seeds and membranes. Cut into thin strips.

To Microwave: Place bell peppers in 1½-quart casserole. Cover tightly and microwave on high 4 to 5 minutes, stirring after 2 minutes, until crisp-tender. Let stand covered 1 minute; drain.

To Serve:
• Serve with grilled sausages or hamburgers.
• Mix with onions and mushrooms for an easy side dish.
• Use as a pizza topping.

Okra with Corn and Tomatoes, Leeks (page 201)

Rice-stuffed Peppers

RICE-STUFFED PEPPERS

MICROWAVE TIME: 11 to 14 minutes

4 medium bell peppers
2 cups chopped tomato
⅔ cup uncooked instant rice
½ cup chopped onion (about 1 medium)
¼ cup raisins
¼ cup chopped fresh parsley
2 tablespoons sunflower nuts
2 tablespoons margarine or butter, melted
¾ teaspoon salt
½ teaspoon curry powder
¼ teaspoon pepper
½ cup water

1. Cut thin slice from stem end of each bell pepper. Remove seeds and membranes; rinse peppers. Arrange in circle in pie plate, 9 × 1¼ inches.

2. Mix remaining ingredients except water. Fill each pepper with about ¾ cup mixture. Spoon 2 tablespoons of the water onto mixture in each pepper.

3. Cover loosely and microwave on high 11 to 14 minutes, rotating pie plate ½ turn after 6 minutes, until peppers are crisp-tender. **4 servings;** 250 calories per serving.

PARSNIPS

1½ POUNDS (6 TO 8 MEDIUM) YIELD 4 SERVINGS; 130 CALORIES PER SERVING.

When Shopping: Look for firm, nicely shaped, unblemished parsnips that are not too big.

To Prepare: Scrape or pare. Cut into ¼-inch slices.

To Microwave: Place ¼ cup water and parsnips in 1-quart casserole. Cover tightly and microwave on high 8 to 12 minutes, stirring after 4 minutes, until tender. Let stand covered 1 minute; drain.

To Serve:
• Sprinkle with ground allspice or ground ginger.
• Sprinkle with brown sugar and drizzle with orange juice.
• Top with a cream or cheese sauce.

•••••••••••

PINEAPPLE PARSNIPS

| MICROWAVE TIME: | 10 to 12 minutes |
| STAND TIME: | 5 minutes |

6 medium parsnips (about 1½ pounds)
1 can (8 ounces) crushed pineapple, drained
½ teaspoon salt
⅛ teaspoon pepper
2 tablespoons margarine or butter

1. Prepare parsnips as directed (above)— except cut into ¼-inch strips. Place parsnips, pineapple, salt and pepper in 2-quart casserole. Dot with margarine.

2. Cover tightly and microwave on high 10 to 12 minutes, stirring after 4 minutes, until parsnips are tender. Let stand covered 5 minutes. **6 servings (about ½ cup each);** 125 calories per serving.

PEA PODS, CHINESE

1 POUND YIELDS 4 SERVINGS; 50 CALORIES PER SERVING.

When Shopping: Look for flat pods with a velvety feel. Pods should be crisp and evenly green.

To Prepare: Wash pea pods; remove tips and strings.

To Microwave: Place pea pods and ¼ cup water in 1½-quart casserole. Cover tightly and microwave on high 5 to 9 minutes, stirring after 1 minute, until crisp-tender; drain.

To Serve:
• Refrigerate pea pods until chilled to add to tossed salads.
• Mix with sliced water chestnuts, and drizzle with small amount of soy sauce.

•••••••••••

PEAS, GREEN

2 POUNDS YIELD 4 SERVINGS; 40 CALORIES PER SERVING.

When Shopping: Look for plump, tender bright green pods.

To Prepare: Wash and shell peas just before microwaving.

To Microwave: Place peas and ¼ cup water in 1-quart casserole. Cover tightly and microwave on high 9 to 11 minutes, stirring after 5 minutes, until tender. Let stand covered 1 minute; drain.

To Serve:
• Sprinkle with chervil, marjoram, thyme or tarragon.
• Add toasted almonds or pine nuts.
• Toss with cooked sliced mushrooms and thin strips of ham.

PEAS AND CAULIFLOWER WITH DILL

MICROWAVE TIME: 12 to 15 minutes

1 tablespoon water
2 teaspoons chopped fresh or ½ teaspoon
   dried dill weed
¼ teaspoon salt
1 tablespoon margarine or butter
1 package (8 ounces) frozen cauliflower
1 package (10 ounces) frozen green peas
2 tablespoons grated Parmesan cheese

1.   Mix water, dill weed and salt in 1½-quart casserole; add margarine and cauliflower. Cover tightly and microwave on high 5 minutes.

2.   Stir in peas. Cover tightly and microwave 7 to 10 minutes, stirring after 5 minutes, until vegetables are tender. Sprinkle with cheese.   **6 servings (about ½ cup each);** 75 calories per serving.

• • • • • • • • • •

PEAS WITH MUSHROOMS AND TOMATO

MICROWAVE TIME: 7 to 9 minutes

1 tablespoon margarine or butter
1½ teaspoons chopped fresh or
   ½ teaspoon dried tarragon
¼ teaspoon salt
⅛ teaspoon pepper
1 package (10 ounces) frozen green peas
1 can (2 ounces) mushroom stems and
   pieces, drained
1 medium tomato, coarsely chopped

1.   Place margarine, tarragon, salt and pepper in 1-quart casserole; add peas and mush-

rooms. Cover tightly and microwave on high 6 to 7 minutes, stirring after 3 minutes, until peas are tender.

2.   Sprinkle with tomato. Cover tightly and microwave 1 to 2 minutes or until tomato is hot.   **4 servings (about ¾ cup each);** 90 calories per serving.

• • • • • • • • • •

POTATOES, SMALL NEW

1½ POUNDS (10 TO 14) YIELD 4 SERVINGS; 135 CALORIES PER SERVING.

When Shopping: Look for nicely shaped, smooth, firm potatoes with unblemished skins, free from discoloration.

To Prepare: Choose potatoes of similar size. Wash potatoes lightly without scrubbing and leave whole. Pare a narrow strip around centers or pierce potatoes with fork to allow steam to escape.

To Microwave: Place ¼ cup water and potatoes, with larger potatoes toward outside edge, in 2-quart casserole. Cover tightly and microwave on high 10 to 15 minutes, stirring after 5 minutes, until tender. Let stand covered 1 minute; drain.

To Serve:
• Drizzle with melted margarine or butter and fresh lemon juice.
• Sprinkle with parsley, chives or green onion.
• Slice potatoes; mix with sour cream or a vinaigrette.

LEMON-DILL NEW POTATOES

Toss these thin-skinned delicacies with a buttery combination of herbs, green onions and lemon zest for a tangy springtime treat.

MICROWAVE TIME: 11 to 16 minutes
STAND TIME: 5 minutes

1½ pounds new potatoes (10 to 14)
2 tablespoons margarine or butter
½ teaspoon grated lemon peel, if desired
1 tablespoon lemon juice
1 teaspoon chopped fresh or ¼ teaspoon dried dill weed
¼ teaspoon salt
⅛ teaspoon pepper
1 green onion, chopped

1. Prepare and microwave potatoes as directed (page 208), paring a narrow strip around centers.

2. Mix remaining ingredients except onion in 1-cup measure. Microwave uncovered on high about 1 minute or until bubbly; stir in onion. Toss with potatoes. **4 servings;** 180 calories per serving.

Barbecued Meat Loaf (page 130), Orange Sweet Potatoes (page 210), Lemon-Dill New Potatoes

POTATOES, SWEET

1½ POUNDS (4 MEDIUM) YIELD 4 SERVINGS; 180 CALORIES PER SERVING.

When Shopping: Look for nicely shaped, smooth, firm potatoes with even-colored skins.

To Prepare: Choose sweet potatoes of similar size. Wash but do not pare. Pierce with fork in several places to allow steam to escape.

To Microwave: Arrange sweet potatoes in circle on paper towel in microwave oven. Microwave uncovered on high 8 to 15 minutes or until tender when pierced with fork. Let stand uncovered 5 minutes.

To Serve:
- Sprinkle with ground cinnamon, cloves, nutmeg or ginger.
- Remove sweet potatoes from skins; mash with butter, and mix with grated orange peel and honey.
- Drizzle with maple syrup.

••••••••••

ORANGE SWEET POTATOES

MICROWAVE TIME: 11 to 21 minutes
STAND TIME: 30 minutes

1½ pounds sweet potatoes (about
    4 medium)*
¼ teaspoon salt
⅓ cup orange marmalade

1. Prepare and microwave sweet potatoes as directed (above)—except cool about 30 minutes or until cool enough to handle. Pare and cut into fourths.

2. Place sweet potatoes in 1-quart casserole; sprinkle with salt. Spoon marmalade onto sweet potatoes.

3. Cover loosely and microwave on high 3 to 6 minutes, stirring and spooning marmalade over sweet potatoes after 4 minutes, until sweet potatoes are hot. **4 servings (about ½ cup each);** 160 calories per serving.

One can (18 ounces) vacuum-packed sweet potatoes, drained, can be substituted for the fresh sweet potatoes.

••••••••••

PINEAPPLE-NUT SWEET POTATOES

MICROWAVE TIME: 16 to 27 minutes
STAND TIME: 30 minutes

1½ pounds sweet potatoes (about
    4 medium)*
1 can (8¼ ounces) crushed pineapple,
    drained
¼ cup coarsely chopped nuts
1 tablespoon packed brown sugar
1 cup miniature marshmallows or 10 or
    11 large marshmallows, cut up
Ground nutmeg

1. Prepare and microwave sweet potatoes as directed (left)—except cool about 30 minutes or until cool enough to handle. Pare and cut into fourths.

2. Layer sweet potatoes, pineapple, nuts, brown sugar and ½ cup of the marshmallows in 1½-quart casserole. Cover and microwave on high 7 to 10 minutes or until hot.

3. Sprinkle with remaining marshmallows. Microwave uncovered 1 to 2 minutes or until marshmallows are puffed. Sprinkle with nutmeg. **4 servings (about ¾ cup each);** 320 calories per serving.

One can (18 ounces) vacuum-packed sweet potatoes, drained, can be substituted for the fresh sweet potatoes.

POTATOES, WHITE

2 POUNDS (4 LARGE) YIELD 4 SERVINGS; 180 CALORIES PER SERVING.

When Shopping: Look for nicely shaped, smooth, firm potatoes, with unblemished skins, free from discoloration.

To Prepare: Choose oval, not long, potatoes of similar size. Scrub potatoes. Pierce whole potatoes with fork to allow steam to escape, or cut into 1-inch pieces.

To Microwave: For 4 whole, arrange potatoes about 1 inch apart in circle on paper towel in microwave oven. Microwave uncovered on high 12 to 18 minutes, turning potatoes over after 6 minutes, until tender. Let stand uncovered 5 minutes. (Potatoes hold their heat well; if microwaving another food, microwave potatoes first.)

For 1 whole, place potato on paper towel in microwave oven. Microwave uncovered on high 4 to 5 minutes, turning potato over after 2 minutes, until tender. Let stand uncovered 5 minutes.

For pieces, place potatoes and ½ cup water in 2-quart casserole. Cover tightly and microwave on high 10 to 16 minutes, stirring after 7 minutes, until tender; drain. Let stand covered 1 minute.

To Serve:
• Top whole potatoes with seasoned sour cream or yogurt.
• Chill potato pieces to use in potato salad.
• Mash potatoes and mix with an egg. Shape into patties; sauté in margarine or butter.
• Sauté potato pieces in margarine or butter with coarsely chopped onion and bell pepper.

SCALLOPED POTATOES WITH CHEDDAR CHEESE

MICROWAVE TIME: 20 to 35 minutes
STAND TIME: 5 minutes

1 can (10¾ ounces) condensed cream
   of chicken soup
¾ cup milk
4 medium potatoes, cut into ⅛-inch slices
   (about 4 cups)
1 cup shredded Cheddar cheese
   (4 ounces)
1 small onion, chopped (about ¼ cup)
⅛ teaspoon salt
⅛ teaspoon pepper

1. Empty soup into 2-quart casserole. Stir in milk gradually. Stir in remaining ingredients.

2. Cover tightly and microwave on high 20 to 35 minutes, stirring every 10 minutes, until potatoes are tender. Let stand covered 5 minutes. **6 servings (about ⅔ cup each);** 235 calories per serving.

STUFFED POTATOES

All four versions of this family favorite can be made ahead and reheated in the microwave just minutes before serving.

MICROWAVE TIME: 15 to 23 minutes
STAND TIME: 5 minutes

4 large baking potatoes (about 2 pounds)
½ to ⅔ cup milk
¼ cup margarine or butter, softened
¼ teaspoon salt
Dash of pepper
¼ cup shredded Cheddar cheese
   (1 ounce)
¼ cup crisply cooked and crumbled
   bacon (about 4 slices)
2 tablespoons chopped fresh chives

1.   Prepare and microwave potatoes as directed (page 211) for 4 whole.

2.   Cut thin lengthwise slice from each potato; scoop out inside, leaving a thin shell. Mash potatoes until no lumps remain. Beat in small amounts of the milk until fluffy. Add margarine, salt and pepper; beat vigorously until mixture is light and fluffy. Stir in cheese. Fill potato shells with potato mixture.

3.   Arrange potatoes in circle on 10-inch plate. Microwave uncovered on high 3 to 5 minutes or until potatoes are hot. Sprinkle with bacon and chives.   **4 servings;** 275 calories per serving.

Blue Cheese Potatoes: Substitute ¼ cup crumbled blue cheese for the Cheddar cheese. Omit chives.   325 calories per serving.

Double Cheese Potatoes: Substitute ¼ cup shredded Swiss cheese for the Cheddar cheese and 2 tablespoons grated Parmesan cheese for the bacon.   305 calories per serving.

Mexican Potatoes: Stir ¼ cup salsa into potato mixture. Substitute ¼ cup shredded mozzarella cheese for the bacon and chives. 305 calories per serving.

• • • • • • • • • • •

EASY POTATO GALETTE

A galette is traditionally a flat, cakelike pastry served on Twelfth Night or Epiphany. It is a French custom that good luck will come to whoever eats the piece with a bean baked into it. This galette is a decorative and delicious side dish.

MICROWAVE TIME: 9 to 12 minutes
STAND TIME: 3 minutes

4 medium potatoes (about 1½ pounds),
   thinly sliced
3 tablespoons olive or vegetable oil
½ teaspoon salt
3 cloves garlic, finely chopped
2 tablespoons grated Parmesan cheese
2 tablespoons chopped fresh parsley

1.   Arrange potato slices, overlapping, in circles in pie plate, 10 × 1½ inches. Mix oil, salt and garlic; spoon evenly over potatoes.

2.   Cover tightly and microwave on high 9 to 12 minutes, rotating pie plate ½ turn after 5 minutes, until potatoes are tender. Let stand covered 3 minutes. Sprinkle with cheese and parsley. Remove from pie plate and garnish with thin tomato wedges if desired.   **4 servings (about 1 cup each);** 250 calories per serving.

Gingered Rutabagas

GINGERED RUTABAGAS

Rutabagas have a kind of funny name, but they also have an assertive earthiness that goes perfectly with ginger. A touch of sugar sweetens the pot.

MICROWAVE TIME: 15 to 20 minutes
STAND TIME: 1 minute

1½ pounds rutabagas (1 large or
   2 medium)
¼ cup water
1 tablespoon sugar

1 tablespoon margarine or butter
½ teaspoon salt
½ teaspoon ground ginger

1.   Prepare rutabagas as directed (page 215). Place rutabagas and remaining ingredients in 1½-quart casserole.

2.   Cover tightly and microwave on high 15 to 20 minutes, stirring every 5 minutes, until tender. Let stand covered 1 minute.   **6 servings;** 40 calories per serving.

RUTABAGAS

1½ POUNDS (1 LARGE OR 2 MEDIUM) YIELD 4 SERVINGS; 60 CALORIES PER SERVING.

When Shopping: Look for rutabagas that are heavy, well shaped (round or elongated) and smooth.

To Prepare: Wash rutabagas and pare thinly. Cut into ½-inch cubes.

To Microwave: Place rutabagas and ½ cup water in 1½-quart casserole. Cover tightly and microwave on high 15 to 20 minutes, stirring every 5 minutes, until tender. Let stand covered 1 minute; drain.

To Serve:
- Sprinkle with dill weed, poppy seed or thyme.
- Mash rutabagas with sour cream; stir in chopped fresh chives.

• • • • • • • • • •

SQUASH, HUBBARD

2 POUNDS YIELD 4 SERVINGS; 95 CALORIES PER SERVING.

When Shopping: Look for good yellow-orange color; hard, tough rinds; squash that is heavy. Available whole or by the piece.

To Prepare: Remove rind and any green portion; remove seeds if necessary. Cut squash into 1½- to 2-inch pieces.

To Microwave: Place squash and 2 tablespoons water in 1-quart casserole. Cover tightly and microwave on high 8 to 10 minutes, stirring every 4 minutes, until tender. Let stand covered 5 minutes; drain.

To Serve:
- Mash with milk or half-and-half; stir in honey.
- Sprinkle pieces with brown sugar and ground cinnamon.

• • • • • • • • • •

SQUASH, SPAGHETTI

2½ POUNDS (1 MEDIUM) YIELD 4 SERVINGS; 60 CALORIES PER SERVING.

When Shopping: Look for good yellow-orange color; hard, tough rinds; squash that is heavy.

To Prepare: Wash squash. Pierce with tip of sharp knife in several places to allow steam to escape.

To Microwave: Place squash on paper towel in microwave oven. Microwave uncovered on high 18 to 23 minutes, turning over after 8 minutes, until tender when pierced with tip of sharp knife. Let stand uncovered 10 minutes. Cut crosswise in half; remove seeds and fibers. Scrape fork across squash to pull flesh into strands.

To Serve:
- Sprinkle with grated Parmesan cheese.
- Sprinkle with ground allspice, ground cinnamon or ground ginger.
- Serve spaghetti sauce or clam sauce over cooked squash.

CROOKNECK SQUASH AND GREEN BELL PEPPER

MICROWAVE TIME: 7 to 10 minutes

1½ pounds crookneck squash
2 tablespoons margarine or butter
½ teaspoon salt
¼ teaspoon ground turmeric
⅓ cup chopped green bell pepper
2 green onions (with tops), sliced

1. Prepare squash as directed for Summer Squash (right), cutting into ½-inch slices. Place squash and remaining ingredients in 1½-quart casserole.

2. Cover tightly and microwave on high 7 to 10 minutes, stirring after 3 minutes, until squash is crisp-tender. **6 servings (about ½ cup each);** 55 calories per serving.

• • • • • • • • • •

ITALIAN ZUCCHINI

MICROWAVE TIME: 6 to 8 minutes

6 small zucchini (about 1½ pounds)
2 tablespoons Italian dressing
⅛ teaspoon Italian herb seasoning
Grated Parmesan cheese

1. Prepare zucchini as directed for Summer Squash (right)—except cut crosswise into halves; cut each half lengthwise into fourths. Place zucchini in 1½-quart casserole. Sprinkle with dressing and herb seasoning.

2. Cover tightly and microwave on high 6 to 8 minutes, stirring after 3 minutes, until crisp-tender. Sprinkle with cheese. **6 servings (about ⅔ cup each);** 50 calories per serving.

SQUASH, SUMMER— CROOKNECK, PATTYPAN, STRAIGHTNECK, YELLOW, ZUCCHINI

1½ POUNDS YIELD 4 SERVINGS; 35 CALORIES PER SERVING.

When Shopping: Look for squash that are heavy in relation to size. Smaller squash are more tender. Skin should be smooth and glossy.

To Prepare: Wash squash; remove stem and blossom ends but do not pare. If squash is small, cut in half; or cut into ½-inch slices or cubes.

To Microwave: Place squash and ¼ cup water in 1½-quart casserole. Cover tightly and microwave on high 8 to 10 minutes (pattypan 9 to 13 minutes), stirring after 4 minutes, until almost tender. Let stand covered 1 minute; drain.

To Serve:
• Sprinkle with basil, marjoram, oregano or rosemary.
• Sprinkle with grated Parmesan or shredded mozzarella cheese.
• Drizzle with mixture of olive oil and crushed garlic.

Crookneck Squash and Green Bell Pepper

NUTTY PATTYPAN SQUASH

Fragile pattypan squash are also known as cymlings or scalloped squash. They're best when tender green and 4 inches or less in diameter. Like all summer squash, pattypan squash has edible skin and it should be stored only for 3 or 4 days. The skin of older squash becomes white and hard. Smaller squash are featured here; cut large ones into 2 or 4 pieces each.

MICROWAVE TIME: 6 to 10 minutes

1 pound 1- to 2-inch pattypan squash
   (25 to 35)
1 tablespoon margarine or butter
2 teaspoons chopped fresh or ¼ teaspoon
   dried thyme
1 tablespoon grated Parmesan cheese
2 tablespoons toasted chopped walnuts

1. Prepare squash as directed for Summer Squash (page 217)—except cut in half. Place squash, margarine and thyme in 1-quart casserole.

2. Cover tightly and microwave on high 6 to 10 minutes, stirring after 4 minutes, until tender. Sprinkle with cheese and walnuts. **4 servings (about ½ cup each);** 75 calories per serving.

ZUCCHINI AND TOMATO CASSEROLE

At the end of the summer, when you've begun to think you can't possibly face another zucchini, this casserole will provide a flavor combination that's still interesting. It tastes new—even if you're bored with the garden's abundance.

MICROWAVE TIME: 5 to 9 minutes

2 medium zucchini (about ½ pound)
1 small onion, chopped (about ¼ cup)
1 teaspoon chopped fresh or ¼ teaspoon
   dried thyme
⅛ teaspoon pepper
1 medium tomato, sliced
½ cup shredded Cheddar cheese
   (2 ounces)
½ cup herb-seasoned stuffing mix

1. Prepare zucchini as directed for Summer Squash (page 217), cutting into slices. Mix zucchini, onion, thyme and pepper in 1½-quart casserole. Cover tightly and microwave on high 4 to 6 minutes, stirring after 3 minutes, until zucchini is almost tender.

2. Arrange tomato on zucchini mixture. Cover tightly and microwave 1 to 2 minutes or until tomato is hot. Sprinkle with cheese and stuffing mix. Microwave uncovered about 30 seconds or until cheese is melted. **4 servings (about ¾ cup each);** 105 calories per serving.

ZUCCHINI AND CORN WITH CHEESE

MICROWAVE TIME: 5 to 7 minutes
STAND TIME: 1 minute

1 medium zucchini (about ¾ pound)
1 can (17 ounces) whole kernel corn,
    drained
⅛ teaspoon salt
⅛ teaspoon pepper
½ cup shredded Cheddar cheese
    (2 ounces)

1. Prepare zucchini as directed for Summer Squash (page 217), cutting into cubes. Mix zucchini, corn, salt and pepper in 1-quart casserole. Cover tightly and microwave on high 5 to 7 minutes, stirring after 2 minutes, until vegetables are hot.

2. Sprinkle with cheese. Cover and let stand 1 minute. **4 servings (about ½ cup each); 140** calories per serving.

• • • • • • • • • • •

SQUASH, WINTER— ACORN, BUTTERCUP, BUTTERNUT

2 POUNDS (1 MEDIUM OR 2 SMALL) YIELD 4 SERVINGS; 90 CALORIES PER SERVING.

When Shopping: Look for hard, tough rinds with no soft spots; good yellow-orange flesh; squash that is heavy.

To Prepare: Wash squash. Pierce with tip of sharp knife in several places to allow steam to escape.

To Microwave: Place squash on paper towel in microwave oven. Microwave uncovered on high 4 to 6 minutes or until squash is hot and rind is firm but easy to cut through; cool

slightly. Carefully cut into halves; remove seeds. Arrange squash halves, cut sides down, on 10-inch plate. Cover tightly and microwave on high 5 to 8 minutes or until squash is tender when pierced with tip of sharp knife. Let stand covered 1 minute.

To Serve:
• Top each squash half with margarine or butter, brown sugar, salt and pepper.
• Remove cooked squash from rind and mash. Stir in half-and-half or orange juice.
• Sprinkle with crumbled cooked bacon and drizzle with maple syrup.

• • • • • • • • • • •

PECAN SQUASH

MICROWAVE TIME: 12 to 20 minutes

2 small acorn squash (about 1 pound
    each)
½ cup graham cracker crumbs
¼ cup coarsely chopped pecans
2 tablespoons margarine or butter, melted
1 tablespoon packed brown sugar
¼ teaspoon ground nutmeg
⅛ teaspoon salt

1. Prepare and microwave squash as directed for Winter Squash (left)—except do not let stand. Remove stems; cut thin slice from pointed ends to prevent tipping.

2. Mix remaining ingredients. Arrange squash halves, cut sides up, on serving plate. Spoon crumb mixture into squash halves. Microwave uncovered on high 3 to 6 minutes or until mixture is hot.

3. Top with cranberry sauce if desired. **4 servings;** 260 calories per serving.

BUTTERNUT SQUASH WITH APPLES

Squash sections with seeds removed form small hollows that become natural containers for seasonings.

MICROWAVE TIME: 10 to 16 minutes

2-pound butternut squash
¼ cup chopped hazelnuts or sliced almonds
1 tablespoon margarine or butter
1 tablespoon honey
¼ teaspoon ground nutmeg
1 red medium unpared all-purpose apple, chopped (about 1 cup)

1. Prepare and microwave squash as directed for Winter Squash (page 219)—except do not let stand.

2. Mix remaining ingredients in small bowl. Cover tightly and microwave on high 1 to 2 minutes or until margarine is melted and mixture is hot; stir. Cut squash halves in half. Spoon apple mixture over squash. **4 servings;** 210 calories per serving.

Butternut Squash with Apples

TOMATOES

1⅓ POUNDS (4 MEDIUM) YIELD 4 SERVINGS; 30 CALORIES PER SERVING.

When Shopping: Look for nicely ripened, well-shaped tomatoes; fully ripe tomatoes should be slightly soft without soft spots; have a rich red color.

To Prepare: Wash tomatoes; cut into 8 wedges or ½-inch slices. Peel tomatoes before cutting if desired. To remove skin easily, dip tomato into boiling water 30 seconds, then into cold water. Or scrape surface of tomato with blade of knife to loosen; peel.

To Microwave: Place tomatoes in 2-quart casserole. Cover tightly and microwave on high, wedges 7 to 9 minutes, gently stirring after 4 minutes, or slices 5 to 7 minutes, gently stirring after 3 minutes, until hot. Let stand covered 1 minute.

To Serve:
- Sprinkle with basil, chives, marjoram, oregano, sage or tarragon.
- Top with Seasoned Croutons (page 254) and mayonnaise.

•••••••••••

SAVORY TOMATOES

MICROWAVE TIME: 5 to 6 minutes

4 medium tomatoes (about 1⅓ pounds)
Salt and pepper to taste
⅓ cup coarsely crushed crumbs, crackers or croutons
1 teaspoon chopped fresh or ¼ teaspoon dried basil
½ cup shredded Cheddar cheese (2 ounces)

1. Remove stem ends from tomatoes; cut tomatoes into halves. Arrange tomatoes, cut sides up, in circle on 10-inch plate. Sprinkle with salt and pepper.

2. Mix crumbs and basil; mound on tomatoes. Microwave uncovered on high 3 minutes.

3. Sprinkle with cheese; rotate plate ½ turn. Microwave uncovered 2 to 3 minutes or until tomatoes are hot and cheese is melted. Garnish with parsley if desired.   **4 servings;** 110 calories per serving.

•••••••••••

TURNIPS

1 POUND (4 MEDIUM) YIELDS 4 SERVINGS; 30 CALORIES PER SERVING.

When Shopping: Look for turnips that are smooth, round and firm, with fresh tops.

To Prepare: Cut off tops if necessary. Wash turnips and pare; cut into ½-inch pieces.

To Microwave: Place turnips and ¼ cup water in 2-quart casserole. Cover tightly and microwave on high 12 to 15 minutes, stirring every 5 minutes, until tender. Let stand covered 1 minute; drain.

To Serve:
- Sprinkle with dill weed or thyme.
- Mash; mix with small amount of half-and-half and ground nutmeg.
- Mix with whipping (heavy) cream; top with shredded Cheddar cheese.

TURNIPS AND CARROTS WITH CHEESE

Turnips and carrots are two root vegetables that go so well together you might decide that this is one case where the whole does exceed the sum of the parts. They cook together in as little as 12 minutes and, with chives and melted cheese, become perhaps the most irresistible vegetable dish ever.

MICROWAVE TIME:	12 to 15 minutes
STAND TIME:	1 minute

1 pound turnips (about 4 medium)
2 medium carrots
2 tablespoons water
1 teaspoon chopped fresh chives
¼ teaspoon salt
⅛ teaspoon pepper
½ cup shredded Cheddar cheese
　　(2 ounces)

1.　Prepare turnips as directed (page 221)—except cut into 1½ × ½-inch strips. Prepare carrots as directed (page 193). Mix water, chives, salt and pepper in 2-quart casserole; stir in turnips and carrots.

2.　Cover tightly and microwave on high 12 to 15 minutes, stirring every 5 minutes, until vegetables are tender; drain.

3.　Stir in cheese. Let stand covered about 1 minute or until cheese is melted. **6 servings (about ½ cup each);** 60 calories per serving.

COLORFUL COLESLAW

Since the ingredients are available all year, you needn't save this recipe for summer barbecues—although it tastes great with chicken and corn on the cob. Jicama, originally from Mexico, looks a lot like a sweet potato and is a staple of Latin American cooking.

MICROWAVE TIME:	2 to 3 minutes
REFRIGERATION TIME:	2 hours

½ small head green cabbage, finely
　　shredded (about 1½ cups)
½ small head red cabbage, finely
　　shredded (about 1½ cups)
1 red medium unpared all-purpose
　　apple, chopped (about 1 cup)
1 cup chopped jicama
¼ cup sugar
¼ cup water
2 tablespoons cider vinegar
½ teaspoon mustard seed
⅛ teaspoon salt

1.　Place green and red cabbage, apple and jicama in large bowl; reserve.

2.　Mix sugar, water and vinegar in 1-cup measure. Cover tightly and microwave on high 1 to 2 minutes or until boiling; stir. Microwave uncovered 30 seconds longer. Stir in mustard seed and salt. Pour over cabbage mixture; toss.

3.　Cover and refrigerate at least 2 hours until chilled. Serve using slotted spoon. **8 servings (about ¾ cup each);** 55 calories per serving.

Chilled Lentil Salad

CHILLED LENTIL SALAD

MICROWAVE TIME: 22 to 28 minutes
REFRIGERATION TIME: 3 hours

1 cup dried lentils, rinsed and drained
3 cups hot water
¼ cup chopped red onion
¼ cup vegetable oil
2 tablespoons red wine vinegar
½ teaspoon salt
¼ teaspoon pepper
1 medium stalk celery, chopped (about
    ½ cup)
1 clove garlic, finely chopped
1 small red bell pepper, chopped (about
    ½ cup)
2 or 3 drops red pepper sauce
Chopped fresh parsley

1. Mix lentils and water in 3-quart casserole. Cover tightly and microwave on high 7 to 10 minutes or until boiling; stir.

2. Cover tightly and microwave on medium (50%) 15 to 18 minutes, stirring every 5 minutes, until tender; drain thoroughly. Stir in remaining ingredients except parsley.

3. Cover and refrigerate at least 3 hours until chilled. Sprinkle with parsley. **6 servings (about ⅔ cup each);** 200 calories per serving.

COUSCOUS SALAD

MICROWAVE TIME: 5 to 9 minutes
REFRIGERATION TIME: 4 hours

1 cup uncooked couscous (wheat-grain
　　semolina)
1½ cups chicken broth
½ cup slivered almonds, toasted
½ cup raisins
½ cup chopped dried peaches
¼ cup sliced green onions (with tops)
1 medium unpared cucumber, seeded
　　and chopped
Curry Dressing (below)

1. Mix couscous and chicken broth in 2-quart casserole. Cover tightly and microwave on high 5 to 9 minutes or until liquid is absorbed. Stir in remaining ingredients except Curry Dressing. Toss couscous mixture and Curry Dressing.

2. Cover and refrigerate at least 4 hours until chilled. Stir before serving. **8 servings (about ¾ cup each)**; 185 calories per serving.

Curry Dressing

2 cups plain yogurt
1 tablespoon lemon juice
2 teaspoons curry powder
2 teaspoons packed brown sugar
¼ teaspoon ground cinnamon
¼ teaspoon ground ginger

Mix all ingredients.

COLD BEET SALAD

MICROWAVE TIME: 19 to 26 minutes
STAND TIME: 5 minutes
REFRIGERATION TIME: 3 hours

1¼ pounds beets (about 5 medium)*
3 tablespoons raspberry or red wine
　　vinegar
2 tablespoons vegetable oil
1 teaspoon sugar
¼ teaspoon salt
2 teaspoons grated orange peel

1. Prepare and microwave beets as directed (page 186). Slice beets.

2. Mix vinegar, oil, sugar and salt in 1½-quart casserole. Microwave uncovered on high about 1 minute or until hot. Stir in beets.

3. Cover and refrigerate at least 3 hours, stirring occasionally, until chilled. Sprinkle with orange peel. **5 servings (about ½ cup each)**; 110 calories per serving.

One can (16 ounces) sliced beets, drained, can be substituted for the cooked fresh beets.

Couscous Salad, Greek Vegetable Salad (page 228)

HOT GERMAN POTATO SALAD

The tang of mustard and vinegar brings out the mellowness of potatoes; the bacon adds a traditional German touch. With microwave help, this unmistakable sweet-sour taste takes only a fraction of the usual preparation time.

MICROWAVE TIME:　　27 to 33 minutes

2 pounds small new potatoes (15 to 18)
¼ cup water
4 slices bacon, cut into 1-inch pieces
1 medium stalk celery chopped (about ½ cup)
1 medium onion, chopped (about ½ cup)
1 tablespoon all-purpose flour
1 tablespoon sugar
½ teaspoon celery seed
½ teaspoon salt
¼ teaspoon pepper
½ cup water
¼ cup cider vinegar
1 teaspoon Dijon mustard
Chopped fresh parsley

1. Pierce potatoes with fork. Place potatoes and ¼ cup water in 2-quart casserole. Cover tightly and microwave on high 14 to 16 minutes, stirring after 6 minutes, until tender; drain. Cool about 15 minutes or until cool enough to handle. Slice potatoes and return to casserole.

2. Place bacon in 4-cup measure. Cover with paper towel and microwave on high 4 to 5 minutes or until crisp. Remove bacon with slotted spoon; reserve.

3. Stir celery and onion into bacon fat in 4-cup measure. Cover loosely and microwave on high 2 to 3 minutes or until celery is crisp-tender. Stir in flour, sugar, celery seed, salt and pepper until well mixed. Stir in ½ cup water, the vinegar and mustard. Cover loosely and microwave 3 to 4 minutes, stirring every minute, until mixture thickens and boils.

4. Sprinkle bacon over potatoes. Pour hot celery mixture over potatoes; stir. Cover tightly and microwave on high 4 to 5 minutes, stirring every 2 minutes, until heated through. Sprinkle with parsley. Serve hot. **6 servings (about ¾ cup each);** 240 calories per serving.

Hot German Potato Salad

GREEK VEGETABLE SALAD

MICROWAVE TIME: 13 to 20 minutes
STAND TIME: 5 minutes
REFRIGERATION TIME: 3 hours

½ cup uncooked regular long grain rice
1 cup water
1 medium unpared cucumber, chopped (about 1 cup)
1 small green bell pepper, chopped (about ½ cup)
12 pitted large ripe olives, cut in half
¼ cup olive or vegetable oil
¼ cup lemon juice
1 tablespoon chopped fresh or 1 teaspoon dried dill weed
½ teaspoon salt
¼ teaspoon pepper
¼ cup crumbled feta cheese

1. Mix rice and water in 2-quart casserole. Cover tightly and microwave on high 3 to 5 minutes or until boiling; stir.

2. Cover tightly and microwave on medium (50%) 10 to 15 minutes or until rice is tender and most of the water is absorbed. Let stand covered 5 minutes or until all water is absorbed.

3. Stir in remaining ingredients except cheese. Cover and refrigerate at least 3 hours until chilled. Sprinkle with cheese. **4 servings (about ¾ cup each)**; 180 calories per serving.

SPINACH SALAD

Popeye would love this. A classic spinach salad with a wonderful, warm bacony dressing is tossed together in well under 10 minutes.

MICROWAVE TIME: 6 to 7 minutes

1 pound spinach, torn into bite-size pieces (about 8 cups)
4 ounces mushrooms, sliced (about 1½ cups)
4 slices bacon, cut into 1-inch pieces
1 small onion, chopped (about ¼ cup)
1 teaspoon sugar
¼ teaspoon dry mustard
¼ teaspoon pepper
¼ cup cider vinegar
¼ cup grated Parmesan cheese
1 hard-cooked egg, finely chopped

1. Mix spinach and mushrooms in large bowl; reserve.

2. Place bacon in 4-cup measure. Cover loosely and microwave on high 4 to 5 minutes or until crisp. Remove bacon with slotted spoon; drain and reserve.

3. Stir onion into bacon fat in 4-cup measure. Cover loosely and microwave about 2 minutes or until soft. Stir in sugar, mustard, pepper and vinegar. Pour over spinach and mushrooms; toss. Sprinkle with bacon, cheese and egg. **6 servings (about 1¼ cups each)**; 160 calories per serving.

SPICY BROWN RICE SALAD

Brown rice tastes wonderful with this blend of apples, currants and spices, and it cooks in about half an hour in the microwave.

MICROWAVE TIME:	41 to 49 minutes
STAND TIME:	5 minutes
REFRIGERATION TIME:	4 hours

1 cup uncooked brown rice
2¾ cups hot water
½ teaspoon salt
1 large unpared all-purpose apple,
    chopped (about 1½ cups)
½ cup currants
¼ cup sliced green onions (with tops)
½ teaspoon ground cinnamon
¼ teaspoon ground cloves
Chutney Dressing (right)

1. Mix rice, water and salt in 3-quart casserole. Cover tightly and microwave on high 6 to 9 minutes or until boiling; stir.

2. Cover tightly and microwave on medium (50%) 35 to 40 minutes, stirring every 15 minutes, until rice is tender and most of the water is absorbed. Let stand covered about 5 minutes or until all water is absorbed. Stir in remaining ingredients except Chutney Dressing. Toss rice mixture with Chutney Dressing.

3. Cover and refrigerate at least 4 hours until chilled. **6 servings (about ¾ cup each);** 265 calories per serving.

Chutney Dressing

⅓ cup chutney
¼ cup vegetable oil
1 teaspoon finely chopped gingerroot

Mix all ingredients.

MICROWAVING FRESH VEGETABLES

For whole vegetables, wash and pierce in several places to allow steam to escape. For vegetable pieces, wash, trim and pare as necessary, then cut into pieces approximately the same size.

Place vegetables (except potatoes) with larger, denser parts toward the outside edge of casserole or dish. For whole white potatoes and sweet potatoes, place uncovered in circle on paper towel in microwave and let stand uncovered.

Add water as directed. Cover tightly and microwave on high until crisp-tender or tender, rotating casserole, stirring, turning over or rearranging food as directed. Let stand covered.

Type	Amount	Water	Time	Stand Time
Asparagus				
spears	1½ pounds	¼ cup	6 to 9 minutes, rotating dish ½ turn after 3 minutes	1 minute
pieces, 1 inch	1½ pounds	¼ cup	6 to 9 minutes, stirring after 3 minutes	1 minute
Beans—Green, Wax				
pieces, 1 inch	1 pound	½ cup	9 to 14 minutes, stirring every 5 minutes	5 minutes
Broccoli				
spears	1½ pounds	1 cup	9 to 12 minutes, rotating dish ½ turn every 4 minutes	5 minutes
pieces, 1 inch	1½ pounds	1 cup	9 to 12 minutes, stirring every 4 minutes	5 minutes
Brussels Sprouts	1 pound	¼ cup	8 to 13 minutes, stirring after 5 minutes	5 minutes
Cabbage—Green, Red, Savoy				
wedges	1 pound	½ cup	10 to 14 minutes, rotating dish ½ turn after 5 minutes	5 minutes
shredded	1 pound	¼ cup	8 to 10 minutes, stirring after 4 minutes	5 minutes
Carrots				
slices, ¼ inch	1 pound	¼ cup	6 to 8 minutes, stirring after 4 minutes	1 minute
Cauliflower				
whole	2 pounds	¼ cup	12 to 14 minutes, rotating dish ½ turn after 6 minutes	1 minute
cauliflowerets	2 pounds	¼ cup	12 to 14 minutes, stirring after 6 minutes	1 minute
Corn	4 ears	¼ cup	9 to 14 minutes, rearranging ears after 5 minutes	5 minutes

TYPE	AMOUNT	WATER	TIME	STAND TIME
Peas, Green	2 pounds	¼ cup	9 to 11 minutes, stirring after 5 minutes	1 minute
Potatoes, White whole	2 pounds	—	12 to 18 minutes, turning over after 6 minutes	5 minutes
pieces	2 pounds	½ cup	10 to 16 minutes, stirring after 7 minutes	1 minute
Potatoes, Sweet (Yams)	1½ pounds	—	8 to 15 minutes, turning over after 4 minutes	5 minutes
Summer Squash— Crookneck, Pattypan, Straightneck, Yellow, Zucchini slices or cubes	1½ pounds	¼ cup	8 to 10 minutes, stirring after 4 minutes; 9 to 13 minutes for pattypan	1 minute
Winter Squash—Acorn, Buttercup, Butternut whole	2 pounds	—	4 to 6 minutes or until rind is easy to cut through; cut in half; microwave 5 to 8 minutes longer	1 minute

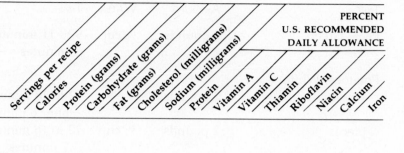

RECIPE, PAGE	Servings per recipe	Calories	Protein (grams)	Carbohydrate (grams)	Fat (grams)	Cholesterol (milligrams)	Sodium (milligrams)	Protein	Vitamin A	Vitamin C	Thiamin	Riboflavin	Niacin	Calcium	Iron

VEGETABLES

RECIPE, PAGE															
Artichokes, Globe, 181	4	75	3	15	1	0	100	4	4	10	6	4	4	5	10
Artichokes, Jerusalem, 181	4	105	1	24	0	2	15	2	0	2	8	10	4	0	2
Asparagus, 181	4	45	5	6	0	0	5	8	30	46	12	12	8	2	6
Asparagus with Cheddar Sauce, 182	6	185	8	11	13	15	270	12	30	26	14	18	10	16	10
Asparagus with Orange Sauce, 182	4	105	2	4	9	0	320	2	20	28	4	4	2	2	8
Asparagus with Water Chestnuts, 183	6	120	5	9	8	0	270	6	28	66	14	12	8	8	6
Beans—Green, Wax, 184	4	40	2	8	0	0	5	2	14	14	6	6	4	4	6
Beets, 186	4	65	2	14	0	0	100	2	0	12	4	0	2	2	6
Beets with Garden Herbs, 186	4	100	1	10	6	0	275	2	4	12	2	0	0	2	4
Blue Cheese Potatoes, 212	4	325	9	39	15	8	385	12	10	18	6	8	14	14	72
Broccoli, 188	4	55	5	9	1	0	45	6	50	100	6	12	4	8	8
Broccoli with Cheese Sauce, 188	4	85	3	7	5	10	335	4	28	40	2	4	2	6	2
Broccoli Mornay, 189	6	75	5	7	3	5	128	6	28	92	4	14	2	16	6
Brussels Sprouts, 189	4	55	4	10	0	0	30	4	20	80	10	6	4	4	8
Butternut Squash with Apples, 220	4	210	5	32	8	0	45	6	100	48	16	8	10	8	8
Cabbage with Bell Pepper and Cheese, 192	4	130	4	9	9	10	220	6	10	65	6	8	2	12	2
Cabbage, Chinese, 191	4	10	1	2	0	0	50	0	44	28	2	2	0	6	2
Cabbage—Green, Red, 191	4	25	1	5	0	0	10	0	0	40	2	0	0	4	2
Carrots, 193	4	50	1	11	0	0	40	0	100	8	6	4	4	2	2
Carrots and Cauliflower, 194	4	90	1	9	6	0	390	2	100	45	2	4	2	2	2
Cauliflower, 197	4	60	4	11	0	0	35	6	0	100	12	8	6	6	6
Cauliflower with Wine-Cheese Sauce, 197	4	155	6	8	9	18	335	8	6	100	6	8	4	14	4
Celery, 193	4	35	1	8	0	0	200	2	4	10	4	4	2	8	6
Chinese Cabbage with Broccoli, 191	8	65	3	9	2	0	285	4	42	84	4	8	4	10	8
Colorful Dilled Vegetables, 194	6	70	3	14	0	0	190	4	100	70	12	4	6	2	8

NUTRITION INFORMATION

PER SERVING OR UNIT

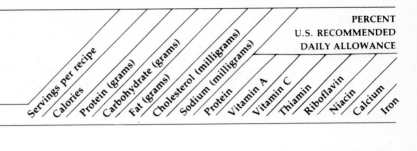

RECIPE, PAGE	Servings per recipe	Calories	Protein (grams)	Carbohydrate (grams)	Fat (grams)	Cholesterol (milligrams)	Sodium (milligrams)	Protein	Vitamin A	Vitamin C	Thiamin	Riboflavin	Niacin	Calcium	Iron
VEGETABLES, *continued*															
Corn, 198	4	90	2	19	1	0	15	2	2	2	10	2	6	0	2
Crookneck Squash and Green Bell Pepper, 217	6	55	1	5	3	0	210	0	10	18	4	2	2	2	2
Dilled Broccoli, 189	4	110	4	8	7	5	155	6	42	65	6	16	4	16	8
Dilled Lima Beans with Water Chestnuts, 186	4	75	4	15	0	0	380	5	0	0	3	0	0	0	9
Dilled Vegetable Platter, 194	4	160	6	10	9	18	335	8	100	64	8	18	10	16	6
Double Cheese Potatoes, 212	4	305	9	39	13	6	368	12	12	20	4	8	12	18	72
Easy Potato Galette, 212	4	250	6	33	11	2	345	10	2	18	4	4	10	12	62
Eggplant, 201	4	30	1	7	0	0	5	0	0	0	6	0	2	4	2
Garlic Corn with Chilies, 198	4	90	2	15	3	0	175	2	8	12	2	2	4	0	0
Garlic Mushrooms, 202	4	70	1	4	6	0	206	2	4	4	2	14	10	0	4
Gingered Rutabagas, 214	6	40	1	11	2	0	226	2	0	45	6	2	4	5	3
Glazed Onions, 203	4	135	2	26	3	0	40	2	2	22	2	2	0	2	2
Green Beans with Almonds, 184	4	95	2	6	7	0	175	4	8	10	2	6	2	4	4
Green Beans Vinaigrette, 184	4	135	2	10	10	0	295	2	12	20	4	6	2	6	6
Greens, 198	4	25	3	4	0	0	90	4	100	26	6	12	4	10	16
Harvard Beets, 188	4	80	1	19	0	0	260	0	0	2	0	2	0	0	0
Herbed Carrots and Zucchini, 196	6	35	1	8	0	0	208	2	100	8	2	2	2	2	2
Hot Pepper Limas, 185	4	165	10	16	7	18	565	15	6	6	4	10	2	20	6
Italian Zucchini, 217	6	50	1	5	3	0	65	2	4	26	4	2	3	2	2
Kohlrabi, 201	4	35	2	7	0	0	25	2	0	58	2	0	2	2	2
Leeks, 201	4	140	3	32	1	0	45	4	4	22	8	4	4	12	26
Lemon-Dill New Potatoes, 209	4	180	5	30	6	0	365	6	6	18	2	4	10	8	56
Lemony Sprouts and Carrots, 190	4	100	3	9	6	0	370	4	100	80	4	4	2	4	4
Mexican Potatoes, 212	4	305	8	40	13	4	446	12	16	22	6	8	14	14	76
Mushrooms, 202	4	30	2	5	0	0	5	2	0	2	6	30	22	0	6
Nutty Pattypan Squash, 218	4	75	2	6	5	0	60	3	7	28	5	3	3	4	4
Okra, 205	4	45	2	9	0	0	10	2	14	18	14	3	4	8	4

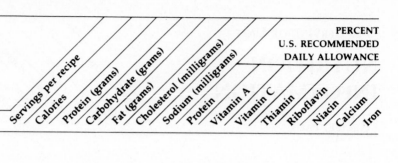

RECIPE, PAGE	Servings per recipe	Calories	Protein (grams)	Carbohydrate (grams)	Fat (grams)	Cholesterol (milligrams)	Sodium (milligrams)	Protein	Vitamin A	Vitamin C	Thiamin	Riboflavin	Niacin	Calcium	Iron
VEGETABLES, *continued*															
Okra with Corn and Tomatoes, 205	6	150	3	11	11	12	130	4	12	22	6	4	4	2	2
Onions—White, Yellow, 202	4	60	2	12	0	0	5	2	0	10	6	0	0	4	2
Orange Sweet Potatoes, 210	4	160	1	39	0	0	175	0	100	16	2	2	0	2	5
Oriental Spinach, 200	4	95	4	12	4	0	350	6	100	56	7	18	9	11	20
Parsnips, 207	4	130	2	31	0	0	20	4	0	24	10	4	4	6	4
Pea Pods, Chinese, 207	4	50	3	9	0	0	5	4	2	56	10	4	2	4	12
Peas and Cauliflower with Dill, 208	6	75	4	9	3	2	220	6	8	46	10	4	6	4	4
Peas, Green, 207	4	40	2	7	0	0	5	2	2	44	8	4	2	2	10
Peas with Mushrooms and Tomato, 208	4	90	4	12	3	0	270	6	18	30	15	4	6	2	6
Pecan Squash, 219	4	260	4	31	13	0	235	6	100	35	15	6	10	6	10
Peppers, Bell, 205	4	25	1	5	0	0	5	0	10	100	6	2	2	0	6
Pineapple-Nut Sweet Potatoes, 210	4	320	4	63	6	0	30	5	100	60	14	16	6	5	9
Pineapple Parsnips, 207	6	125	1	22	4	0	235	0	2	20	6	2	2	2	2
Potatoes, New, 208	4	135	3	31	0	0	10	4	0	26	10	4	12	0	6
Potatoes, Sweet, 210	4	180	3	41	1	0	25	4	100	32	6	14	4	2	4
Potatoes, White, 211	4	180	5	41	0	0	15	6	0	36	12	4	16	0	8
Rutabagas, 215	4	60	2	14	0	0	35	2	0	34	10	4	4	6	4
Rice-stuffed Peppers, 206	4	250	5	36	10	3	230	7	40	100	25	8	10	2	20
Savory Cabbage, 193	6	40	1	4	2	1	135	0	2	30	2	2	0	4	0
Savory Tomatoes, 221	4	110	5	10	6	14	440	8	32	38	5	7	5	11	6
Scalloped Potatoes with Cheddar Cheese, 211	6	235	10	27	10	25	595	16	9	12	4	1	9	24	43
Spinach with Bacon, 200	3	60	3	5	3	4	290	4	98	16	4	6	2	8	6
Spinach and Broccoli, 200	6	40	2	4	2	0	425	2	64	34	2	4	0	6	4
Squash, Hubbard, 215	4	95	3	20	1	0	10	4	100	22	14	4	8	6	6
Squash, Spaghetti, 215	4	60	3	12	0	0	5	4	10	34	10	6	6	4	6
Squash, Summer, 217	4	35	2	7	0	0	5	2	6	20	6	4	4	2	4
Squash, Winter, 219	4	90	3	20	1	0	10	4	100	22	14	4	8	6	6
Stuffed Potatoes, 212	4	275	12	39	8	22	325	18	6	20	6	12	14	24	72

PER SERVING OR UNIT **NUTRITION INFORMATION** RECIPE, PAGE	Servings per recipe	Calories	Protein (grams)	Carbohydrate (grams)	Fat (grams)	Cholesterol (milligrams)	Sodium (milligrams)	PERCENT U.S. RECOMMENDED DAILY ALLOWANCE							
								Protein	Vitamin A	Vitamin C	Thiamin	Riboflavin	Niacin	Calcium	Iron
VEGETABLES, *continued*															
Tomatoes, 221	4	30	1	9	0	0	15	2	38	24	6	4	4	0	4
Turnips, 221	4	30	1	7	0	0	75	0	0	18	2	2	2	2	0
Turnips and Carrots with Cheese, 222	6	60	3	5	3	10	190	4	100	10	0	2	0	8	0
Zucchini and Corn with Cheese, 219	4	140	6	17	6	15	160	8	8	2	0	4	0	10	4
Zucchini and Tomato Casserole, 218	4	105	5	10	5	15	185	8	16	15	6	6	4	12	6
SALADS															
Chilled Lentil Salad, 223	6	200	9	20	9	0	190	14	0	30	10	5	4	2	16
Cold Beet Salad, 225	5	110	2	13	6	0	190	2	0	20	2	0	2	2	4
Colorful Coleslaw, 222	8	55	1	13	0	0	45	0	0	30	0	0	0	0	2
Couscous Salad, 225	8	185	6	25	7	8	180	8	8	8	4	12	8	10	14
Greek Vegetable Salad, 228	4	180	2	4	18	10	470	3	2	48	9	4	5	7	8
Hot German Potato Salad, 226	6	240	6	31	10	10	255	8	0	15	4	4	10	7	50
Spicy Brown Rice Salad, 229	6	265	3	40	10	0	210	4	4	34	8	0	8	2	5
Spinach Salad, 228	6	160	6	6	13	60	170	9	100	38	7	16	7	12	14

BREADS AND GRAINS

Most people deny that the microwave has a bread-making function beyond reheating a muffin or thawing a frankfurter roll. While it is true that yeast breads require dry heat for best results, quick breads cooked in the microwave turn out moist and tender and, best of all, they really are quick. Microwave muffins can be ready to eat in just six minutes. Try Bacon-Cheddar Muffins (page 242) for breakfast, Easy Pizza Muffins (page 243) to go with dinner. We've selected ingredients and toppings to enhance the appearance of microwaved baked goods, and frequently serve cakes and muffins inverted to reveal golden crumbs or nuts baked right into the surface.

- To promote even cooking, we use ring-shaped muffin cups, and the cooking dishes for cakes and loaves are set on inverted dinner plates to raise them off the oven floor, so that the bottom of the loaf gets its fair share of microwave energy. We use lower power settings for some breads for more even cooking and tender results. Don't be tempted to overcook; excess moisture, which sometimes is evident around the edges of muffins or on the top of cakes, usually disappears after the recommended standing time.

- Rice is among the things the microwave cooks very nicely. In fact, just about all grains cook to perfection in the microwave without sticking or burning. Even wild rice is tamed in less time than usual, as the flavorful Mushroom and Wild Rice Casserole (page 265) shows. Parboiled, brown and wild rices are initially cooked at high power to bring the cooking liquid to a boil, then finished at medium power to prevent boiling over and to ensure that all the liquid is absorbed. Instant rice, couscous, grits, bulgur and oatmeal absorb liquid so quickly that they need only the first brief burst of high power to cook. Be sure to cover all grains tightly to retain moisture and flavor.

- Although there is little time-saving benefit to microwaving pasta, we have developed some microwave pasta recipes that work exceptionally well, such as lush Noodles Romanoff (page 265), worthy of the Czar himself. And, of course, if you have any leftovers, the microwave is a master at gentle reheating.

Cranberry-Orange Muffins (page 241), Herbed Biscuit Ring (page 252), Couscous with Spinach (page 260)

PEANUT BUTTER MUFFINS

MICROWAVE TIME: 2 to 4 minutes
STAND TIME: 2 minutes

¼ cup milk
2 tablespoons sugar
2 tablespoons peanut butter
2 tablespoons vegetable oil
1 egg
1 cup variety baking mix

1. Line 6-cup muffin ring with paper baking cups.

2. Beat all ingredients except baking mix in medium bowl with wire whisk or hand beater until well blended. Stir in baking mix just until moistened. Fill each cup with scant ¼ cup batter.

3. Microwave uncovered on high 2 to 4 minutes, rotating ring ¼ turn every minute, until tops are almost dry and wooden pick inserted in centers comes out clean. (Parts of muffins may appear slightly moist but will continue to cook while standing.)

4. Immediately remove muffins from ring. Let stand uncovered on wire rack 2 minutes. Serve warm and, if desired, with jelly. **6 muffins;** 185 calories per muffin.

REFRIGERATED OAT BRAN MUFFINS

Mix up the muffin batter and keep it on hand for breakfast on the run. Nutmeg and dates make these muffins good-tasting; oat bran makes them good for you.

MICROWAVE TIME: 6 to 12 minutes
STAND TIME: 2 minutes

1 cup uncooked oat bran cereal
1 cup buttermilk
½ cup packed brown sugar
½ cup vegetable oil
1 cup all-purpose flour
1 teaspoon baking soda
½ teaspoon ground nutmeg
¼ teaspoon salt
½ cup chopped dates or raisins
3 eggs

1. Mix cereal and buttermilk in large bowl with fork; beat in brown sugar and oil. Stir in remaining ingredients except eggs, all at once, just until flour is moistened. Use immediately as directed below, or cover tightly and refrigerate up to 4 days.

2. For 6 muffins, place 1 cup of the batter in medium bowl; beat in 1 egg. Cover tightly and refrigerate remaining batter. Line 6-cup muffin ring with paper baking cups. Fill each cup with scant ¼ cup batter.

3. Microwave uncovered on high 2 to 4 minutes, rotating ring ¼ turn every minute, until tops are almost dry and wooden pick inserted in centers comes out clean. (Parts of muffins may appear slightly moist but will continue to cook while standing.)

4. Immediately remove muffins from ring. Let stand uncovered on wire rack 2 minutes. Serve warm. Repeat with remaining batter and eggs.   **18 muffins;** 150 calories per muffin.

RAISIN-NUT MUFFINS

Here is a good, basic recipe for microwave muffins; its variation possibilities are nearly unlimited. Try the apple, blueberry or cranberry versions, or substitute the same amounts of spices and fresh or dried fruits of your own choosing.

MICROWAVE TIME: 2 to 4 minutes
STAND TIME: 2 minutes

¼ cup milk
3 tablespoons sugar
3 tablespoons vegetable oil
1 egg
¾ cup all-purpose flour
1 teaspoon baking powder
¼ teaspoon ground cinnamon
⅛ teaspoon salt
¼ cup raisins
2 tablespoons chopped nuts
Cinnamon-Nut Topping (right)

1. Line 6-cup muffin ring with paper baking cups.

2. Beat milk, sugar, oil and egg in medium bowl with fork. Stir in remaining ingredients except Cinnamon-Nut Topping, all at once, just until flour is moistened. Fill each cup with scant ¼ cup batter. Sprinkle with Cinnamon-Nut Topping.

3. Microwave uncovered on high 2 to 4 minutes, rotating ring ¼ turn every minute, until tops are almost dry and wooden pick inserted in centers comes out clean. (Parts of muffins may appear slightly moist but will continue to cook while standing.)

4. Immediately remove muffins from ring. Let stand uncovered on wire rack 2 minutes. Serve warm.   **6 muffins;** 210 calories per muffin.

Cinnamon-Nut Topping

2 teaspoons sugar
1 tablespoon finely chopped nuts
⅛ teaspoon ground cinnamon

Mix all ingredients.

Apple-Nut Muffins: Substitute ⅓ cup applesauce for the milk.   210 calories per muffin.

Blueberry Muffins: Omit raisins and 2 tablespoons nuts. Fold ⅓ cup fresh or frozen (thawed and drained) blueberries into batter.   175 calories per muffin.

Cranberry-Orange Muffins: Substitute ½ teaspoon grated orange peel for the ¼ teaspoon cinnamon. Substitute ⅓ cup cranberry halves for the raisins and 2 tablespoons nuts.   175 calories per muffin.

Cranberry-Orange Muffins, Refrigerated Oat Bran Muffins (page 239), Peanut Butter Muffins (page 239)

BACON-CHEDDAR MUFFINS

MICROWAVE TIME: 2 to 3 minutes
STAND TIME: 2 minutes

¼ cup milk
3 tablespoons vegetable oil
1 egg
¾ cup all-purpose flour
¼ cup shredded Cheddar cheese
    (2 ounces)
1 teaspoon baking powder
¼ teaspoon salt
3 slices bacon, crisply cooked and
    crumbled
Paprika or ground red pepper (cayenne)

1. Line 6-cup muffin ring with paper baking cups.

2. Beat milk, oil and egg in medium bowl with fork. Stir in remaining ingredients except paprika, all at once, just until flour is moistened. Fill each cup with scant ¼ cup batter. Sprinkle with paprika.

3. Microwave uncovered on high 2 to 3 minutes, rotating ring ¼ turn every minute, until tops are almost dry and wooden pick inserted in centers comes out clean. (Parts of muffins may appear slightly moist but will continue to cook while standing.)

4. Immediately remove muffins from ring. Let stand uncovered on wire rack 2 minutes. Serve warm.   **6 muffins;** 165 calories per muffin.

Bacon-Cheddar Muffins, Sour Cream and Chive Muffins (page 243)

EASY PIZZA MUFFINS

MICROWAVE TIME: 3 to 5 minutes

¼ cup milk
¼ cup vegetable oil
1 egg
¾ cup all-purpose flour
¼ cup finely chopped pepperoni (about
    1 ounce)
1 teaspoon baking powder
¼ teaspoons salt
1 teaspoon chopped fresh or ¼ teaspoon
    dried oregano
2 tablespoons pizza sauce
¼ cup shredded mozzarella cheese
    (1 ounce)

1. Line 6-cup muffin ring with paper baking cups.

2. Beat milk, oil and egg in medium bowl with fork. Stir in remaining ingredients except pizza sauce and cheese, all at once, just until flour is moistened. Fill each cup with scant ¼ cup batter. Spread 1 teaspoon pizza sauce over batter in each cup.

3. Microwave uncovered on high 2 to 4 minutes, rotating ring ¼ turn every minute, until wooden pick inserted in centers comes out clean.

4. Sprinkle with cheese. Microwave uncovered 30 to 60 seconds or until cheese is melted. Immediately remove muffins from ring. Serve hot.   **6 muffins;** 190 calories per muffin.

SOUR CREAM AND CHIVE MUFFINS

MICROWAVE TIME: 2 to 4 minutes
STAND TIME: 2 minutes

¼ cup sour cream
¼ cup milk
¼ cup vegetable oil
1 egg
¾ cup all-purpose flour
2 tablespoons chopped fresh chives
¾ teaspoon baking powder
¼ teaspoon baking soda
¼ teaspoon salt

1. Line 6-cup muffin ring with paper baking cups.

2. Beat sour cream, milk, oil and egg in medium bowl with fork. Stir in remaining ingredients, all at once, just until flour is moistened. Fill each cup with scant ¼ cup batter. Sprinkle with additional chopped fresh chives if desired.

3. Microwave uncovered on high 2 to 4 minutes, rotating ring ¼ turn every minute, until tops are almost dry and wooden pick inserted in centers comes out clean. (Parts of muffins may appear slightly moist but will continue to cook while standing.)

4. Immediately remove muffins from ring. Let stand uncovered on wire rack 2 minutes. Serve warm.   **6 muffins;** 170 calories per muffin.

APPLE-WALNUT COFFEE CAKE

MICROWAVE TIME: 12 to 14 minutes
STAND TIME: 5 minutes

⅔ cup sugar
½ cup buttermilk
⅓ cup vegetable oil
1 egg
1¼ cups all-purpose flour
½ teaspoon baking soda
½ teaspoon ground nutmeg
¼ teaspoon salt
1 red medium unpared all-purpose
    apple, chopped (about 1 cup)
1 red medium unpared all-purpose
    apple, thinly sliced
Walnut Topping (right)

1. Lightly grease bottom only of round dish, 8 × 1½ inches. Beat sugar, buttermilk, oil and egg in medium bowl with fork. Stir in remaining ingredients except sliced apple and Walnut Topping just until moistened. Spread batter evenly in dish.

2. Microwave uncovered on medium (50%) 9 to 10 minutes; rotating dish ½ turn after 5 minutes, until top edge of cake is set but still moist. Arrange apple slices spoke fashion on coffee cake; sprinkle evenly with Walnut Topping.

3. Microwave uncovered on high 3 to 4 minutes, rotating dish ½ turn after 2 minutes, until apple slices are slightly tender and wooden pick inserted in center of cake comes out clean. Let stand uncovered 5 minutes. Serve warm. **1 coffee cake (8 servings);** 300 calories per serving.

A 500-watt microwave is not recommended.

Walnut Topping

¼ cup packed brown sugar
¼ cup chopped walnuts
1 tablespoon margarine or butter,
    softened

Mix all ingredients with fork until crumbly.

• • • • • • • • • •

BROWN SUGAR–PECAN COFFEE CAKE

MICROWAVE TIME: 4 to 6 minutes
STAND TIME: 1 minute

¼ cup margarine or butter
¼ cup packed brown sugar
½ cup coarsley chopped pecans
1½ cups variety baking mix
½ cup milk
½ teaspoon ground cinnamon

1. Place margarine in 6-cup ring dish. Microwave uncovered on high about 45 seconds or until melted. Sprinkle brown sugar and pecans evenly over margarine. Microwave uncovered 45 seconds to 1 minute or until hot and bubbly.

2. Mix baking mix, milk and cinnamon until soft dough forms; beat vigorously 30 seconds. Drop dough by 6 spoonsfuls into hot mixture in dish.

3. Microwave uncovered 2 to 4 minutes, rotating dish ½ turn after 1 minute, until top appears dry and springs back when touched lightly.

4. Immediately invert onto heatproof serving plate; leave dish over coffee cake 1 minute. Serve warm. **1 coffee cake (6 servings);** 305 calories per serving.

Apple-Walnut Coffee Cake

RAISIN-RICE COFFEE CAKE

MICROWAVE TIME: 9 to 10 minutes
STAND TIME: 2 minutes

2 tablespoons sugar
½ teaspoon ground cinnamon
1 cup cooked rice
¼ cup raisins
½ cup milk
⅓ cup margarine or butter, melted
1 egg
1½ cups all-purpose flour
½ cup sugar
½ cup raisins
1½ teaspoons baking powder
½ teaspoon ground cinnamon
¼ teaspoon salt

1.   Grease 6-cup ring dish. Mix 2 table-spoons sugar and ½ teaspoon cinnamon; sprinkle evenly over bottom and sides of dish. Mix rice and ¼ cup raisins; spread evenly in bottom of dish.

2.   Beat milk, margarine and egg in large bowl; stir in remaining ingredients, all at once, just until flour is moistened. Spread batter evenly over rice mixture.

3.   Elevate ring dish on inverted dinner plate in microwave oven. Microwave uncovered on medium (50%) 7 minutes, rotating dish ¼ turn after 3 minutes.

4.   Rotate dish ¼ turn. Microwave uncovered on high 2 to 3 minutes, rotating dish ¼ turn after 1 minute, until wooden pick inserted in center comes out clean. (Parts of surface may appear moist but will continue to cook while standing.) Let stand uncovered on heatproof surface 2 minutes. Invert onto heatproof serving plate. Serve warm.   **1 coffee cake (12 servings);** 200 calories per serving.

A 500-watt microwave is not recommended.

BLUEBERRY COFFEE CAKE

MICROWAVE TIME: 12 to 14 minutes
STAND TIME: 10 minutes

¼ cup graham cracker crumbs
Streusel Coffee Cake batter (page 249)
2 cups fresh or frozen (thawed and drained) blueberries
Lemon Glaze (below)

1.   Generously grease 12-cup bundt cake dish; coat with graham cracker crumbs.

2.   Prepare Streusel Coffee Cake batter as directed. Spread half of the batter in dish; sprinkle with half of the blueberries. Repeat with remaining batter and blueberries.

3.   Microwave uncovered on high 12 to 14 minutes, rotating dish ¼ turn every 4 minutes, until top springs back when touched lightly.

4.   Let stand uncovered on heatproof surface 10 minutes. Invert onto serving plate. Drizzle with Lemon Glaze.   **1 coffee cake (12 servings);** 260 calories per serving.

A 500-watt microwave is not recommended.

Lemon Glaze

1 cup powdered sugar
¼ teaspoon grated lemon peel
1 tablespoon lemon juice

Mix all ingredients until smooth. Stir in a few drops additional lemon juice, if necessary, until glaze is the consistency of syrup.

GLAZED SOUR CREAM COFFEE CAKE

A lovely, traditional coffee cake. The glaze and nut filling make it delicious served warm for a coffee klatch or special breakfast.

MICROWAVE TIME:	7 to 10 minutes
STAND TIME:	10 minutes

½ cup sugar
¼ cup margarine or butter, softened
½ teaspoon vanilla
1 egg
1 cup all-purpose flour
½ teaspoon baking powder
½ teaspoon baking soda
¾ cup sour cream
Nut Filling (right)
Browned Butter Glaze (right)

1. Beat sugar, margarine, vanilla and egg in small bowl on medium speed 2 minutes, scraping bowl occasionally.

2. Beat in flour, baking powder and baking soda alternately with sour cream on low speed.

3. Spread half of the batter in ungreased round dish, 8 × 1½ inches; sprinkle with half of the Nut Filling. Repeat layers.

4. Microwave uncovered on high 5 to 7 minutes or until top springs back when touched lightly.

5. Let stand uncovered on heatproof surface 10 minutes. Drizzle with Browned Butter Glaze. **1 coffee cake (6 servings);** 400 calories per serving.

Nut Filling

3 tablespoons packed brown sugar
3 tablespoons chopped nuts
½ teaspoon ground cinnamon

Mix all ingredients.

Browned Butter Glaze

2 tablespoons margarine or butter
1 cup powdered sugar
½ teaspoon vanilla
2 to 3 teaspoons milk

Place margarine in 2-cup measure. Microwave uncovered on high 2 to 3 minutes or until melted and brown. Stir in powdered sugar and vanilla. Mix in milk, 1 teaspoon at a time, until glaze is the consistency of syrup.

Zucchini Bread, Orange-Date Nut Bread (page 249)

ZUCCHINI BREAD

MICROWAVE TIME: 12 to 14 minutes
STAND TIME: 10 minutes

¼ cup graham cracker crumbs
1⅓ cups all-purpose flour
1⅓ cups sugar
1 medium zucchini, shredded (about
   1½ cups)
⅓ cup shortening
⅓ cup water
1 teaspoon baking soda
¾ teaspoon salt
½ teaspoon ground cinnamon
¼ teaspoon baking powder
¼ teaspoon ground cloves
2 eggs
⅓ cup coarsely chopped nuts
⅓ cup raisins

1. Generously grease 10-cup ring dish; coat with graham cracker crumbs.

2. Mix remaining ingredients except nuts and raisins; beat until well blended. Stir in nuts and raisins. Pour batter into ring dish.

3. Elevate ring dish on inverted dinner plate in microwave. Cover with waxed paper and microwave on medium-high (70%) 12 to 14 minutes, rotating dish ½ turn after 6 minutes, until top of bread is dry and springs back when touched lightly. Let stand uncovered on heatproof surface 10 minutes.

4. Invert onto serving plate; cool completely before slicing. To store, wrap and refrigerate up to 10 days. **1 bread ring (14 servings);** 200 calories per serving.

A 500-watt microwave is not recommended.

STREUSEL COFFEE CAKE

MICROWAVE TIME:	12 to 14 minutes
STAND TIME:	10 minutes

¼ cup graham cracker crumbs
2 cups all-purpose flour
1 cup sugar
3 teaspoons baking powder
1 teaspoon salt
⅓ cup margarine or butter, softened
1 cup milk
1 egg
Streusel (below)
Powdered sugar

1.   Generously grease 12-cup bundt cake dish; coat with graham cracker crumbs.

2.   Beat remaining ingredients except Streusel and powdered sugar in large bowl on low speed 30 seconds. Beat on medium speed 2 minutes, scraping bowl occasionally.

3.   Spread half of the batter in dish; sprinkle with 1½ cups of the Streusel. Repeat with remaining batter and Streusel.

4.   Microwave uncovered on high 12 to 14 minutes, rotating dish ¼ turn every 4 minutes, until top springs back when touched lightly.

5.   Let stand uncovered on heatproof surface 10 minutes. Invert onto serving plate. Sprinkle with powdered sugar.   **1 coffee cake (12 servings);** 375 calories per serving.

A 500-watt microwave is not recommended.

Streusel

⅔ cup chopped nuts
½ cup packed brown sugar
⅓ cup all-purpose flour
¼ cup firm margarine or butter
¾ teaspoon ground cinnamon

Mix all ingredients until crumbly.

ORANGE-DATE NUT BREAD

MICROWAVE TIME:	8 to 10 minutes
STAND TIME:	5 minutes

⅓ cup finely chopped nuts
1¼ cups all-purpose flour
½ cup chopped nuts
½ cup cut-up dates
¼ cup sugar
½ cup milk
⅓ cup vegetable oil
¼ cup honey
2 teaspoons grated orange peel
1¾ teaspoons baking powder
½ teaspoon salt
1 egg

1.   Generously grease 6-cup ring dish; coat with ⅓ cup finely chopped nuts.

2.   Mix remaining ingredients; beat 30 seconds. Pour batter into ring dish.

3.   Microwave uncovered on medium-high (70%) 8 to 10 minutes, rotating dish ¼ turn every 3 minutes, until wooden pick inserted in center comes out clean. Let stand uncovered on heatproof surface 5 minutes.

4.   Invert onto serving plate; cool completely before slicing. To store, wrap and refrigerate up to 10 days.   **1 bread ring (12 servings);** 220 calories per serving.

A 500-watt microwave is not recommended.

BAGELS WITH CREAM CHEESE SPREAD

With half the calories of butter or margarine, cream cheese is a wonder for the weight-conscious; these recipes add lots of extra flavor with very few extra calories. They're simple enough for kids to make after school, quick enough for busy-day breakfasts.

MICROWAVE TIME: 30 to 40 seconds

Bagels
Cream Cheese Spreads (right)

1. For each serving, split a bagel; place on plate. Microwave uncovered on high 15 to 20 seconds or until warm.

2. Spread each bagel half with about 1 tablespoon of one of the Cream Cheese Spreads.

3. Microwave uncovered 15 to 20 seconds or until spread is warm. Cover and refrigerate any remaining Cream Cheese Spread up to 3 days.

Cream Cheese Spreads

Mix 1 container (4 ounces) whipped cream cheese with one of the following:

Apricot: 2 tablespoons apricot preserves. 195 calories per bagel with spread.

Herb: 1 teaspoon chopped fresh or ½ teaspoon dried dill weed and 1 small clove garlic, finely chopped. 170 calories per bagel with spread.

Bagels with Cream Cheese Spreads

Onion-Chili: 1 teaspoon instant minced onion and ½ teaspoon chili powder. 170 calories per bagel with spread.

Peanut Butter: 2 tablespoons peanut butter. 195 calories per bagel with spread.

Strawberry: ¼ cup chopped fresh strawberries and 1 tablespoon powdered sugar. 185 calories per bagel with spread.

• • • • • • • • • •

APRICOT STREUSEL BREAD

MICROWAVE TIME: 9 to 11 minutes

1 package (13.5 ounces) cinnamon streusel
    muffin mix
⅔ cup milk
2 eggs
¾ cup chopped dried apricots

1.   Grease 6-cup ring dish. Sprinkle with ¼ cup of the streusel, spreading excess evenly in bottom of dish.

2.   Beat milk and eggs in medium bowl with fork; stir in muffin mix and apricots just until moistened. Spread half of the batter (about 1 cup) in ring dish. Sprinkle with remaining streusel; top with remaining batter.

3.   Elevate ring dish on inverted dinner plate in microwave oven. Microwave uncovered on medium (50%) 7 minutes, rotating dish ¼ turn after 3 minutes.

4.   Microwave uncovered on high 2 to 4 minutes longer or until surface appears almost dry and wooden pick inserted in center comes out clean. Immediately invert onto heatproof serving plate. Serve warm.   **1 bread ring (12 servings);** 200 calories per serving.

A 500-watt microwave is not recommended.

BLUEBERRY-ORANGE BREAD

MICROWAVE TIME: 10 to 12 minutes
STAND TIME: 1 minute

1 package (13 ounces) wild blueberry
    muffin mix
¾ cup orange juice
2 eggs
½ cup chopped walnuts

1.   Grease 6-cup ring dish. Drain blueberries; rinse and set aside.

2.   Beat orange juice and eggs in medium bowl with fork; stir in muffin mix just until moistened (batter will be lumpy). Fold in blueberries and walnuts. Pour batter into ring dish.

3.   Elevate ring dish on inverted dinner plate in microwave oven. Microwave uncovered on medium (50%) 7 minutes, rotating dish ¼ turn after 3 minutes.

4.   Microwave uncovered on high 3 to 5 minutes longer, rotating dish ¼ turn after 2 minutes, until wooden pick inserted in center comes out clean. (Parts of surface may appear slightly moist but will continue to cook while standing.) Let stand on heatproof surface 1 minute. Invert onto heatproof serving plate. Serve warm.   **1 bread ring (12 servings);** 140 calories per serving.

A 500-watt microwave is not recommended.

HERBED BISCUIT RING

MICROWAVE TIME: 8 to 11 minutes

½ cup grated Parmesan cheese
¾ teaspoon Italian seasoning
½ teaspoon paprika
¼ cup margarine or butter
2 cups variety baking mix
⅔ cup milk

1. Mix cheese, Italian seasoning and paprika; set aside. Place margarine in smalll bowl. Cover loosely and microwave on high about 45 seconds or until melted.

2. Mix baking mix and milk until soft dough forms; beat vigorously 30 seconds. Turn dough onto surface well floured with baking mix; turn to coat with baking mix. Knead 10 times. Divide dough into 6 equal parts. Dip each part into margarine, coating all sides. Roll in cheese mixture. Place in ungreased 6-cup ring dish.

3. Elevate ring dish on inverted dinner plate in microwave oven. Microwave uncovered on medium (50%) 7 to 10 minutes, rotating dish ½ turn after 4 minutes, until no longer doughy. Immediately invert onto heatproof serving plate. Serve warm. **1 biscuit ring (6 servings);** 270 calories per serving.

SAVORY FRENCH BREAD

Make the most of a store-bought loaf and coordinate its flavor with your menu: Serve the Cheese 'n Chilies version with a Tex-Mex feast, the Garlic Spread with an Italian dinner.

MICROWAVE TIME: 3 to 4 minutes

Seasoned Spreads (below)
½ loaf French bread or 6 French rolls

1. Prepare one of the Seasoned Spreads. Cut bread into 12 slices, or split rolls. Spread one side of each with one of the Seasoned Spreads.

2. Reassemble loaf or rolls; place in napkin-lined basket or on dinner plate. Cover with paper towel.

3. Microwave on medium (50%) 2 to 3 minutes, rotating basket ½ turn after 1 minute, until bread is warm. **12 slices bread.**

Seasoned Spreads

Place ¼ cup margarine or butter in smalll bowl. Microwave uncovered on medium-low (30%) 15 to 30 seconds or until softened. Mix with one of the following:

Cheese 'n Chilies: ½ cup shredded sharp Cheddar cheese (2 ounces), 1 tablespoon chopped green chilies and ½ teaspoon Worcestershire sauce. 110 calories per slice with spread.

Parmesan-Herb: 2 teaspoons grated Parmesan cheese, ½ teaspoon chopped fresh parsley, ⅛ teaspoon dried oregano and dash of garlic salt. 90 calories per slice with spread.

Garlic: 1 small clove garlic, finely chopped. 90 calories per slice with spread.

Onion: ¼ teaspoon instant minced onion or 1 teaspoon chopped fresh chives. 90 calories per slice with spread.

CRUSTY BLUE CHEESE SLICES

MICROWAVE TIME: 3 to 4 minutes

3 tablespoons margarine or butter
2 tablespoons crumbled blue cheese
1 tablespoon grated Parmesan cheese
½ loaf (½ pound) French bread, cut
   diagonally into 12 slices

1.   Place margarine and blue cheese in small bowl. Microwave uncovered on medium-low (30%) 15 to 30 seconds or until softened. Stir in Parmesan cheese; spread mixture on one side of each slice bread.

2.   Reassemble loaf; place in napkin-lined basket or on dinner plate. Cover with paper towel.

3.   Microwave on medium (50%) 2 to 3 minutes, rotating basket ½ turn after 1 minute, until bread is warm.   **12 slices bread;** 85 calories per slice.

Crusty Blue Cheese Slices

CHEDDAR FRENCH BREAD

MICROWAVE TIME: 2 to 3 minutes

½ cup shredded sharp Cheddar cheese
    (2 ounces)
¼ cup mayonnaise or salad dressing
2 teaspoons chopped fresh parsley
1 teaspoon prepared mustard
½ loaf (½ pound) French bread, cut
    diagonally into 12 slices

1. Mix all ingredients except bread; spread mixture on one side of each slice bread.

2. Reassemble loaf; place in napkin-lined basket or on dinner plate. Cover with paper towel.

3. Microwave on medium (50%) 2 to 3 minutes, rotating basket ½ turn after 1 minute, until bread is warm and cheese begins to melt.   **12 slices bread;** 110 calories per slice.

• • • • • • • • • • •

SEASONED CROUTONS

MICROWAVE TIME: 5 to 8 minutes

2 tablespoons margarine or butter
½ teaspoon parsley flakes
⅛ teaspoon garlic salt
⅛ teaspoon paprika
2 slices bread, cut into ½-inch cubes
    (2 cups)

1. Place margarine in square dish, 8 × 8 × 2 inches. Cover loosely and microwave on medium (50%) 1 to 2 minutes or until melted.

2. Stir in parsley flakes, garlic salt and paprika. Add bread cubes; toss to coat. Microwave uncovered on high 3 minutes 30 seconds to 5 minutes 30 seconds, stirring every minute, until golden brown and crisp; cool.   **4 servings (about ¼ cup each);** 85 calories per serving.

ORANGE PILAF

MICROWAVE TIME: 27 to 35 minutes

1 cup uncooked parboiled rice
1½ cups water
1 cup orange juice
¼ cup sliced green onions (with tops)
1 tablespoon margarine or butter
¼ teaspoon salt
1 teaspoon grated orange peel
½ teaspoon chopped fresh or ¼ teaspoon
    dried thyme
1 medium orange, pared and sectioned

1. Mix rice, water, juice, onions, margarine and salt in 2-quart casserole. Cover tightly and microwave on high 5 minutes; stir.

2. Cover tightly and microwave on medium (50%) 22 to 30 minutes, stirring after 15 minutes, until rice is tender and liquid is absorbed. Stir in remaining ingredients.   **6 servings (about ½ cup each);** 100 calories per serving.

• • • • • • • • • • •

LEMON RICE

MICROWAVE TIME: 9 to 10 minutes

2 cups uncooked instant rice
2 cups chicken broth
½ cup sliced celery
2 tablespoons margarine or butter
¼ teaspoon salt
1 tablespoon chopped fresh parsley
2 teaspoons grated lemon peel
1 tablespoon lemon juice

1. Mix rice, broth, celery, margarine and salt in 2-quart casserole.

2. Cover tightly and microwave on high 9 to 10 minutes or until rice is tender and liquid is absorbed. Stir in remaining ingredients.   **6 servings (about ⅔ cup each);** 205 calories per serving.

Sour Cream Rice with Chilies

SOUR CREAM RICE WITH CHILIES

MICROWAVE TIME: 11 to 13 minutes
STAND TIME: 4 minutes

2 cups uncooked instant rice
2 cups chicken broth
⅛ teaspoon garlic powder
1 cup shredded Cheddar cheese
  (4 ounces)
½ cup sour cream
1 can (4 ounces) chopped mild green
  chilies, drained

1. Mix rice, broth and garlic powder in 2-quart casserole. Cover tightly and microwave on high 9 to 10 minutes or until rice is tender and liquid is absorbed.

2. Stir in ½ cup of the cheese, the sour cream and chilies. Cover tightly and microwave 2 to 3 minutes or until heated through.

3. Sprinkle with remaining cheese. Cover and let stand about 4 minutes or until cheese is melted.   **6 servings (about ⅔ cup each);** 350 calories per serving.

APPLE AND WILD RICE DRESSING

Unique texture and flavor set this aquatic, grainlike seed apart from true rice. Wild rice is also exceptionally high in protein and low in fat. Combined with apples and almonds, it becomes the perfect accompaniment to the sightly sweet fruitiness of Apricot-glazed Grilled Turkey (page 62).

MICROWAVE TIME: 32 to 40 minutes
STAND TIME: 5 minutes

½ cup uncooked wild rice
1 cup hot water
2 tablespoons margarine or butter
½ teaspoon salt
1 small onion, finely chopped (about ¼ cup)
1 cup unseasoned croutons
½ cup slivered almonds
½ teaspoon ground cinnamon
1 medium unpared all-purpose apple, chopped (about 1 cup)
⅓ cup apple juice

1. Mix wild rice, water, margarine and salt in 2-quart casserole. Cover tightly and microwave on high 3 to 5 minutes or until boiling.

2. Microwave on medium (50%) 25 to 30 minutes or until wild rice is tender and liquid is absorbed. Stir in onion. Cover and let stand 5 minutes.

3. Stir in remaining ingredients except apple juice. Add apple juice, 1 tablespoon at a time, tossing until croutons are moistened.

4. Cover tightly and microwave on high 4 to 5 minutes or until hot.   **8 servings (about ½ cup each)**; 150 calories per serving.

500-watt microwave: You may need to increase microwave times.

•••••••••••

PARSLEY-MUSHROOM RICE

MICROWAVE TIME: 10 to 11 minutes

1½ cups uncooked instant rice
1½ cups hot water
2 tablespoons margarine or butter
¼ cup finely chopped onion
1 small clove garlic, finely chopped
2 teaspoons chicken bouillon granules
2 teaspoons chopped fresh or ¼ teaspoon dried basil
1 can (4 ounces) mushrooms stems and pieces, drained
2 tablespoons chopped fresh parsley

1. Mix all ingredients except mushrooms and parsley in 1½-quart casserole. Cover tightly and microwave on high 7 minutes.

2. Stir in mushrooms. Cover tightly and microwave 3 to 4 minutes or until rice is tender and liquid is absorbed. Stir in parsley.   **6 servings (about ½ cup each)**; 125 calories per serving.

CURRIED RICE WITH ALMONDS

MICROWAVE TIME: 17 to 20 minutes
STAND TIME: 10 minutes

1 small onion, chopped (about ¼ cup)
2 tablespoons margarine or butter
¾ cup uncooked regular long grain rice
1½ teaspoons chicken bouillon granules
¼ teaspoon ground allspice
¼ teaspoon ground tumeric
⅛ to ¼ teaspoon curry powder
Dash of pepper
2⅔ cups hot water
¼ cup slivered almonds, toasted

1. Place onion and margarine in 3-quart casserole. Cover tightly and microwave on high 2 to 3 minutes or until crisp-tender.

2. Stir in remaining ingredients except water and almonds. Stir in water. Cover tightly and microwave 15 to 17 minutes, stirring after 7 minutes, until most of the liquid is absorbed.

3. Let stand covered 10 minutes (rice will absorb liquid while standing). Stir in almonds. **4 servings (about ¾ cup each);** 175 calories per serving.

500-watt microwave: You may need to increase microwave times.

SPANISH RICE

MICROWAVE TIME: 12 to 15 minutes

2 slices bacon, cut into ½-inch pieces
1½ cups uncooked instant rice
1⅓ cups water
1 tablespoon finely chopped onion or
    1 teaspoon instant minced onion
1 teaspoon chopped fresh or ¼ teaspoon
    dried oregano
½ teaspoon chili powder
¼ teaspoon salt
⅛ teaspoon pepper
1 small green bell pepper, chopped
1 can (16 ounces) stewed tomatoes,
    undrained

1. Place bacon in 1½-quart casserole. Cover with paper towel and microwave on high 2 to 3 minutes or until crisp.

2. Stir in remaining ingredients. Cover tightly and microwave 10 to 12 minutes, stirring after 5 minutes, until rice is tender and liquid is absorbed. **6 servings (about ¾ cup each);** 155 calories per serving.

500-watt microwave: You may need to increase microwave times.

CHINESE RICE

The microwave does most of the work with this dish, and gives authentic stir-fried flavor without added oil and practically without stirring.

MICROWAVE TIME: 9 to 13 minutes

6 ounces Chinese pea pods*
1 cup uncooked instant rice
1 cup hot water
½ cup chopped celery
1 tablespoon margarine or butter
1 teaspoon finely chopped gingerroot
1 clove garlic, finely chopped
1 tablespoon soy sauce
1 can (8 ounces) sliced water chestnuts, drained
2 eggs

1. Rinse frozen pea pods under cold running water to separate; drain and reserve.

2. Mix remaining ingredients except soy sauce, water chestnuts and eggs in 2-quart casserole. Cover tightly and microwave on high 6 to 8 minutes or until rice is tender and liquid is absorbed.

3. Stir in pea pods, soy sauce and water chestnuts. Cover tightly and microwave 2 to 3 minutes or until pea pods are crisp-tender. Let stand covered.

4. Beat eggs in small bowl with fork. Microwave uncovered on high 1 minute to 1 minute 30 seconds, stiring every 30 seconds, until set. Break up eggs; stir into rice mixture. Serve with additional soy sauce if desired. **6 servings (about ⅔ cup each);** 140 calories per serving.

One package (6 ounces) frozen Chinese pea pods, rinsed and drained, can be substituted for the fresh pea pods.

Chinese Rice, Black Beans and Rice

BLACK BEANS AND RICE

MICROWAVE TIME: 12 to 15 minutes

¾ cup uncooked instant rice
½ cup hot water
¼ teaspoon salt
½ medium green bell pepper, chopped
1 small onion, chopped (about ¼ cup)
1 clove garlic, finely chopped
1 can (16 ounces) stewed tomatoes, undrained
1 can (15 ounces) black beans, drained

1. Mix all ingredients in 2-quart casserole.

2. Cover tightly and microwave on high 12 to 15 minutes, stirring every 5 minutes, until rice is tender and liquid is absorbed. **6 servings (about ⅔ cup each);** 125 calories per serving.

• • • • • • • • • • •

CHICKEN-FLAVORED RICE

MICROWAVE TIME: 10 to 12 minutes
STAND TIME: 5 minutes

2 cups uncooked instant rice
1 can (10½ ounces) condensed chicken broth (about 1¼ cups)
1 small onion, chopped (about ¼ cup)
¼ cup dry white wine
Dash of ground turmeric
1 to 2 tablespoons margarine or butter
Grated Parmesan cheese, if desired

1. Mix all ingredients except margarine and cheese in 2-quart casserole. Cover tightly and microwave on high 10 to 12 minutes, stirring after 5 minutes, until rice is tender and liquid is absorbed.

2. Stir in margarine. Cover and let stand 5 minutes. Sprinkle with cheese. **4 servings (about ¾ cup each);** 220 calories per serving.

500-watt microwave: You may need to increase microwave times.

ITALIAN RISOTTO

Microwave risotto is fast and easy to make—no constant stirring as with conventional cooking—yet you still achieve the luxurious texture and almost saucelike creaminess that make this dish a worldwide favorite.

MICROWAVE TIME: 18 to 25 minutes
STAND TIME: 5 minutes

2 tablespoons margarine or butter
1 small onion, finely chopped (about ¼ cup)
1 cup uncooked Arborio or short grain rice
1¾ cups chicken broth
⅓ cup freshly grated Parmesan cheese

1. Place margarine and onion in 2-quart casserole. Cover tightly and microwave on high 2 to 3 minutes or until onion is soft. Add rice; stir to coat with margarine.

2. Place broth in 2-cup measure. Microwave uncovered 3 to 4 minutes or until hot (do not boil). Stir broth into rice mixture.

3. Cover tightly and microwave on high 3 to 5 minutes or until boiling; stir.

4. Cover tightly and microwave on medium (50%) 10 to 13 minutes or until rice is almost tender and most of the liquid is absorbed. Stir in cheese. Let stand covered 5 minutes. **6 servings (about ½ cup each);** 180 calories per serving.

Risotto with Artichoke Hearts: Just before serving, stir in 1 package (9 ounces) frozen artichoke hearts, cooked and drained. **6 servings (about ⅔ cup each);** 195 calories per serving.

Risotto with Peas: Just before serving, stir in 1 package (10 ounces) frozen green peas, cooked and drained. **6 servings (about 1¼ cups each);** 210 calories per serving.

Risotto with Artichoke Hearts, Pear Chutney (page 333)

Risotto with Zucchini: Stir in 1 medium zucchini, shredded (about 1½ cups), with the Parmesan cheese. **6 servings (about ¾ cup each);** 185 calories per serving.

• • • • • • • • • • •

MUSHROOM AND WILD RICE CASSEROLE

MICROWAVE TIME: 36 to 43 minutes
STAND TIME: 5 minutes

¾ cup uncooked wild rice
2 tablespoons dry white wine
1 tablespoon margarine or butter
1½ teaspoons chopped fresh or ½ teaspoon dried thyme
1 small onion, chopped (about ¼ cup)
1 can (10¾ ounces) condensed chicken broth
1 can (8 ounces) sliced water chestnuts, drained
1 can (4 ounces) sliced mushrooms, drained

1. Mix all ingredients in 2-quart casserole. Cover tightly and microwave on high 6 to 8 minutes or until boiling.

2. Microwave on medium (50%) 30 to 35 minutes or until rice is tender and liquid is absorbed. Let stand covered 5 minutes. **6 servings (about ½ cup each);** 150 calories per serving.

500-watt microwave: You may need to increase microwave times.

CHEDDAR GRITS

MICROWAVE TIME: 8 to 10 minutes

1 tablespoon margarine or butter
2 tablespoons sliced green onion
   (with top)
2 cups milk
½ cup white hominy quick grits
¼ teaspoon salt
⅛ teaspoon pepper
½ cup shredded Cheddar cheese
   (2 ounces)*

1.   Place margarine and onion in 3-quart cas-serole. Cover tightly and microwave on high 1 to 2 minutes or until margarine is bubbly.

2.   Stir in milk, grits, salt and pepper. Cover tightly and microwave 7 to 8 minutes, stir-ring every 3 minutes, until mixture is thick-ened and liquid is absorbed. Stir in cheese.   **5 servings (about ½ cup each)**; 175 calories per serving.

½ cup shredded Colby or Monterey Jack cheese can be substituted for the Cheddar cheese.

BULGUR WITH PEAS

MICROWAVE TIME: 19 to 24 minutes

1 cup uncooked bulgur
2¼ cups hot water
1 medium onion, chopped (about ½ cup)
1 clove garlic, finely chopped
2 tablespoons margarine or butter
2 teaspoons beef or chicken bouillon
   granules
2 teaspoons chopped fresh or ½ teaspoon
   dried dill weed
½ teaspoon salt
1 package (10 ounces) frozen green peas

1.   Mix all ingredients except peas in 2-quart casserole. Cover tightly and microwave on high 12 minutes.

2.   Add peas; stir to break apart. Cover tightly and microwave 7 to 12 minutes or until bulgur is tender and liquid is absorbed; stir.   **8 servings (about ½ cup each)**; 140 calories per serving.

Cheddar Grits

COUSCOUS WITH SPINACH

Traditionally, couscous undergoes a lengthy steaming process, but the microwave puts that on fast forward and gets it done in minutes. The finely cracked wheat or millet grain from which coucous is made has a subtle, nutty flavor that complements a wide variety of foods, including the spinach and dill featured here.

Microwave Time: 12 to 15 minutes

1 package (10 ounces) frozen chopped spinach
Couscous (page 266)
1 tablespoon chopped fresh or 1 teaspoon dried dill weed
¼ teaspoon salt
2 tablespoons lemon juice

1. Microwave spinach as directed on package; drain thoroughly.

2. Prepare couscous as directed.

3. Stir spinach, dill weed and salt into couscous. Cover tightly and microwave on high 2 to 3 minutes or until hot. Stir in lemon juice. **6 servings (about ⅔ cup each);** 140 calories per serving.

NOODLES ROMANOFF

Microwave Time: 4 to 5 minutes

2 cups uncooked medium egg noodles
1 cup sour cream
¼ cup grated Parmesan cheese
2 tablespoons milk
1 tablespoon chopped fresh chives
¼ teaspoon garlic salt
Dash of pepper
¼ teaspoon paprika

1. Cook noodles as directed on package; drain. Stir in remaining ingredients except 2 tablespoons of the cheese and the paprika in 1-quart casserole. Mix remaining cheese and paprika; sprinkle over noodle mixture.

2. Cover tightly and microwave on high 4 to 5 minutes or until hot. **4 servings (about ½ cup each);** 325 calories per serving.

500-watt microwave: You may need to increase microwave time.

GREEK PASTA

Orzo, also known as rosamarina, looks like rice but is really a type of pasta. This recipe couldn't be much simpler to make, and it provides an appropriate side dish for the Greek-inspired Meatballs with Mint (page 158).

MICROWAVE TIME: 18 to 22 minutes

½ cup uncooked orzo
⅓ cup water
½ teaspoon salt
Dash of ground red pepper (cayenne)
1 can (14½ ounces) stewed tomatoes, undrained
1 can (2½ ounces) sliced ripe olives, drained
1 medium zucchini, cut lengthwise into halves
¼ cup plain yogurt

1. Mix all ingredients except zucchini and yogurt in 2-quart casserole. Cover tightly and microwave on high 4 minutes; stir.

2. Cover tightly and microwave 12 to 15 minutes, stirring every 3 minutes, until orzo is tender.

3. Cut zucchini halves into ½-inch slices. Stir zucchini into orzo mixture. Cover tightly and microwave 2 to 3 minutes or until zucchini is crisp-tender. Serve with plain yogurt. **4 servings (about ⅔ cup each);** 105 calories per serving.

MACARONI AND CHEESE WITH TOMATO

MICROWAVE TIME: 18 to 21 minutes

4 slices bacon, cut into 1-inch pieces
1 medium onion, chopped (about ½ cup)
1 medium green bell pepper, chopped (about 1 cup)
1 package (7 ounces) uncooked elbow macaroni (2 cups)
1 can (10¾ ounces) condensed tomato soup
1¾ cups hot water
2 cups shredded American or Colby cheese (8 ounces)
Buttered bread crumbs or cracker crumbs, if desired

1. Place bacon in 3-quart casserole. Cover loosely and microwave on high 4 to 5 minutes or until crisp. Stir in onion, bell pepper, macaroni, soup and water.

2. Cover tightly and microwave 14 to 16 minutes, stirring every 4 minutes, until macaroni is tender. Stir in cheese until melted. Top with bread crumbs.   **4 servings (about 1¼ cups each);** 640 calories per serving.

500-watt microwave: You may need to increase microwave times.

Greek Pasta, Meatballs with Mint (page 158)

MICROWAVING GRAINS

Mix grain and water in 2-quart casserole. Cover tightly and microwave as directed or until tender, stirring at least once. After starting on high, some grains require lower power settings to finish cooking for a tender result.

TYPE	AMOUNT	WATER	POWER LEVEL/TIME	STAND TIME
Bulgur	1 cup	2¼ cups hot	High 7 to 12 minutes, stirring after 5 minutes	
Couscous (wheat-grain semolina)	1 cup	1½ cups hot	High 5 to 7 minutes, stirring after 3 minutes	
Grits, Quick-cooking	½ cup	2 cups	High 7 to 8 minutes, stirring every 3 minutes	
Oatmeal, Quick-cooking	⅓ cup	⅔ cup	High 2 to 3 minutes, stirring after 1 minute	
Rice, Brown	1 cup	2¾ cups	High 6 to 9 minutes; medium (50%) 35 to 40 minutes, stirring after 20 minutes	5 minutes
Rice, Instant	2 cups	2 cups hot	High 9 to 10 minutes	2 minutes
Rice, Parboiled	1 cup	2½ cups	High 5 minutes; medium (50%) 18 to 22 minutes, stirring after 10 minutes	5 minutes
Rice, Wild	½ cup	1 cup hot	High 5 minutes; medium (50%) 25 to 30 minutes, stirring after 15 minutes	5 minutes

RECIPE, PAGE	Servings per recipe	Calories	Protein (grams)	Carbohydrate (grams)	Fat (grams)	Cholesterol (milligrams)	Sodium (milligrams)	PERCENT U.S. RECOMMENDED DAILY ALLOWANCE Protein	Vitamin A	Vitamin C	Thiamin	Riboflavin	Niacin	Calcium	Iron

PER SERVING OR UNIT

NUTRITION INFORMATION

MUFFINS

RECIPE, PAGE	Servings	Calories	Protein	Carb	Fat	Chol	Sodium	Protein	Vit A	Vit C	Thiamin	Riboflavin	Niacin	Calcium	Iron
Apple-Nut Muffins, 241	6	210	3	27	10	48	130	4	0	0	6	4	4	4	4
Bacon-Cheddar Muffins, 242	6	165	5	12	11	55	230	6	2	0	4	6	4	8	2
Blueberry Muffins, 241	6	175	3	20	9	48	130	4	0	0	4	4	4	6	2
Cranberry-Orange Muffins, 241	6	175	3	21	9	48	135	4	0	4	4	4	4	6	2
Easy Pizza Muffins, 243	6	190	5	13	13	50	325	6	2	2	6	6	4	8	4
Peanut Butter Muffins, 239	6	185	4	18	11	48	275	6	0	0	8	6	6	4	4
Raisin-Nut Muffins, 241	6	210	4	25	11	48	135	4	0	0	6	4	4	6	4
Refrigerated Oat Bran Muffins, 239	18	150	3	18	8	48	120	4	0	0	6	4	2	2	4
Sour Cream and Chive Muffins, 243	6	170	3	12	12	50	210	4	4	0	4	4	2	6	2

COFFEE CAKES

RECIPE, PAGE	Servings	Calories	Protein	Carb	Fat	Chol	Sodium	Protein	Vit A	Vit C	Thiamin	Riboflavin	Niacin	Calcium	Iron
Apple-Walnut Coffee Cake, 244	8	300	3	43	13	35	180	4	2	2	6	4	4	2	4
Blueberry Coffee Cake, 246	12	260	3	48	6	25	375	4	4	6	6	6	6	8	4
Brown Sugar–Pecan Coffee Cake, 244	6	305	4	30	19	2	450	4	6	0	18	10	6	8	8
Glazed Sour Cream Coffee Cake, 247	6	400	4	54	19	60	295	6	14	0	6	6	4	4	4
Raisin-Rice Coffee Cake, 246	12	200	3	34	6	25	230	4	4	0	6	4	4	4	4
Streusel Coffee Cake, 249	12	375	5	57	14	25	425	6	8	0	10	6	8	10	8

LOAVES

RECIPE, PAGE	Servings	Calories	Protein	Carb	Fat	Chol	Sodium	Protein	Vit A	Vit C	Thiamin	Riboflavin	Niacin	Calcium	Iron
Apricot Streusel Bread, 251	12	200	4	30	7	48	200	4	24	0	8	6	4	4	8
Blueberry-Orange Bread, 251	12	140	3	18	6	48	145	4	0	0	8	6	2	2	2
Herbed Biscuit Ring, 252	6	270	7	26	15	0	970	10	10	0	16	14	8	20	6
Orange-Date Nut Bread, 249	12	220	4	26	12	25	165	6	0	0	8	2	4	6	4
Zucchini Bread, 248	14	200	3	32	8	40	225	4	2	0	6	2	2	0	4

PER SERVING OR UNIT **NUTRITION INFORMATION** RECIPE, PAGE	Servings per recipe	Calories	Protein (grams)	Carbohydrate (grams)	Fat (grams)	Cholesterol (milligrams)	Sodium (milligrams)	PERCENT U.S. RECOMMENDED DAILY ALLOWANCE						
								Protein	Vitamin A	Vitamin C	Thiamin	Riboflavin	Niacin	Calcium	Iron

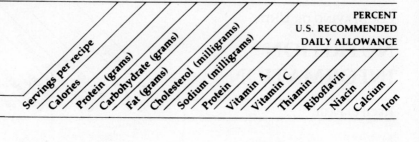

FIX-UPS

Bagels with Cream Cheese Spread															
Apricot, 250	1	195	4	29	7	20	250	6	4	2	8	6	8	2	6
Herb, 250	1	170	4	22	7	20	250	6	4	0	8	6	8	2	6
Onion-Chili, 251	1	170	4	23	7	20	250	6	8	0	8	8	8	2	6
Peanut Butter, 251	1	195	5	23	9	18	250	8	4	0	8	6	12	2	6
Strawberry, 251	1	185	4	26	7	20	250	6	4	8	8	8	8	2	6
Cheddar French Bread, 254	12	110	3	11	6	5	220	4	0	0	2	2	2	4	2
Cheese 'n Chilies French Bread, 252	12	110	3	11	6	5	190	4	4	0	2	2	2	4	2
Crusty Blue Cheese Slices, 253	12	85	2	10	4	2	170	2	2	0	2	2	2	2	2
Garlic French Bread, 252	12	90	2	11	4	0	155	2	2	0	2	2	2	0	2
Onion French Bread, 252	12	90	2	11	4	0	155	2	2	0	2	2	2	0	2
Parmesan-Herb French Bread, 252	12	90	2	11	4	0	185	2	2	0	2	2	2	0	2
Seasoned Croutons, 254	4	85	1	7	6	0	165	0	4	0	2	2	2	0	2

RICE

Black Beans and Rice, 259	6	125	6	26	0	0	285	8	8	40	10	4	6	4	12
Chicken-flavored Rice, 259	4	220	7	38	4	0	350	10	2	2	14	2	16	0	10
Chinese Rice, 259	6	140	6	20	4	95	225	8	6	12	12	6	6	2	8
Curried Rice with Almonds, 257	4	175	3	17	10	0	290	4	4	2	6	2	4	2	4
Italian Risotto, 261	6	180	5	26	6	4	205	8	2	0	8	12	10	8	6
Risotto with Artichoke Hearts, 261	6	195	7	29	6	4	215	10	4	4	10	16	12	8	6
Risotto with Peas, 261	6	210	8	32	6	4	225	12	8	8	16	14	12	8	8
Risotto with Zucchini, 261	6	185	6	27	6	4	205	8	4	8	10	14	10	8	6
Lemon Rice, 254	6	205	4	37	4	0	210	6	2	4	12	0	12	0	8

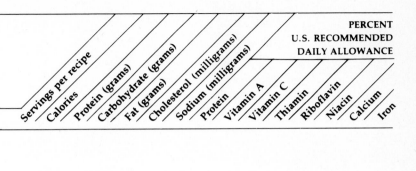

RECIPE, PAGE	Servings per recipe	Calories	Protein (grams)	Carbohydrate (grams)	Fat (grams)	Cholesterol (milligrams)	Sodium (milligrams)	Protein	Vitamin A	Vitamin C	Thiamin	Riboflavin	Niacin	Calcium	Iron
RICE, *continued*															
Orange Pilaf, 254	6	100	2	19	2	0	115	2	8	50	8	0	2	0	4
Parsley-Mushroom Rice, 256	6	125	3	20	4	0	245	4	4	2	6	0	4	0	4
Sour Cream Rice with Chilies, 255	6	350	11	51	11	30	395	16	8	8	18	28	16	18	10
Spanish Rice, 257	6	155	3	24	5	6	575	4	10	35	10	2	6	2	8
GRAINS															
Apple and Wild Rice Dressing, 256	8	150	4	19	7	0	240	6	2	2	4	8	4	2	4
Bulgar with Peas, 262	8	140	5	23	3	0	320	6	6	18	12	4	10	2	8
Cheddar Grits, 262	5	175	7	18	8	20	255	10	8	2	8	14	4	20	4
Couscous with Spinach, 263	6	140	6	30	0	0	135	8	74	14	10	6	6	4	8
Mushroom and Wild Rice Casserole, 261	6	150	6	24	3	0	300	8	0	0	8	10	14	0	10
PASTA															
Greek Pasta, 265	4	105	4	17	2	0	520	6	16	20	12	6	8	6	6
Macaroni and Cheese with Tomato, 265	4	640	22	59	35	70	1395	34	26	100	40	28	22	36	20
Noodles Romanoff, 263	4	325	8	44	13	28	395	12	12	2	18	14	10	10	8

6

DESSERTS

Desserts are the grace notes that can make a meal memorable. They may be comforting or elegant, simple or simply stunning, but for most of us they are delicious indulgences. Desserts have always held a place of honor at the dinner table, but they are just as often enjoyed as pick-me-ups or as luxurious leftovers, too. One thing has changed: With the microwave, preparing desserts is easier than ever.

- Microwave-cooked cakes fit today's lifestyle to a T, so quick to make and often a more convenient size. We've even dressed up a handful of convenience mixes for ultra-fast gratification. Puddings and custards in the microwave don't demand constant stirring as they do on the stove top. We cook them gently at 50% power just until they "set."

- Fruit was made for the microwave. Warm, even hot, fruit desserts are especially luscious with intense, sweet flavor. Whole fruits can be microwave "poached" without becoming mushy, with the advantage of a cool kitchen rather than a hot, steamy one. Finally, because ordinary, flour-based crusts bake better conventionally, we've developed some scrumptious alternative crusts: buttery chocolate crumb, toasty coconut, even meringue. Just turn to these pages when you are looking for something sweet, something new, something fast.

Raspberry Pear Cobbler (page 285), Pecan Fingers (page 289)

APPLESAUCE SNACK CAKE

| MICROWAVE TIME: | 19 to 22 minutes |
| STAND TIME: | 10 minutes |

1⅔ cups all-purpose flour
1 cup packed brown sugar
1½ teaspoons ground allspice
1 teaspoon baking soda
¼ teaspoon salt
½ cup applesauce
⅓ cup chopped nuts
½ cup water
⅓ cup vegetable oil
1 teaspoon vinegar
Apple Cider Sauce (right)

1. Mix flour, brown sugar, allspice, baking soda and salt in round dish, 8 × 1½ inches, using fork. Mix in remaining ingredients except Apple Cider Sauce.

2. Elevate dish on inverted 9-inch pie plate, in microwave oven. Microwave uncovered on medium (50%) 15 to 17 minutes, rotating dish ¼ turn every 5 minutes, until top springs back when touched lightly. (Parts of surface may appear wet but will continue to cook while standing.)

3. Let stand uncovered on flat, heatproof surface (not wire rack) 10 minutes. Prepare Apple Cider Sauce; serve warm sauce with cake. Refrigerate any remaining sauce **8 servings;** 435 calories per serving.

Apple Cider Sauce

½ cup packed brown sugar
¼ cup margarine or butter
2 tablespoons apple cider or orange juice
2 tablespoons whipping (heavy) cream

1. Place all ingredients in 4-cup measure. Microwave uncovered on high 1 to 2 minutes or just until boiling; stir.

2. Microwave uncovered 2 to 3 minutes longer, stirring every minute, until thickened.

Applesauce Snack Cake

CHOCOLATE CHIP–DATE CAKE

MICROWAVE TIME: 10 to 11 minutes
STAND TIME: 15 minutes

⅔ cup hot water
½ cup cut-up dates
½ teaspoon baking soda
⅓ cup vegetable oil
1 egg
1 cup all-purpose flour
½ cup semisweet miniature chocolate chips
¼ cup granulated sugar
¼ cup packed brown sugar
½ teaspoon baking soda
½ teaspoon vanilla
¼ teaspoon salt
Chocolate Chip–Nut Topping (right)

1. Pour hot water over dates in medium bowl; stir in ½ teaspoon baking soda. Let stand 5 minutes.

2. Stir remaining ingredients except Chocolate Chip–Nut Topping into date mixture. Pour batter into round dish, 8 × 1½ inches; sprinkle with topping.

3. Elevate dish on inverted 9-inch pie plate in microwave oven. Microwave uncovered on medium (50%) 6 minutes, rotating dish ¼ turn every 3 minutes.

4. Microwave uncovered on high 3 minutes 30 seconds to 4 minutes 30 seconds, rotating dish ½ turn after 2 minutes, until wooden pick inserted in center comes out clean. (Parts of surface may appear wet but will continue to cook while standing.)

5. Let stand uncovered on flat, heatproof surface (not wire rack) 10 minutes; cool on wire rack.   **8 servings**; 400 calories per serving.

Chocolate Chip–Nut Topping

½ cup chopped nuts
½ cup miniature semisweet chocolate chips
2 tablespoons packed brown sugar

Mix all ingredients.

••••••••••

CHOCOLATE SUNDAE CAKE

Pudding cakes that make up their own spoonable sauces are perfect for microwaving. Serve each portion with a generous drizzle of chocolate sauce from the bottom of the dish.

MICROWAVE TIME: 14 to 16 minutes

1 cup all-purpose flour
¾ cup sugar
2 tablespoons cocoa
2 teaspoon baking powder
¼ teaspoon salt
1 cup chopped walnuts
½ cup milk
2 tablespoons vegetable oil
1 teaspoon vanilla
1 cup packed brown sugar
¼ cup cocoa
1¾ cups hot water

1. Mix flour, sugar, 2 tablespoons cocoa, the baking powder and salt in 2-quart casserole. Stir in walnuts, milk, oil and vanilla.

2. Sprinkle with brown sugar and ¼ cup cocoa. Pour hot water over batter. Microwave uncovered on medium (50%) 9 minutes; rotate casserole ½ turn.

3. Microwave uncovered on high 5 to 7 minutes or until top is almost dry. Serve warm. Spoon into dessert dishes and top with ice cream if desired. Spoon sauce over ice cream.
9 servings; 390 calories per serving.

Butterscotch Sundae Cake: Stir in 1 package (6 ounces) butterscotch chips (1 cup) with the milk. Decrease brown sugar to ½ cup and the ¼ cup cocoa to 2 tablespoons. 410 calories per serving.

Marshmallow-Fudge Sundae Cake: Stir in ½ cup chopped nuts and ½ cup miniature marshmallows with the milk. Decrease brown sugar to ½ cup. 315 calories per serving.

Peanut Butter Sundae Cake: Substitute ½ cup peanut butter for the walnuts. 400 calories per serving.

Raisin Sundae Cake: Stir in 1 cup raisins with the milk. Decrease brown sugar to ½ cup. 365 calories per serving.

••••••••••

LEMON-COCONUT PUDDING CAKE

MICROWAVE TIME: 10 to 12 minutes

2 eggs, separated
¼ teaspoon cream of tartar
1 teaspoon grated lemon peel
¼ cup lemon juice
1 cup milk
1 cup sugar
¼ cup all-purpose flour
¼ teaspoon salt
¼ cup flaked or shredded coconut, toasted

1. Beat egg whites and cream of tartar in small bowl until stiff peaks form; reserve. Beat egg yolks slightly in small bowl. Beat in lemon peel, lemon juice and milk; beat in sugar, flour and salt. Fold into egg white mixture. Pour into 1-quart casserole; sprinkle with coconut.

2. Pour 1 cup very hot water into 1½-quart casserole in microwave. Place casserole of pudding mixture carefully in casserole of hot water. Microwave uncovered on medium-high (70%) 10 to 12 minutes or until wooden pick inserted in center comes out clean. Serve warm and top each serving with whipped cream if desired. **6 servings;** 230 calories per serving.

••••••••••

DATE CAKE

MICROWAVE TIME: 7 to 10 minutes
STAND TIME: 5 minutes

1 package (14 ounces) date bar mix
½ cup hot water
2 eggs
1 teaspoon baking powder
½ cup chopped walnuts
½ cup raisins, if desired
Lemon-Scotch Topping (below)

1. Grease square dish, 8 × 8 × 2 inches. Mix date mix and hot water in small bowl. Stir in crumb mix, eggs, baking powder, walnuts and raisins. Spread in dish.

2. Microwave uncovered on high 6 to 8 minutes, rotating dish ¼ turn every 2 minutes, until top springs back when touched lightly. Let stand uncovered on flat, heatproof surface (not wire rack) 5 minutes. Prepare Lemon-Scotch Topping; spread over warm cake. **9 servings;** 415 calories per serving.

Lemon-Scotch Topping

⅔ cup packed brown sugar
½ cup finely chopped walnuts
2 tablespoons lemon juice
2 tablespoon margarine or butter

Mix all ingredients in 4-cup measure. Microwave uncovered on high 1 to 2 minutes or until hot and bubbly.

APRICOT UPSIDE-DOWN GINGERBREAD

MICROWAVE TIME: 11 to 13 minutes
STAND TIME: 5 minutes

¼ cup margarine or butter
½ cup packed brown sugar
9 maraschino cherry halves
1 can (17 ounces) apricot halves, drained
1 package (14.5 ounces) gingerbread mix

1. Place margarine in square dish, 8 × 8 × 2 inches. Microwave uncovered on high 45 to 60 seconds or until melted. Sprinkle brown sugar over margarine. Arrange cherries and apricots on top.

2. Prepare gingerbread mix as directed on package—except decrease water to ¾ cup. Pour batter over fruit. Elevate dish on inverted 9-inch pie plate in microwave oven. Microwave uncovered on high 10 to 12 minutes, rotating dish ½ turn after 5 minutes, until gingerbread begins to pull away from sides of dish.

3. Let stand uncovered 5 minutes. Invert dish onto plate; leave dish over cake 5 minutes. Serve with ice cream if desired.   **9 servings;** 345 calories per serving.

Apple Upside-down Gingerbread: Substitute 2 cups thinly sliced pared all-purpose apples (about 2 medium) for the apricots. Overlap in 3 rows in dish.   345 calories per serving.

Lemon Upside-down Gingerbread: Substitute 9 very thin slices lemon (about ⅛ inch thick), cut into fourths, for the apricot halves. **9 servings;** 325 calories per serving.

BLUEBERRY CAKE WITH LEMON CUSTARD SAUCE

MICROWAVE TIME: 8 to 10 minutes
REFRIGERATION TIME: 1 hour
STAND TIME: 10 minutes

Lemon Custard Sauce (below)
1 package (13½ ounces) wild blueberry muffin mix
2 tablespoons sugar
1 tablespoon grated lemon peel
¾ teaspoon ground nutmeg
1 tablespoon graham cracker crumbs

1. Prepare Lemon Custard Sauce. Prepare muffin mix as directed on package—except stir in sugar, lemon peel and nutmeg with the muffin mix. Pour batter into round dish, 8 × 1½ inches. Sprinkle graham cracker crumbs over batter.

2. Microwave uncovered on high 4 to 5 minutes, rotating dish ½ turn after 2 minutes, until top springs back when touched lightly. Let stand on flat, heatproof surface (not wire rack) 10 minutes. Serve with Lemon Custard Sauce. Refrigerate any remaining sauce. **8 servings;** 290 calories per serving.

Lemon Custard Sauce

1 egg
¾ cup milk
2 tablespoons sugar
2 teaspoons grated lemon peel

1. Beat egg slightly in 2-cup measure. Mix in remaining ingredients. Microwave uncovered on medium-high (70%) 3 minutes 30 seconds to 4 minutes 30 seconds, briskly stirring with fork every minute, until thick.

2. Stir; cover and refrigerate about 1 hour or until chilled.

Apricot Upside-down Gingerbread

CHOCOLATE-ALMOND PUDDING

MICROWAVE TIME: 8 to 13 minutes
REFRIGERATION TIME: 1 hour

¾ cup sugar
2 tablespoons cornstarch
Dash of salt
2 cups milk
2 ounces unsweetened chocolate,
   chopped
1 egg yolk, slightly beaten
2 tablespoons margarine or butter,
   softened
1½ teaspoons vanilla
1 teaspoon almond extract

1. Mix sugar, cornstarch and salt in 4-cup measure. Gradually stir in milk; stir in chocolate. Microwave uncovered on high 6 to 10 minutes, stirring every 2 minutes, until boiling.

2. Gradually stir at least half of the hot mixture into egg yolk. Stir into hot mixture in measure. Microwave uncovered on medium (50%) 2 to 3 minutes or until boiling. Stir in margarine, vanilla and almond extract.

3. Pour into 5 dessert dishes. Press plastic wrap onto pudding; refrigerate about 1 hour until chilled. Immediately refrigerate any remaining pudding. **5 servings (about ½ cup each);** 290 calories per serving.

Butterscotch Pudding: Omit chocolate and almond extract. Substitute packed brown sugar for the sugar.   245 calories per serving.

Vanilla Pudding: Omit chocolate and almond extract.   230 calories per serving.

RICE PUDDING

MICROWAVE TIME: 13 to 16 minutes
STAND TIME: 10 minutes

1 cup uncooked instant rice
1 cup water
1½ cups milk
¼ cup sugar
2 eggs, slightly beaten
½ cup golden raisins
1 teaspoon vanilla
¼ teaspoon ground nutmeg

1. Mix rice and water in 2-quart casserole. Cover tightly and microwave on high 5 to 6 minutes or until water is absorbed.

2. Stir milk and sugar into hot rice; gradually stir in eggs. Stir in raisins, vanilla and nutmeg.

3. Elevate casserole on inverted 9-inch pie plate in microwave oven. Microwave uncovered on medium (50%) 8 to 10 minutes, stirring every 3 minutes, just until creamy. (Pudding will continue to cook while standing.) Let stand uncovered on flat, heatproof surface (not wire rack) 10 minutes. Serve warm or cold and with cream if desired. Immediately refrigerate any remaining pudding. **6 servings (about ½ cup each);** 185 calories per serving.

LEMON TAPIOCA WITH FRESH BERRIES

Lemon and berries are delicious together, a refreshing combination for a summer treat. The microwave cooks tapioca quickly, without long stirring over a hot range.

MICROWAVE TIME:	6 to 8 minutes
STAND TIME:	5 minutes
REFRIGERATION TIME:	15 minutes

2 cups milk
⅓ cup sugar
3 tablespoons quick-cooking tapioca
1 egg

1 tablespoon grated lemon peel
¼ teaspoon vanilla
1 cup fresh berries

1. Beat milk, sugar, tapioca and egg in 4-cup measure, using wire whisk or hand beater, until well blended. Microwave uncovered on high 6 to 8 minutes, stiring every 2 minutes, until boiling. Stir in lemon peel and vanilla. Let stand uncovered 5 minutes; stir.

2. Pour into 4 dessert dishes. Cover and refrigerate about 15 minutes or until set. Serve warm or cold with berries. Immediately refrigerate any remaining tapioca. **4 servings (about ½ cup each);** 180 calories per serving.

500-watt microwave: You may need to increase microwave times.

Lemon Tapioca with Fresh Berries

RAISIN-NUT BREAD PUDDING

MICROWAVE TIME: 10 to 13 minutes
STAND TIME: 10 minutes

1¾ cups milk
3 eggs
¼ cup sugar
1 teaspoon ground cinnamon
½ cup raisins
¼ cup chopped pecans
4 slices bread, cut into ½-inch cubes
    (about 3 cups)

1. Microwave milk uncovered in 4-cup measure on high 2 to 3 minutes or until hot but not boiling. Beat eggs slightly in 2-quart casserole; stir in milk and remaining ingredients.

2. Cover tightly and microwave on medium (50%) 8 to 10 minutes, stirring after 4 minutes, until center is set. Let stand uncovered on flat, heatproof surface (not wire rack) 10 minutes. Serve warm or cold with cream if desired. Immediately refrigerate any remaining pudding. **6 servings (about ½ cup each);** 230 calories per serving.

500-watt microwave: You may need to increase microwave times.

BANANA FLANS

These Spanish custards are flavored with rum and prettily garnished with banana slices. Allspice provides a gentle, warm note.

MICROWAVE TIME: 7 to 10 minutes
REFRIGERATION TIME: 2 hours

1 tablespoon sugar
¼ teaspoon ground allspice
1¼ cups milk
3 eggs
¼ cup sugar
1 tablespoon dark rum
Dash of salt
2 medium bananas, sliced

1. Grease four 6-ounce custard cups lightly. Mix 1 tablespoon sugar and the allspice. Sprinkle about 1 teaspoon mixture on bottom and side of each custard cup.

2. Microwave milk uncovered on high 3 to 4 minutes or until hot but not boiling. Beat eggs slightly in 4-cup measure using wire whisk or hand beater. Beat in ¼ cup sugar, the rum and salt until foamy and well blended. Beat in hot milk gradually. Pour into custard cups. Arrange custard cups on 10-inch plate.

3. Microwave uncovered on medium (50%) 4 to 6 minutes, rotating custard cups and plate ½ turn after 2 minutes, just until set. (Tops will appear slightly wet but will set completely during refrigeration.) Refrigerate 2 hours or until well chilled.

4. Unmold flans on dessert plates. Top each with 3 banana slices. Arrange remaining banana slices around edges of flans. Immediately refrigerate any remaining flans. **4 servings (about ½ cup each);** 220 calories per serving.

Tangerine Mousse

TANGERINE MOUSSE

Citrus mousses taste every bit as light as they indeed are. If tangerines aren't available, use limes for a tropical-tasting alternative.

MICROWAVE TIME: 1 to 2 minutes
REFRIGERATION TIME: 1 hour 45 minutes

1 envelope unflavored gelatin
¼ cup cold water
¼ cup sugar
½ cup frozen tangerine juice concentrate, thawed
2 teaspoons grated tangerine peel
1 cup whipping (heavy) cream
1 tangerine, peeled and sectioned

1. Sprinkle gelatin on cold water in 4-cup measure. Let stand 5 minutes. Stir in sugar and tangerine juice concentrate. Microwave uncovered on high 1 to 2 minutes or until sugar and gelatin are dissolved. Stir in tangerine peel. Refrigerate about 45 minutes, stirring occasionally, until mixture mounds slightly when dropped from spoon.

2. Beat whipping cream in chilled medium bowl until soft peaks form. Beat gelatin mixture until slightly foamy; fold into whipped cream. Spoon into 5 dessert dishes. Refrigerate about 1 hour or until set. Garnish with tangerine sections and drizzle with Raspberry Sauce (page 328) if desired. **5 servings (about ½ cup each);** 220 calories per serving.

Lime Mousse: Substitute limeade concentrate for the tangerine juice concentrate. Substitute 1 teaspoon grated lime peel for the tangerine peel. Omit tangerine. Garnish with mint leaves if desired. 260 calories per serving.

Orange Mousse: Substitute orange juice concentrate for the tangerine juice concentrate. Substitute orange peel and orange sections for the tangerine peel and tangerine sections. 225 calories per serving.

• • • • • • • • • • •

MOCHA MOUSSE

MICROWAVE TIME:	2 to 3 minutes
REFRIGERATION TIME:	2 hours

2 tablespoons sugar
2 teaspoons cornstarch
1 cup whipping (heavy) cream
¼ cup semisweet chocolate chips
1 tablespoon coffee liqueur

1. Mix sugar and cornstarch in 4-cup measure. Gradually stir in ½ cup of the whipping cream. Stir in chocolate chips. Microwave uncovered on medium (50%) 2 to 3 minutes, stirring every 30 seconds, until chocolate is melted and can be stirred smooth. Stir in liqueur. Refrigerate about 30 minutes or until chilled.

2. Beat remaining cream in chilled small bowl until soft peaks form. Fold chocolate mixture into whipped cream. Spoon into 4 small soufflé dishes. Cover and refrigerate at least 1 hour 30 minutes until set. Garnish with chocolate curls if desired. **4 servings (about ½ cup each);** 330 calories per serving.

EGG CUSTARDS

MICROWAVE TIME:	7 to 10 minutes
REFRIGERATION TIME:	15 minutes

1¼ cups milk
3 eggs
¼ cup sugar
1 teaspoon vanilla
Dash of salt
Nutmeg

1. Microwave milk uncovered on high 3 to 4 minutes or until hot but not boiling.

2. Beat eggs slightly in 4-cup measure, using wire whisk or hand beater. Beat in sugar, vanilla and salt until slightly foamy and well blended. Gradually beat in hot milk. Pour into four 6-ounce custard cups. Sprinkle with nutmeg. Arrange custard cups on 10-inch plate.

3. Microwave uncovered on medium (50%) 4 to 6 minutes, rotating custard cups and plate ½ turn after 2 minutes, just until set. (Tops will appear slightly wet but will set completely during refrigeration.) Refrigerate at least 15 minutes. Unmold to serve warm or cold. Immediately refrigerate any remaining custards. **4 servings (about ½ cup each);** 150 calories per serving.

500-watt microwave: You may need to increase microwave times.

Hazelnut Custards: Substitute 1 teaspoon hazelnut-flavored liqueur for the vanilla. Omit nutmeg; sprinkle each custard with 1 tablespoon chopped hazelnuts before serving. 200 calories per serving.

APPLE CRISP

MICROWAVE TIME: 7 to 10 minutes
STAND TIME: 10 minutes

3 medium tart cooking apples, pared and
   sliced (about 3 cups)
2 tablespoons lemon juice
⅔ cup quick-cooking oats
⅔ cup packed brown sugar
½ cup all-purpose flour
⅓ cup margarine or butter, softened
¾ teaspoon ground cinnamon

1. Place apples in square dish, 8 × 8 × 2 inches. Sprinkle with lemon juice. Mix remaining ingredients with fork until crumbly; sprinkle over apples.

2. Microwave uncovered on high 7 to 10 minutes or until apples are tender. Let stand uncovered 10 minutes. Serve warm and with half-and-half or ice cream if desired.   **6 servings;** 295 calories per serving.

Berry Crisp: Substitute 3 cups raspberries or blueberries for the apples.   280 calories per serving.

Apple Crisp

RASPBERRY-PEAR COBBLER

Cobblers are cozy fruit desserts. This cobbler features a rich, crumbly almond topping rather than the traditional biscuit one. Almonds and pears are especially delicious together.

MICROWAVE TIME:　　6 to 10 minutes

3 firm medium pears, pared and sliced
3 tablespoons sugar
1 tablespoon cornstarch
1 pint raspberries
Almond Topping (below)

1. Place pears in square dish, 8 × 8 × 2 inches. Mix sugar and cornstarch; toss with pears. Carefully stir in raspberries. Sprinkle Almond Topping over fruit.

2. Microwave uncovered on high 6 to 10 minutes, rotating dish ½ turn after 4 minutes, until fruit is tender. Serve warm. **6 servings (about ½ cup each);** 230 calories per serving.

500-watt microwave: You may need to increase microwave time.

Almond Topping

½ cup finely ground almonds
¼ cup all-purpose flour
2 tablespoons sugar
2 tablespoons margarine or butter, softened
¼ teaspoon ground ginger

Mix all ingredients until crumbly.

BLUEBERRY COBBLER

MICROWAVE TIME:　　8 to 10 minutes
STAND TIME:　　10 minutes

1 can (21 ounces) blueberry pie filling
½ teaspoon grated orange peel
1 cup variety baking mix
¼ cup milk
1 tablespoon sugar
1 tablespoon margarine or butter, softened
2 tablespoons slivered almonds, toasted
Ground cinnamon

1. Mix pie filling and orange peel in 1½-quart casserole. Microwave uncovered in medium-high (70%) 4 minutes; stir. Mix baking mix, milk, sugar and margarine until soft dough forms; beat vigorously 20 strokes. Stir in almonds. Drop dough by 6 spoonfuls onto hot blueberry mixture around edge of casserole. Sprinkle with cinnamon.

2. Microwave uncovered 4 to 6 minutes, rotating dish ½ turn after 2 minutes, until biscuits are no longer doughy. Let stand uncovered 10 minutes. Serve with half-and-half if desired. **6 servings;** 245 calories per serving.

DOUBLE CHERRY CRUMBLE

MICROWAVE TIME: 7 to 10 minutes
STAND TIME: 10 minutes

1 can (21 ounces) cherry pie filling
1 can (about 16 ounces) pitted dark sweet
 cherries, drained
⅔ cup quick-cooking oats
½ cup packed brown sugar
½ cup variety baking mix
¼ cup firm margarine or butter
¼ cup chopped nuts, if desired
1 teaspoon ground cinnamon

1. Mix pie filling and cherries in square dish, 8 × 8 × 2 inches. Mix remaining ingredients with fork until crumbly; sprinkle over fruit.

2. Microwave uncovered on high 7 to 10 minutes or until fruit is hot and bubbly. Let stand uncovered 10 minutes. Serve warm. **8 servings;** 290 calories per serving.

• • • • • • • • • • •

SPICY PEACH CRUMBLE

MICROWAVE TIME: 10 to 15 minutes
STAND TIME: 10 minutes

4 medium peaches, peeled and sliced,
 or 1 package (16 ounces) frozen sliced
 peaches, thawed and drained
3 tablespoons packed brown sugar
2 tablespoons cornstarch
½ teaspoon ground cinnamon
¼ teaspoon ground ginger
¼ teaspoon ground allspice
Crumb Topping (right)

1. Place peaches in round dish, 8 × 1½ inches. Mix remaining ingredients except Crumb Topping; toss with peaches. Sprinkle topping over peaches.

2. Microwave uncovered on high 10 to 15 minutes, rotating dish ½ turn every 5 minutes, until peaches are hot and bubbly. Let stand uncovered 10 minutes. Serve warm and with whipped cream if desired. **6 servings;** 190 calories per serving.

500-watt microwave: You may need to increase microwave time.

Crumb Topping

½ cup all-purpose flour
⅓ cup packed brown sugar
2 tablespoons margarine or butter,
 softened

Mix all ingredients until crumbly.

• • • • • • • • • • •

APPLE BROWN BETTY

MICROWAVE TIME: 15 to 17 minutes

3 tablespoons margarine or butter
2 cups soft bread crumbs (about 4 slices
 bread)
½ cup packed brown sugar
¼ cup orange juice
1 teaspoon ground nutmeg
5 medium tart cooking apples, pared and
 sliced (about 6 cups)

1. Place margarine in medium bowl. Microwave uncovered on high 30 to 60 seconds or until melted. Add bread crumbs; toss until well coated with margarine.

2. Mix remaining ingredients. Arrange half of the apple mixture in square dish, 8 × 8 × 2 inches. Top with half of the bread crumb mixture. Repeat with remaining apple and bread crumb mixtures.

3. Microwave uncovered on high 14 to 16 minutes, rotating dish ½ turn every 5 minutes, until apples are tender. Serve warm and with ice cream if desired. **6 servings;** 260 calories per serving.

500-watt microwave: You may need to increase microwave times.

Fruit and Dumplings

FRUIT AND DUMPLINGS

MICROWAVE TIME: 11 to 13 minutes

1 package (10 ounces) frozen raspberries, thawed, drained and liquid reserved
1 can (16 ounces) sliced pears, drained and liquid reserved
2 tablespoons cornstarch
1 teaspoon ground cinnamon
⅓ cup sugar
¾ cup variety baking mix
2 tablespoons sugar
¼ cup sour cream
1 egg

1. Pour reserved liquids into 4-cup measure; add enough water to measure 1½ cups. Stir in cornstarch, cinnamon and ⅓ cup sugar. Microwave uncovered on high 4 to 5 minutes, stirring after 2 minutes, until mixture boils and thickens. Mix with fruits in round dish, 8 × 1½ inches.

2. Mix remaining ingredients; spoon onto fruit mixture, forming a ring around edge of dish. (Dumplings will cook more toward center.) Spoon some of fruit mixture over dumplings. Microwave uncovered on high 6 minutes 30 seconds to 7 minutes 30 seconds, rotating dish ¼ turn after 3 minutes, until dumplings are no longer doughy. Serve warm. **5 servings;** 265 calories per serving.

RHUBARB CRUNCH

MICROWAVE TIME: 15 to 18 minutes

1 pound rhubarb, sliced (about 4 cups)
1 cup sugar
⅛ teaspoon almond extract
¼ cup margarine or butter
4 slices bread, cut into ¼-inch cubes
¼ cup sugar
½ cup chopped almonds
1 teaspoon grated orange peel

1.   Mix rhubarb and 1 cup sugar in 2-quart casserole. Cover and microwave on high 7 to 9 minutes or until rhubarb is tender. Stir in almond extract; cool.

2.   Place margarine in pie plate, 10 × 1½ inches. Microwave uncovered on high 30 to 60 seconds or until melted. Stir in bread cubes, ¼ cup sugar and the almonds until well coated with margarine. Microwave uncovered 7 to 8 minutes, stirring every 2 minutes, until toasted. Stir in orange peel. Spoon rhubarb mixture into dessert dishes; top with bread mixture. Serve warm.   **6 servings;** 350 calories per serving.

Applesauce Crunch: Substitute 2½ to 3 cups applesauce for the cooked rhubarb mixture.   270 calories per serving.

CHERRY-PECAN SHORTBREAD BARS

These are sophisticated cookies. The combination of bittersweet chocolate and preserves or jam is very European.

MICROWAVE TIME: 4 to 5 minutes
STAND TIME: 34 minutes

1 cup all-purpose flour
½ cup sugar
½ cup margarine or butter, softened
¼ cup finely chopped pecans
⅓ cup semisweet chocolate chips
½ cup cherry preserves

1.   Mix flour, sugar, margarine and pecans until crumbly. Press mixture in bottom of ungreased square dish, 8 × 8 × 2 inches.

2.   Microwave uncovered on high 4 to 5 minutes, rotating dish ¼ turn after 2 minutes, until slightly puffed and set.

3.   Sprinkle chocolate chips evenly over hot layer; let stand uncovered 3 to 4 minutes or until chips are shiny. Carefully spread to cover; cool about 30 minutes or until chocolate is slightly set. Spread preserves over chocolate. Cut into about 1¾ × 1¼-inch bars.   **24 bars;** 105 calories per bar.

FROSTED LEMON TREATS

MICROWAVE TIME: 3 to 4 minutes

½ cup margarine or butter, softened
¼ cup sugar
3 tablespoons milk
1 teaspoon grated lemon peel
1 egg
1¼ cups all-purpose flour
½ teaspoon baking powder
½ teaspoon salt
Lemon Frosting (below)

1. Grease bottom only of square dish, 10 × 6 × ½ inches. Mix margarine, sugar, milk, lemon peel and egg in medium bowl. Stir in flour, baking powder and salt. Spread evenly in dish.

2. Microwave uncovered on high 3 to 4 minutes, rotating dish ½ turn after 2 minutes, until no longer doughy; cool. Frost with Lemon Frosting. Cut into about 2 × 1½-inch bars. **18 bars;** 130 calories per bar.

Lemon Frosting

3 tablespoons margarine or butter, softened
¾ cup powdered sugar
1 teaspoon lemon juice

Beat all ingredients until smooth.

PECAN FINGERS

MICROWAVE TIME: 10 to 12 minutes

¾ cup powdered sugar
⅓ cup shortening
⅓ cup margarine or butter, softened
1½ cups all-purpose flour
½ teaspoon salt
2 eggs
1 cup packed brown sugar
1 cup chopped pecans
2 tablespoons all-purpose flour
½ teaspoon baking powder
½ teaspoon salt
½ teaspoon vanilla
Powdered sugar

1. Mix powdered sugar, shortening and margarine in large bowl thoroughly. Stir in 1½ cups flour and ½ teaspoon salt. Press mixture firmly in rectangular dish, 11 × 7 × 1½ inches. Microwave uncovered on high 4 to 6 minutes, rotating dish ¼ turn after 2 minutes, until no longer doughy.

2. Mix remaining ingredients; spread over hot layer. Microwave uncovered 6 minutes, rotating dish ¼ turn after 3 minutes; cool completely. Sprinkle with powdered sugar. Cut into about 3 × 1-inch bars. **28 bars;** 145 calories per bar.

Chocolate-covered Pecan Fingers: Immediately sprinkle warm bars with 1 package (6 ounces) semisweet chocolate chips. Microwave uncovered about 1 minute or until chocolate is melted; spread over bars. 180 calories per bar.

CHOCOLATE TOFFEE BARS

MICROWAVE TIME: 12 to 17 minutes
STAND TIME: 10 minutes
REFRIGERATION TIME: 30 minutes

¼ cup packed brown sugar
3 tablespoons margarine or butter
½ cup all-purpose flour
1 egg, beaten
½ cup packed brown sugar
1 tablespoon all-purpose flour
½ teaspoon baking powder
½ teaspoon vanilla
¼ teaspoon salt
½ cup semisweet chocolate chips
½ cup chopped nuts
Chocolate Glaze (right)

1. Mix ¼ cup brown sugar and the margarine. Stir in ½ cup flour. Press firmly and evenly in bottom of square dish, 8 × 8 × 2 inches. Elevate dish on inverted dinner plate in microwave oven. Microwave uncovered on medium (50%) 4 to 6 minutes, rotating dish ¼ turn after 2 minutes, until mixture appears almost dry. Let stand uncovered 5 minutes.

2. Mix egg, ½ cup brown sugar, 1 tablespoon flour, the baking powder, vanilla and salt. Stir in chocolate chips and nuts. Spread over cooked layer. Microwave uncovered on medium (50%) 7 to 10 minutes, rotating dish ¼ turn every 3 minutes, until top begins to lose glossiness. Cover loosely and let stand 5 minutes.

3. Prepare Chocolate Glaze; drizzle over top. Cut into about 2 × 1¼-inch bars. Refrigerate about 30 minutes or until chocolate is firm. **24 bars;** 105 calories per bar.

Chocolate Glaze

1 tablespoon cocoa
1 tablespoon margarine or butter
1 tablespoon water
½ cup powdered sugar

1. Place cocoa, margarine and water in 2-cup measure.

2. Microwave uncovered on high 20 to 30 seconds or until margarine is melted; stir. Mix in powdered sugar until smooth.

• • • • • • • • • • •

LINZER SQUARES

Linzer Squares are a variation on the famous Linzer torte, named for the Austrian city of Linz that lies by the blue Danube. This very easy cookie is enhanced with the deep flavor of hazelnuts.

MICROWAVE TIME: 12 to 16 minutes

½ cup packed brown sugar
½ cup margarine or butter, softened
1 cup all-purpose flour
1 cup quick-cooking oats
¼ teaspoon salt
1 jar (12 ounces) raspberry preserves
¼ cup chopped hazelnuts or almonds

1. Mix brown sugar and margarine in medium bowl. Stir in flour, oats and salt until crumbly. Reserve 1 cup mixture. Press remaining mixture in bottom of square dish, 8 × 8 × 2 inches.

2. Elevate dish on inverted dinner plate in microwave oven. Microwave uncovered on medium (50%) 8 to 10 minutes, rotating dish ¼ turn every 2 minutes, until hot and slightly bubbly around edges.

3. Carefully spread preserves over hot layer. Sprinkle with reserved oat mixture and the hazelnuts. Elevate dish on inverted dinner

plate in microwave oven. Microwave uncovered on high 4 to 6 minutes, rotating dish ½ turn after 3 minutes, until bubbly; cool. Cut into about 1¼-inch squares. **36 squares;** 85 calories per square.

500-watt microwave: You may need to increase microwave times.

Date Squares: Place 1 package (8 ounces) chopped dates, 2 tablespoons sugar and ½ cup water in 4-cup measure. Microwave uncovered on high 3 to 5 minutes, stirring every 2 minutes, until boiling and thickened. Substitute date mixture for the raspberry preserves. **36 squares;** 80 calories per square.

• • • • • • • • • •

BANANA SPLIT SQUARES

Here are the gooey ingredients of a banana split: bananas, chocolate, pecans, whipped cream and even maraschino cherries. This is ice cream fountain decadence in a cookie.

MICROWAVE TIME: 11 to 14 minutes

¼ cup margarine or butter
1½ cups vanilla wafer crumbs
2 bananas, sliced
1 package (6 ounces) semisweet chocolate chips (1 cup)
1 can (14 ounces) sweetened condensed milk
1 cup chopped pecans
1 cup whipped cream
20 maraschino cherries

1. Place margarine in rectangular dish, 11 × 7 × 1½ inches. Microwave uncovered on high 1 minute to 1 minute 30 seconds or until melted. Sprinkle wafer crumbs evenly over margarine. Arrange banana slices over crumbs.

2. Mix chocolate chips and milk in 4-cup measure. Microwave on medium-high (70%) 2 to 3 minutes or until chips are melted; stir.

Pour over bananas; sprinkle pecans evenly over top.

3. Microwave uncovered on high 8 to 9 minutes or until set; cool. Cut into about 2-inch squares. Top each serving with a dollop of whipped cream and a cherry. **20 squares;** 255 calories per square.

• • • • • • • • • •

MARMALADE PEARS

MICROWAVE TIME: 4 to 7 minutes
STAND TIME: 3 minutes
REFRIGERATION TIME: 1 hour

¼ cup orange marmalade
¼ cup orange juice
2 large pears, cut into halves and cored
¼ cup sour cream
1 tablespoon orange marmalade

1. Mix ¼ cup marmalade and the orange juice in square dish, 8 × 8 × 2 inches, or round dish, 8 × 1½ inches. Arrange pears, cut sides down, in mixture in dish. Cover tightly and microwave on high 4 to 7 minutes or until almost tender when pierced with fork. Let stand covered 3 minutes. Spoon into 4 dessert dishes. Cover and refrigerate about 1 hour or until slightly chilled.

2. Swirl sour cream and 1 tablespoon orange marmalade; spoon over pears. Garnish with mint leaves if desired. **4 servings;** 145 calories per serving.

PLUMS IN PARCHMENT

This simple dessert is ideal for entertaining guests. The presentation is dramatic, the dessert is light. Ice cream is delicious with the warm red or purple plums.

MICROWAVE TIME: 8 to 10 minutes

4 teaspoons margarine or butter
Four 12-inch circles cooking parchment paper
8 large plums, cut into fourths
¼ cup packed brown sugar
¼ cup chopped pecans
½ teaspoon ground cinnamon

1. Place 1 teaspoon margarine on half of each parchment circle. Arrange 8 plum pieces on margarine on each circle. Mix remaining ingredients; sprinkle over plums. Fold other half of circle over plum; mixture.

2. Beginning at one end of semicircle, roll edge up tightly 2 or 3 times to seal. Twist each end several times to secure. Arrange packets in circle in microwave.

3. Microwave on high 8 to 10 minutes, rearranging packets after 5 minutes, until plums are tender.

4. Place each packet on plate. To serve, cut a large X shape on top of each packet; fold back corners. Serve warm with ice cream if desired. **4 servings;** 190 calories per serving.

500-watt microwave: You may need to increase microwave times.

Apples in Parchment: Substitute 4 medium cooking apples, pared and thinly sliced, for the plums. 220 calories per serving.

APRICOT-FIG COMPOTE

MICROWAVE TIME: 9 to 11 minutes
STAND TIME: 30 minutes

1½ cups dried apricots, apples, peaches, pears or prunes, cut into bite-size pieces
¾ cup dried figs, cut into bite-size pieces
½ cup raisins
3 cups water
2 tablespoons honey
2 tablespoons lemon juice
Lemon Whipped Cream (below)

1. Place apricots, figs, raisins and water in 2-quart casserole. Cover tightly and microwave on high 9 to 11 minutes, stirring after 5 minutes, until almost tender when pierced with fork. Stir in honey and lemon juice. Cover and let stand 30 minutes.

2. Place fruit in dessert dishes, using slotted spoon. Top with Lemon Whipped Cream and, if desired, sliced almonds. **6 servings (about ½ cup each);** 270 calories per serving.

Lemon Whipped Cream

½ cup whipping (heavy) cream
1 tablespoon sugar
1 teaspoon grated lemon peel

Beat all ingredients until stiff.

ROSY APPLES

MICROWAVE TIME: 5 to 10 minutes

4 large tart unpared eating apples
¼ cup red cinnamon candies
¼ cup packed brown sugar
1 tablespoon chopped nuts, if desired

1. Core apples. Pare 1-inch strip of skin around top of each apple. Place each apple upright in 10-ounce dish or custard cup. Place 1 tablespoon candies and 1 tablespoon brown sugar in center of each apple, pressing firmly. Arrange dishes in circle in microwave.

2. Microwave uncovered on high 5 to 10 minutes, rotating dishes ½ turn after 3 minutes, until apples are tender when pierced with knife. Spoon syrup in dishes over apples; sprinkle with nuts. Serve warm or cold and with half-and-half if desired.   **4 servings;** 165 calories per serving.

Maple Apples: Omit red cinnamon candies. Pour 1 tablespoon maple-flavored syrup over each apple before microwaving.   195 calories per serving.

Raisin-Nut Apples: Omit red cinnamon candies and brown sugar. Fill each apple with 2 teaspoons raisins and 2 teaspoons chopped nuts. Pour 1 tablespoon apple juice over each apple before microwaving.   150 calories per serving.

COCONUT PINEAPPLE

MICROWAVE TIME: 4 to 6 minutes

4 cups pineapple chunks (about
    1 medium)
1 can (11 ounces) mandarin orange
    segments, drained
⅓ cup packed brown sugar
¼ cup rum
2 tablespoons margarine or butter
⅓ cup shredded coconut, toasted

1. Mix all ingredients except coconut in 1½-quart casserole.

2. Cover tightly and microwave on high 4 to 6 minutes or until bubbly; stir. Sprinkle with coconut. Serve warm.   **6 servings (about ⅔ cup each);** 230 calories per serving.

• • • • • • • • • • •

RHUBARB WITH STRAWBERRIES

MICROWAVE TIME: 8 to 10 minutes

4 cups 1-inch pieces rhubarb (about
    1 pound)
¾ to 1 cup sugar
2 tablespoons water
1 cup strawberry halves

1. Mix rhubarb, sugar and water in 2-quart casserole.

2. Cover tightly and microwave on high 8 to 10 minutes, stirring after 5 minutes, until rhubarb is tender and slightly transparent. Stir in strawberries. Serve warm or cold. **6 servings (about ½ cup each);** 115 calories per serving.

ALMOND-STUFFED PEACHES

MICROWAVE TIME: 4 to 6 minutes
STAND TIME: 10 minutes

2 firm ripe peaches, cut into halves
2 crisp macaroon cookies, crushed (about ¼ cup)
2 tablespoons chopped almonds
1 tablespoon sugar
2 tablespoons almond-flavored liqueur
4 teaspoons margarine or butter

1. Place each peach half in 6-ounce custard cup or small bowl. Mix remaining ingredients except margarine until well blended. Fill each peach half with about 1 tablespoon macaroon mixture. Top each with 1 teaspoon margarine. Arrange custard cups on 10-inch plate.

2. Cover with waxed paper and microwave on medium (50%) 4 to 6 minutes, rotating plate ½ turn after 3 minutes, until peaches are tender when pierced with fork. Let stand uncovered 10 minutes. Serve warm or cold and with ice cream if desired.   **4 servings;** 170 calories per serving.

Winter Almond-stuffed Peaches: Substitute 4 canned peach halves, well drained, for the fresh peaches.   170 calories per serving.

GLAZED ORANGES WITH KIWIFRUIT

STAND TIME: 10 minutes
MICROWAVE TIME: 2 to 3 minutes
REFRIGERATION TIME: 1 hour

3 large seedless oranges
¼ cup sugar
2 teaspoons cornstarch
½ cup water
1 kiwifruit, pared and sliced, or ½ cup raspberries or blueberries

1. Cut enough thin slivers of peel from 1 orange with vegetable parer or sharp knife to measure 2 tablespoons, being careful not to cut into white membrane. Cover orange peel with boiling water. Let stand 5 minutes; drain.

2. Mix sugar and cornstarch in 2-cup measure. Stir in ½ cup water and the orange peel. Microwave uncovered on high 2 to 3 minutes, stirring every minute, until mixture thickens and boils. Let stand uncovered 5 minutes.

3. Pare oranges, removing all white membrane. Cut into slices; place in large bowl. Pour sugar mixture over oranges. Cover and refrigerate about 1 hour or until chilled. Just before serving, fold in kiwifruit.   **4 servings (about ⅔ cup each);** 110 calories per serving.

POACHED PEARS WITH HOT FUDGE SAUCE

For a calorie shortcut, serve the pears with the poaching liquid spooned over them instead of Hot Fudge Sauce.

MICROWAVE TIME: 17 to 24 minutes
STAND TIME: 45 minutes

4 medium pears
2 tablespoons lemon juice
1 cup dry white wine, rosé wine or water
½ cup sugar
½ cup Hot Fudge Sauce (page 327)

1. Core pears from the bottom, leaving stems intact. Pare pears; brush with lemon juice.

2. Mix wine and sugar in 3-quart casserole. Microwave uncovered on high 3 to 6 minutes or until boiling; stir until sugar is dissolved. Place pears upright in wine mixture. Spoon wine mixture over pears.

3. Cover tightly and microwave on high 10 to 12 minutes, rotating casserole ½ turn and spooning wine mixture over pears after 5 minutes, until pears are soft but not mushy.

4. Let pears stand covered in wine mixture about 45 minutes or until warm. Serve warm or cold with Hot Fudge Sauce. **4 servings;** 445 calories per serving.

500-watt microwave: You may need to increase microwave times.

•••••••••••

BERRY COMPOTE

MICROWAVE TIME: 4 to 6 minutes

½ cup sugar
¼ cup kirsch or cherry juice
2 cups strawberry halves
1 cup raspberries
1 cup blueberries or blackberries

1. Mix sugar and kirsch in 2-quart casserole. Microwave uncovered on high 2 to 3 minutes, stirring after 1 minute, until boiling. Carefully stir in berries.

2. Microwave uncovered 2 to 3 minutes, stirring after 1 minute, until berries are warm. Serve warm and with whipped cream or ice cream if desired. **4 servings (about ½ cup each);** 240 calories per serving.

500-watt microwave: You may need to increase microwave times.

•••••••••••

TWO-FRUIT SHORTCAKES

MICROWAVE TIME: 2 to 3 minutes
REFRIGERATION TIME: 1 hour

2 tablespoons packed brown sugar
1 tablespoon cornstarch
½ cup orange juice
¼ cup water
2 cups raspberries, strawberry halves
 or blueberries
2 firm large bananas, sliced
4 angel food or pound cake slices
¼ cup whipped cream

1. Mix brown sugar and cornstarch in 4-cup measure; stir in orange juice and water. Microwave uncovered on high 2 to 3 minutes, stirring every minute, until boiling. Cover and refrigerate about 1 hour or until cool.

2. Fold raspberries and bananas into orange sauce. Spoon over cake slices; top each with 1 tablespoon of whipped cream. **4 servings;** 280 calories per serving.

Poached Pears with Hot Fudge Sauce, Berry Compote

FRUIT TORTILLAS

Soft flour tortillas quickly become crisp in the microwave. Here they form a pretty shell to hold fruit and chocolate, an unusual dessert.

MICROWAVE TIME: 4 to 8 minutes
REFRIGERATION TIME: 10 minutes

4 flour tortillas (about 7 inches in diameter)
½ cup semisweet chocolate chips
2 teaspoons shortening
1 cup raspberries or blueberries
3 medium peaches or nectarines, peeled and sliced
½ cup peach yogurt

1.   Press each tortilla into 10-ounce custard cup, forming a shell. Microwave uncovered on high 2 to 5 minutes, rotating custard cups ½ turn after 2 minutes, until tortillas feel dry. Remove from custard cups.

2.   Place chocolate chips and shortening in pie plate, 9 × 1¼ inches. Microwave uncovered on high 2 to 3 minutes or until melted; stir until smooth. Dip edges of tortillas into melted chocolate. Drizzle remaining chocolate mixture on inside of tortillas. Refrigerate about 10 minutes or until chocolate is firm.

3.   Mix raspberries and peaches; spoon into tortillas. Top with yogurt.   **4 servings;** 255 calories per serving.

500-watt microwave: You may need to increase microwave times.

Fruit Tortillas

FLAMING FRUIT

MICROWAVE TIME: 4 to 6 minutes

1 jar (10 ounces) currant jelly
1 cup canned pitted dark sweet
    cherries, drained and 2 tablespoons
    syrup reserved
1 can (11 ounces) mandarin orange
    segments, drained
¼ cup rum
1 teaspoon grated orange peel
¼ cup brandy
8 scoops vanilla ice cream (about ½ cup
    each)

1. Place jelly in 1-quart casserole. Microwave uncovered on high 2 to 3 minutes, stirring every minute, until melted.

2. Stir in cherries, reserved syrup, the orange segments, rum and orange peel. Microwave uncovered 1 to 2 minutes or until hot.

3. Measure brandy in 1-cup measure. Microwave uncovered on high about 15 seconds or until warm. Fill metal ladle with about 1 tablespoon warm brandy; pour remaining brandy over cherries and oranges. Ignite brandy in ladle; pour over fruit. Serve hot over ice cream.   **8 servings;** 310 calories per serving.

• • • • • • • • • • •

BANANA SUNDAES

MICROWAVE TIME: 4 to 6 minutes

⅓ cup packed brown sugar
2 tablespoons margarine or butter
½ teaspoon ground cinnamon
¼ cup coffee liqueur or strong coffee
4 firm medium bananas, cut into ½-inch
    diagonal slices
4 scoops vanilla ice cream (about ½ cup
    each)

1. Place brown sugar, margarine and cinnamon in 2-quart casserole. Microwave uncovered on high 2 to 3 minutes, stirring after 1 minute, until hot and bubbly. Stir in liqueur. Microwave uncovered about 1 minutes or until bubbly.

2. Carefully stir in bananas. Microwave uncovered 1 to 2 minutes or until bananas are hot. Serve warm over ice cream. Garnish each serving with maraschino cherry if desired.   **4 servings;** 450 calories per serving.

• • • • • • • • • • •

BUTTERSCOTCH-APPLE SUNDAES

MICROWAVE TIME: 8 to 10 minutes

3 medium tart unpared cooking
    apples, sliced
⅓ cup packed brown sugar
1 tablespoon margarine or butter
6 scoops cinnamon or vanilla ice cream
    (about ½ cup each)

1. Mix all ingredients except ice cream in 2-quart casserole.

2. Cover tightly and microwave on high 8 to 10 minutes, stirring after 4 minutes, until apples are almost tender when pierced with fork. Serve warm over ice cream.   **6 servings (about ½ cup each);** 240 calories per serving.

Butterscotch-Pear Sundaes: Substitute 3 firm medium pears, pared and sliced, for the apples.   235 calories per serving.

FLAMING PECAN BANANAS

MICROWAVE TIME: 3 to 4 minutes

2 tablespoons margarine or butter
2 tablespoons honey
¼ teaspoon ground nutmeg
2 firm bananas, cut lengthwise in half
and halves cut crosswise in half
2 tablespoons chopped pecans
2 tablespoons dark rum

1. Place margarine in 2-quart casserole. Microwave uncovered on high 20 to 30 seconds or until melted. Stir in honey and nutmeg. Place bananas in honey mixture; turn to coat. Sprinkle with pecans. Microwave uncovered 2 to 3 minutes or until hot.

2. Place rum in 1-cup measure. Microwave uncovered on high about 15 seconds or until warm. Pour into metal serving spoon. Ignite rum in spoon; pour over bananas. Serve warm. **4 servings**; 180 calories per serving.

Flaming Pecan Bananas

SOUTHERN BLUEBERRY PIE

MICROWAVE TIME: 6 to 7 minutes
REFRIGERATION TIME: 2 hours

Graham Cracker Crust (below)
3 cups fresh or frozen (thawed and drained) blueberries
½ cup sugar
2 tablespoons cornstarch
¼ teaspoon salt
¼ teaspoon ground cinnamon
¾ cup water
2 tablespoons grenadine syrup
1 tablespoon lemon juice
Sour Cream Topping (right)

1. Prepare Graham Cracker Crust. Spread blueberries in crust. Mix sugar, cornstarch, salt and cinnamon in 4-cup measure. Stir in water. Microwave uncovered on high 3 to 4 minutes, stirring every minute, until thickened and clear.

2. Stir in grenadine syrup and lemon juice. Pour over blueberries. Refrigerate at least 2 hours. Serve with Sour Cream Topping. **8 servings;** 300 calories per serving.

Graham Cracker Crust

¼ cup margarine or butter
1 cup graham cracker crumbs (about 12 squares)
2 tablespoons sugar

1. Place margarine in pie plate, 9 × 1¼ inches. Microwave uncovered on high 30 to 45 seconds or until melted. Stir in cracker crumbs and sugar until crumbs are well coated.

2. Press mixture firmly and evenly on bottom and against side of pie plate. Microwave uncovered 1 minute 30 seconds to 2 minutes or until set; cool.

Sour Cream Topping

1 cup sour cream
2 tablespoons sugar
1 teaspoon vanilla

Mix all ingredients.

•••••••••

IMPOSSIBLE FRENCH APPLE PIE

MICROWAVE TIME: 24 to 28 minutes

6 cups sliced pared tart cooking apples
1¼ teaspoons ground cinnamon
¼ teaspoon ground nutmeg
½ cup milk
2 tablespoons margarine or butter, softened
2 eggs
1 cup sugar
⅓ cup variety baking mix
Streusel (below)

1. Grease pie plate, 10 × 1½ inches. Mix apples and spices; turn into pie plate. Beat remaining ingredients except Streusel 15 seconds in blender on high speed or 1 minute with hand beater, until smooth.

2. Pour over apples. Sprinkle with Streusel and, if desired, ground cinnamon. Microwave on medium-high (70%) 24 to 28 minutes, rotating pie plate ¼ turn every 8 minutes, until knife inserted in center comes out clean. Cool on flat, heatproof surface (not wire rack).   **10 servings;** 340 calories per serving.

Streusel

1 cup variety baking mix
½ cup chopped nuts
⅓ cup packed brown sugar
3 tablespoons firm margarine or butter

Mix all ingredients until crumbly.

DOUBLE COCONUT CREAM PIE

The *dessert for coconut lovers. The crust for this rich confection is simply chewy-crunchy coconut. The custard filling is fully cooked in as little as 8 minutes.*

MICROWAVE TIME: 13 to 20 minutes
REFRIGERATION TIME: 4 hours

Coconut Crust (right)
½ cup sugar
2 tablespoons cornstarch
1¾ cups milk
2 egg yolks, slightly beaten
2 tablespoons margarine or butter, softened
1 teaspoon coconut extract
2 cups whipped cream

1.   Prepare Coconut Crust. Mix sugar and cornstarch in 4-cup measure. Gradually stir in milk. Microwave uncovered on high 6 to 10 minutes, stirring every 2 minutes, until boiling.

2.   Gradually stir at least half of the hot mixture into egg yolks. Stir into hot mixture in measure. Microwave uncovered on medium (50%) 2 to 3 minutes or until boiling.

Stir in reserved ½ cup shredded coconut, the margarine and coconut extract until margarine is melted. Pour into crust; press plastic wrap onto filling. Refrigerate at least 4 hours until chilled.

3.   Top with whipped cream and reserved 2 tablespoons toasted coconut. Immediately refrigerate any remaining pie.   **8 servings;** 460 calories per serving.

Coconut Crust

1 package (7 ounces) shredded coconut
1 tablespoon margarine or butter, melted

1.   Empty coconut into pie plate, 9 × 1¼ inches; reserve ½ cup for filling. Microwave remaining coconut in pie plate uncovered on high 4 to 6 minutes, stirring every 30 seconds, until brown. (Watch carefully so coconut does not burn.) Remove 2 tablespoons of the toasted coconut; reserve for top of pie.

2.   Toss remaining coconut and margarine until coconut is well coated. Press mixture evenly against bottom and side of pie plate. Microwave uncovered 1 minute; cool.

500-watt microwave: You may need to increase microwave times.

MINI PUMPKIN PIES

The little gingersnap cookies on top of the filling become soft after cooking. Every spoonful mixes gingery "crust" with smooth pumpkin cream.

MICROWAVE TIME:	16 to 18 minutes
STAND TIME:	10 minutes
REFRIGERATION TIME:	1 hour

2 eggs
¾ cup sugar
1 can (16 ounces) pumpkin
1 cup evaporated milk
1 teaspoon ground cinnamon
½ teaspoon ground ginger
¼ teaspoon salt
¼ teaspoon ground cloves
8 gingersnaps

1. Beat eggs slightly in large bowl, using wire whisk or hand beater. Beat in remaining ingredients except gingersnaps. Divide mixture among eight 6-ounce custard cups or soufflé dishes. Place gingersnap on each.

2. Arrange 4 custard cups on 10-inch plate. Elevate plate on inverted 10-inch plate in microwave oven. Microwave uncovered on medium (50%) 8 to 9 minutes, rotating custard cups ¼ turn every 2 minutes, until knife inserted near center comes out clean (remove pies one at a time as they finish cooking).

3. Repeat with remaining custard cups. Let stand uncovered 10 minutes. Refrigerate uncovered at least 1 hour until chilled. Serve with whipped cream if desired. Immediately refrigerate any remaining pies. **8 servings;** 185 calories per serving.

CHOCOLATE-TOPPED PEANUT PIE

MICROWAVE TIME:	19 to 27 minutes
STAND TIME:	30 minutes
REFRIGERATION TIME:	2 hours

Cookie Crust (below)
⅓ cup margarine or butter, melted
1 cup corn syrup
⅔ cup sugar
1 tablespoon all-purpose flour
½ teaspoon salt
3 eggs
1 cup salted peanuts, coarsely chopped
½ cup semisweet chocolate chips

1. Prepare Cookie Crust. Beat margarine, corn syrup, sugar, flour, salt and eggs in medium bowl, using hand beater, until smooth. Stir in peanuts. Microwave uncovered on medium (50%) 5 to 7 minutes, stirring every 2 minutes, until hot.

2. Pour mixture into crust. Elevate pie plate on inverted dinner plate in microwave oven. Microwave uncovered on medium (50%) 9 to 13 minutes, rotating pie plate ¼ turn every 3 minutes, until filling is almost set.

3. Sprinkle with chocolate chips. Let stand uncovered 30 minutes. Refrigerate at least 2 hours. **8 servings;** 640 calories per serving.

Cookie Crust

½ cup margarine or butter, softened
1 cup all-purpose flour
¼ cup finely chopped peanuts
¼ cup powdered sugar

1. Mix all ingredients with hands until soft dough forms. Press firmly and evenly on bottom and against side of pie plate, 9 × 1¼ inches, using floured fingers.

2.   Elevate pie plate on inverted dinner plate in microwave oven. Microwave uncovered on high 5 to 7 minutes, rotating pie plate ½ turn after 3 minutes, until dry and flaky. Cool on flat, heatproof surface (not wire rack).

• • • • • • • • • •

FROSTY CHOCOLATE-CARAMEL PIE

MICROWAVE TIME:	6 to 9 minutes
STAND TIME:	10 minutes
FREEZE TIME:	4 hours

Graham Cracker Crust (page 301)
¼ cup graham cracker crumbs
1 package (6 ounces) semisweet chocolate chips (1 cup)
3 tablespoons water
1 teaspoon vanilla
1 container (9 ounces) frozen whipped
   topping, thawed (about 4 cups)
28 caramels
¼ cup water
⅓ cup pecan halves

1.   Prepare Graham Cracker Crust, adding ¼ cup graham cracker crumbs. Place chocolate chips and 3 tablespoons water in large bowl or 2½-quart casserole. Microwave uncovered on high 1 minute to 1 minute 30 seconds or until chocolate is softened. Stir until smooth. Let stand 10 minutes.

2.   Stir in vanilla; fold in whipped topping. Spoon into crust. Freeze at least 4 hours until firm.

3.   Place caramels and ¼ cup water in 4-cup measure. Microwave uncovered on high 1 minute 30 seconds to 2 minutes 30 seconds or until caramels are softened. Stir until smooth. Stir in pecans; cool. Pour over pie. **8 servings;** 505 calories per serving.

CREAMY CHEESECAKE WITH CRANBERRY TOPPING

MICROWAVE TIME:	17 to 20 minutes
REFRIGERATION TIME:	2 hours

Cranberry Topping (below)
Graham Cracker Crust (page 301)
¼ cup graham cracker crumbs
2 packages (8 ounces each) cream cheese,
   softened
2 eggs
¾ cup sugar
1 tablespoon grated orange peel
2 teaspoons vanilla
1 cup sour cream
2 tablespoons sugar
2 teaspoons vanilla

1.   Prepare Cranberry Topping. Prepare Graham Cracker Crust, adding ¼ cup graham cracker crumbs.

2.   Beat cream cheese, eggs, sugar, orange peel and 2 teaspoons vanilla in large bowl on high speed about 2 minutes or until smooth. Microwave uncovered on medium (50%) 8 to 9 minutes, stirring every 2 minutes, until hot and thickened. Pour into crust.

3.   Mix remaining ingredients; spread carefully over filling. Refrigerate about 2 hours or until chilled. Serve with Cranberry Topping. Immediately refrigerate any remaining cheesecake.   **8 servings;** 635 calories per serving.

Cranberry Topping

½ cup sugar
½ cup corn syrup
2 cups cranberries

1.   Mix all ingredients in 1-quart caserole.

2.   Cover tightly and microwave on high 6 to 7 minutes, stirring after 4 minutes, until sugar is dissolved and mixture boils; cool.

Fresh Fruit Tart

FRESH FRUIT TART

MICROWAVE TIME: 4 to 5 minutes
REFRIGERATION TIME: 4 hours

Graham Cracker Crust (page 301)
1 package (8 ounces) cream cheese,
    softened
½ cup apricot preserves
1 tablespoon milk
2 nectarines or peaches, peeled and
    thinly sliced
2 plums, thinly sliced
½ cup seedless grapes

1.   Prepare Graham Cracker Crust as directed except stir ½ teaspoon ground cinnamon into the melted margarine and press crumb mixture firmly and evenly in bottom of 10-inch dinner plate, quiche dish or pie plate.

2.   Beat cream cheese, ¼ cup of the preserves and the milk on medium speed until well blended. Spread evenly over crust. Arrange fruit on cream cheese mixture.

3.   Place remaining ¼ cup preserves in 1-cup measure. Microwave uncovered on high 30 to 60 seconds or until hot; spoon over fruit. Refrigerate at least 4 hours until chilled. **8 servings;** 310 calories per serving.

500-microwave: You may need to increase microwave times.

BLACK-BOTTOM BANANA TART

Microwavable tart pans are available now, some even with classic, fluted sides. Quiche dishes and pie plates work beautifully, too, of course. This rich chocolate crumb crust filled with banana cream is irresistible.

MICROWAVE TIME:	10 to 16 minutes
STAND TIME:	5 minutes
REFRIGERATION TIME:	3 hours

Chocolate Crumb Crust (right)
½ cup sugar
2 tablespoons cornstarch
2 cups milk
3 egg yolks, slightly beaten
2 tablespoons margarine or butter, softened
1 teaspoon vanilla
3 firm large bananas
1 tablespoon chocolate wafer crumbs

1. Prepare Chocolate Crumb Crust. Mix sugar and cornstarch in 4-cup measure. Gradually stir in milk. Microwave uncovered on high 6 to 10 minutes, stirring every 2 minutes, until boiling.

2. Gradually stir at least half of the hot mixture into egg yolks; stir into hot mixture in measure. Microwave uncovered on medium (50%) 2 to 3 minutes, stirring every minute, until boiling. Add margarine and vanilla; stir until margarine is melted. Press plastic wrap onto filling; let stand 5 minutes. Slice 2 bananas into crumb crust. Pour filling over bananas; press plastic wrap into filling. Refrigerate at least 3 hours until chilled.

3. Sprinkle wafer crumbs over filling. Slice remaining banana; arrange on top. Immediately refrigerate any remaining tart. **8 servings;** 310 calories per serving.

Chocolate Crumb Crust

¼ cup margarine or butter
1¼ cups chocolate wafer crumbs (about 20 chocolate wafers)

1. Place margarine in quiche dish or pie plate, 9 × 1¼ inches. Microwave uncovered on high 1 to 2 minutes or until melted.

2. Stir in wafer crumbs until well coated. Press mixture evenly against bottom and side of pie plate. Microwave uncovered on high 30 seconds; cool.

500-watt microwave: You may need to increase microwave times.

• • • • • • • • • • •

DESSERT OMELET WITH FRESH FRUIT

MICROWAVE TIME:	2 minutes

2 eggs, separated
2 tablespoons sugar
1 cup sliced strawberries
1 small kiwifruit, pared and sliced
1 teaspoon powdered sugar

1. Beat egg whites in medium bowl on high speed until stiff but not dry. Beat egg yolks and sugar in small bowl on high speed about 2 minutes or until thick and lemon colored. Fold egg yolk mixture into egg whites.

2. Pour into pie plate, 9 × 1¼ inches. Microwave uncovered on high 2 minutes or until center is set but still moist.

3. Spoon strawberries and kiwifruit onto half of omelet. Loosen edge of omelet; fold just to center. Slide omelet onto serving plate. Sprinkle with powdered sugar. Serve immediately. **4 servings;** 90 calories per serving.

500-watt microwave: You may need to increase microwave times.

Chocolate-Almond Cheesecake

CHOCOLATE-ALMOND CHEESECAKE

The filling for this cheesecake is cooked separately, then poured into the crust.

MICROWAVE TIME:	11 to 13 minutes
REFRIGERATION TIME:	4 hours

Vanilla Wafer Crust (right)
2 packages (8 ounces each) cream cheese, softened
2 eggs
¾ cup sugar
1 teaspoon vanilla
½ teaspoon almond extract
Rich Chocolate Glaze (page 309)
¼ cup sliced almonds

1. Prepare Vanilla Wafer Crust. Beat cream cheese, eggs, sugar, vanilla and almond extract on medium speed until smooth.

2. Microwave uncovered on medium (50%) 8 to 9 minutes, stirring every 2 minutes, until hot and thickened. Pour into shell. Refrigerate uncovered 1 hour or until cool.

3. Prepare Chocolate Glaze. Pour over top of cheesecake; garnish with almonds. Refrigerate at least 3 hours until chilled. Immediately refrigerate any remaining cheesecake. **10 servings;** 420 calories per serving.

Vanilla Wafer Crust

¼ cup margarine or butter
1¼ cups vanilla wafer crumbs (about 30 wafers)

1. Place margarine in quiche dish, 9 × 1½ inches, or pie plate, 9 × 1¼ inches. Microwave uncovered on high 30 to 45 seconds or until melted. Stir in crumbs.

2. Press mixture evenly on bottom and against side of dish. Microwave uncovered 1 minute.

Rich Chocolate Glaze

½ cup whipping (heavy) cream
½ cup semisweet chocolate chips

1. Measure whipping cream in 1-cup measure. Microwave uncovered on high 1 to 2 minutes or until hot (do not boil).

2. Stir in chocolate chips until smooth and thickened; cool.

500-watt microwave: You may need to increase microwave times.

INDIVIDUAL LEMON CHEESECAKES

MICROWAVE TIME: 4 to 5 minutes
REFRIGERATION TIME: 1 hour 30 minutes

6 gingersnaps, crushed
1 package (8 ounces) cream cheese, softened
⅓ cup sugar
1 egg
2 teaspoons grated lemon peel
1 teaspoon vanilla
Cheesecake Topping (below)

1. Sprinkle about 1 tablespoon gingersnap crumbs in each of six 6-ounce custard cups.

2. Beat cream cheese, sugar, egg, lemon peel and vanilla in medium bowl with hand beater about 2 minutes or until blended. Microwave uncovered on medium (50%) 4 to 5 minutes, stirring every 2 minutes, until hot and thickened.

3. Spread about ¼ cup cheese mixture over gingersnap crumbs in each custard cup. Refrigerate uncovered 30 minutes.

4. Carefully spread Cheesecake Topping over cheesecakes. Refrigerate about 1 hour or until chilled. Serve with fresh strawberries if desired. Immediately refrigerate any remaining cheesecake. **6 servings;** 275 calories per serving.

Cheesecake Topping

½ cup sour cream
1 tablespoon sugar
1 teaspoon vanilla

Mix all ingredients.

TRIFLE

MICROWAVE TIME: 6 to 10 minutes
REFRIGERATION TIME: 3 hours

2 cups milk
1 package (3⅛ ounces) vanilla regular
    pudding and pie filling (dry)
1 package (3 ounces) ladyfingers (12)
3 tablespoons rum or 1 teaspoon rum
    extract
2 cups sliced strawberries
1 cup whipping (heavy) cream
¼ cup packed brown sugar
½ teaspoon vanilla
2 tablespoons slivered almonds, toasted

1. Measure milk in 4-cup measure; stir in
pudding and pie filling. Microwave uncovered on high 3 minutes; stir. Microwave uncovered 3 to 7 minutes, stirring every minute,
until boiling. Press plastic wrap onto pudding. Refrigerate about 2 hours or until cool.

2. Split ladyfingers lengthwise; arrange cut
sides to center in 2-quart serving bowl, using
as many as needed to line bowl. Sprinkle
rum over ladyfingers. Layer pudding, strawberries and remaining ladyfingers in bowl.

3. Beat whipping cream, brown sugar and
vanilla in chilled medium bowl until stiff.
Spread over trifle; sprinkle with almonds.
Refrigerate at least 1 hour but no longer than
6 hours.   **10 servings;** 240 calories per serving.

BRANDIED BUTTERSCOTCH FONDUE

MICROWAVE TIME: 3 to 4 minutes

1 package (14 ounces) caramels
    (about 48)
⅓ cup whipping (heavy) cream
½ teaspoon salt
¼ cup brandy
Dippers (pineapple chunks, banana
    slices, seedless grapes or cake cubes)

1. Place caramels, whipping cream and salt
in 4-cup measure. Microwave uncovered on
high 3 to 4 minutes, stirring after 2 minutes,
until caramels can be stirred smooth. Stir in
brandy.

2. Pour into fondue or chafing dish to keep
warm. Spear Dippers with fondue forks; dip
and swirl in fondue with stirring motion.
6 servings (about ⅓ cup each); 455 calories per
serving.

SPICED CHOCOLATE FONDUE

MICROWAVE TIME: 4 to 8 minutes

1 package (12 ounces) semisweet
   chocolate chips
½ cup light corn syrup
¼ cup milk
2 tablespoons coffee liqueur or strong
   coffee
¼ teaspoon ground cinnamon
Dippers (angel food cake cubes, cake
   doughnut slices, banana slices,
   cherries, marshmallows or pretzels)

1. Place chocolate chips and corn syrup in
4-cup measure. Microwave uncovered on medium (50%) 1 minute 30 seconds to 3 minutes 30 seconds or until mixture can be stirred
smooth.

2. Stir in milk, liqueur and cinnamon. Microwave uncovered 2 to 4 minutes, stirring
every minute, until warm. Pour into fondue
or chafing dish to keep warm. (If mixture
become too thick, stir in small amount of
milk.) Spear Dippers with fondue forks; dip
and swirl in fondue with stirring motion.
6 servings (about ⅓ cup each); 585 calories per
serving.

FROZEN MOCHA MALLOW

MICROWAVE TIME: 3 to 4 minutes
REFRIGERATION TIME: 20 minutes
FREEZER TIME: 3 hours

3 cups miniature marshmallows
½ cup water
1 to 2 tablespoons powdered instant
   coffee (dry)
½ teaspoon ground nutmeg
1 cup whipping (heavy) cream
½ cup whipping (heavy) cream
2 tablespoons packed brown sugar
½ teaspoon vanilla
1 cup sliced peaches or nectarines

1. Mix marshmallows, water, coffee and nutmeg in 3-quart casserole. Cover tightly and
microwave on high 3 to 4 minutes, stirring
every minute, until smooth. Refrigerate about
20 minutes or until mixture mounds slightly
when dropped from spoon.

2. Beat 1 cup whipping cream in chilled
large bowl until stiff. Fold marshmallow mixture into whipped cream. Pour into square
pan, 8 × 8 × 2 inches. Freeze about 3 hours
or until firm.

3. Beat ½ cup whipping cream, the brown
sugar and vanilla until stiff. Top each serving with whipped cream mixture and peaches.
9 servings; 210 calories per serving.

TROPICAL PARFAITS

Wine glasses are a respectable substitute for tall parfait glasses. The layers of fruit and cream are what make parfaits unique.

MICROWAVE TIME: 8 to 13 minutes
REFRIGERATION TIME: 2 hours

¾ cup sugar
2 tablespoons cornstarch
Dash of salt
2 cups milk
1 egg yolk, slightly beaten
1 tablespoon magarine or butter, softened
½ teaspoon vanilla
1 can (20 ounces) pineapple tidbits, drained
¼ cup chopped macadamia nuts, toasted

1. Mix sugar, cornstarch and salt in 8-cup measure. Gradually stir in milk. Microwave uncovered on high 6 to 10 minutes, stirring every 2 minutes, until boiling.

2. Gradually stir at least half of the hot mixture into egg yolk; stir into hot mixture in measure. Microwave uncovered on medium (50%) 2 to 3 minutes or until boiling. Stir in margarine and vanilla until margarine is melted. Press plastic wrap onto pudding. Refrigerate at least 2 hours until chilled.

3. Layer pineapple and pudding in each of 4 parfait glasses or dessert dishes, topping with pudding. Sprinkle with nuts. **4 servings;** 365 calories per serving.

500-watt Microwave: You may need to increase microwave times.

CHOCOLATE-MINT PARFAITS

MICROWAVE TIME: 4 to 5 minutes
REFRIGERATION TIME: 1 hour 20 minutes
STAND TIME: 10 minutes

24 large marshmallows
½ cup milk
1 teaspoon vanilla
⅛ teaspoon salt
6 drops peppermint extract
6 drops red or green food color
¾ cup chocolate wafer crumbs (about 14 chocolate wafers)
2 tablespoons margarine or butter
1 tablespoon sugar
1 cup whipping (heavy) cream

1. Place marshmallows and milk in 3-quart casserole. Cover tightly and microwave on high 3 to 4 minutes or until marshmallows are melted. Stir in vanilla, salt, peppermint extract and food color. Refrigerate about 20 minutes, stirring occasionally, until mixture mounds slightly when dropped from spoon.

2. Mix wafer crumbs, margarine and sugar in 2-cup measure. Microwave uncovered on high about 1 minute or until margarine is melted; stir. Let stand uncovered 10 minutes.

3. Beat whipping cream in chilled small bowl until stiff. Stir marshmallow mixture until smooth; fold into whipped cream. Layer whipped cream mixture and crumb mixture in each of 6 parfait glasses, using about 2 tablespoons crumb mixture for each glass, topping with crumb mixture. Refrigerate at least 1 hour until chilled. **6 servings;** 385 calories per serving.

RECIPE, PAGE	Servings per recipe	Calories	Protein (grams)	Carbohydrate (grams)	Fat (grams)	Cholesterol (milligrams)	Sodium (milligrams)	Protein	Vitamin A	Vitamin C	Thiamin	Riboflavin	Niacin	Calcium	Iron

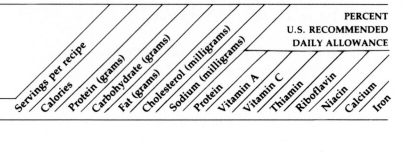

PER SERVING OR UNIT

NUTRITION INFORMATION

PERCENT U.S. RECOMMENDED DAILY ALLOWANCE

CAKES

RECIPE, PAGE	Serv	Cal	Prot	Carb	Fat	Chol	Sod	Prot%	VitA	VitC	Thia	Ribo	Niac	Calc	Iron
Applesauce Snack Cake, 273	8	435	4	64	19	5	360	4	4	0	8	4	8	4	12
Apple Upside-down Gingerbread, 277	9	345	2	57	12	0	390	2	4	0	6	6	4	2	12
Apricot Upside-down Gingerbread, 277	9	345	2	57	12	0	390	2	12	0	6	6	4	2	12
Blueberry Cake with Lemon Custard Sauce, 277	8	290	5	44	9	35	325	8	0	0	8	10	4	10	4
Butterscotch Sundae Cake, 275	9	410	5	67	14	15	190	6	2	0	6	8	4	12	6
Chocolate Chip–Date Cake, 274	8	400	5	50	21	35	225	6	0	0	8	4	6	2	10
Chocolate Sundae Cake, 274	9	390	5	62	14	15	195	8	2	0	6	10	4	14	10
Date Cake, 275	9	415	5	58	18	60	225	8	2	0	4	2	0	6	6
Lemon-Coconut Pudding Cake, 275	6	230	4	43	5	95	150	6	2	2	4	6	0	6	2
Lemon Upside-down Gingerbread, 277	9	325	2	53	12	0	390	2	4	4	6	6	4	2	12
Marshmallow-Fudge Sundae Cake, 275	9	315	5	51	11	15	195	6	2	0	6	8	4	12	8
Peanut Butter Sundae Cake, 275	9	400	7	63	15	15	265	10	2	0	6	10	12	14	10
Raisin Sundae Cake, 275	9	365	5	64	11	15	195	8	2	0	8	8	4	14	10

COOKIES

RECIPE, PAGE	Serv	Cal	Prot	Carb	Fat	Chol	Sod	Prot%	VitA	VitC	Thia	Ribo	Niac	Calc	Iron
Banana Split Squares, 291	20	255	3	26	16	25	85	4	6	2	4	6	0	6	2
Cherry-Pecan Shortbread Bars, 288	24	105	1	14	5	0	45	0	2	0	2	0	0	0	0
Chocolate-covered Pecan Fingers, 289	28	180	2	21	10	20	150	2	4	0	4	2	2	0	4
Chocolate Toffee Bars, 290	24	105	1	14	5	10	60	0	0	0	2	0	0	0	2
Date Squares, 291	36	80	1	12	3	0	45	0	2	0	2	0	0	0	2
Frosted Lemon Treats, 289	18	130	1	14	7	15	160	2	6	0	2	2	2	0	2
Linzer Squares, 290	36	85	1	14	3	0	50	0	2	0	2	0	0	0	2
Pecan Fingers, 289	28	145	1	17	8	20	150	2	4	0	4	2	2	0	2

PUDDINGS, CUSTARDS AND MOUSSES

RECIPE, PAGE	Serv	Cal	Prot	Carb	Fat	Chol	Sod	Prot%	VitA	VitC	Thia	Ribo	Niac	Calc	Iron
Banana Flans, 280	4	220	8	33	6	210	160	10	8	10	4	16	2	10	4
Butterscotch Pudding, 278	5	245	4	40	8	55	170	4	8	0	2	10	0	14	6

RECIPE, PAGE	Servings per recipe	Calories	Protein (grams)	Carbohydrate (grams)	Fat (grams)	Cholesterol (milligrams)	Sodium (milligrams)	Protein	Vitamin A	Vitamin C	Thiamin	Riboflavin	Niacin	Calcium	Iron

PER SERVING OR UNIT

NUTRITION INFORMATION

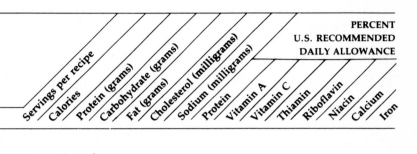

PERCENT U.S. RECOMMENDED DAILY ALLOWANCE

PUDDINGS, CUSTARDS AND MOUSSES, *continued*

RECIPE, PAGE	Servings	Calories	Protein	Carb	Fat	Cholesterol	Sodium	Protein %	Vit A	Vit C	Thiamin	Riboflavin	Niacin	Calcium	Iron
Chocolate-Almond Pudding, 278	5	290	5	40	14	55	160	6	8	0	2	10	0	12	4
Chocolate-Mint Parfaits, 313	6	385	3	36	25	55	260	4	14	0	4	10	2	6	4
Egg Custards, 283	4	150	7	16	6	210	160	10	6	0	2	12	0	10	4
Hazelnut Custards, 283	4	200	8	18	10	210	160	12	6	0	6	14	2	12	6
Lemon Tapioca with Fresh Berries, 279	4	180	6	31	4	80	80	8	6	40	2	14	0	16	2
Lime Mousse, 282	5	260	2	26	18	65	20	2	14	8	0	2	0	2	0
Mocha Mousse, 283	4	330	2	21	25	80	25	2	16	0	0	4	0	4	2
Orange Mousse, 282	5	225	2	16	18	65	20	2	14	34	2	2	0	2	0
Raisin-Nut Bread Pudding, 280	6	230	8	33	8	145	165	12	4	0	10	14	4	12	8
Rice Pudding, 278	6	185	6	34	3	95	55	8	4	0	8	8	2	8	6
Tangerine Mousse, 282	5	220	2	14	18	65	20	2	18	14	2	2	0	2	0
Tropical Parfaits, 313	4	365	6	59	13	70	190	8	8	12	8	14	2	16	4
Vanilla Pudding, 278	5	230	4	37	8	55	160	4	8	0	2	10	0	12	0

COBBLERS AND CRISPS

RECIPE, PAGE	Servings	Calories	Protein	Carb	Fat	Cholesterol	Sodium	Protein %	Vit A	Vit C	Thiamin	Riboflavin	Niacin	Calcium	Iron
Apple Brown Betty, 286	6	260	2	51	7	0	165	2	6	8	6	4	4	4	6
Apple Crisp, 284	6	295	3	49	11	0	125	4	8	2	8	2	2	2	8
Applesauce Crunch, 288	6	270	4	35	14	0	185	6	6	2	6	10	6	6	6
Berry Crisp, 284	6	280	3	45	11	0	125	4	10	12	8	6	2	4	10
Blueberry Cobbler, 285	6	245	2	45	6	0	300	2	2	0	8	6	4	6	8
Double Cherry Crumble, 286	8	290	2	52	10	0	170	4	12	0	8	2	2	4	10
Fruit and Dumplings, 287	5	265	3	51	6	60	235	4	2	4	8	8	4	6	6
Raspberry-Pear Cobbler, 285	6	230	3	34	10	0	45	4	4	10	4	8	4	4	4
Rhubarb Crunch, 288	6	350	4	55	14	0	185	6	6	4	6	8	6	12	6
Spicy Peach Crumble, 286	6	190	2	38	4	0	50	2	12	4	4	4	6	2	6

FRUIT DESSERTS

RECIPE, PAGE	Servings	Calories	Protein	Carb	Fat	Cholesterol	Sodium	Protein %	Vit A	Vit C	Thiamin	Riboflavin	Niacin	Calcium	Iron
Almond-stuffed Peaches, 295	4	170	1	21	7	0	65	2	8	2	2	2	2	0	0
Apples in Parchment, 293	4	220	1	37	9	0	50	0	4	4	6	0	0	2	4

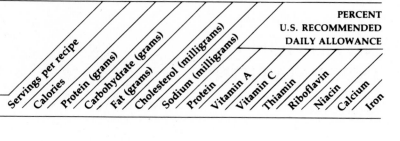

Per Serving or Unit **NUTRITION INFORMATION** RECIPE, PAGE	Servings per recipe	Calories	Protein (grams)	Carbohydrate (grams)	Fat (grams)	Cholesterol (milligrams)	Sodium (milligrams)	Protein	Vitamin A	Vitamin C	Thiamin	Riboflavin	Niacin	Calcium	Iron
FRUIT DESSERTS, *continued*															
Apricot-Fig Compote, 293	6	270	3	53	8	30	15	4	52	2	2	4	6	6	12
Banana Sundaes, 299	4	450	4	74	14	30	135	4	12	10	4	16	2	10	6
Berry Compote, 297	4	240	1	50	1	0	5	0	0	44	2	4	2	0	2
Butterscotch-Apple Sundaes, 299	6	240	2	39	9	30	85	2	6	2	2	10	0	10	2
Butterscotch-Pear Sundaes, 299	6	235	3	38	9	30	85	4	6	2	2	10	0	10	2
Coconut Pineapple, 294	6	230	1	39	6	0	70	0	4	24	12	4	4	2	6
Flaming Fruit, 299	8	310	3	51	7	30	65	4	6	6	2	10	0	10	4
Flaming Pecan Bananas, 300	4	180	1	23	9	0	70	0	4	4	4	4	0	0	0
Fruit Tortillas, 298	4	255	5	41	9	2	45	6	12	24	4	8	6	10	8
Glazed Oranges with Kiwifruit, 295	4	110	1	28	0	0	0	0	4	100	6	2	0	4	0
Maple Apples, 294	4	195	0	50	0	0	40	0	0	4	2	0	0	0	2
Marmalade Pears, 291	4	145	1	30	3	5	10	0	2	10	2	2	0	2	2
Plums in Parchment, 293	4	190	1	28	9	0	50	2	8	8	6	6	2	2	4
Poached Pears with Hot Fudge Sauce, 297	4	445	2	65	6	5	40	2	0	6	2	6	0	6	8
Raisin-Nut Apples, 294	4	150	1	30	4	0	5	2	0	4	4	0	0	0	2
Rhubarb with Strawberries, 294	6	115	1	29	0	0	5	0	0	20	0	2	0	6	0
Rosy Apples, 294	4	165	0	43	0	0	5	0	0	4	2	0	0	0	2
Two-Fruit Shortcakes, 297	4	280	5	67	1	0	90	6	2	74	4	10	2	8	4
Winter Almond-stuffed Peaches, 295	4	170	1	21	7	0	65	2	8	2	2	2	2	0	0
PIES AND TARTS															
Black-Bottom Banana Tart, 307	8	310	5	41	15	95	235	6	10	6	4	12	4	8	6
Chocolate-topped Peanut Pie, 304	8	640	10	73	35	105	690	14	16	0	10	8	22	4	18
Double Coconut Cream Pie, 302	8	460	5	29	37	145	180	6	24	0	2	10	0	12	2
Fresh Fruit Tart, 306	8	310	4	36	18	30	245	4	16	6	2	8	4	2	6
Frosty Chocolate–Caramel Pie, 305	8	505	3	63	24	0	190	4	8	0	4	4	4	0	6
Impossible French Apple Pie, 301	10	340	4	53	14	55	305	6	6	2	12	8	4	8	8
Mini Pumpkin Pies, 304	8	185	4	31	6	80	160	6	100	2	2	10	2	10	8
Southern Blueberry Pie, 301	8	300	2	43	14	15	245	2	10	6	2	6	2	42	2

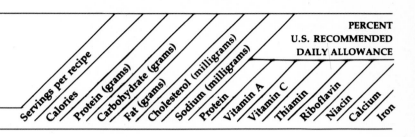

PER SERVING OR UNIT NUTRITION INFORMATION RECIPE, PAGE	Servings per recipe	Calories	Protein (grams)	Carbohydrate (grams)	Fat (grams)	Cholesterol (milligrams)	Sodium (milligrams)	Protein	Vitamin A	Vitamin C	Thiamin	Riboflavin	Niacin	Calcium	Iron

SPECIAL DESSERTS

RECIPE, PAGE	Servings	Calories	Protein	Carb	Fat	Chol	Sodium	Protein	Vit A	Vit C	Thiamin	Riboflavin	Niacin	Calcium	Iron
Brandied Butterscotch Fondue, 310	6	455	2	79	5	15	220	2	4	6	2	6	2	2	0
Chocolate-Almond Cheesecake, 308	10	420	6	31	30	115	235	10	20	0	2	8	2	6	6
Creamy Cheesecake with Cranberry Topping, 305	8	635	8	73	35	145	395	12	26	4	2	18	4	10	14
Dessert Omelet with Fresh Fruit, 307	4	90	3	13	3	135	35	4	2	70	2	6	0	2	4
Frozen Mocha Mallow, 311	9	210	1	19	15	55	25	2	12	2	0	2	0	2	2
Individual Lemon Cheesecakes, 309	6	275	5	20	20	100	170	6	14	0	0	6	0	6	4
Spiced Chocolate Fondue, 311	6	585	7	100	17	0	130	10	0	0	2	8	0	10	16
Trifle, 310	10	240	4	27	12	70	90	4	8	14	2	8	2	8	2

7

SAUCES, RELISHES AND PRESERVES

In the microwave, most sauces are cooked uncovered. That way, liquid evaporates, intensifying flavor and thickening the sauce at the same time. A few tips for successful saucemaking include:

- Sauces are easiest to handle when microwaved in measuring cups. Liquid can be measured in the cup and the handle makes it easy to move in and out of the microwave when stirring.

- A wire whisk or table fork works most efficiently when stirring sauces in the microwave.

- When converting your own conventional sauce recipes, reduce the liquid by about 1 tablespoon per cup so the finished sauce is not too thin. It's easier to thin a sauce after cooking by adding more liquid than it is to thicken it.

Putting up vegetables and fruit in small batches means that preparation is quick and easy. Microwaves make crisp relishes and pickles a snap, and they make quick work of jellies, jams and preserves without vigilant stirring. In just a single afternoon you can prepare a wide variety of preserves to store in the refrigerator. The small amounts made in the microwave fit perfectly with the ripe harvest of a small garden or a splurge at the farmer's market.

Be sure to use the recommended size container when cooking fruit and sugar, as these mixtures will boil over if cooked in one that is too small.

Liquid or powdered fruit pectin is always used when making preserves in the microwave. Since there is no direct heat to evaporate moisture as quickly as in conventional cooking, the fruit-sugar mixture would take forever to thicken without the use of pectin.

Bread and Butter Pickles (page 331), Lemon-Orange Marmalade (page 333), Mixed Berry Jam (page 334)

GARLIC TOMATO SAUCE

Microwave Time: 4 to 6 minutes

1 can (8 ounces) tomato sauce
¾ cup finely chopped tomato
   (about 1 medium)
2 cloves garlic, finely chopped
1 tablespoon lemon juice
⅛ teaspoon ground cumin
⅛ teaspoon salt

1.   Mix all ingredients in 4-cup measure.

2.   Cover tightly and microwave on high 4 to 6 minutes, stirring after 2 minutes, until hot and bubbly.   **About 1¾ cups sauce;** 5 calories per tablespoon.

LEMON-DILL SAUCE

Microwave Time: 4 to 5 minutes

1 tablespoon margarine or butter
1 tablespoon all-purpose flour
1 teaspoon chicken bouillon granules
1 tablespoon chopped fresh or 1 teaspoon
   dried dill weed
⅔ cup water
1 tablespoon lemon juice

1.   Place margarine in 2-cup measure. Microwave uncovered on high 15 to 30 seconds or until melted.

2.   Stir in flour, bouillon granules and dill weed. Stir in water and lemon juice. Microwave uncovered 3 to 4 minutes, stirring every minute, until mixture thickens and boils. **About ¾ cup sauce;** 15 calories per tablespoon.

Tangy Orange Sauce (page 324), Garlic Tomato Sauce

Hollandaise Sauce

HOLLANDAISE SAUCE

Be certain that the melted butter is just warm—not hot—when the egg yolks are added. Otherwise, the eggs will curdle. Whisk or stir this sauce thoroughly. When it is done it will have thickened.

MICROWAVE TIME: 2 to 4 minutes

½ cup butter*
1 tablespoon lemon juice
1 tablespoon water
3 egg yolks, slightly beaten

1. Place butter in 2-cup measure. Microwave uncovered on medium (50%) 1 minute to 1 minute 15 seconds or until partially melted. Stir until completely melted. (Butter should be warm but not hot.)

2. Add lemon juice and water. Gradually beat in egg yolks with fork. Microwave uncovered 45 seconds; stir. Microwave uncovered 30 seconds to 1 minute 15 seconds longer, stirring every 15 seconds, until thickened. (Do not overcook or sauce will curdle.) Cover and refrigerate any remaining sauce. **About ¾ cup sauce;** 85 calories per tablespoon.

We do not recommend margarine for this recipe.

CHEDDAR CHEESE SAUCE

MICROWAVE TIME: 4 to 5 minutes

2 tablespoons margarine or butter
2 tablespoons all-purpose flour
1 teaspoon chicken bouillon granules
Dash of ground nutmeg
Dash of ground red pepper (cayenne)
1 cup milk
⅔ cup shredded Cheddar cheese

1.   Place margarine in 4-cup measure. Microwave uncovered on high 15 to 20 seconds or until melted; stir in flour, bouillon granules, nutmeg and red pepper until blended. Stir in milk.

2.   Microwave uncovered 3 to 4 minutes, stirring every minute, until thickened. Stir in cheese until melted.   **About 1½ cups sauce;** 30 calories per tablespoon.

• • • • • • • • • •

MOZZARELLA SAUCE

MICROWAVE TIME: 4 to 5 minutes

1 tablespoon margarine or butter
1 tablespoon all-purpose flour
⅛ teaspoon ground red pepper (cayenne)
½ cup chicken broth
½ cup half-and-half
½ cup shredded mozzarella cheese
    (2 ounces)

1.   Place margarine in 4-cup measure. Microwave uncovered on high about 45 seconds or until melted. Stir in flour, red pepper, broth and half-and-half.

2.   Microwave uncovered 3 to 4 minutes or until thickened. Stir in cheese until melted. **About 1½ cups sauce;** 15 calories per tablespoon.

RED CHILI SAUCE

MICROWAVE TIME: 1 to 2 minutes

1 cup chili sauce
2 teaspoons prepared horseradish
2 teaspoons lemon juice
¼ teaspoon Worcestershire sauce
⅛ teaspoon salt

1.   Mix all ingredients in 2-cup measure.

2.   Microwave uncovered on high 1 to 2 minutes or until hot. Stir before serving.   **About 1 cup sauce;** 15 calories per tablespoon.

• • • • • • • • • •

RED WINE SAUCE

MICROWAVE TIME: 3 to 4 minutes

3 tablespoons cornstarch
¼ cup water
1 can (10½ ounces) condensed beef broth
⅓ cup dry red wine
1 tablespoon soy sauce

1.   Mix cornstarch and water in 4-cup measure. Gradually stir in remaining ingredients.

2.   Microwave uncovered on high 3 to 4 minutes, stirring every minute, until boiling. **About 2 cups sauce;** 10 calories per tablespoon.

TANGY ORANGE SAUCE

MICROWAVE TIME: 2 to 4 minutes

½ cup orange juice
¼ cup orange marmalade
1 tablespoon lemon juice
⅛ teaspoon ground ginger
2 teaspoons cornstarch
1 tablespoon cold water
1 orange, pared and sectioned

1. Mix orange juice, marmalade, lemon juice and ginger in 2-cup measure. Microwave uncovered on high 1 to 2 minutes or until boiling.

2. Mix cornstarch and water; stir into orange juice mixture. Microwave uncovered on medium-high (70%) 1 to 2 minutes, stirring every minute, until mixture thickens and boils. Stir in orange. Serve warm. **About 1 cup sauce;** 25 calories per tablespoon.

• • • • • • • • • •

ZESTY BARBECUE SAUCE

This is basting sauce at its simplest; it can even be prepared ahead of time. After grilling or broiling, just heat the remaining sauce to boiling and serve it for dipping.

MICROWAVE TIME: 2 minutes

½ cup ketchup
3 tablespoons packed brown sugar
1 tablespoon lemon juice
1 teaspoon Worcestershire sauce
1 clove garlic, crushed

1. Mix all ingredients in 2-cup measure.

2. Cover loosely and microwave on high 1 minute 30 seconds to 2 minutes, stirring after 1 minute, until hot and bubbly. **About ¾ cup sauce;** 15 calories per tablespoon.

SHRIMP SAUCE

MICROWAVE TIME: 6 to 8 minutes

2 tablespoons margarine or butter
1 tablespoon all-purpose flour
1 cup milk
1 egg yolk, slightly beaten
1 can (4¼ ounces) shrimp, rinsed and drained
⅓ cup finely chopped cucumber
⅛ teaspoon chili powder
Dash of pepper

1. Place margarine in 4-cup measure. Microwave uncovered on high 15 to 20 seconds or until melted. Stir in flour and milk. Microwave uncovered 2 to 3 minutes, stirring every minute, until thickened.

2. Stir at least half of the hot mixture into egg yolk. Stir egg mixture into remaining hot mixture. Stir in remaining ingredients. Microwave uncovered on medium (50%) 3 to 4 minutes, stirring after 2 minutes, until hot. Cover and refrigerate any remaining sauce. **About 2 cups sauce;** 20 calories per tablespoon.

• • • • • • • • • •

APRICOT-HONEY SAUCE

This sweet-tart sauce is especially good with crisp, fried chicken and chicken nuggets.

MICROWAVE TIME: 2 minutes

½ cup apricot jam
2 tablespoons honey
2 tablespoons Dijon mustard
1 tablespoon vinegar

1. Mix all ingredients in 2-cup measure.

2. Microwave uncovered on high about 2 minutes or until hot. **About 1 cup sauce;** 40 calories per tablespoon.

Shrimp Sauce

CREAMY ALMOND SAUCE

As good with fresh fruit as with pound cake, this pale almond-scented sauce is a quick dessert dress-up.

MICROWAVE TIME: 3 to 5 minutes

¼ cup sugar
1 tablespoon cornstarch
1½ cups milk
2 eggs
¼ teaspoon almond extract

1. Mix sugar and cornstarch in medium bowl. Gradually stir in milk. Beat in eggs with wire whisk or hand beater.

2. Microwave uncovered on high 3 to 5 minutes, stirring briskly with wire whisk every minute, until mixture coats a spoon. Stir in almond extract. Serve warm or chilled. Cover and refrigerate any remaining sauce. **About 1¾ cups sauce;** 20 calories per tablespoon.

• • • • • • • • • •

BUTTERSCOTCH SAUCE

MICROWAVE TIME: 3 minutes

⅔ cup packed brown sugar
⅓ cup light corn syrup
¼ cup margarine or butter
¼ cup milk
½ teaspoon vanilla

1. Mix all ingredients except vanilla in 4-cup measure.

2. Microwave uncovered on high 2 minutes 30 seconds to 3 minutes, stirring after 1 minute, until boiling rapidly. Stir in vanilla. Serve warm. **About 1¼ cups sauce;** 65 calories per tablespoon.

Creamy Almond Sauce, Butterscotch Sauce

MARSHMALLOW SAUCE

MICROWAVE TIME: 4 minutes

⅔ cup sugar
¼ cup water
3 tablespoons light corn syrup
2 cups miniature marshmallows
¾ teaspoon vanilla

1. Mix sugar, water and corn syrup in 2-quart casserole. Microwave uncovered on high 2 minutes 30 seconds to 3 minutes or until boiling. Stir in marshmallows.

2. Microwave uncovered 1 minute. Stir in vanilla; continue stirring until marshmallows are melted and mixture is smooth. Serve warm. **About 2 cups sauce;** 30 calories per tablespoon.

• • • • • • • • • •

HOT FUDGE SAUCE

MICROWAVE TIME: 4 to 6 minutes

1 can (5⅓ ounces) evaporated milk (⅔ cup)
1 package (6 ounces) semisweet chocolate chips (1 cup)
½ cup sugar
2 teaspoons margarine or butter
½ teaspoon vanilla

1. Mix milk, chocolate chips and sugar in 2-cup measure. Microwave uncovered on medium (50%) 4 to 6 minutes, stirring every 2 minutes, until boiling.

2. Add margarine and vanilla; stir vigorously until margarine is melted and sauce is smooth. Serve warm. **About 1½ cups sauce;** 65 calories per tablespoon.

Lemon Sauce, Raspberry Sauce

LEMON SAUCE

MICROWAVE TIME: 2 to 3 minutes

¼ cup sugar
1 tablespoon cornstarch
1 teaspoon grated lemon peel
¾ cup lemon juice

1.   Mix sugar and cornstarch in 4-cup measure. Stir in lemon peel and lemon juice.

2.   Microwave uncovered on high 2 minutes to 2 minutes 30 seconds, stirring after 1 minute, until boiling. Serve warm.   **About ¾ cup sauce;** 25 calories per tablespoon.

RASPBERRY SAUCE

Raspberries make one of the most beautiful and versatile fruit sauces. Serve it with fresh cantaloupe, peaches or apricots, or sorbet or plain cake.

MICROWAVE TIME: 2 to 3 minutes

¼ cup currant jelly
1 tablespoon cornstarch
1 package (10 ounces) frozen raspberries, thawed, drained and ½ cup syrup reserved

1.   Mix jelly and cornstarch in 4-cup measure until well blended. Gradually stir in reserved raspberry syrup.

2.   Microwave uncovered on high 2 to 3 minutes, stirring every minute, until boiling. Stir in raspberries. Serve warm or chilled.   **About 1 cup sauce;** 15 calories per tablespoon.

RUM SAUCE

MICROWAVE TIME: 3 to 5 minutes

¾ cup sugar
¾ cup whipping (heavy) cream
¼ cup milk
1 tablespoon cornstarch
½ cup margarine or butter
1 teaspoon rum flavoring or 1 tablespoon
   rum

1. Mix sugar, whipping cream, milk and cornstarch in 4-cup measure. Add margarine.

2. Microwave uncovered on high 3 to 5 minutes, stirring after 3 minutes, until boiling. Serve warm. **About 1¼ cups sauce;** 105 calories per tablespoon.

CRANBERRY RELISH

MICROWAVE TIME: 10 to 12 minutes
REFRIGERATION TIME: 3 hours

¾ pound fresh cranberries (about
   3 cups)
1¼ to 1⅓ cups sugar
½ cup water
Grated peel of 1 orange

1. Mix all ingredients in 3-quart casserole. Cover tightly and microwave on high 5 minutes; stir.

2. Cover tightly and microwave on medium (50%) 5 to 7 minutes or until boiling. Cover and refrigerate at least 3 hours to blend flavors. **About 2 cups relish;** 35 calories per tablespoon.

Scalloped Potatoes with Cheddar Cheese (page 211), Cranberry Relish

CORN RELISH

MICROWAVE TIME: 2 to 3 minutes
REFRIGERATION TIME: 2 days

½ cup sugar
⅓ cup vinegar
½ teaspoon salt
½ teaspoon celery seed
¼ teaspoon mustard seed
¼ teaspoon red pepper sauce
1 can (17 ounces) whole kernel corn, drained
2 tablespoons chopped green or red bell pepper
2 tablespoons chopped celery
2 tablespoons finely chopped fresh or 1 tablespoon instant minced onion

1. Mix sugar, vinegar, salt, celery seed, mustard seed and pepper sauce in 1½-quart casserole. Microwave uncovered on high 2 to 3 minutes or until boiling; stir.

2. Stir in remaining ingredients. Cover and refrigerate at least 2 days to blend flavors. **About 2 cups relish;** 30 calories per tablespoon.

APRICOT-BRANDY BUTTER

This is a classic fruit "butter," thick and tart with fresh apricots, wonderful with hot buttery toast, biscuits or scones. The microwave cuts the cooking time in half.

MICROWAVE TIME: 40 to 52 minutes

2 pounds ripe apricots, unpared and sliced (about 8 cups)
½ cup brandy
2 cups sugar
½ teaspoon ground cinnamon
¼ teaspoon ground nutmeg

1. Mix apricots and brandy in 3-quart casserole. Microwave uncovered on high 10 to 12 minutes, stirring after 5 minutes, until tender. Place mixture in blender container or in food processor workbowl fitted with steel blade; cover and blend until smooth.

2. Return mixture to casserole. Stir in sugar, cinnamon and nutmeg. Microwave uncovered on high 30 to 40 minutes, stirring every 10 minutes, until slightly thickened. Immediately pour into hot, sterilized jars, leaving ¼-inch headspace. Wipe rims of jars. Seal and refrigerate up to 3 weeks. Or seal and freeze up to 6 months. Thaw and stir before using. **About 4 half-pints butter;** 15 calories per tablespoon.

Bread and Butter Pickles

BREAD AND BUTTER PICKLES

You can make Bread and Butter Pickles in the morning and enjoy them at noon. Store these old-fashioned pickles in the refrigerator.

STAND TIME: 3 hours
MICROWAVE TIME: 18 to 22 minutes

1½ quarts thinly sliced unpared
   cucumbers (about 2 pounds)
3 cups thinly sliced onions (about
   1 pound)
½ medium red bell pepper, cut into strips
½ medium green bell pepper, cut into
   strips
¼ cup pickling or noniodized salt
1 cup water
1½ cups sugar
1¼ cups cider or white wine vinegar
1 tablespoon mustard seed
½ teaspoon celery seed
½ teaspoon ground turmeric

1. Mix cucumbers, onions and bell peppers. Dissolve salt in water; pour over vegetables. Place a solid layer of ice cubes or crushed ice over vegetables. Weight with heavy object; let stand 3 hours.

2. Drain vegetables thoroughly. Mix remaining ingredients in 3-quart casserole. Microwave uncovered on high 6 minutes; stir until sugar is dissolved. Stir in vegetables. Cover tightly and microwave 11 minutes 30 seconds to 16 minutes or until boiling.

3. Immediately pack mixture in hot, sterilized jars, leaving ¼-inch headspace. Wipe rims of jars. Seal and refrigerate up to 3 weeks. Or seal and freeze up to 6 months. Thaw before serving. **About 3½ pints pickles;** 55 calories per ¼ cup.

PEACH CHUTNEY

MICROWAVE TIME: 10 to 12 minutes
REFRIGERATION TIME: 2 hours

2 cups coarsely chopped peaches (about
  2 large)
1 cup raisins
1 cup packed brown sugar
⅓ cup lemon juice
1 jar (2½ ounces) crystallized ginger,
  finely chopped
1 clove garlic, finely chopped
¼ teaspoon salt

1.   Mix all ingredients in 2-quart casserole.
Cover tightly and microwave on high 10 to
12 minutes, stirring after 5 minutes, until
peaches are transparent and mixture is syrupy.

2.   Refrigerate at least 2 hours until chilled.
Cover and refrigerate any remaining chutney
up to 2 weeks.   **About 2½ cups chutney;** 40
calories per tablespoon.

• • • • • • • • • •

PEAR CHUTNEY

MICROWAVE TIME: 10 to 12 minutes
REFRIGERATION TIME: 2 hours

1½ cups sliced pears (about 2 medium)
½ cup sugar
⅓ cup vinegar
3 tablespoons raisins
1 to 2 tablespoons finely chopped
  crystallized ginger
1 tablespoon finely chopped green bell
  pepper
3 whole cloves
3 whole allspice
1 three-inch stick cinnamon

1.   Mix all ingredients in 1½-quart casserole.
Cover tightly and microwave on high 10 to

Peach Chutney, Pear Chutney

12 minutes, stirring after 5 minutes, until
pears are transparent.

2.   Refrigerate at least 2 hours until chilled.
Cover and refrigerate any remaining chutney up to 2 weeks.   **About 1¼ cups chutney;**
35 calories per tablespoon.

• • • • • • • • • •

LEMON-ORANGE MARMALADE

MICROWAVE TIME: 24 to 28 minutes

2 medium unpared oranges, cut into
  fourths and thinly sliced
1 small unpared lemon, cut into fourths
  and thinly sliced
1 cup water
4 cups sugar
½ package (6-ounce size) liquid fruit
  pectin (1 three-ounce pouch)

1.   Mix oranges, lemon and water in 3-quart
casserole. Cover tightly and microwave on
high 13 to 15 minutes or until fruit peels are
tender. Stir in sugar.

2.   Microwave uncovered 10 to 12 minutes,
stirring after 5 minutes, until entire surface
of mixture is boiling. Microwave uncovered
1 minute longer. Stir in pectin thoroughly.
Immediately pour into hot, sterilized jars,
leaving ¼-inch headspace. Wipe rims of jars.
Seal and refrigerate up to 3 weeks. Or seal and
freeze up to 6 months. Thaw and stir before
serving.   **About 3 pints marmalade;** 40 calories
per tablespoon.

FREEZER BLUEBERRY JAM

The blueberries in this recipe aren't cooked, just crushed and flavored with orange peel.

STAND TIME: 20 minutes
MICROWAVE TIME: 3 to 4 minutes

2½ cups mashed blueberries (about
  2 pints)
3 cups sugar
1 teaspoon grated orange peel
1 package (1¾ ounces) powdered fruit
  pectin
½ cup water

1. Mix blueberries, sugar and orange peel in bowl; let stand 20 minutes, stirring occasionally.

2. Mix pectin and water in 4-cup measure. Microwave uncovered on high 2 minutes to 2 minutes 30 seconds or until boiling; stir. Microwave uncovered 1 minute longer; stir thoroughly.

3. Pour over blueberry mixture; stir 3 minutes. Pour mixture into freezerproof containers, leaving ½-inch headspace. Seal and freeze up to 6 months. Thaw and stir before serving. **About 5 half-pints jam;** 30 calories per tablespoon.

• • • • • • • • • •

MIXED BERRY JAM

MICROWAVE TIME: 11 to 13 minutes

1 cup crushed strawberries (about
  1 pint)
1 cup crushed raspberries (about 1 pint)
3 cups sugar
½ teaspoon grated lemon peel
1 tablespoon lemon juice
½ package (6-ounce size) liquid fruit
  pectin

1. Mix all ingredients except pectin in 3-quart casserole. Microwave uncovered on high 11 to 13 minutes, stirring after 5 minutes, until boiling; stir until sugar is dissolved.

2. Stir in pectin thoroughly; skim off foam. Immediately pour into hot, sterilized jars, leaving ¼-inch headspace. Wipe rims of jars. Seal and refrigerate up to 3 weeks. Or seal and freeze up to 6 months. Thaw and stir before serving. **About 4 half-pints jam;** 30 calories per tablespoon.

• • • • • • • • • •

ROSY GRAPE JELLY

Here is a quick jelly that uses ready-made fruit juice—no messy, stained cheesecloth bags needed. This jelly can be enjoyed just as soon as it has finished cooking.

MICROWAVE TIME: 9 to 14 minutes

1 cup cranberry juice
½ cup grape juice
½ package (1¾-ounce size) powdered
  fruit pectin (2 tablespoons plus
  1½ teaspoons)
1¾ cups sugar

1. Mix cranberry juice, grape juice and pectin in 2-quart casserole. Microwave uncovered on high 4 to 7 minutes or until boiling. Stir in sugar.

2. Microwave uncovered 5 to 7 minutes, stirring after 3 minutes to dissolve sugar, until mixture coats a metal spoon. Skim off foam. Immediately pour into hot, sterilized jars. Wipe rims of jars. Seal and refrigerate up to 3 weeks. Or seal and freeze up to 6 months. Thaw before serving. **About 1½ cups jelly;** 65 calories per tablespoon.

Fresh Peach Jam, Rosy Grape Jelly (page 334)

FRESH PEACH JAM

MICROWAVE TIME: 9 to 13 minutes

2 cups chopped peeled peaches (about
   1 pound)
1 tablespoon lemon juice
½ package (1¾-ounce size) powdered
   fruit pectin (2 tablespoons plus
   1½ teaspoons)
1½ cups sugar

1. Mix peaches, lemon juice and pectin in
3-quart casserole. Cover tightly and microwave on high 5 to 8 minutes or to rolling
boil; stir. Stir in sugar.

2. Microwave uncovered 3 minutes 30 seconds to 5 minutes or until boiling; skim off
foam. Stir 3 minutes. Immediately pour into
hot, sterilized jars, leaving ¼-inch headspace.
Wipe rims of jars. Seal and refrigerate up to
3 weeks. Or seal and freeze up to 6 months.
Thaw and stir before serving.   **About 3 half-
pints jam;** 25 calories per tablespoon.

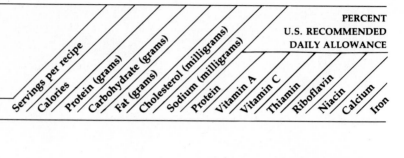

RECIPE, PAGE	Servings per recipe	Calories	Protein (grams)	Carbohydrate (grams)	Fat (grams)	Cholesterol (milligrams)	Sodium (milligrams)	Protein	Vitamin A	Vitamin C	Thiamin	Riboflavin	Niacin	Calcium	Iron
SAVORY SAUCES															
Apricot-Honey Sauce, 324	16	40	0	10	0	0	25	0	0	0	0	0	0	0	0
Cheddar Cheese Sauce, 323	24	30	1	1	2	5	50	0	0	0	0	0	0	2	0
Garlic Tomato Sauce, 321	28	5	0	1	0	0	55	0	2	4	0	0	0	0	0
Hollandaise Sauce, 322	12	85	1	0	9	80	80	0	6	0	0	0	0	0	0
Lemon-Dill Sauce, 321	20	15	0	1	1	0	45	0	0	0	0	0	0	0	0
Mozzarella Sauce, 323	16	15	0	0	1	2	25	0	0	0	0	0	0	0	0
Red Chili Sauce, 323	16	15	0	4	0	0	220	0	4	2	0	0	0	0	0
Red Wine Sauce, 323	32	10	0	2	0	0	105	0	2	0	0	0	0	0	0
Shrimp Sauce, 324	32	20	1	1	1	15	20	0	0	0	0	0	0	0	0
Tangy Orange Sauce, 324	16	25	0	6	0	0	0	0	0	12	0	0	0	0	0
Zesty Barbecue Sauce, 324	16	15	0	4	0	0	80	0	2	0	0	0	0	0	0
DESSERT SAUCES															
Butterscotch Sauce, 327	20	65	0	11	2	0	40	0	2	0	0	0	0	0	0
Creamy Almond Sauce, 327	28	20	1	3	1	20	10	0	0	0	0	0	0	0	0
Hot Fudge Sauce, 327	24	65	1	9	3	2	15	0	0	0	0	0	0	2	0
Lemon Sauce, 328	12	25	0	6	0	0	0	0	0	8	0	0	0	0	0
Marshmallow Sauce, 327	32	30	0	8	0	0	5	0	0	0	0	0	0	0	0
Raspberry Sauce, 328	32	15	0	3	0	0	0	0	0	0	0	0	8	8	8
Rum Sauce, 329	20	105	0	8	8	12	60	0	6	0	0	0	0	0	0
RELISHES															
Bread and Butter Pickles, 331	28	55	1	14	0	0	235	0	2	14	0	0	0	0	0
Corn Relish, 330	32	30	0	6	0	0	260	0	0	0	0	2	0	0	0
Cranberry Relish, 329	32	35	0	9	0	0	0	0	0	0	0	0	0	0	0
Peach Chutney, 333	40	40	0	10	0	0	15	0	0	0	0	0	0	0	0
Pear Chutney, 333	20	35	0	9	0	0	0	0	0	0	0	0	0	0	0

NUTRITION INFORMATION

PER SERVING OR UNIT

RECIPE, PAGE

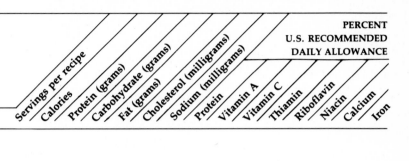

Recipe, page	Servings per recipe	Calories	Protein (grams)	Carbohydrate (grams)	Fat (grams)	Cholesterol (milligrams)	Sodium (milligrams)	Protein	Vitamin A	Vitamin C	Thiamin	Riboflavin	Niacin	Calcium	Iron
PRESERVES															
Apricot-Brandy Butter, 330	64	15	0	2	0	0	0	0	10	0	0	0	0	0	0
Freezer Blueberry Jam, 334	80	30	0	8	0	0	0	0	0	0	0	0	0	0	0
Fresh Peach Jam, 335	48	25	0	7	0	0	0	0	0	0	0	0	0	0	0
Lemon-Orange Marmalade, 333	80	40	0	10	0	0	0	0	0	2	0	0	0	0	0
Mixed Berry Jam, 334	64	30	0	7	0	0	0	0	0	4	0	0	0	0	0
Rosy Grape Jelly, 334	24	65	0	16	0	0	0	0	0	2	0	0	0	0	0

································ 8 ································

SPECIAL HELPS

MICROWAVE SAFETY

Like other appliances in the home, the microwave should always be used properly. Some basic guidelines for safe use of the microwave follow.

1. Read and follow all directions in the use and care manual.

2. Keep children away from the microwave when hot foods are being removed.

3. Any food heated for a young child should be sampled before being given to the child. Sometimes food heats unevenly and may be much hotter at the outside edges than in the middle or at the top.

4. Use caution when removing coverings/lids from foods. Turn back one corner of plastic wrap before cooking to allow some of the steam to escape.

5. Do not use the microwave for deep fat frying. The temperature of the oil could climb high enough to reach the "flash point," causing the oil to burst into flames. The design of many microwaves makes it awkward to lift out heavy containers, and that can be especially dangerous with hot oil.

6. To heat a baby bottle in the microwave, remove the cap and nipple. Watch the time. Plastic bag liners may burst if heated too long. Cover and shake bottles before testing them for an appropriate lukewarm temperature. Babies cannot tolerate foods as hot as those adults can.

When heating baby food from a jar, remove a portion and heat in a dish. (Bacteria from a used baby's spoon can contaminate the food in the jar. That makes the remaining food in the jar unsafe to refrigerate for later use.) Stir food before testing.

7. Always refer to your use and care manual to determine whether the use of aluminum foil and other metal is recommended in your microwave.

8. When using a meat thermometer, make sure it is designed for the microwave (with no metal parts).

9. Use tea bags without staples when making tea in the microwave. The metal staple could cause arcing.

10. Do not use the microwave as a substitute for a hot water bath in home canning. Pressure can build up rapidly in jars and cause them to explode.

11. Never heat an unopened bottle or jar in the microwave. Uneven heating and glass that is not heat tempered pose safety hazards in heating any foods in bottles or jars.

12. Avoid using paper napkins to cover foods. Some are made from low quality paper and are printed with dyes that could get into foods.

13. Use caution and follow directions precisely when preparing microwave popcorn.

Carefully open the bag, since the temperature of steam inside the bag can exceed 180° and cause burns.

14. When heating water for coffee or tea, watch carefully. Add a pinch of instant tea or coffee before heating and stir occasionally. Whenever possible use measuring cups.

Their slanted sides will help to avoid heating water to a temperature above the boiling point, causing it to erupt.

15. When microwaving pasta, do not add cooking oil to the water. Oil may form a film over the water surface, causing the boiling water underneath to erupt.

FOOD SAFETY

Keep Food Hot or Cold

The most perishable foods are those containing eggs, milk (creamed foods, cream pies), seafood (seafood salads), meats and poultry. When you shop, pick up your meat and poultry selections last. Take them straight home and refrigerate or freeze.

Don't allow hot or cold foods to remain at room temperature for more than 2 hours. Bacteria thrive in lukewarm food, and are especially dangerous because they seldom change the taste, odor or appearance of food. A standard rule, recommended by the U.S. Department of Agriculture, is to keep hot foods at a temperature above 140° and cold foods cold, below 40°.

Once food has been cooked, keep it hot until serving time or refrigerate as soon as possible. Hot food can be placed immediately in the refrigerator.

Keep Food Clean

Germs are a natural part of the environment. Keep utensils, dishes, countertops and hands soap-and-water clean. Don't handle food if you have open cuts or sores on your hands; or you can use plastic gloves.

Be careful not to transfer germs from raw meat to cooked meat. Do not, for example, carry raw hamburgers to the grill on a platter, then serve the cooked hamburgers on the same, unwashed platter.

Do not use wooden cutting boards for raw meat or poultry. A nonporous plastic cutting board is safer for meats. Wash boards with a mixture of 2 teaspoons chlorine bleach and 1 teaspoon vinegar to a gallon of water.

Use disposable paper towels when working with or cleaning up after raw foods.

Keep pets out of the kitchen. After playing with pets, teach children to wash their hands before handling food.

Food Safety Tips

Eggs. Eggs are a perishable food and require proper storage and cooking to prevent the growth of potentially harmful bacteria. Avoid eating raw eggs and foods containing raw eggs. Cook eggs thoroughly. Foods containing cooked eggs (such as cheesecakes, cream fillings, custards, quiches and potato salads) must be served hot or cold, with leftovers refrigerated immediately. Storage for "do-ahead" recipes should not exceed 48 hours.

Ground Meat. Cook thoroughly—it's handled frequently in preparation, an open invitation to germs. Don't eat raw ground meat—it's not safe!

Ham. Know what kind of ham you're buying; most hams are fully cooked but others need cooking. Check the label. (If you have any doubts, cook it.)

Luncheon Meat, Frankfurters. Refrigerate; use within a week. Use a fork or tongs to handle.

Poultry. Cook all poultry products as long as directions require. Refrigerate cooked poultry, stuffing and giblets as soon as possible in separate containers; use within a few days or freeze.

Canned Foods. Do not buy or use food from leaking, bulging or dented cans or jars with cracks or loose or bulging lids. If you are in doubt about a can of food, don't taste it! Return it to your grocer and report it to your local health authority.

Milk. Fresh milk products are highly perishable; refrigerate them as soon after purchase as possible. Unopened evaporated milk and nonfat dry milk may be stored in a cool area for several months. Unopened dry whole milk, which contains fat, should be refrigerated; use within a few weeks.

Keep Food Safe at Buffets

Serve food in small dishes, refilling frequently from stove or refrigerator. Or keep food hot in an electric skillet or chafing dish or on a hot tray. Don't depend on warming units with candles. Refrigerate salads made with seafood, poultry or meat. Chill both food and dish before serving. Serve cold foods over crushed ice.

Pack Safe Lunches

- Wash fruits and vegetables before packing.
- Use fully cooked foods (frankfurters, canned meats and poultry). They keep well.
- Wash vacuum bottles and rinse with boiling water after each use. Be sure hot foods are boiling hot when poured into vacuum bottles.
- Lunch boxes insulate better than lunch bags.

Note: For a free copy of the Home and Garden Bulletin Safe Food Book, write to The Meat and Poultry Hotline, USDA-FSIS, Rm. 1165-S, Washington, D.C. 20250

MICROWAVE COOKING FOR CHILDREN

The microwave is one of the safest cooking appliances in the kitchen, and children love to cook! Teach your children some simple rules so they can fix their own snacks and help prepare meals safely. You are the best judge of the age at which your children should be allowed to use the microwave. They need to understand that, even though the appliance doesn't get hot, the food does. Follow these simple steps to help your children microwave safely:

1. There should always be adult supervision when children use the microwave, unless they have been given permission to use it unsupervised.

2. The microwave should be placed where it is easy for children to reach. If they can't reach the microwave, be sure a sturdy stool is available for them to climb on.

3. Children should be taught how to operate and use the microwave safely, following the

recommendations in the use and care manual, safe food-preparation techniques, and, how to handle hot foods.

4. It is important that microwave dishes used by children have handles, since the heat from food can quickly transfer to the dish itself, possibly causing accidents or even burns. Dishes should be of a size easy for them to manage. Encourage the use of pot holders and be sure they are available in a size easy to use for smaller, less adept hands.

5. Help children learn to judge how hot food is, since they don't like food as hot as adults usually do. Teach them to stir those foods that can be stirred before tasting, and to taste those foods that can't with caution. Depending on the food, the inside could be hotter than the outside. The jelly in a doughnut gets hot much more quickly than the surrounding doughnut.

6. Easy recipes with few ingredients, using foods children are especially fond of, are good choices for beginning microwavers. We suggest the recipes at right:

MICROWAVE TO GRILL

Grilling was once reserved for summer days, but today it's a cooking method enjoyed by many year-round. By combining the talents of your microwave with those of your grill, you can cut grilling time almost in half. Foods are enhanced by the smoky flavor of grilling, while a microwave head start retains natural juiciness. An additional convenience is that much of the fat in such foods as sausages will "cook out" in the microwave, causing fewer flare-ups on the grill.

Heat the grill according to the manufacturer's directions. Whether you use a gas or electric grill, it is important to keep the heat as even as possible throughout the grilling period. If you're not getting a sizzle, the fire may be too cool. You can regulate the heat by spreading the coals or raking them together, opening or closing the vents or adjusting the control on a gas or electric grill. Heat can also be controlled by raising or lowering the cooking grill or covering it.

While the grill is heating to the right temperature, you can complete the necessary microwave cooking steps. Three important points to remember when using the Microwave-to-Grill method:

1. Plan preparation time so that foods can go directly from the microwave to the grill.

Have coals ready by the time foods are partially cooked in the microwave.

2. Pay close attention to foods on the grill and follow the doneness tests to avoid underdone or overcooked foods.

3. A rule of thumb: Foods should be microwaved only half of their total microwave time if they are to finish cooking on the grill.

Lemon-Herb Grilled Chicken (page 45) microwaved before grilling

Lemon-Herb Grilled Chicken on the grill.

The following recipes were developed especially for Microwave-to-Grill cooking:

Apricot-glazed Grilled Turkey, 62
Lemon-Herb Grilled Chicken, 45
Gourmet Grilled Steak, 117

Grilled Pork Tenderloins, 137
Grilled Pork and Fruit Kabobs, 145
Currant-glazed Grilled Pork Ribs, 140
Grilled Ham with Plum Glaze, 147
Grilled Italian Sausage Kabobs, 152

HIGH-ALTITUDE COOKING IN THE MICROWAVE

Microwave cooking at high altitude (3,500 to 6,500 feet elevation), like its conventional counterpart, requires special considerations. As a general rule most recipes will use similar high-altitude adjustments for microwaving as for conventional preparation.

Because air is thinner at higher altitudes, water boils at a lower temperature, resulting in greater expansion of gases and faster evaporation of water. This means that foods that puff or rise will expand more at high altitudes. You may need to use larger containers for beverage, cake, cereal, sauce, soup and bread recipes. This also means you will need to increase cooking times for recipes cooked with a high proportion of liquid, such as vegetables, rice, soups and stews.

Following are some general guidelines for high-altitude microwave cooking:

Baked Goods. Adjust sugar, leavening, liquid in similar proportion as for conventional recipes.

Yeast Breads. Microwave proofing times will be shorter.

Batters and Doughs. Larger bowls and dishes are needed for greater expansion.

Microwave Cake Mixes. No adjustment needed.

Conventional Cake Mixes. Follow package directions for high altitude and generally increase microwave times.

Muffins. Fill muffin cups no more than half. This will increase yield; microwave only six muffins at a time. Microwave times will be slightly longer than package directions if a mix is used.

Main Dishes. Increase cooking times. Increase the amount of cooking water for pasta, rice and vegetables.

Cereals, Beverages and Sauces. Increase size of dish or bowl.

Frozen Main Dishes (or Other Dense Foods). Thaw first; cooking from frozen state is not satisfactory.

SPECIAL MICROWAVE EQUIPMENT

There is a variety of equipment specifically designed for use in the microwave. Some pieces are conventional favorites (baking sheets, for example) just now available in microwavable materials. Some may include metal parts along with unique microwave features or designs. Because microwave appliances vary in size, it's a good idea to measure your microwave before purchasing special equipment, to be certain it will fit. Follow the directions carefully. Be sure to refer to your microwave manufacturer's use and care manual to determine if metal utensils may be used in your microwave. New specialty microwave products are introduced periodically; shop wisely to determine whether they meet your microwave needs. This is a sampling of the specialty microwave products on the market.

1. *Baking sheets.* Like conventional baking sheets, but made of plastic or glass. Provide large surface for foods cooked or heated in quantity. Sizes vary.

2. *Bundt cake dishes.* Traditional fluted shape allows for high volume of microwave cakes. Made of plastic or glass.

3. *Browning dishes or grills.* Special coating allows bottom of the dish to absorb microwave energy and reach temperature of 500° to 600°. Sizes vary. Refer to recipes using browning dish, Pepper Tuna Steaks (page 93) and Brandy Beef Steaks (page 117).

4. *Portable turntables.* Turntables rotate food automatically through the microwave field. Helpful for foods that otherwise would need rotation. Available in windup or battery-operated models. Sizes vary.

5. *Popcorn poppers.* Plastic popper allows you to make your own popcorn with or without oil. Special design concentrates the popcorn in a cup or cone shape so microwaves are more easily absorbed. Holds up to 3 quarts and most can also be used for steaming.

6. *Coffeepots and teapots.* Made with no metal parts; will brew up to 5 cups.

7. *Pressure cookers.* Tender pressure-cooker results with the speed of the microwave. Cooks food under pressure, seals in moisture.

NUTRITION

Today's cooking emphasizes good taste. However, new information linking certain foods with the cause or prevention of health problems is changing the way we cook and the foods we choose for our daily meals. We are becoming interested in eating more foods that provide complex carbohydrates and fiber, and eating fewer foods high in fat, sugar and sodium. Yesterday's favorite ingredients are re-proportioned in today's recipes to reflect concerns about good nutrition and physical fitness. The key to healthful eating remains the same, however—eat a varied, balanced diet that includes appropriate amounts of all necessary nutrients.

Nutrients in Food

Protein. Protein occurs naturally in foods of animal and plant origin and is necessary for growth and maintenance of body tissues. Careful combinations of whole grains, vegetables and legumes can provide the protein we need less expensively and without contributing as much fat as some sources of animal protein.

Carbohydrates. Carbohydrates, the body's main source of energy, are of two types—simple and complex.

Simple carbohydrates include sugars found naturally in some foods and sweeteners. Regardless of whether a sugar is added to food or occurs naturally in food, it is used in the same way the body.

Complex carbohydrates are found in vegetables, fruits, dried beans and peas, and whole grain foods and cereal products. An increased use of complex carbohydrate foods as substitutes for foods high in fat is thought to be an important factor in reducing the risk of such health problems as heart disease, obesity and certain cancers. Complex carbohydrates also contribute fiber.

Fiber is the nondigestible portion of foods derived from plants. Foods often contain both soluble and insoluble fiber, and both types are important in a well-balanced diet. Soluble fiber, which dissolves easily in water, has been shown to play a role in helping to lower blood cholesterol when part of a low-fat diet. Some foods high in soluble fiber include whole-grain oats, oat bran, whole-grain barley, apples, oranges and legumes. Information suggesting a link between some soluble fiber foods such as oat bran with the lowering of cholesterol levels in the blood has increased their popularity.

Insoluble fiber, which does not dissolve in water, is best known for promoting regularity. Wheat, corn bran, whole grains, vegetables and nuts are good sources of insoluble fiber.

Fat and Cholesterol. Fat, found in many foods, supplies energy, provides essential fatty acids and aids in the transport of the fat-soluble vitamins A, D, E and K. The body needs fat to insulate and cushion the organs.

Our bodies manufacture cholesterol, and we also get it from the foods we eat. Cholesterol is involved in manufacturing certain hormones and is an essential part of the nervous system and the brain.

The concern today about the relationship of dietary fat and cholesterol to heart disease has prompted recommendations that total fat intake be limited to 30 percent or less of daily calories, and that cholesterol not exceed 300 milligrams per day.

There are three types of fat—saturated, monounsaturated and polyunsaturated. Saturated fat is thought to be the major contributor of elevated blood cholesterol levels. It is recommended that saturated fats contribute no more than 10 percent of daily calories. Saturated fats are primarily found in animal sources such as meat, eggs and dairy products. Fats and oils that contain primarily monounsaturated and polyunsaturated fats are liquid at room temperature and found most commonly in vegetable or plant sources.

Sodium. Common table salt is a combination of sodium and chloride, both of which are needed to help regulate the balance of water in the body. Sodium occurs naturally in some foods, and much of our sodium is from the salt used in food preparation and at the table.

Vitamins. Vitamins are compounds necessary for growth, development and maintenance of health. They are found in varying amounts in the food we eat. The vitamins most easily lost during cooking are the B vitamins (thiamine, riboflavin, niacin, B_6 and B_{12}) and vitamin C. Cooking foods, especially vegetables, in only a small amount of water saves the greatest amount of these vitamins. For example, very little water is required when vegetables are steamed or cooked in the microwave.

Minerals. Minerals also are important to the body, essential for a rigid skeleton, healthy nerves and muscles and oxygen transport.

The most prevalent minerals are calcium, phosphorus, sodium, potassium and magnesium. The trace minerals—those needed in smaller amounts—are iron, zinc, manganese, copper and iodine. Calcium and iron typically are consumed at less-than-adequate levels by many groups, especially teenage girls and adult women.

Calcium has received a lot of publicity recently as a contributing factor in the prevention of osteoporosis, a disease that causes bones to become brittle and fragile. Postmenopausal women are especially susceptible to osteoporosis.

Water—The Forgotten Nutrient

Water makes up about 70 percent of the human body and is second only to oxygen as being essential for life. We can survive only four days without water.

Because water is involved in so many body functions, maintenance of water balance is crucial. Balance is attained when we ingest at least as much water as we lose. Drinking six to eight or more cups of liquids—including juices and broths—per day helps provide some of the water that is needed to maintain water balance. Sodium and potassium are the principal minerals responsible for the body's water balance along with adequate protein.

GUIDE TO NUTRITION INFORMATION ON RECIPES

The United States Recommended Daily Allowance (U.S. RDA) is based on Recommended Dietary Allowances established by the Food and Nutrition Board of the National Academy of Sciences and National Research Council. The dietary allowances determined for adults represent the average nutrient requirement plus an added margin to cover individual variations.

Low-fat (2%) milk is used in all recipe calculations. Calories per serving as well as protein, carbohydrates, fat, cholesterol and sodium have been calculated for each recipe. Also included are the percent U.S. RDA for protein, vitamin A, vitamin C, thiamine, riboflavin, niacin, calcium and iron.

- If an alternative ingredient choice is offered, the ingredient given first is the one on which the nutrition information is calculated. For example, when "dry sherry or apple juice" is indicated, the nutrition content has been determined based on dry sherry.
- When a range is given for the amount of an ingredient, or more than one serving is indicated, the lower amount or smaller serving size has been used to calculate the nutrition content.
- "If desired" ingredients are not included in the nutrition calculations. For example, for "top with strawberries and, if desired, whipped cream," the nutrition information has been determined using strawberries only.

MICROWAVE MENU IDEAS

Family Supper for 6
Impossible Lasagne Pie (page 124)
Green Salad
Italian Zucchini (page 217)
Apple Crisp (page 284)

Weekend Brunch for 4
Garden Harvest Frittata (page 16)
Apricot-Streusel Bread (page 251)
Fresh Fruit
Coffee, Milk or Juice

Gourmet Italian Dinner for 4
Hot Artichoke Dip (page 15)
Turkey Scallopini (page 65)
Italian Risotto (page 261)
Nutty Pattypan Squash (page 218)
Plums in Parchment (page 293)

Outdoor Barbecue for 6
Lemon-Herb Grilled Chicken (page 45)
Colorful Coleslaw (page 222)
Corn (page 198)
Savory French Bread (page 252)
Raspberry-Pear Cobbler (page 285)

Luncheon for 6
Tropical Rumaki (page 20)
Wild Rice and Turkey Salad (page 70)
Orange Dip with Fresh Fruit (page 17)
Crusty Rolls
Iced Tea

Winter Skating Party for 4
Green Chili (page 144) or Beer-Cheese
  Soup (page 172)
Spinach Salad (page 228)
Raisin-Nut Muffins (page 241)
Rosy Apples (page 294)
Hot Chocolate (page 33)

Family Breakfast for 4
Anytime Scrambled Eggs (page 163)
Bagels with Cream Cheese Spread (page 250)
Refrigerated Oat Bran Muffins (page 239)
Coffee, Milk or Juice

Formal Dinner Party for 6
Brie with Almonds (page 18)
Salmon-stuffed Flounder (page 78)
Broccoli Mornay (page 189)
Flaming Fruit (page 299)

Thanksgiving Dinner for 8
Apricot-glazed Grilled Turkey (page 62)
Apple and Wild Rice Dressing (page 256)
Cranberry Relish (page 329)
Winter Squash (page 219)
Stuffed Potatoes (page 212)
Mini Pumpkin Pies (page 304)

Southwest Appetizer Party for 12
Spicy Cheese Dip (page 15)
Appetizer Burritos (page 23)
Stacked Quesadillas (page 24)
Spicy Shrimp Appetizer (page 26)
Chorizo-filled Breads (page 24)
Cranberry-Orange Punch (page 34)

Hot Chocolate (page 33), Raisin-Nut Muffins (page 241), Spinach Salad (page 228), Beer-Cheese Soup (page 172), Rosy Apples (page 294)

CANADIAN METRIC
CONVERSION TABLES

Dry and Liquid Measurements

Temperatures

IMPERIAL	METRIC		FAHRENHEIT	CELSIUS
¼ teaspoon	1 mL		32°F	0°C
½ teaspoon	2 mL		212°F	100°C
1 teaspoon	5 mL		250°F	121°C
1 tablespoon	15 mL		275°F	140°C
2 tablespoons	25 mL		300°F	150°C
3 tablespoons	50 mL		325°F	160°C
¼ cup	50 mL		350°F	180°C
⅓ cup	75 mL		375°F	190°C
½ cup	125 mL		400°F	200°C
⅔ cup	150 mL		425°F	220°C
¾ cup	175 mL		450°F	230°C
1 cup	250 mL		475°F	240°C

COMMON COOKING AND BAKING UTENSIL EQUIVALENTS

BAKEWARE	IMPERIAL	METRIC
Round Pan	8 × 1½ inches	20 × 4 cm
	9 × 1½ inches	22 × 4 cm
Square Pan	8 × 8 × 2 inches	22 × 22 × 5 cm
	9 × 9 × 2 inches	23 × 23 × 5 cm
Baking Dishes	11 × 7 × 1½ inches	28 × 18 × 4 cm
	12 × 7½ × 2 inches	30 × 19 × 5 cm
	13 × 9 × 2 inches	33 × 23 × 5 cm
Loaf Pan	8½ × 4½ × 2½ inches	22 × 11 × 6 cm
	9 × 5 × 3 inches	23 × 13 × 8 cm
Tube Pan	10 × 4 inches	25 × 10 cm
Jelly Roll Pan	15½ × 10½ × 1 inch	39 × 27 × 2.5 cm
Pie Plate	9 × 1¼ inches	23 × 3.2 cm
	10 × 1½ inches	25 × 4 cm
Muffin Cups	2½ × 1¼ inches	6 × 3.2 cm
	3 × 1½ inches	8 × 4 cm
Skillet	10 inches	25 cm
Casseroles and Saucepans	1 quart	1 L
	1½ quart	1.5 L
	2 quarts	2 L
	2½ quarts	2.5 L
	3 quarts	3 L
	4 quarts	4 L

NOTE: The recipes in this cookbook have not been developed or tested in Canadian metric measures. When converting to Canadian metric, some variations in recipe quality may be noted.

GLOSSARY

· · · · · · · · · · ·

MICROWAVE TERMS
AND TECHNIQUES

Arcing: Whitish flashes or sparks accompanied by sharp, crackling sounds. Arcing can damage your microwave or dishes. To avoid arcing, do not use dishes that have metal trim, metal skewers, metal twist ties on a plastic bag or aluminum foil that is not molded smoothly over a food or the container.

Arrange: To place food in a particular pattern to cook more evenly. Such foods as potatoes cook more evenly when arranged in a circle, so that all sides of food are exposed to equal amounts of microwaves.

Brown: The surface of microwaved food does not usually brown, unless the food has a high fat content or is cooked for a long period of time. To achieve browning in the microwave, use a browning dish, sauces, glazes, coatings or toppings.

Browning dish or grill: A microwave accessory available in many shapes and sizes used to sear or brown foods. The dish is coated or contains special substances that absorb microwave energy and become very hot when preheated before adding the food.

Coat: To evenly cover food with crumbs or a sauce to give color, crispness and flavor. Flour or flour-based batters are generally not used for coating when microwaving. Fish and chicken are foods commonly coated.

Cooking or roasting rack: A microwave accessory that elevates foods above their cooking juices and allows for circulation of air, resulting in drier surfaces of foods.

Cover loosely: To cover a container or food with a loose cover that will prevent spattering and/or hold in heat. Use waxed paper or casserole lid (left slightly ajar).

Cover tightly: To cover a container of food with a tightly fitting lid or cover that will prevent most moisture or steam from escaping, to speed cooking and reduce spattering. Use casserole lid, plate or plastic wrap with one corner turned back.

Elevate: To lift food or dish off the floor of the microwave. This assures doneness on the bottom of sensitive foods. Place foods on an inverted microwavable plate or dish.

Food placement: Placement of food affects the way it will cook. Place foods in center of oven. Place small, thin or tender portions of foods in the center of the dish. Arrange foods of uniform size in a ring shape to promote even cooking.

Let stand: To complete cooking by heat conduction after the food has been microwaved. This can take place inside (without microwave power) or outside the microwave. In some cases, standing also helps develop flavor. foods in the center of the dish. Arrange foods

Microwavable: Food, package or cookware appropriate for use in the microwave.

Microwave: To cook, heat or defrost food in a microwave oven.

Pierce: To puncture with fork or knife a skin or membrane covering a food to prevent bursting. Foods such as whole egg yolks (out of the shell) and whole vegetables (potatoes or winter squash, for example) should be pierced before microwaving.

Power level settings: Setting on the microwave that controls the percentage of power introduced into the oven cavity as microwave energy.

Rearrange: To reposition foods in the same dish for even cooking. This is important for foods of uneven thickness and some foods that cannot be stirred (kabobs or barbecued ribs, for example). Move foods from the center of the dish toward the outside, foods from the outside toward the center.

Rotate: To reposition dish either one quarter or one half turn in order to cook food more evenly. This is important for foods that cannot be stirred, rearranged or turned over.

Shield: To protect sensitive areas of foods from overcooking. Pieces or strips of aluminum foil deflect microwave energy; use aluminum foil only where recommended by the manufacturer of your appliance.

Stand time: A period of time after microwaving specified for certain foods to complete heating or cooking in the center and in thicker areas. This can take place inside (without microwave power) or outside the microwave.

Stir: To help foods cook more quickly and to equalize the food temperature. Stir from the outside to center; food heats and cooks faster on the outside. Stirring is usually done midway or after evenly divided periods through the cooking time.

Turn over: To even cooking from top to bottom for foods such as burgers, steaks and chops. Allows top and bottom surfaces to be reversed.

Vent: To turn plastic wrap back slightly at dish edge or corner or to leave a lid or cover ajar allowing excess steam to escape.

GENERAL COOKING TERMS

Baste: Spoon liquid over food during cooking to keep it moist.

Beat: Mix ingredients vigorously with spoon, hand beater or electric mixer until smooth.

Blanch: Plunge food into boiling water for brief time to preserve color, texture, and nutritional value, or to remove skins from fruits or nuts.

Blend: Mix ingredients until they are smooth and uniform.

Boil: Heat liquid until bubbles rise continuously and break on the surface. For rolling boil, the bubbles form rapidly.

Brown: Cook until surface of food changes color, usually over medium heat.

Caramelize: To melt sugar slowly over low heat until it becomes brown in color.

Chill: Refrigerate food to make cold.

Chop: Cut into irregular pieces. A knife, food chopper or food processor may be used.

Coat: To evenly cover food with crumbs or a thickened liquid.

Cool: Allow hot food to come to room temperature.

Crisp-tender: To cook food until it is tender but retains some of the crisp texture of the raw food.

Crush: Grind into fine particles or press to extract juice. For example, crush clove of garlic using chef's knife or garlic press.

Cube: Cut into squares ½ inch or larger with knife.

Cut in: Distribute solid fat in dry ingredients by cutting with pastry blender with a rolling motion or cutting with two knives until particles are desired size.

Cut up: Cut into pieces with scissors or knife. To prevent sticking of such sticky foods as dried apricots, dip blade into water or coat lightly with vegetable oil.

Dash: Less than ⅛ teaspoon of an ingredient.

Dice: Cut into squares smaller than ½ inch.

Finely chop: Cut into very tiny pieces.

Fold: Combine ingredients lightly using two motions: First, cut vertically through mixture with rubber spatula; next, slide spatula across bottom of bowl and up the side, turning the mixture over. Continue down-across-up-over motion while rotating bowl a quarter turn with each series of strokes.

Garnish: To decorate food with additional foods that have distinctive color or texture. Parsley, fresh berries, and carrot curls are common garnishes that enhance some foods' appearance.

Glaze: To brush or drizzle a mixture on a food to give it a glossy appearance or hard finish.

Grate: Cut into tiny particles using small holes of grater or food processor.

Julienne: To cut fruits, vegetables or meats into matchlike strips using knife or food processor.

Marinate: Let food stand in a savory, usually acidic liquid, for several hours to add flavor or to tenderize. Marinade is the savory liquid in which the food is marinated.

Mix: Combine ingredients to distribute them evenly.

Pare: Cut off outer covering with knife or vegetable parer. Apples and carrots are "pared."

Peel: Strip off outer covering using fingers, such as for bananas or oranges.

Poach: Cook in hot liquid just below the boiling point.

Reduce: Boil liquid uncovered to evaporate liquid until desired consistency and to intensify flavor.

Scald: Heat liquid to just below the boiling point. Tiny bubbles form at the edge.

Score: Cut surface of food about ¼ inch deep with knife to facilitate cooking, flavoring or tenderizing.

Shred: Cut into long, thin pieces using large holes of grater, a knife or food processor.

Slice: Cut into same size flat pieces.

Sliver: Cut into long, thin pieces.

Soften: Let cold margarine, butter or cream cheese stand at room temperature or microwave at low power setting until soft.

Soft peaks: To beat egg whites until peaks are rounded or curled when beaters are lifted from bowl, but are still moist and glossy.

Stiff peaks: To beat egg whites until peaks stand up straight when beaters are lifted from bowl, but are still moist and glossy.

Stir: Mix ingredients with circular or figure-eight motion until of uniform consistency.

Tear: Break into pieces using fingers.

Toss: Tumble ingredients lightly with a lifting motion.

INDEX

Defrosting Poultry, Seafood and Meats

Defrost in microwavable wrapper or place in shallow dish. Pierce tightly closed packages allowing steam to escape. Cover seafood. After half the time, separate, turn over, break up or rearrange in dish. Arrange thickest parts to outside edge if possible.

Microwave on defrost setting as directed until few ice crystals remain in center. Edges should not begin to cook. Let stand 5 to 15 minutes to complete defrosting.

POULTRY (see Chapter 2 for additional information)

TYPE	AMOUNT	TIME (defrost)
Chicken		
Broiler-fryer, cut up	3 to 3½ pounds	20 to 25 min, turning over and separating every 10 min
Breast halves (2), with skin and bones	1¼ pounds	12 to 15 min, turning over and separating after 8 min
Breast halves (4), skinless, boneless	1½ pounds	15 to 20 min, turning over and separating after 10 min
Drumsticks, thighs and wings	2 pounds	12 to 15 min, separating after 8 min
Turkey		
Tenderloins (2)	1½ pounds	10 to 12 min, separating and turning over after 5 min
Breast slices	1 pound	8 to 10 min, separating and turning over after 4 min
Rock Cornish hen (1)	1½ pounds	10 to 12 min, turning over after 5 min; let stand 30 min in cold water

SEAFOOD (see Chapter 2 for additional information)

TYPE	AMOUNT	TIME (defrost)
Fish fillets, ½ to ¾ inch	1 pound	6 to 8 min, separating and rearranging after 3 min
Fish steaks (2), 1 inch	1 pound	6 to 8 min, separating and rearranging after 3 min
Crabmeat	6 to 8 ounces	4 to 7 min, breaking up after 2 min
Lobster tails (4)	2 pounds	8 to 10 min, rotating dish ½ turn after 5 min
Scallops	1 pound	8 to 10 min, stirring after 4 min
Shrimp, in shells or peeled and deveined	1 pound	6 to 8 min, stirring after 3 min

MEATS—Beef, Veal, Pork, Lamb (see Chapter 3 for additional information)

TYPE	AMOUNT	TIME (defrost)
Steaks, ½ to 1 inch	1 pound	7 to 11 min, separating and turning over after 4 min
Chops (4), ½ inch	1 pound	6 to 9 min, separating and rearranging after 4 min
Ribs, back	1 pound	7 to 9 min, separating and rearranging after 4 min
Ground		
bulk	1 pound	8 to 10 min, breaking up and removing thawed meat after 4 min
patties (4), ¾ inch	1 pound	8 to 10 min, separating and turning over after 4 min
Bacon, sliced	1 pound	5 to 6 min
Frankfurters (10)	1 pound	5 to 7 min, turning over after 3 min
Sausages (6), uncooked or cooked (bratwurst, Italian, Polish)	1 pound	6 to 8 min, turning over after 3 min

Microwaving Fresh Vegetables
(See Chapter 4 for additional information)

For whole, wash and pierce in several places allowing steam to escape. For pieces, wash, trim and pare as necessary; cut into pieces about the same size.

Place vegetables with larger, denser parts toward the outside edge of casserole. For whole potatoes or unhusked corn, place uncovered (potatoes in circle) on paper towel in microwave; let stand uncovered.

Add water as directed. Cover tightly and microwave on high until crisp-tender or tender, stirring, rotating casserole, turning over or rearranging food as directed. Let stand covered.

Type	Amount	Water	Time (high)	Stand Time
Asparagus				
spears	1½ pounds	¼ cup	6 to 9 min, rotating dish ½ turn after 3 min	1 min
pieces, 1 inch	1½ pounds	¼ cup	6 to 9 min, stirring after 3 min	1 min
Beans—Green, Wax				
pieces, 1 inch	1 pound	½ cup	9 to 14 min, stirring every 5 min	5 min
Broccoli				
spears	1½ pounds	1 cup	9 to 12 min, rotating dish ½ turn every 4 min	5 min
pieces, 1 inch	1½ pounds	1 cup	9 to 12 min, stirring every 4 min	5 min
Brussels Sprouts	1 pound	¼ cup	8 to 13 min, stirring after 5 min	5 min
Cabbage—Green, Red, Savoy				
wedges	1 pound	½ cup	10 to 14 min, rotating dish ½ turn after 5 min	5 min
shredded	1 pound	¼ cup	8 to 10 min, stirring after 4 min	5 min
Carrots				
slices, ¼ inch	1 pound	¼ cup	6 to 8 min, stirring after 4 min	1 min
Cauliflower				
whole	2 pounds	¼ cup	12 to 14 min, rotating dish ½ turn after 6 min	1 min
cauliflowerets	2 pounds	¼ cup	12 to 14 min, stirring after 6 min	
Corn				
husked	4 ears	¼ cup	9 to 14 min, rearranging after 5 min	5 min
unhusked	4 ears	—	9 to 14 min, rearranging after 5 min	5 min
Peas, Green	2 pounds	¼ cup	9 to 11 min, stirring after 5 min	1 min
Potatoes, White				
whole (4)	2 pounds	—	12 to 18 min, turning over after 6 min	5 min
pieces	2 pounds	½ cup	10 to 16 min, stirring after 7 min	1 min
Potatoes, Sweet (Yams)	1½ pounds	—	8 to 15 min, turning over after 4 min	5 min
Summer Squash— Crookneck, Pattypan, Straightneck, Zucchini				
slices or cubes	1½ pounds	¼ cup	8 to 10 min, stirring after 4 min	1 min
Winter Squash— Acorn, Buttercup, Butternut				
whole or piece	2 pounds	—	4 to 6 min or until rind is easy to cut through; cut in half, microwave 5 to 8 min longer	1 min

COOK'S NOTES

· · · · · · · · · · · ·

COOK'S NOTES

· · · · · · · · · · · ·

COOK'S NOTES

· · · · · · · · · · · ·

COOK'S NOTES

• • • • • • • • • • •

COOK'S NOTES

· · · · · · · · · · ·

COOK'S NOTES

· · · · · · · · · · · ·

COOK'S NOTES

···········